WOMEN REMAKING AMERICAN JUDAISM

WOMEN REMAKING AMERICAN JUDAISM

Edited by Riv-Ellen Prell

With a Foreword by David Weinberg

Wayne State University Press
Detroit

 Manufactured in the United States of America.
11 10 09 08 07 5 4 3 2 1

Library of Congress Cataloging-in-Publication Data

Women remaking American Judaism / edited by Riv-Ellen Prell.
p. cm.
Includes bibliographical references and index.
ISBN-13: 978-0-8143-3280-1 (pbk. : alk. paper)
ISBN-10: 0-8143-3280-3 (pbk. : alk. paper)
1. Jewish women—United States—Religious life. 2. Women in Judaism—United States. 3. Feminism—Religious aspects—Judaism. 4. Judaism—United States. I. Prell, Riv-Ellen, 1947–
BM729.W6W69 2007
296.082′0973—dc22

2007006907

♾ The paper used in this publication meets the minimum requirements of the American National Standard for Information Sciences—Permanence of Paper for Printed Library Materials, ANSI Z39.48-1984.

Chava Weissler's "Meanings of Shekhinah in the 'Jewish Renewal' Movement" first appeared as an article in *Nashim* 10, no. 1 (1995): 53–83, and is included here with the permission of Indiana University Press. The current version has been slightly revised and updated for publication in this volume.

Portions of Deborah Dash Moore and Andrew Bush's "Mitzvah, Gender, and Reconstructionist Judaism" first appeared in Deborah Dash Moore, "Judaism as a Gendered Civilization: The Legacy of Mordecaim Kaplan's Magnum Opus," *Jewish Social Studies: History, Culture, Society* 12, no. 2 (2006): 172–86.

Grateful acknowledgment is made to the Pearl and George M. Zelter Endowment Fund for its generous support of the publication of this volume.

Designed and typeset by The Composing Room of Michigan, Inc.
Composed in Adobe Garamond

To Isa Aron, Sara M. Evans, and Elaine Tyler May
Teachers, study partners, and generous friends for more than thirty years

"Seek out a teacher (rav). Acquire a study partner. When judging others, tip the balance in their favor."
—Pirke Avot 1:6

CONTENTS

Foreword by David Weinberg ix
Acknowledgments xi

Introduction
Feminism and the Remaking of American Judaism 1
Riv-Ellen Prell

PART ONE: REENVISIONING JUDAISM

Chapter One
"Her Mouth Is Full of Wisdom": Reflections on Jewish Feminist Theology 27
Rochelle L. Millen

Chapter Two
Meanings of Shekhinah in the "Jewish Renewal" Movement 51
Chava Weissler

Chapter Three
A Tent of One's Own: Feminist Biblical Scholarship, a Popular Novel, and the Fate of the Biblical Text 83
Adriane B. Leveen

PART TWO: REDEFINING JUDAISM

Chapter Four
Women in Reform Judaism: Between Rhetoric and Reality 109
Karla Goldman

Chapter Five
Mitzvah, Gender, and Reconstructionist Judaism 135
DEBORAH DASH MOORE AND ANDREW BUSH

Chapter Six
The Tensions That Merit Our Attention: Women in Conservative Judaism 153
SHULY RUBIN SCHWARTZ

Chapter Seven
Women in Orthodoxy: Conventional and Contentious 181
NORMA BAUMEL JOSEPH

Chapter Eight
Bridges to "A Judaism Transformed by Women's Wisdom": The First Generation of Women Rabbis 211
PAMELA S. NADELL

PART THREE: REFRAMING JUDAISM

Chapter Nine
Phasing In: Rosh Hodesh Ceremonies in American Jewish Life 231
JODY MYERS

Chapter Ten
Miriam's Object Lesson: Ritualizing the Presence of Miriam 257
VANESSA L. OCHS

Chapter Eleven
Finding Her Right Place in the Synagogue: The Rite of Adult Bat Mitzvah 279
LISA D. GRANT

Timeline of Jewish and U.S. Feminism 303
Contributors 317
Index 321

FOREWORD

The present volume is an outgrowth of a conference titled "The Changing Role of Women in American Jewish Religious Life," which was organized by the Cohn-Haddow Center for Judaic Studies in May 2004 on the campus of Wayne State University in Detroit. Generated by both scholarship being conducted at the university and serious interest within the Jewish community of the greater Detroit Jewish community, the topic reflected the basic mission of the Cohn-Haddow Center—to bring the best of Jewish scholarship to the Wayne State campus and to the Detroit community.

For a day and a half, nine renowned scholars from throughout the United States addressed a series of questions relevant to the topic. What are the internal and external factors that have led to the growing visibility of women and women's issues in American Judaism? How specifically has the increased role of women affected Jewish belief, practices, and institutions? What does the increased role of women and of the influence of feminist consciousness in American Jewish life suggest about the future of Judaism in the United States? How has the distinctively American phenomenon of Jewish feminism affected religious life and thought in other parts of the globe?

The present volume represents both a distillation and an expansion of the major themes discussed at the conference. Under the able guidance and editorship of Professor Riv-Ellen Prell of the University of Minnesota, who also served as the keynote speaker at the conference, the collection brings together the scholarly perspectives of all of the participants, as well as those of several individuals who were invited to write on topics that expanded the scope of the volume. The result is one of the first assessments of the impact of thirty years of feminism on American Judaism, a richly informative compendium of information and insight on a central theme in modern American Jewish life.

As director of the Cohn-Haddow Center for Judaic Studies, I am honored that Wayne State University is publishing this work. It is an important contribution to the Press's already impressive Judaica reading list, and I have little doubt that it will prove to be of inestimable value to scholars, students, and general readers.

I wish to thank Kathy Wildfong of the Wayne State University Press for her assistance throughout the editing and publishing process. *Yasher koach* to Sandy Loeffler, the Administrative Assistant of the Cohn-Haddow Center, whose tireless work made the conference an outstanding success.

I am extremely grateful to the Chaim, Fanny, Louis, Benjamin and Anne Florence Kaufman Memorial Trust, and to John (*z"l*) and Rita Haddow for their financial support of the conference.

* * *

Finally, my special appreciation goes to Pearl (*z"l*) and Mike Zeltzer, whose generous contribution helped the volume to become a reality. Sadly, Pearl passed away only a few months before its publication. She was an enthusiastic supporter for the project from the beginning and was so looking forward to seeing the work in print. May Pearl's memory be a blessing.

David Weinberg

ACKNOWLEDGMENTS

I appreciate the opportunity that David Weinberg extended to me when he asked me to edit the papers from the conference he organized in 2004 at the Cohn-Haddow Center for Judaic Studies at Wayne State University. I attended the conference because I was interested in learning what new and insightful things my colleagues might have to say about American Jewish feminism. It seemed to me, as I anticipated the event, that the Jewish feminist analysis had already been effectively made some decades before, whether it concerned Jewish law or the organization of the American Jewish community. I was unprepared for the excitement I felt as I listened to papers that documented a major transformation in American Jewish life, and theorized how this was accomplished. Many of the presenters also discussed the vulnerabilities of these achievements, and speculated about what would lie ahead. The weight and intelligence of these papers were palpable over the long day spent not only with scholars but with an avid and excited audience of people interested in American Jewish women and Judaism. It was a true pleasure to work with David Weinberg on this undertaking and to have the able assistance of Sandy Loeffler of the center, as well as the support of Kathryn Wildfong, the acquisition editor with whom we were fortunate to work at the Press.

First and foremost I appreciate the commitment of the contributors to this volume: those who attended the conference and those who were later invited to join our work. We corresponded over two years, and each author willingly engaged with her or his contribution many times to effectively communicate its contents and to orient it to the purpose of the book.

In preparing the illustrations for the volume I was ably assisted by Karin Kugel, who not only found images but helped me to put them in the appropriate formats. Choosing these illustrations put me into e-mail contact with many exciting American Jewish artists—photographers, painters, and creators of ritual objects—as well as archivists. Their enthusiasm for this book and their generosity in allowing me to reproduce the images were an especially rewarding part of editing the volume. I especially thank Kevin Proffitt of the Marcus Center of the American Jewish Archives, whose staff assisted me in finding interesting images.

I appreciate the support that I received from both the Cohn-Haddow Center and the College of Liberal Arts of the University of Minnesota, which provided funds for research-related costs for this book.

Inevitably, a book on Jewish feminism puts me and my colleagues in mind of those early thinkers and activists who created this movement. I would like to acknowledge some of the people to whom I feel particularly indebted, despite the fact that I have only encountered a few of them in their written work. Rachel Adler, Paula Hyman, Blu Greenberg, Rabbi Laura Geller, Rachel Biale, Norma Baumel Joseph, Judith Plaskow, and Rabbi Saul Berman, among so many others, laid the foundations for a world on which this volume is based. I particularly recall my teacher and friend, Barbara Myerhoff, whose work on ritual and storytelling was so influential. It is a source of deep satisfaction that more than twenty years after her tragic death her work influences so many of the essays in this volume. Our gratitude to them, and so many others whom the reader will encounter in this book, is enormous. Many have come after them, and continue to do so, and that is the most important legacy of those who came first.

Rabbi Morris J. Allen gave a sermon a number of years ago about the ways in which Jewish feminism created a revolution and demonstrated that change was truly possible. I thought about that sermon many times, and his point, so powerfully put, motivated me to want to edit this book. I thank him not only for that but for all that he has done to allow Conservative Judaism to live up to its ideals.

I am especially grateful to Steven S. Foldes, who not only provided extensive comments on the book's introduction but also reviewed and helped me format many of the illustrations. His remarkable eye is surpassed only by his generous heart, which enriches all that I do, and words cannot begin to express my gratitude to him.

I dedicate this book to three remarkable women: my dear friends Isa Aron, Elaine Tyler May, and Sara M. Evans. Not only have they enriched my life immeasurably by sharing it with me for more than three decades, but each as a feminist scholar and activist has helped make our world a better place.

INTRODUCTION

Feminism and the Remaking of American Judaism

RIV-ELLEN PRELL

This book was born from the thirty-five-year gestation of American Jewish feminism, a movement that marks a revolution in American Judaism as well as American religion. Jewish feminism, which grew from both Second Wave feminism, which began at the very end of the 1960s, and the American counterculture, which slightly preceded it, had an extraordinary impact on the leadership, organizations, practices, and beliefs of American Jews.[1] Jewish feminism remains a broad cultural umbrella under which to gather the ideas, institutional and communal structures, aesthetics, political activism, ritual and liturgical innovations, theologies, and new sacred objects associated with it.[2] Seminaries' decisions to ordain women rabbis and cantors (as well as the women who now fill those roles), liturgists who revise and create prayer books (as well as the men and women who pray those words), institutions created to train women to study Talmud (as well as the women who study there), and artists who design prayer garments and objects (as well as the men and women who wear and use them) have engaged in that revolution. Activists who demand expanded roles for women leaders in national Jewish organizations that are political, communal, and religious, as well as those filling roles never held by women before, and Jewish feminists who build political coalitions around gay rights, Israel, antiracism, and the environment are only a small sample of how Jewish feminism has reshaped American Judaism.[3]

The Jewish feminist vision is so pervasive today that many of its accomplishments have been disassociated from it. One may participate in Jewish life in a way that was largely created by Jewish feminism—women taking public roles in a synagogue and men and women using gender-neutral language in prayers—and not care to stand under its umbrella or recall the storms against which it provided shelter. Jewish feminism, then, is very

Queen Esther tambourine, by Betsy Teutsch (http://www.kavanahcards.com/tambourines). This tambourine casts Rosie the Riveter as the Purim heroine Queen Esther, combining muscle, power, and alluring beauty. Rosie the Riveter was an icon of women's homefront patriotism. She was portrayed as a shipyard worker who exclaimed, "We can do it." Second Wave feminism widely disseminated this image to focus on the history of women in the workplace and to provide counterimages to domestic women. Teutsch writes, "Both are icons of strength, capability, and determination. Queen Esther's job requires more jewelry!" Used with permission. Photo credit: Benj Kamm.

much like Second Wave feminism and no different from other social movements in the United States and elsewhere that bring about transformations whose origins are often forgotten and whose claims are imagined to have been unnecessary.

Jewish feminism's detractors and critics are no less engaged with its issues than are its advocates. Those who dismiss Jewish feminism, which over time have largely been concentrated in the right wing of Conservative Judaism and in most Orthodox Jewish communities, engage its discourse at length, dismiss its vision aggressively, and declare it alien to Judaism in their legal decisions. Their vehement rationalizations underscore how powerfully Jewish feminism continues to reshape American Jewish practices and ideas.

It is particularly challenging to assess and explain a revolution in the context of an American Judaism that is highly decentralized and in some sense radically democratic. Within Judaism, no single authority determines what is or is not Jewish, or how to interpret Jewish law or customs. Jewish denominations do not even determine everything that happens in each synagogue, let alone in each Jewish home. However, if a Jew wishes to remain in a community or movement, such as Reform or Conservative, each denomination's authority and power are entirely real. Each denomination determines how Jewish law and custom may be interpreted and thus decides who can serve as a rabbi or cantor, who can marry as a Jew, and the limits of inclusion or exclusion from communal prayer and study. It goes without saying that in the United States the state has no control over Jewish practices against which activists are forced to mobilize; Congress cannot demand religious equality for Jewish women.

In the dual context of American religious pluralism and a decentralized American Judaism, Jewish feminists brought about a religious and cultural transformation by using the tools (and on occasion weapons) of educating, organizing, sharing personal stories, and creating alternative rituals within a variety of movements, organizations, and institutions. Their revolution was, therefore, fomented first within conferences, in groups that met in homes, in articles written in Jewish magazines, newspapers, and later books, as well as in novels, theological works, and new liturgies, which in turn were shared, discussed, and debated in print, in communal gatherings, and among women informally. Jewish feminism changed Judaism by mobilizing women who themselves changed and challenged power in their own communities and denominations. Jewish feminism is then best studied "locally" within particular Jewish movements, synagogues, and communities, as well as in the settings where women met to teach one another how to lead prayer and study Talmud, and to conduct and share what came to be called women-centered rituals, such as celebrating the new moon. At the same time one must see the ways in which that local work was translated into the national context of institutions that were most often, but not always, changed to bring about more, if by no means complete, equality for women.

Jewish feminism is unquestionably transnational. American Jewish feminists were key activists in the campaign to create a space for women to worship publicly at the Western Wall in Jerusalem, which ultimately became the basis of a Supreme Court case in Israel.[4] North American Jewish feminism inspired and outraged Jewish communities throughout Europe, Central and Latin America, and Israel. In time, Jewish feminist scholarship, theology, and gatherings created mutual influence that transcended national lines. Although American Jewish feminism and feminists reach out across the globe, the context of this book, the United States, centers activism in synagogues, national denominations, organizations, homes, and schools.

Not only is Jewish feminism global, national, and local, it was and remains anything but monolithic. A (somewhat) shared feminist analysis did not create a single set of demands, interests, or ideas. Many feminist Judaisms did and will exist. For example, Orthodox feminism does not look like Reconstructionist feminism, but they share an important assumption about Judaism: it must afford gender equality, however that is defined.

Jewish feminism also inspired and led to subsequent challenges to Jewish law and Jewish communal practices. Its impact stretched well beyond its initial goals. In particular, gay and lesbian Jews' demands to be included fully in Jewish life, to be ordained and to marry within the Jewish community, were in part shaped and generated by Jewish feminism. Movements devoted to Jewish spirituality, to health and healing, and to experimental worship also draw on Jewish feminism.[5]

There are now three generations of Jewish feminists in the United States, as well as a variety of Jewish practices and organized groups that they have created. The visions of the pioneer generation described in several of these essays were often challenged not only by those who felt Judaism was under attack but also by those who felt that feminism did not go far enough. Jewish feminism is therefore best understood as dynamic and constantly changing, intelligible only within a variety of social and historical contexts.

Women Remaking American Judaism describes the transformations of Judaism beginning in the 1970s and provides a context for understanding these remarkable changes. The essays in this book allow us to pose questions about gender and religious change, about authority and religious experience, and about the yearning for equality within a religious framework. They describe and analyze why Jewish women who embraced Jewish feminism stayed within a system that they believe oppressed them to transform it rather than leave it.

JEWISH FEMINISM AND ITS REDEFINITION OF WOMEN'S EQUALITY

Jewish feminism, in its many manifestations, asserts the right of Jewish women to participate fully in Judaism and in Jewish life, a right denied to them in Jewish law and in Jewish denominations prior to the last third of the twentieth century. This revolutionary proposition may ultimately have as radical an impact on Judaism and Jewish practice as the ideas of the Enlightenment did on modern Jewish culture.[6] Like the Enlightenment, Jewish feminism challenges the assumptions on which Judaism is based, including that gender is a key principle in determining Jewish rights and obligations.[7] If men and women are not fundamentally different from one another, Jewish feminism then undermines the foundation of the legal structure that shapes Jewish practice.[8] The ideas of both the Enlightenment and feminism apply Western principles to Judaism that emphasize the importance of equality. The responses of Jewish leaders, thinkers, and ordinary Jews to those ideas and movements remake Judaism.

Indeed, Jewish feminism is a product of the Enlightenment and shares its complexities and contradictions.[9] The demand for gender equality, asserting the rights of any Jew, regardless of gender, to Jewish competence and literacy, and the yearning to pursue any practice, including those leading to rabbinical ordination, advanced scholarship, and full participation in Jewish life, are grounded in an ideology of equal rights, and one of its latter-day versions, personal empowerment. Jewish feminists' demands for halakhic (legal) equality in Judaism resonate with a vision of Jews as "citizens" of their tradition. Similarly, sacred places such as synagogues and study halls are also regarded as "civic" spaces that should allow equal access, evoking something like a gender-neutral public sphere. Despite the fact that the European Enlightenment hardly delivered on its promise of citizenship or a shared public life for either Jews or women in Europe, its ideal remains visible in a feminist vision for a Judaism in which women are actors who are equal to men, however that is defined by different feminist movements within Judaism.[10]

The Enlightenment analogy is richly ironic when applied to Judaism as a "religion." The Enlightenment championed reason over any belief that manifests itself as a coercive dogma. It prized the imagined dispassion of the male citizen and relegated emotion and belief to the weaker, female sex. Nevertheless, Jewish thinkers and leaders from the late seventeenth century onward attempted to reformulate Judaism in light of the principles of a universalist, rationalist understanding of religion. Jewish intellectuals and rabbis claimed that, like Protestantism, Judaism might be a sphere of experience rather than an all-encompassing way of life. The various formulations of the relationship between Judaism and the larger society across the denominations shared at least one conviction: Judaism was compatible and even congruent with rationality and science, and ultimately modernity.[11] That conviction, with all of its ironies, had important consequences for women.

The transformation in Judaism engendered by the Enlightenment engaged issues of women and gender from the outset in two important ways. First, the Enlightenment was initially tied to Jews' increasing access to the larger societies in which they lived through emancipation in western and then eastern Europe, and citizenship in the United States in the eighteenth and nineteenth centuries.[12] Jewish intellectuals, activists, and rabbis eager to claim the mantle of the Enlightenment broached the question of how women might live as Jews, because women's status became bound up with ideas of bourgeois respectability, modernity, and Westernization—goals sought by Jews who embraced Enlightenment principles. The more that Jews imagined themselves as belonging to the larger culture in which they lived, the more they had to address how Jewish religious principles and practices that concerned women comported with the German, British, American, or French ones that surrounded them, particularly among a new bourgeoisie.[13] Jewish women's right to participate in religious services and receive Jewish and secular educations were among the issues that the Enlightenment, and its subsequent translation to modernity, raised for Jews. Therefore, equality for women in Judaism may be understood as part of what the distinguished feminist historian Paula Hyman terms "the project of assimilation," Jewish communal leaders' vision for how to integrate Jews into larger societies that offered them citizenship.[14]

Containing and redefining the meaning of equality for women was the second way in which the Enlightenment was linked to the "project of assimilation." One of the most important strategies used by European and subsequently American Jews to claim a place within Western societies was to portray the Jewish family as the embodiment of Western values. Community leaders—rabbis, writers, and intellectuals—were constantly called on to demonstrate the worthiness of Jews for membership in society throughout the eighteenth, nineteenth, and even twentieth centuries. Their assertion that the Jewish family was the source of morality and responsibility for Jews was one of their key rationales for Jewish membership in civil society. They cast the Jewish mother and wife as the embodiment of those virtues. Her moral guidance and her domestic disposition assured the bourgeoisie of Berlin, New York, Budapest, and other cosmopolitan capitals that Jews could assimilate to Western culture. Therefore, neither in the Enlightenment nor during the period of emancipation and modernity were Jewish women imagined as true equals by Jews in the sense of having access to all rights and opportunities available to men. They were first and foremost imagined as mothers and wives. Their education, increasing presence, and even rights in the synagogue, as well as other opportunities, were linked to and limited by a cultural commitment to the domestication of Jewish women.

Notions of equality within Judaism over the last three centuries, therefore, have always existed within the cultural imperatives of how women's lives are understood by the larger society in which Jews have lived. The same cultural and historical moment might well give rise to opposition to, and support for, women's participation in civic life. That participation might mean a robust education or a particular role in the family through cooking and childrearing. Nevertheless, most of the changes demanded by and for women in Judaism—gender-mixed seating in worship, women's parallel organizations in the synagogue, limited participation in public Jewish worship, and protections around divorce and spousal abandonment—reflect the norms of the societies in which they lived. Jewish feminism, in fact, intervened in an American Judaism whose leaders, by the late 1960s, were quite confident that women had already succeeded in becoming equal participants in Judaism.[15] They had a greater role and even presence in synagogue and Jewish life than had their foremothers. On the whole they received more years of religious and secular education than had previous generations of Jewish young women. Judaism, it appeared, could respond to America and include women.

However, Jewish feminists in the context of Second Wave American feminism did not find these visions of equality sufficient. A woman could not become a rabbi or the president of an organization outside a separate women's sphere. Women did not count in the prayer quorum required for prayer for Conservative or Orthodox Jews, and in many cases they were not even considered members of their synagogues. Nor were women allowed, with rare exceptions, to engage in the most prestigious and demanding forms of study so highly valued by the Jewish tradition. In short, women's aspirations were limited by Jewish law or by American customs for the Jewish denominations that did not accept Jewish law as the final authority.[16] Feminists argued that as injurious as social exclusion was, there was a far more bitter marginalization because the foundational texts of Judaism (the Bible, Talmud, and commentaries) ignored women and their experiences at best, and at worst minimized and demonized them. For Orthodox women, it then followed that in Jewish law some of their most basic rights, such as divorce, left them vulnerable to male power.[17] The American Jewish writer Cynthia Ozick put the issue in a succinct cri de coeur in the feminist magazine *Lilith* in 1979: "We look into the Torah with regard to women, and we see that women are perceived as lesser, are thereby dehumanized."[18] When Jewish feminists began to address these injustices they made the boldest and most far-reaching claims on Judaism yet. Feminists across all denominations questioned whether normative Judaism as it was presently constituted could allow women to have all the rights and privileges of men. They argued that prior attempts to create equality for Jewish women had failed.[19]

Women Remaking American Judaism offers an analysis of the meanings of equality that emerged after 1970 in the practice of Judaism, an equality that looked quite different from previous visions espoused by postwar suburbanites, interwar activists, and late nineteenth-century reformers in the United States. Not unlike their Enlightenment predecessors, feminists challenged normative tradition as the final authority. However, unlike their predecessors who sought to re-create a Judaism built on principles of Western society, Jewish feminists in their most radical claims challenged the very principles on which *both* Judaism and the Enlightenment were founded. Feminists refused to accept the existence of the fundamental difference between men and women and the legitimacy of social hierarchy that followed from that. Jewish feminists, across many other ideological divides, asserted that a God of justice, compassion, and love neither could nor would want to exclude women. Feminists' dual claims to justice and a personal experience of God were radical rationales for transforming Judaism.

The context of American Jewish feminism—Second Wave feminism—occurred during a period when notions of cultural, political, and religious authority, ideas about the self and meaning, and the translation of both into religious and social institutions underwent radical change. Jewish feminism came of age not in the modern period but on the edge of postmodernity, a period marked by contradictory ideas and identities all held simultaneously. Jewish feminists, many of whom were raised in traditional Jewish homes and institutions that also embraced political activism and Zionism, and others brought to it from families steeped in secularism and left-wing politics who were antireligious found common cause in their desire to transform Judaism to be inclusive of women. In an exceptionally insightful analysis of Second Wave feminism, the historian Matthew Jacobson argues that its intellectual weave was made on the warp of ethnic roots and the woof of alienation from the larger American society. Jewish Americans, as well as Irish and Italian Americans, some from religious backgrounds, some from the working class, and many from both, found that their own sense of difference from American society prepared them to develop a feminist critique of cultural, religious, and political power in everything from New Left political leadership to churches and synagogues. A striking number of the leaders of Second Wave feminism were children and grandchildren of immigrants, with strong ties to those communities. These feminist writers and activists often uncovered or re-created their histories and religious traditions to provide distance from a society increasingly viewed as racist and oppressive. At the same time, they took those traditions to task and worked to dismantle the male power of those traditions. Like many Jewish feminists they claimed that male power was not the quotidian of one's culture or religion but something that could be changed.[20]

Jewish feminism reveals the true complexity of the changing meaning of equality for women and Jews over three centuries. The dream of equality for Jewish women was, by necessity, inevitably tied to the social and political movements of the cultures in which Jews have lived and continued to live. The Jewish feminist revolution is as indebted to the Enlightenment and emancipation as it is to the cultural and identity politics launched by Second Wave feminism and the related movements of civil rights and the American counterculture. It has embraced the core ideas of Western culture, equality and rights, and rejected the idealization of neutrality and rationalism that led some of the heirs of the Enlightenment to dismiss religion as an element of culture and identity. By the late twentieth century, Jewish feminism was inextricably linked to a search for an "authentic" Judaism grounded in a rejection of hierarchy that was an important foundation of Judaism.

THE (PARADOXICAL) MEANINGS OF A JEWISH FEMINIST REVOLUTION

The essays in this volume offer a paradoxical understanding of Jewish feminism as both *radical,* in the sense of challenging and engaging Jewish power and authority, and *accommodationist,* in the sense of focusing on issues and experiences that do not require dismantling Jewish law or community. Jewish feminism's radical critique questions the nature of Jewish authority and demands a place for women in any and all Jewish practices, especially knowledge of all classical texts and methods of study. Even its Orthodox thinkers suggest that by the late twentieth century there could be no defense of inequality based on gender in any Jewish undertaking.[21] Non-Orthodox and some Orthodox feminists have worked to remake Judaism by rewriting prayer language, creating new rituals, and insisting on women's leadership. They articulate the radical critique in the language of rights and equality, and thus evoke Enlightenment notions of citizenship and the exercise of obligations and privileges of adult members of a community. They envision men and women as equal before Jewish law.

Several contributors to this volume argue that some of the most widespread feminist practices in Judaism—New Moon ceremonies, women's bat mitzvah classes, and the explosion of images of the biblical Miriam on ritual objects used by women—may be more inclusive of women but are accepted because they are compatible with liberal denominations or traditional ideas about women. These feminist practices are less concerned with challenging Jewish authority because they are more deeply engaged with bringing women's personal experience into Judaism. These new feminist rituals, new interpretations of texts, and use of newly created sacred objects appear primarily to demonstrate that women have an important and central place in Judaism. They do not depend on a discourse of equality and rights; they draw on a vocabulary of meaning, empowerment, and inclusion. They seek continuity; they find biblical figures to fashion as role models for empowered women. They look to the body, aesthetics, personal stories, and the life cycle, as well as female role models, to assert women's place in Judaism.

Jewish feminism shares with other social movements not only differences in how to go about bringing social change but also the nature of the change sought. The student Left in the 1960s, for example, included those who argued that they created cultural transformation by living alternative lifestyles, moving to the "land," and abandoning the family and monogamous marriage. Others in the movement were avowedly political and interested in a fundamental transformation of power in society. Similarly, Second Wave feminism included an impressive array of groups who were devoted to different ways of dismantling patriarchy, and with that racism and economic inequity, through socialism, communism, and radicalism, to name only a few strategies and ideas that guided them. But there were also powerful movements within feminism devoted to creating women's music and women's art, as well as providing women-only cultural and sexual spaces that reflected fully and exclusively women's experiences.

Feminism within Judaism sought, to some extent, a narrower scope of social and cultural change than the entire Second Wave, but its approaches were still related to the social movements of the day and equally varied. Similarly, they shared with many other American religious traditions the challenge of how to maintain and transform institutions, sacred texts, and cultural ideas that were at once personally powerful and virtually inseparable from a history of male domination. Many Second Wave feminists declared that no woman could or should remain within patriarchal religion, and hence women-based traditions of Wicca or goddess worship emerged in this period as part of women's liberation, and they continue to provide a vision of a female-centered worship community. However, feminists who challenged and reformed American religions far outnumbered those who created new ones.[22]

Feminist transformations of Judaism, then, reveal important insights into the complexity of remaking American religion in general and Judaism in particular. The ways in which a frankly hierarchical, patriarchal Judaism continued to command and structure the experience of some women, to shape the desire to create community, and finally to provide workable models of women's power suggest that religions operate on many levels and create complex meanings.[23] Feminists certainly engaged in bringing about institutional change and in challenging traditional structures of power. However, they also invented rituals that responded to experiences on which their tradition had been silent, created new approaches to the study of traditional and ancient texts, and created new sacred objects that were integrated into ritual. Though some may have been more "radical" and others more "accommodationist," all feminist-inspired changes in some sense radically challenged traditional authority *and* sought to make Jewish prayer, ritual, and texts reflect women's lives.[24] Women redefined gender roles and religious practices simultaneously and inextricably from one another. At the same time, the theologians, biblical scholars, and observers of Jewish life who are described in these pages retain a strong investment in and commitment to Judaism. They translate their feminist critiques into Jewish practices—ritual, liturgical, or textual. Over time the practices become "authentically" Jewish. New objects become a part of the cycle of rituals; they take on the trappings of the familiar and hence the traditional. Invention can be made sacred. The sacred can become alienating. The paradox of feminism reshaping tradition is that the media of religion in Judaism—liturgy, ritual, home and life cycle celebrations, and inherited texts—can be remade in both radical and accommodating fashions. Change can serve a variety of ends.

No single vision emerged from a feminist critique of Judaism; no single set of practices developed. However, these essays reveal three broad new formulations of Judaism that emerged and they provide the structure for the volume. Jewish feminists, over more than three decades, have *reenvisioned* Judaism, they have *redefined* Judaism, and they have *reframed* it. In each of these formulations the reader will find examples of Jewish thought and practice, institutional change, and radical as well as moderate visions for change.

REENVISIONING JUDAISM

At its most radical, Jewish feminism reenvisions Judaism because it questions how Jewish law and practice define Jewish personhood; it challenges the fundamental categories of Judaism. Feminists reject hierarchic distinction between men and women as a basis for observance and instead insist on the legitimacy of women's inclusion among adult Jews who are obligated to adhere to Jewish law. Not all Orthodox feminists embrace the full critique. Nor did all feminist Jews articulate their feminism through engagement with normative Judaism. However, this very critique sets contemporary Jewish feminism apart from any other previous effort to be gender inclusive in Judaism. Feminists who choose to reenvision Judaism by changing Jewish law are both the most traditional and perhaps the most radical. The essays in part 1, therefore, look at the foundational formulations of Judaism in Jewish theology, law, and the Bible.

Rochelle L. Millen's essay, "'Her Mouth Is Full of Wisdom': Reflections on Jewish Feminist Theology," examines the emergence of a Jewish feminist theology, a particularly interesting development since theology was rarely an elaborated aspect of Jewish thought until recently. She closely reads the work of three feminist theologians: Judith Plaskow, whom she suggests offers a Reconstructionist view, Tamar Ross, an Orthodox Jewish Israeli, and Rachel Adler, from a Reform point of view, and finds striking continuity in their work. Her essay maps the terrain of how each addresses the theological problems raised by feminism. Millen holds that the Jewish legal system remains critical to each, albeit in different ways. As such, their feminism challenges the bedrock assumptions of the systems of Jewish law and thought. Millen's discussion turns on their shared critique of hierarchy. The theologians' uniform rejection of this fundamental source of human differentiation particularly reveals the extent to which a feminist theology demands profound transformation of Judaism, whether the outlook is "liberal" or "traditional."

Chava Weissler's analysis of the Jewish Renewal movement offers a study of the complexity of consciously attempting to address the gendered nature of God within practice. "Meanings of Shekhinah in the 'Jewish Renewal' Movement" analyzes the translation of feminist ideas into an emerging movement among North American Jews: Jewish Renewal. While Renewal was founded on principles that include the equality of men and women, Renewal's leadership further asserts that the "feminine" is currently emergent in Jewish practice and theology, particularly in elaborating the importance of the kabbalistic notion of a female emanation of God, the Shekhinah. Weissler's research complicates what many regard as Renewal's radical reenvisioning of Judaism by exploring the varied ways in which equality and gender, as well as Shekhinah, are understood. Though Renewal Jews may be willing to boldly rethink Judaism in their theology and practices, they do not agree on what equality means or what precisely constitutes the feminine nature of God. Weissler learns that there is debate among the movement's rabbis and laypeople, some advocating for a theology that equates the feminine with classical, even stereotypical ideas about God's softness and nurturance. Others argue for liberating men and women from any traditional notions about gender in order to be free of culturally bound constraints and ideas about God or religious life. Renewal Jews' aspirations for equality and their willingness to push the boundaries of normative Judaism farther than other movements have not freed them from a number of struggles. Their challenge is how to translate a radical critique of what they take to be hierarchic and male ideas into a new understanding shared among participants of how to envision God as well as community. Weissler offers an important framework for linking the reenvisioning of Judaism to lived experience.

Perhaps the most pervasive reenvisioning of Judaism has occurred within biblical studies. Feminist readings of the Bible began among activists as well as scholars as soon as feminist ideas first surfaced in popular articles and Jewish women began forming consciousness-raising groups. Adriane B. Leveen engages Jewish feminist biblical approaches in "A Tent of One's Own: Feminist Biblical Scholarship, a Popular Novel, and the Fate of the Biblical Text." She notes the paradoxical position of feminist biblical criticism in her helpful review of the literature. Feminist scholars note the patriarchal foundations of the Bible, as they have similarly found women's lives and voices within the text. They work to bring marginalized women to the center of understanding the Bible, and in so doing reenvision the Bible's narratives and reengage, rather than reject, the text.

Leveen explores another world of feminists engaged with the Bible through her analysis of Anita Diament's retelling of the story of the patriarch Jacob, his wives Rachel and Leah, and their children in *The Red Tent.* A book that offers a fictionalized story of biblical women whose sales top three million is not only a publishing phenomenon but a cultural one that invites interpretation. Leveen argues that Diament, as well as her readers, some of whose Web-based conversations she analyzes, also seek to bring the voices of women from the margins to the center of biblical narrative. Leveen discovers that both readers and the author of *The Red Tent,* in the end, are happy to rewrite the biblical narrative. She argues that reinvented scenarios and rereading the motivations and actions of biblical characters often result in demonizing figures, inventing motivations for relationships, and abandoning the narrative. Rather than simply drawing a distinction between scholarly and popular readings, Leveen focuses on the power and meaning of textuality. Engagement with the narrative results in a radical reenvisioning of Judaism. Retelling and inventing its stories dismisses the Bible and cannot actually engage Judaism.

These three essays examine contemporary feminist thought on the foundational texts of Jewish life. Theologians and biblical critics rethink and retell these texts, and in so doing reenvision them. Nevertheless, Millen, Weissler, and Leveen note an ongoing engagement with those very texts. Millen and Leveen argue that Jewish feminists do not approach the Bible, for example, as Christian feminists do, and that not all feminist readings are coterminous with Jewish feminism. The reenvisioning of Judaism as a task related to its textual tradition demands a radical critique rather than abandonment. Weissler's essay emphasizes that radical reenvisioning remains a complex process within Judaism.

REDEFINING JUDAISM

The translation of feminism into Jewish practice (or the refusal to do so) ultimately became the work of the four American Jewish denominations—their law committees, seminaries, rabbinic courts, lay organizations, rabbis, and synagogues. Each movement's earlier encounter with modernity, in Europe and the United States, began the process of transforming women's participation in Jewish life, as noted above. The strength of both Second Wave feminism and Jewish feminism in American Jewish life led all movements to respond further to the place of women within Judaism. As a whole, the essays in part 2 describe and assess the process by which feminists and feminism challenged and shaped the denominations in the last third of the twentieth century. Feminists called on these denominations to be inclusive. In distinctive ways, they sought the full participation of women in religious life. In all but the Orthodox movement they demanded the ordination of women as rabbis and cantors. They fought battles for gender-inclusive language. The tensions over the equality of women persist (except in Reconstructionist Judaism, the smallest movement in America), and the essays note both an unimagined elasticity in virtually all of the movements and points of resistance to change.

What is at work in the redefinition of Judaism is the ability of institutions and leaders to negotiate competing ideas. What was unthinkable in one year or in one era became possible and even desirable in the next. The essays demonstrate that the process of redefinition often draws on tradition, but it also draws on competing ideas of contemporary life. What is self-evident in the present redefines the past, even within the language of normative tradition.

Reform Judaism was the first movement to integrate women as a premise of its re-formation. Karla Goldman's discussion of Reform Judaism, "Women in Reform Judaism: Between Rhetoric and Reality," charts the movement's long history of engagement with issues of gender equality. She describes more than a century of developments that brought women into ritual activity in the synagogue, organizational leadership, education, and effective philanthropic work. At every point that women made substantial gains in access to newly envisioned equality throughout the twentieth century they also suffered losses due to unrealized promises. These ongoing struggles persist in the twenty-first century, she argues, because Reform Judaism has demonstrated a persistent male-centered institutional culture, even as it has made substantial changes. Goldman's essay is an important cautionary tale about the complexity of change, even within a religious movement singularly committed to the transformation of traditional Jewish gender roles.

Deborah Dash Moore and Andrew Bush offer an analysis of Reconstructionist Judaism and the thought of its founder, Mordecai Kaplan, in "Mitzvah, Gender, and Reconstructionist Judaism." They argue that Kaplan replaced traditional Jewish authority, the mitzvot (obligations), with what he termed "folkways" that were based on the values and culture of contemporary Jewish people, and were an American formulation of how to structure Judaism. His inclusion of women as educated, active participants in Jewish life was a powerful example of how folkways operated. Though not sanctioned by the tradition, equality was an important democratic principle of American life that supported Judaism's ends. Moore and Bush argue that Kaplan's development of folkways as the foundation for authority in Jewish life remains an important forerunner of feminist thought and practice in Judaism. American ideals of equality and pluralism were essential to Kaplan's reimagining of American Judaism and provided the groundwork for virtually every important change in women's participation in Jewish life that followed.

Shuly Rubin Schwartz analyzes the contours of the Conservative movement's response to women's growing involvement in Judaism in the twentieth century in "The Tensions That Merit Our Attention: Women in Conservative Judaism." She argues that in the middle third of the century the movement easily incorporated organizational and educational opportunities for women. These accommodations to what was perceived as modernity did not challenge Jewish law and therefore supported the fundamental premise of Conservative Judaism that tradition coexists amicably with contemporary life. Schwartz suggests that the movement confronted more wrenching challenges to this synthesis as women lobbied for greater equality, first around legal issues related to *agunah* (the abandonment of married women by their husbands) and then rabbinic ordination. She charts, in the journals and magazines of Conservative Judaism from the 1970s, a remarkable transformation of opinion that shifted from opposition to acceptance of women's rights to equality to acceptance of them. Schwartz concludes, however, with issues concerning gender equality that continue to challenge the movement.

In "Women in Orthodoxy: Conventional and Contentious," Norma Baumel Joseph analyzes the tensions generated in Orthodox Judaism by the rise of what she terms "religious feminism" in the 1970s. She compares the reception of three profound changes in Orthodox women's Jewish lives. In contemporary times the first two—women's access to religious education and increased ritual practice in the Orthodox community—have received little opposition. Women's *tefillah* (prayer) groups have, by contrast, evoked a firestorm. Joseph investigates what caused these different responses from rabbinic leadership. She argues that newly emerging women's communities constitute a challenge to traditional authority, even when the participants do not intend to attack the principle of rabbinic authority. Do Orthodox feminists then signal a new formulation of Orthodoxy? Joseph suggests that the movement for egalitarianism within a commitment to Jewish law constitutes a profound challenge to Orthodox Judaism as it is currently practiced.

Finally, Pamela S. Nadell looks across American Jewish denominations in her discussion of the experiences of women rabbis in the United States in "Bridges to 'A Judaism Transformed by Wisdom': The First Generation of Women Rabbis." She finds surprising commonalities among them despite substantial differences in their understanding and practice of Judaism. She suggests that though few of them originated a feminist critique of Judaism, they nevertheless have been the key translators of those ideas for the majority of America's Jews. Women rabbis pioneered rituals that responded to previously unmarked life passages of women. They sought bridges between classical texts and the experience of women. They have, to a far greater extent then their male counterparts, brought their life experiences into their reflections on Judaism and the rabbinate. Nadell persuasively argues that not only their gender but the historical position of women in normative Judaism created a shared perspective that transcended other differences among women rabbis.

Feminists institutionally redefined Judaism by opening Jewish life to women in new ways. Taken as a whole, the essays in part 2 demonstrate the tensions between the transformation and accommodation of change. Redefining American Jewish life took many forms, from promoting women's participation as a way to join American society, to ordaining women, to creating alternative structures. However, these essays also attest to the ways in which different denominations set limits on women's full access to Jewish life and leadership.

REFRAMING JUDAISM

Denominations were not the only translators of Jewish feminism into Jewish life. The essays in part 3 address feminist innovations that in some cases took place outside the synagogue. The authors argue that innovative rituals, objects, and settings for study did not provide a critique of Judaism and did not challenge authority as it was defined in liberal or progressive Judaism. Rather, they reframed Judaism and reimagined it in women's voices, objects, and ritual gatherings. These innovators, for example, evoked the biblical Miriam as a model of powerful Jewish womanhood, eschewing more marginal and often rebellious women in sacred Jewish literature like the demoness Lilith.

The new feminist objects and rituals led women to experience Judaism in new ways and to heighten their own sense of themselves as Jews. Women who gathered to mark the new moon, to gain Hebrew skills, or to use a tambourine bearing the image of Miriam, the prophet, in worship sought a Jewish experience that more directly and personally reflected their lives. In these acts they remade a Judaism that was gender inclusive. They were less concerned with conflicts over rights or limits of Jewish law. Instead, they created a Judaism that represented them and therefore asserted that Jewish women's aesthetics and lives had an uncontested place within Judaism.[25]

Jody Myers's essay, "Phasing In: Rosh Hodesh Ceremonies in American Jewish Life," charts the thirty-year development of New Moon ceremonies, one of the earliest, most popular, and ubiquitous rituals to emerge from Jewish feminism. These innovative rituals, grounded in classical texts, provide her the opportunity to speculate on the different Jewish feminisms that exist simultaneously and, on occasion, overlap. She reads the gathering of Jewish women who meet to mark the appearance of the new moon as a classical example of a "cultural" rather than "political" feminism. These rituals do not challenge Jewish law, or even male dominance. However, they provide visibility for women and the ritualization of the experience of women in Judaism. Myers speculates about the limits and possibilities of a cultural

Jewish feminism. At the same time, she argues that the fact that ritual may create visibility rather than community or transformation is a feature that is often overlooked by scholars.

Vanessa L. Ochs's essay, "Miriam's Object Lesson: Ritualizing the Presence of Miriam," examines another of the most tangible expressions of feminism in Jewish observance: the emergence of new ritual objects. The two that have proven to be most popular are a cup associated with the biblical Miriam that is used on the seder table at Passover, and a tambourine, also associated with Miriam. The image of Miriam playing her tambourine with dancing Israelite women also appears on a variety of ritual objects chosen and used by women, from seder plates to prayer shawls. Like Myers, Ochs analyzes these objects within the context of understanding how rituals change. She argues that they allow women to stay "safely" within the tradition, behaving in a fashion that will not alienate their larger communities even as they engage in resisting normative Judaism: they are used outside the synagogue. She notes that the feminist Miriam is the product of rewriting traditional narratives and imaginative engagement with the texts by scholars and writers who attempt to make Miriam and hence Jewish women central actors in Jewish life. Further, Ochs argues that the biblical Miriam emerged as a role model for Jewish women from the 1980s onward precisely because she is situated within the tradition, facilitating and supporting others, never challenging authority or traditional power. The heroine who preceded Miriam for the first decade of Jewish feminism was Lilith, a product of rabbinic legend. She was Adam's first "wife" and was cast from the garden for unbecoming behavior. She was powerful, dangerous, and destructive, and hence an ideal role model for the first generation of Jewish feminists—journalists, poets, writers, and activists—who were drawn to an image that embodied the demand for equality. Lilith became a demon when she was forced out of the garden, and her danger appealed to feminists as well.

Lisa D. Grant looks at the phenomenon of the adult bat mitzvah in "Finding Her Right Place in the Synagogue: The Rite of Adult Bat Mitzvah." She notes that this rite of passage can certainly be located within an ever-expanding range of Jewish innovations to mark women's life experiences and to include women's voices. In addition, however, it encourages women to seek legitimacy within the existing traditions of a Jewish movement. Grant describes the experiences of five Conservative Jewish women who studied to become bat mitzvah. She learned that as they became more confident and active Jews, their expectations for their community changed as well. Their participation transformed them and in effect encouraged them to transform their communities. Grant notes both the "conservative" and "transformative" aspects of this ritual.

CONCLUSION

When the religious studies scholar Elizabeth Castelli writes that each of the "terms—women, gender, and religion—is inherently unstable," she suggests that a study of American Jewish feminism is only intelligible in the context of specific historical moments and particular political conditions.[26] Jewish women have sought a place on the stage of Jewish life for more than three centuries. However, what precisely they sought, and what it meant to be a Jew and a woman, can only be understood within particular contexts. To complicate matters, there has never been a monolithic meaning to Jewish womanhood, for all Jews in a single place or time. The purpose of this volume, therefore, is to illuminate the ways that Jewish women have sought to define themselves as full participants in Judaism. These essays uncover those meanings by scrutinizing the ideas, institutions, relationships, practices, and material objects launched by feminism that define multiple ways of being a Jewish woman.

The Enlightenment, emancipation, and modernity fundamentally changed Judaism and Jews who drew on Western political and social thought to reshape their understanding and experience of Jewish law, worship, architecture, governance, family, and work. Feminism did no less. Jewish feminist thinkers and activists posed foundation-shaking questions and principles. Can women be fully Jewish if they are not obligated by all Jewish laws, if they are barred from leadership, if texts and rituals are indifferent to their life cycles and experiences? Feminists remade American Judaism by asking these questions and then by offering answers that insisted on exploring Judaisms that in a variety of ways became more inclusive. Feminism did not remake Judaism by creating a perfect and uniform equality for all Jews. Rather, its questions led to a surprisingly complex and broad set of possibilities. Those answers were played in many registers, including theology, law, ritual, an emerging focus on spirituality, new life cycle rituals, a new appreciation of the power of personal stories and experience, and recovering long-lost traditions and ideas.

Feminism was itself a product and engine of broad cultural change. As ideas of authority were loosened and challenged in the United States following World War II, feminism became possible. Similarly, with feminism's Second Wave, issues of gender and sexuality rode the crest of that radical rethinking of power and authority. Women and religion then became the eye of a cultural hurricane that remade American Jewish life. These essays invite the reader to consider the many forms that religious and cultural revolutions may take, their limits and their possibilities, their promises and their setbacks. In the end they reveal a panoramic view of feminism's encounter with the Enlightenment on the terrain of contemporary Judaism.

NOTES

I would like to thank my colleagues who took time from their many responsibilities to read and comment on this essay. The insights of Rabbi Morris Allen, Isa Aron, Ra'anan Boustan, Sara Evans, Lila Foldes, Elaine Tyler May, Deborah Dash Moore, and especially Steven Foldes were critical in thinking about these issues. I also appreciated an invitation from Professor Louis Newman to deliver the Forkosh Lecture at Carleton College where I spoke about these issues as well.

1. For an overview of Second Wave feminism, see Sara M. Evans, *Tidal Wave: How Women Changed America at Century's End* (New York: Free Press, 2003).

2. Discussions of Jewish feminism may be found in Sylvia Barack Fishman, *A Breath of Life: Feminism in the American Jewish Community* (New York: Free Press, 1993), and Joyce Antler, *The Journey Home: Jewish Women and the American Century* (New York: Free Press, 1997). See also Hasia Diner and Beryl Lieff Benderly, *Her Works Praise Her: A History of Jewish Women in America from Colonial Times to the Present* (New York: Basic Books, 2002), and Paula E. Hyman, "Jewish Feminism," in *Jewish Women in America: An Historical Encyclopedia,* ed. Paula E. Hyman and Deborah Dash Moore (New York: Routledge, 1997), 694–98. Reflections on the next generation may be found in Danya Ruttenberg, *Yentl's Revenge: The Next Wave of Jewish Feminism* (Seattle: Seal Press, 2001). The early writings articulating a Jewish feminism appeared in a variety of journals and magazines published by baby boomer Jews. Many of these articles were gathered into a few collections such as Elizabeth Koltun, ed., *The Jewish Woman in America: New Perspectives* (New York: Schocken, 1976), and Susannah Heschel, ed., *On Being a Jewish Feminist* (New York: Schocken, 1983). The first full-length book on the subject was Charlotte Baum, Paula Hyman, and Sonya Michel's *The Jewish Woman in America* (New York: Plume, 1979).

3. There are many Jewish feminisms. This book addresses the ways in which Jewish feminism expresses itself within the practice of Judaism. Jewish anarchists, socialists, and communists inspired by feminism as well could and should be included under the umbrella of Jewish feminism. The avowedly antireligious Emma Goldman is claimed by Jewish feminists as a role model and beloved ancestor for that reason. Similarly, Zionists certainly engaged issues of feminism, struggling with issues of socialism and nationalism. This book addresses Jewish femi-

nism in the context of Judaism as a religious practice engaged with Jewish religious law, halakhah, though Jewish feminism encompasses far more than this.

4. See Phyllis Chelser and Rivka Haut, eds., *Women of the Wall: Claiming Sacred Ground at Judaism's Holy Site* (Woodstock, VT: Jewish Lights, 2003).

5. See Rebecca T. Alpert, Sue Levi Elwell, and Shirley Idelson, eds., *Lesbian Rabbis: The First Generation* (New Brunswick: Rutgers University Press, 2001), which describes the experience and legal issues faced by lesbians seeking ordination. The first work by a gay Orthodox rabbi closely examines issues of halakhah. Steve Greenberg, *Wrestling with God and Man: Homosexuality in the Jewish Tradition* (Madison: University of Wisconsin Press, 2004).

6. Classic works on Jews and the Enlightenment include Michael A. Meyer, *Jewish Identity in the Modern World* (Seattle: University of Washington Press, 1990), and Jacob Katz, *Tradition and Crisis: Jewish Society at the End of the Middle Ages,* trans. Bernard Dov Cooperman (New York: Schocken, 1993).

7. Paula E. Hyman also notes the roots of egalitarianism in Enlightenment views ("Jewish Feminism," 695).

8. See Rachel Adler, *Engendering Judaism: An Inclusive Theology and Ethics* (Philadelphia: Jewish Publication Society, 1998), and Judith Hauptman, *Rereading the Rabbis: A Woman's Voice* (Boulder: Westview Press, 1998), for an important discussion of Jewish law and gender.

9. Historians of Jewish women who have noted this complex relationship are Paula Hyman, *Gender and Assimilation in Modern Jewish History: The Roles and Representation of Women* (Seattle: University of Washington Press, 1995), and Marion Kaplan, *The Making of the Jewish Middle Class: Women, Family and Identity in Imperial Germany* (New York: Oxford University Press, 1991).

10. See Carole Pateman, *Sexual Contract* (Palo Alto: Stanford University Press, 1988), for a classic discussion of these issues.

11. Meyer, *Jewish Identity in the Modern World.*

12. The Enlightenment affected Jews in different parts of the world at a different pace, beginning in the West and ultimately affecting the Mizrachi Jews of Arab lands. See Pierre Birnbaum and Ira Katznelson, eds., *Paths of Emancipation: Jews, States, and Citizenship* (Princeton: Princeton University Press, 1995).

13. David Biale, *Eros and the Jews: From Biblical Israel to Contemporary America* (New York: Basic Books, 1992).

14. Hyman, *Gender and Assimilation,* 13–15. Hyman notes that the project of assimilation always implied acculturation, which included the maintenance of a distinctive Jewish culture or identity within a larger society.

15. Jewish feminism's development consistently paralleled the processes of feminist change in the larger American culture. Not surprisingly, American feminism consistently developed in the context of historical periods in which women were regarded as having achieved unprecedented opportunities.

16. See Riv-Ellen Prell, "The Vision of Woman in Classical Reform Judaism," *Journal of the American Academy of Religion* 50 (1983): 576–89, for a discussion of the ways in which custom puts even greater limits on women's rights in Judaism.

17. Jewish divorce is initiated by the husband. If he cannot initiate a divorce because he disappears or dies without a witness, a woman cannot be divorced and hence remarry. She is called an agunah (chained woman). If a man refuses to give a woman a divorce, she cannot win her suit for divorce.

18. Cynthia Ozick, "Notes toward Finding the Right Question: A Vindication of the Rights of Jewish Women," *Lilith* 6 (1979): 29.

19. Karla Goldman, *Beyond the Synagogue: Finding a Place for Women in American Judaism* (Cambridge, MA: Harvard University Press, 2000); Jenna Weissman Joselit, *New York's Jewish Jews: The Orthodox Community in the Interwar Years* (Bloomington: Indiana University Press, 1990), 97–115, 122. See also the essays in this volume devoted to denominations.

20. Jacobson's point is more profound and complex than this key insight. His larger argument suggests that insofar as Second Wave feminism drew on ethnic and immigrant roots as foundational to its analysis and vision, it often set its course in conflict with women-of-color feminism that had no foundation in the experience of immigration or ethnicity. Matthew Frye Jacobson, *Roots Too: White Ethnic Revival in Post—Civil Rights America* (Cambridge, MA: Harvard University Press, 2006), 246–311.

21. See, for example, Tamar Ross, *Expanding the Palace of Torah: Orthodoxy and Feminism* (Hanover, NH: Brandeis University Press, 2004).

22. Carol Christ, ed., *Womanspirit Rising: A Feminist Reader in Religion* (San Francisco: Harper and Row, 1992). Christ has also written a variety of books on goddess worship and women's spirituality.

23. Elizabeth A. Castelli, ed., *Women, Gender, Religion: A Reader* (New York: Palgrave 2001); Catherine Bell, *Ritual Perspectives and Dimensions* (Oxford: Oxford University Press, 1997).

24. Feminists were reinvesting in their religious traditions at the very moment that scholars of religion were beginning to challenge some of the assumptions about religion that dominated the scholarship of 1960s. That scholarship suggested that the church or synagogue would have little influence over individuals or culture in an environment of volunteerism and pluralism. The classic discussion of these issues is in Thomas Luckmann, *The Invisible Religion: The Problem of Religion in Modern Society* (New York: Macmillan, 1967). A discussion of the viability of religion in such a society is in Peter Berger, *The Sacred Canopy: Elements of a Sociological Theory of Religion* (New York: Anchor 1969). David Martin, *A General Theory of Secularization* (New York: Harper and Row, 1978), examines the secularization debate. A discussion of these assumptions and why they did not effectively explain religious change in this period appears in Riv-Ellen Prell, *Prayer and Community: The Havurah in American Judaism* (Detroit: Wayne State University Press, 1989), 161–65.

Feminists' refusal to abandon "traditional" religions and denominations in the United States bolsters the view that traditions continued to hold meaning even in the act of reshaping them. The long history of radical innovation, and conservative backlash, was not going to disappear from American religious life. As noted above, Matthew Jacobson argues that these religious identities were deeply embedded in a critique of American society.

25. Clifford Geertz argued long ago that ritual succeeded when the world as imagined and the world as lived were united in ritual. See Geertz, "Religion as a Cultural System," in *The Interpretation of Cultures* (New York: Basic Books, 1973). However, Catherine Bell has observed that invented rituals often focus on these personal dimensions as important resources at the expense of the experience of the divine and the obligatory. Bell, *Ritual Perspectives and Dimensions,* 241.

26. Castelli, *Women, Gender, Religion.*

PART ONE

REENVISIONING JUDAISM

CHAPTER ONE

"HER MOUTH IS FULL OF WISDOM"

Reflections on Jewish Feminist Theology

ROCHELLE L. MILLEN

It is no coincidence that Rosemary Ruether's groundbreaking work in Christian feminist theology and Judith Plaskow's formulations of Jewish feminist theology were published within a few years of each other. The first edition of Ruether's book, *Sexism and God-Talk: Toward a Feminist Theology*, came out in 1983.[1] Parts of Plaskow's *Standing Again at Sinai: Judaism from a Feminist Perspective* were published in various journals in 1986 and 1987, with the volume appearing in 1990.[2] Changes wrought by the feminist movement in the 1970s and 1980s made ripe the time for measured reflections on their impact on religious life.

This essay will trace the development of Jewish feminist theology through the writings of Judith Plaskow, Marcia Falk, Tamar Ross, and Rachel Adler. It will consider the implications of the varied transformations in legal status, theology, and liturgy that have developed over the last decades: how they are intertwined and how we, individually and collectively, live our lives as Jews in light of the fresh thinking and behaviors regarding feminism with which all denominations of Judaism have had to struggle. While Plaskow, Ross, and Adler are theologians, Falk is a poet and liturgist whose liturgical reconfigurings articulate and are undergirded by essential theological notions. Jewish feminist theology as it has evolved over the past decades is transnational, as is the Jewish community. Americans (in this essay, Judith Plaskow, Marcia Falk, and Rachel Adler), Israelis (Tamar Ross), and some Europeans have all been involved in explicating the meanings of the interfacing between feminism and Judaism. As Ross makes clear in her recently published book, "The women's question in Judaism . . . is an ideological enterprise of major proportions."[3] This was true in the Reform movement and its debates over women's ordination, as well as in the lengthy conversations among members of the law committee, the faculty at the Jewish Theological Seminary, and the Rabbinical Assembly in the Conservative movement.[4] Now the "women's question" pervades Orthodoxy with urgency.[5] But while Plaskow identifies as Reconstructionist, Adler as Reform, and Ross as Orthodox, denominational labels, in my view, do not radically affect the theology each espouses. Exploring the meanings of being both Jewish and female draws together these theologies, despite their differences.

The publication of Plaskow's *Standing Again at Sinai* signaled the entry into academic discourse of a sustained, carefully worked out blueprint for a new way of thinking about Judaism and the Jewish community. Plaskow's articulate formulations both sum up the work of Jewish feminism in the previous decades, from the late 1960s onward, and help set the agenda for the future.

It is important to place Plaskow in historical context. She is writing after the founding of Ezrat Nashim in the early 1970s; subsequent to the ordination of women in the Reform movement in 1972 and in the Conservative movement in 1984; and after the founding of Drisha in 1979 and the publication of Saul Berman's groundbreaking article, "The Status of Women in Halakhic Judaism," in the Orthodox journal *Tradition* in 1973.[6] By 1990, Elizabeth Koltun and Susannah Heschel had both edited anthologies of Jewish feminist writings, the documentary *Half the Kingdom* had been produced and widely disseminated, and even right-wing women were thinking about b'not mitzvah for their daughters, considering reciting kaddish when appropriate, and committing to advanced Torah learning.[7] *Kol ishah,* the voices of women, were no longer as restricted or silent. Women had begun the journey in Judaism started earlier in other arenas: the move from private to public areas of involvement, competency, ritual, and participation.

Plaskow was the first to put the various strands of Jewish feminism into an organized framework that forms a theology. She appropriates the methodology of the "hermeneutics of suspicion" and the "hermeneutics of remembrance" from Elisabeth Schussler Fiorenza,[8] insisting on a deep respect for the very tradition her theology sets out to critique and transform. Plaskow attempts to maintain a precarious balance. While acknowledging the important changes that had already taken place in regard to women and Jewish ritual, she insists that the time had come to investigate and reconstruct the fundamental conceptual assumptions upon which categories of Jewish thought, as they define male and female social roles, were based. In order for concrete changes to be more than piecemeal accommodations or

Women "Supporting" Scholars: cover of *Lilith,* no. 6 (1979). This issue features some of its most important articles—on women's ordination in Conservative Judaism and a call for women's rights by Cynthia Ozick. The cover image conveys not only women's lack of access to Jewish study and knowledge but also the fact that without women's labor and support men could not study. Reprinted with permission from *Lilith* magazine—independent, Jewish, and frankly feminist. http://www.Lililth.org. Paula J. Gordon, artist.

ad hoc permutations, fundamental transformations need to occur. "Reform always begins in conviction and vision," Plaskow states. "An established system can become self-perpetuating and lose its ability for introspection and re-examination of basic premises."[9] The formula set out by Plaskow is followed by Ross and Adler as well.

In each of the essential areas of Torah, Israel, and God, according to Plaskow, women's history, experience, and perspective have been put aside and do not determine the forms articulated by and practiced within the tradition. Even at the crucial moment of revelation at Mount Sinai, although the text speaks of *ha-am* (the people), the instructions given by Moses in Exodus 19:15 state: "Be ready on the third day; come not near a woman." That is, Moses's admonition is not spoken to men and women, asking that they refrain from sexual intimacy, but is addressed only to men. The exclusion of women as subjects at such a moment is painful indeed.[10] The new theology would recover female history, experience, and perspective. Without the participation and input of women's voices, Judaism would remain truncated and woman only, and always, as Other.

A reclaiming of Torah to include a feminist perspective is a sine qua non for Plaskow. Only through so doing can the truly patriarchal character of the Jewish past and Jewish sources be acknowledged and women's invisibility dealt with. It is insufficient to fill positions of leadership and authority with women or to create new liturgy.[11] Since memory is such a crucial aspect of Jewish tradition, the content of memory itself must be transformed; essential to such transformation is halakhah and its methodology. Plaskow argues, "Any halakhah that is part of a feminist Judaism would have to look very different from halakhah as it has been. . . . It would begin with the assumption of women's equality and humanity and legislate only on that basis."[12] Women would be co-shapers of the legal tradition, determining, together with men, both the issues raised and the responses formulated. She asserts that "we must also be suspicious of the claim that only halakhic change is legitimate, that without halakhah there is no Judaism," and concludes that "the deeper question of the compatibility of feminism and the law must be left open."[13] This is an issue that both Ross and Adler continue to develop. One might say that Jewish feminist theology hinges on an understanding of halakhic process. Does Plaskow's theology necessitate overturning old tables so as to leave Judaism unrecognizable? I believe not; Plaskow is exploring possibilities, not creating new certainties.

In *Standing Again at Sinai* Plaskow both affirms and demonstrates a claim she made in an earlier essay written in response to an essay by Cynthia Ozick.[14] Ozick defined feminism in Judaism as a sociological issue, a delineation Plaskow found insufficient. For not only is increased inclusion in both ritual and leadership positions at stake, but also—and more fundamentally—the foundational assumptions about women as persons. Jewish feminism, maintains Plaskow in her response to Ozick, must be more than a civil rights movement, more than lobbying for a larger piece of the pie of power and participation.[15] Rather, it must be a truly liberating movement, one that rethinks presuppositions and grapples with their historical embeddedness and implications. Thus theology and the ramifications of the centrality of halakhah become central in her thinking.

Indeed, this centrality creates a focal, theological conundrum for feminist theologians. Given the androcentric perspective forged in halakhic texts, in what ways can they be used to formulate a "hermeneutics of remembrance"? In such a process, what is lost and what is gained?

Plaskow questions whether, when women's voices are added to tradition, their female timbre will express itself through the venue of halakhah.[16] Here Plaskow echoes issues brought forward by Carol Gilligan[17] and indicates three problems. First, "what is the changing historical relationship of women"[18] to the halakhic system? Second, what is the relationship between women's experience and halakhah? And third, in what ways would/do feminist rituals nurture an openness and focus on relations perhaps minimized in halakhic formulations? Plaskow's analysis of these issues is astute. She questions whether "an emphasis on relationship is inherently nonnomian"[19] and is carefully attuned to the bases of the halakhic system that are concerned with one's relationship with God, both individually and through human connections. She recognizes the possible pitfalls of a moral order and religious sensitivity rooted in legal obligation. Much like the critique of prophetic literature,[20] she knows that attention to detail can become an end in itself, truncated from its moral context, blurring its rootedness in one's relationship with God[21] and in the concrete, lived reality. Yet without boundaries, human nature and the political community wander, unguided, lacking parameters. Each path, that of legal obligation and that which emphasizes subjective choice, has its difficulty.

For Plaskow, how does a Jewish feminist regard halakhah? S/he views it as that which provides "structure and content to a human religious and social vision" at the same time as this vision is "humane."[22] In the feminist view of halakhah, according to Plaskow, the possibility of radical halakhic change must somehow mesh with the notion that perhaps a feminist Judaism can exist without halakhic normative guidelines as they are known in the tradition. She writes, "[S]ince feminism questions any definition of 'normative' Judaism that excludes women's experience, it cannot accept the idea that a Judaism that includes women's experience will necessarily fall within certain predetermined boundaries."[23] While recognizing Jewish law as central to Jewish living, Plaskow nonetheless acknowledges that a feminist Jewish theology would differ from classical Judaism in its understanding of both the content and methodology of legal development. The formation of such a theology, she knows, "is just beginning" and therefore must remain open to further elucidation and analysis. Plaskow wrote this in 1990, and, indeed, the deepening understanding of the relationship between feminist Jewish theology and halakhah continues to be explored. The writings of Ross and Adler exemplify this ongoing examination. Even Ellen Umansky, who writes from a Reform perspective and some of whose writings seem incompatible with the halakhic viewpoint, maintains that a feminist Judaism, to be Jewish, must be halakhic.[24] The continuing discussion of how and in what way(s) Jewish feminist theology can remain connected with halakhah will be further explicated when the works of Ross and Adler are analyzed. But Plaskow probes several other issues related to feminist theology and they are briefly presented here. As part of the reexamination of hierarchical dualism, the same hierarchy that establishes male as dominant and female as subordinate, Plaskow explores the differences between "chosenness" and "distinctness."[25] Her critique of hierarchy is a challenge to the fundamental conceptual basis of Western thinking: the binary or oppositional mode of cognition. Is hierarchical dualism necessarily male? Does it necessarily lead to a power nexus in which women are subjugated and exploited? Can we as human beings use reason in any other way? On a societal level, can we function without hierarchy in terms of axiology or morality?[26] While problem solving can be contextual and relational as well as hierarchical, need it be an either/or? Is not feminism itself advocating particular values when it argues for one perspective over another, for the values of feminism which, unlike those of Western culture, do not subjugate women? What is the construct of the hermeneutic advocated by Plaskow, and to what extent is "remembrance" impeded by suspicion? These important questions as formulated by Plaskow are also further explored by Ross and Adler.

Parallel to the discussion of broadening Jewish memory in the area of Torah and acknowledging the diversity of the Jewish community is Plaskow's carefully constructed argument for the use of a plurality of images and metaphors for God. Plaskow here joins many others in demonstrating the effect on community and individual consciousness of the predominance of androcentric images of God. She suggests as a possible linguistic and conceptual alternative that God's might could be construed as empowering rather than dominating.[27] As there are "seventy faces to Torah" so may there be at least seventy—indeed an infinite number—of names or metaphors for God. God need not be imaged in terms of hierarchical domination but understood as the Being who "cherishes diversity," who acknowledges and values difference. The critique of hierarchy thus profoundly affects how Plaskow articulates the issue of God-language; indeed, it may possibly be understood as a critique of the very concept of God's transcendence. Plaskow is correct that given the one-sided emphasis on masculine metaphor (e.g., God as King, He, Father), the corrective, at the very least, must be an incorporation of female metaphor into how we talk about God (e.g., God as Mother, Nurturer, Immanent Presence). But surely the philosophical difficulty does not entail a permanent either/or.

The interconnection between liturgical language and theology is a significant aspect of current Jewish feminist theology that Plaskow addresses. Ross alludes to and Adler directly discusses the use of male metaphor and language in constructing a universe of discourse and social reality in which maleness is normative, domination is acceptable, and woman remains Other. The theological challenges of traditional liturgy have been explored in the work of Marcia Falk, whose *Book of Blessings*[28] remains the premier reworking of Jewish liturgy seen through the lens of feminist theology. Its poetry, translations, and transfigurations represent spiritual texts as highly developed, sensitive, poignant searchings. For instance, in place of the ancient formulation, "*Baruch ata hashem* etc.," Falk gives God the appellation *Eyn hachaim* (source of life). She sometimes begins a blessing with the first-person plural grammatical form of *Nevarech* (let us bless) or *nekadesh* (let us sanctify or hallow). The theological metaphor of Eyn hachaim is intended to acknowledge God as provider and nurturer, and Falk offers a detailed description of how this phrase came to be. As a deeply religious poet, Falk sees her task not only as the poetic expression of the meanings of the traditional formulations but also as a means to sculpt the language of liturgy. Such aesthetic-literary sculpting would modify the male imagery of God, making the divine, in human speech, truly gender free. Falk's renderings and essays make an important contribution to the development of Jewish feminist theology through liturgy and language.

As Plaskow comments, "[I]f the Jewish community is to become truly inclusive and the liturgy is to reflect and foster inclusiveness, then women's presence will need to be . . . brought fully into the foreground of awareness." Such foregrounding is intrinsic to Falk's work, which contributes to Jewish feminist theology through its linguistic embodiments of feminist theological conversations. Falk's work realizes a previously unarticulated understanding of the sacred. She insists that "the dismantling of hierarchical dualisms is not to be confused with the abolition of distinction."[29] Falk makes explicit the underlying theological disputes intrinsic to Jewish liturgy. Her prayers and their commentary offer a probing theological critique of fundamental issues of Jewish feminism. The 1997 discussion of *The Book of Blessings* by four theologians—Adler, Rebecca Alpert, Aryeh Cohen, and Plaskow—testifies to its theological impact.[30]

In her delineation of feminist Jewish theology into God, Torah, and Israel—one might rename them Divinity, Law/Instruction, and Community—Plaskow has established the foundation for all further explorations of Jewish feminist approaches to the theological underpinnings of Judaism. Melding her insights into Judaism and rabbinic literature with her wide-ranging knowledge of theology and feminist literature, she has elaborated on the possible philosophical ramifications for Jewish feminist theology of the centrality of halakhah. She has explored the notion of hierarchy and examined its implications, and she has commented on the difficult issue of God-language. In these ways, Plaskow has set the stage for all subsequent deliberations regarding Jewish feminist theology. Ross continues the investigation from a different denominational and philosophical framework.

Ross has articulated her feminist theological position over a number of years in presentations she has given at conferences of Edah and the Jewish Orthodox Feminist Alliance (JOFA)[31] beginning in the late 1990s, in an essay published in the journal *Judaism* in 1993,[32] and in a series of Hebrew articles she wrote during her student days, the 1960s, before, as she writes, "the terms 'feminism' or even 'women's lib' were common currency." Her position is clearly put forth in "Modern Orthodoxy and the Challenge of Feminism"[33] and in her recent book, *Expanding the Palace of Torah: Orthodoxy and Feminism.*[34] "I have little patience," she writes, "for the arbitrary exclusion of women from traditionally male-based centers of power. People who listen to me," Ross continues, "say I have become more radical, although I'm not sure that I would agree."[35]

Ross gives three reasons for what she calls her "change of heart." First is the extent to which the "changed perception of women's roles in Western society has taken hold" within large segments of the Orthodox community, both in terms of advanced Torah learning and new avenues of practical expression. Second is her increased sensitivity to what she calls the "male bias" in Jewish tradition and the courage to express that bias. There is, she claims, "significance to the fact that halakhah has been molded primarily by men," and it is important to explore that significance. The traditional process of decision making in halakhah "almost by definition leaves no scope for the direct input of independent women's practical experience, expertise, and self-knowledge."[36] Women's voices, perspectives, and feelings, when part of a decision, are interpreted through a male lens. And third, Ross says she has become much more aware of possibilities and options within the halakhic system. She attributes this increased cognizance to female scholars and "their male sympathizers."[37] These three factors impel Ross to pursue and distill the philosophical and sociological ramifications of halakhic decision making, halakhic decisions, and the fears of feminism expressed in contemporary Jewish legal literature.

Ross's analysis begins by affirming that Jewish tradition is based on a hierarchical view of society. A significant social division is *cohen, levi,* and *yisrael*—the priests, levites, and laypeople—each of whom is given a different designated function. Another—equally significant—distinction is that of gender, that is, male and female. Despite apologetics to the contrary, it is obvious that the male is what Ross terms "the representative" Jew.[38] This vision of women's place in Jewish society is, as Ross says, "in direct opposition to Western democratic ideals and to the modern notions regarding the nature of gender distinction."[39] Despite the seeming omnipresence of "hierarchy" in just about all philosophical systems—Plato is an obvious example—the spread of democratic social ideals coupled with increasing gender egalitarianism within democratic societies has rendered anachronistic the earlier division of male in the public arena, female in the private domain. To what extent this dichotomy can continue to be maintained in Orthodox tradition is one of the questions posed by Ross.[40]

Ross thus begins, as does Plaskow, by questioning the very concept of hierarchy, especially the hierarchical structure of the halakhic system in regard to gender division. The second issue she deals with is the nature of the halakhic process itself, especially the unwieldy circumlocutions of decision making. Here she incorporates analyses of subjectivity, creativity, and autonomy as well as the impact of the gradual erosion of the *kahal,*[41] or centralized Jewish community authority.

Ross believes that any revamping of Judaism to further diminish or eliminate its androcentrism cannot discount the "entire body of law, lore, and literature that has developed in its wake—including various accommodations, compromises, and trade-offs for women," something that, in her reading, Plaskow does. Rather, she claims, "I think it would be fair to say that the ultimate message of Judaism, over and above the notion of monotheism, is the centrality of *halakhah* to the religious way of life."[42] At various times in Jewish history, beginning with the formulation of what became Pauline Christianity, the centrality of law to religious life was scrutinized. Ross maintains that "[a]ttempts at preserving Judaism without reference to *halakhah* as an essential bridge to the divine never remained Jewish for very long."[43] Thus, she argues, Plaskow's model, while significant, may not be workable. Rather, suggests Ross, the sociological approach, on one level, may be correct. But any corrective—or historical movement—she claims, whether sociological or theological, requires development of a new paradigm of theological thinking. This model is explicated by Ross after her examination of related essential issues.

In contradistinction to those who would claim an absolute, value-free method of rabbinic decision making, in tandem with modern philosophical thinking, Ross clearly demonstrates that such a methodology is impossible. No decision, even the seemingly most cut-and-dried legal pronouncement, is "value-free." Ross is also careful to note that the function of halakhic decision making—indeed, one might compare briefs from various U.S. courts to this process[44]—is such as to always weigh the moral and practical repercussions of a responsum, as far as one is able to make such a judgment. That element of the posek (legal decisor) often enhances authority, especially in the ultra-Orthodox world. In that context there exists a strong allegiance not only to the content of the *p'sak* (legal decision) but also to the very form of what is understood as a sanctified legal tradition.

Ross goes on to investigate the apologetics found in Orthodox literature and to examine its reliance on essentialism as a philosophical claim. She explores "overarching halakhic principles" as they have led to women's greater participation in the public arena, in activities previously tagged with a "men only" sign. Also used by halakhic decisors—although infrequently—is the practice of simply ignoring earlier halakhic precedents. The well-known example given by Ross is found in the writings of Rabbi Moshe Sternbuch, a contemporary decisor, who wonders why the prohibition against unmarried men and all women—both married and unmarried—teaching young children is blatantly ignored. The original prohibition was based on the fear of the intermingling of the sexes. Rabbi Sternbuch asks: Why is this halakhah so obviously neglected? "Could it be that it is the influence of the widespread mixing of the sexes in the modern marketplace?"[45] The very question contains the answer: surely the change has come about because of an altered social environment.

Ross's essay continues by exploring public policy and political factors, the uniqueness of the "woman question," feminism as a perceived threat, and the implications of feminism for halakhic reality. Each of these categories is more fully analyzed in her recent book, in which nuanced philosophical ramifications are meticulously explored. Let us deal with each briefly. Concerns for the possible long-range—and broad—implications of specific legal rulings can lead to conservative decisions. For example, while Rabbi Moshe Feinstein permits women to *daven* (pray) in a tallit (prayer shawl), he does so with some reluctance.[46] Others argue about female recitation of kaddish (the memorial prayer for the dead),[47] or *sheva berachot* (the blessings said during the marriage ceremony and at subsequent celebrations for the bride and groom),[48] or reading of the Book of Esther on Purim.[49] In the clash between conservative tendencies and religious change, "issues of public policy remain the most elastic and open to debate." Some argue "that the integrity of the halakhic system demands unswerving allegiance to the status quo,"[50] but others recognize that such inflexibility will alienate women—and men—from tradition.[51]

Given the significance of public policy considerations in legal decisions, why the special alert in regard to issues relating to women? In the history of Jewish law there appears to have been no such difficulties when the legal modifications of selling *chametz* (unleavened products) on Passover or taking interest (*heter iskah*)[52] developed. Ross puts forth three possible reasons for the sense of threat that accompanies rethinking of women's status. First, she sees the situation as pressing, even urgent. The dissonance between women's status in the Western world, including in Conservative and Reform Judaism, and that of women in Orthodoxy is powerful. Second, issues relating to women involve deep moral sensibilities. They encompass "the nature of sexuality, the Jewish family, and the community at large."[53] The risks of vitiating gender differences entrenched in our history have to be weighed against the benefits of greater autonomy and self-fulfillment for women. And third is "the fact that in addition to the centrality of the issue in and of itself, its solution ultimately involves an ideological enterprise of . . . major proportions."[54] That is, the conscious acceptance of feminism—in its variegated permutations—as a legitimate and explicit influence on Jewish life cannot be gradual and indirect. By its very nature, it is straightforward and incisive.

Feminist thinking, as Plaskow perceived so well, challenges traditional Jewish theology. Indeed, it sees itself as generating "a spiritual revolution," one that envisions alternative ways of understanding God, the human being, and history. Feminism suggests that the fundamental halakhic model of male-female relations is culturally determined. That the Jewish legal system is constructed entirely from a male perspective "seems to relativize its legitimacy,"[55] Ross states. The feminist critique thus points to a devaluation of the halakhic mind-set. Feminist theology goes beyond woman's initially slow entry into advanced Jewish learning or the proliferation of women's *tefillah* (prayer) groups or the larger number of women in high managerial positions in federations. Yet the impact of the current explosion in women's advanced Torah learning cannot be underestimated. Knowledge—Jewish literacy—"is the great democratic equalizer."[56] Male rabbinic authorities can no longer ignore the voices of women, voices that now speak with an expertise that can match their own. Through the development of a critical mass of learned women, feminism in Orthodoxy now includes a religious spirituality through intellectual rigor available to women in ways never dreamed of by Glueckel of Hameln,[57] Rayna Batya,[58] and other women of the last centuries.

All this having been said, how can traditional theological categories accommodate concepts of social conditioning and the influences of history? The answer is: not very well. If aspects of the Torah, such as patriarchal institutions and viewpoints, are conditioned by historical context (as indeed Maimonides argued in regard to sacrifices),[59] then the concept of divine revelation is challenged. Indeed, echoing Cynthia Ozick's lament,[60] "What sort of God is it who ignores women's voices and experiences?" queries Ross. How can Orthodox Judaism respond to this challenge?

Other than intensifying an isolationist approach—which obscures rather than meets the challenge—Ross suggests a theological solution that takes into account the many precedents in Jewish tradition that would allow "the new-found reluctance of both men and women to maintain patriarchy as the ideal societal mode"[61] and would, in addition, be regarded positively. That is, rather than lament about change and "the way things were," one would welcome transformations that increase not only the autonomy, leadership, and creativity of women, but also the substantial potential contributions of women to Jewish religious life.

Ross's feminist theology is based on the concept of revelation of Rabbi Avraham Yitzchak Kook, which views the divine word as gradually unfolding over time. History is the backdrop to this cumulative revealing of divine intention. Since human beings are placed in time and space, "all receptions of the word (including the one at Sinai) are time and culture-bound" (emphasis in original).[62] The conditions of history are not accidental. There is divine significance to their sequence and development; human needs continue to be met and moral sensibilities refined. Thus sacrifice and slavery were superseded by prayer and social freedom. The legal status of women improved—mostly—over the centuries. Revelation at Sinai can still be understood as "an immutable element in the Jewish foundational canon" even as aspects of its content are seen as culturally outmoded.

Based on her study of Rabbi Kook's philosophy, Ross meets the challenges of feminism by embracing a doctrine of cumulative revelations through the movements of history rather than a one-time proclamation from God at Sinai. Indeed, she sees the ultimate theological question as "Is the Torah from Heaven?"[63] This parallels theological conflicts in other religious groups, all of which are compelled to deal with the fundamental issue of how revelation can accommodate historical change and development.[64] Ross scrutinizes halakhah as carefully as Plaskow does, in ways both similar and different, and with full cognizance that Orthodoxy must not shield itself from confronting feminism. Women who play out the tension of modernity within the Orthodox community often are advocates for change by the very activities they have developed within that community. Their involvement in prenuptial agreements, prayer groups, the creation of new rituals, the training of women leaders, and the establishment of places of Torah study for women all help create the necessary conditions for new meanings of female spirituality within the established traditional community. Controversies of the past have demonstrated that the criteria for separating "a legitimate from a questionable legal ruling is often the retroactive decree of history as it unfolds within the halakhic community."[65] Such a "wait and see" attitude is summed up in the well-known quip of Rabbi Yehiel Weinberg in regard to women voting: "Time, not logical debate, will resolve the controversy."[66] To me that seems a vote—male and rabbinical—for history and historicism.

As others before her, Ross clearly demonstrates that halakhah has always encouraged creativity, which is understood as elaboration on the texts' original meaning. She writes, "The idea of accumulating revelation may be regarded as a natural outgrowth of this traditional understanding of the nature of rabbinic interpretation and its relationship to the Written Torah. What it adds is merely the conviction that if these free-flung interpretations of the Torah have evolved in a certain way, there is likely to be something of significance to be derived from this particular involvement."[67] Such a fluid notion of Torah presents the Sinaitic revelation not as Martin Buber's "moment God"[68] nor as outlined by Plaskow, whose groundbreaking work begins the process of rethinking its conception from a feminist perspective. As Ross notes, Plaskow departs from Reconstructionist formulations in that she leans toward a dialectical theology rather than denying any supernatural element in history.[69] Much like Buber, Plaskow puts forward the notion of "moments of intense religious experience."[70] In contrast, Ross's fluid notion of revelation suggests Sinai as revealing God's word through initiating "a series of revelations in the form of inspired interpretations throughout the ages. The ideal meaning of the Sinaitic revelation is eked out only with these accumulated interpretations."[71] While Ross's notion of the successive unfolding of God's plan has echoes of Hegel,[72] it remains rooted not in abstract process but in the practical—and messy—lived experience of the religious community. Ross maintains, "For the believer, if any particular idea or social form, no matter what its source, takes hold and informs the life of Jews committed to Torah, this is a sign that it stems from God and was meant to be."[73] Both audacious and undaunted, Ross proclaims that Jewish theology not only can combine with feminism but is also more truly revelatory when it does.

Plaskow delineates the parameters of Jewish feminist theology by affirming that "[w]omen's halakhah . . . and women's self-defined relation to halakhah await the present and the future."[74] Ross, writing more than a decade later, outlines a theology of halakhah that incorporates the future. Citing some of the many instances in which Jewish law has accommodated historical change, Ross advocates the inclusion of feminism, in its broadest sense, as a legitimate and positive transforming element in the tradition.

Rachel Adler's 1998 study, *Engendering Judaism: An Inclusive Theology and Ethics,*[75] builds on Plaskow's analyses of God, Torah, and Israel, as well as Ross's framework of "cumulative unfolding" as conceptual doors through which feminism can comfortably enter Jewish theology. What follows is an analysis of one theoretical aspect of Adler's Jewish feminist theology as well as a foundational, practical example of how the theory can be stunningly applied in Jewish life.

Adler is well aware that halakhah—whatever its shortcomings with regard to women—cannot be easily dismissed. One must wrestle with its underlying attitudes and essentialisms in terms of gender, perspectives, and specific laws. "An authentic modern Jewish theology," she writes, "has to account for the norms and praxis of Judaism."[76] Theology requires a method that can connect what we believe with what we do.[77] A profound dimension of the halakhic system is to bind human physicality with the cognitive/spiritual/moral element. We think, imagine, and make choices, all of which are realized though action; as thinking influences action, required action influences thinking.[78] The legal system of Judaism, Adler says, must therefore be "engendered"; that is, it is no longer acceptable to presume that while women are represented in Judaism, they constitute a separate category. To engender Judaism means to understand the impact of gender as a category in Jewish texts, subtexts, and contexts, and to struggle with the ethical task of reexamining priorities, assumptions, and axiologies.[79] In an engendered Jewish community, women, like men, will be

Rachel Adler being honored at a 1984 Los Angeles conference titled "Illuminating the Unwritten Scroll: Women's Spirituality and Jewish Tradition." The conference was organized by Rabbis Laura Geller and Patricia Karlin-Neumann to address the following question: "What is the nature of women's religious experience?" Adler is dancing with the representation of the "other" scroll that would reflect a Judaism that takes women's experience seriously. Used with the permission of Alexis Krasilovsky, http://www.csun.edu.

normative members of the community. The private domain and public arena will be gender-neutral spaces. Equal access or equal obligation, as Adler sees them, are band-aids that avoid the problems in the system's own categories, terms, and structures. She sees the goal of liberal halakhah as repairing "the inadequacies of classical *halakhah* exposed by modernity while leaving the system basically intact."[80] Even more, halakhah must be proactive. Adler explains this through the theoretical legal formulations of the philosopher of law Robert Cover, who uses the metaphor of a bridge to convey the delicate equilibrium required as legal development and historical reality are interwoven to create the social fabric, as classical and liberal versions of halakhah—and their feminist critics—enter into conversation.[81] The bridge connects the story of a tradition with committed praxis. As Adler writes, "Ultimately, law is maintained or remade not by orthodoxies or visions but by commitments of communities either to obey the law as it stands or to resist and reject it in order to live out some alternative legal vision."[82]

Adler draws on Cover's work, especially his "Nomos and Narrative,"[83] as a paradigm for how the halakhic system can be inclusive of women. Cover maintains that no legal system is systematized in a static body of law to which the community adapts and adheres. Rather, as the narratives of the community reflect its history and moral visions, its legal traditions articulate the norms and values embedded in the narratives. Narrative and law, or nomos, are in a dialectical relationship. There is a dynamic equilibrium, one that may shift, but that nonetheless permits the bridge to safely carry out its connecting function. The responsibility for this balance rests not only with the legal establishment but also—and primarily—on the community of practitioners. Indeed, Adler focuses on the community as a central source of halakhic development. Cover's principle is already present in rabbinic law in the category of custom (minhag)[84] and in the notion of taking an obligation upon oneself, such as women establishing as a requirement the hearing of shofar on Rosh Hashanah.[85] Does Adler advocate a broad—if not "complete"—interpretive freedom? Tamar Ross thinks so.[86] She claims that Adler is "writing [the halakhic system] . . . off altogether";[87] I am not so sure. Surely Adler, who for years was Orthodox and then reestablished herself within the Reform movement, has used her considerable acumen both to observe and articulate two very different perspectives on the same essential—and thorny—question. But complete interpretive freedom would lead to anarchy in any legal system.

A good way to clarify Adler's complex theory of reconstructing halakhah is to examine the concrete practical example she investigates, an instance of legal alteration she regards as foundational for an engendered Judaism: marriage. Rejecting a Judaism in which women's public voices are silenced, Adler maintains that women must be full dialogical partners in the public conversations of the Jewish people. Marriage, with all it entails, is the perfect place to begin the transformation.

Adler anchors her analysis in the ketubah (Jewish wedding contract). She argues that the traditional Jewish legal concept of kinyan (acquisition) in marriage—that is, the man acquiring the woman—is solely a commercial transaction. In other words, the marriage contract conveys the woman from the domain of one male—usually the father—to another—the husband. Here we must be clear: this transaction is in terms of the woman's sexuality. In other areas women are treated as autonomous persons.[88] But exclusion from the realm of public religious expression drastically limits autonomy. Adler's meticulous analysis of the texts shows how the biblical language of marriage as "taking" is transmuted by the rabbinic use of *kiddushin* and *hekdesh* as primary metaphors of marriage. Biblical acquisition is softened, but not invalidated. And it is the woman who must be acquired because only the woman undergoes a status change: she will belong exclusively to the man. The man will not belong to the woman in the same way because, in relationships, men are subjects and never objects, unless they are slaves.[89] A woman is no longer purchased, but she is still acquired.[90]

Adler designs a marriage contract very different from the traditional ketubah. She calls it a *brit ahuvim* (covenant of lovers), designating a marriage of two subjects. Such a marriage would follow the laws of a partnership, not the acquiring of property, and would incorporate the rabbinic understanding of partnership. Adler rewrites all the documents of the traditional marriage ceremony, wishing to avoid any intimation of kiddushin, or acquisition. Through the brit document a partnership of equals, of subjects, is effected. Like other partnerships, the brit could be dissolved at the initiative of either partner. Basing a marriage on partnership law, *hilkhot stutafut,* reflects the economic as well as social bases of marriage, "[b]ut unlike the ketubah, which presumes that most economic power and resources belong to the male, the *brit ahuvim* presumes communal resources and requires joint decisions about their distribution."[91] This is a stunning suggestion. In one fell swoop, it disarms the hierarchical categories that haunt the halakhic marriage relationship as well as empowering both spouses to regard themselves and each other as equal partners in all respects. Transforming the legal parameters of marriage reconfigures male-female relationships and provides a powerful strategy—both conceptual and practical—for the implanting of egalitarianism within the tradition.

Adler's creative transformation of the legal bases of Jewish marriage is supported by some documents of early Jewish history. It represents a clear, decisive, and significant rethinking of the foundation of the Jewish family and gender relations within Jewish society as a whole. The brit ahuvim engenders Jewish law for both men and women, recognizing differences between two equal subjects.

Indeed, law (halakhah), together with liturgy and language, constitutes the foundation upon which the multistoried building of Jewish feminist theory continues to be constructed. How does the tradition deal with the text in Exodus 19:15, "come not near a woman," as Plaskow queries? Can the Jewish community, individually and institutionally, learn to pray in nongendered liturgical language, thus helping to weaken deeply embedded patterns of social hierarchy? Can the concept of cumulative revelation, based on the writings of Rabbi Kook and articulated by Tamar Ross, be accepted in the still male-dominated world of halakhic decisors? Will legal egalitarianism as explicated in Adler's brit ahuvim become an integral part of the Jewish wedding ceremony?

Based on the theologies explored here, I believe it is reasonable, long term, to look toward a Jewish future in which maleness as normative, domination as acceptable, and woman as Other will be part of our past historical narrative and no longer central to the lived tradition. Inspired and influenced by the work of thinkers such as Judith Plaskow, Marcia Falk, Tamar Ross, and Rachel Adler, Judaism would continue its ever-present process of change, innovation, and adaptation.

In rethinking Jewish theology, Jewish feminism has forced us to explore some of our deepest assumptions. It has challenged us to transform memory, to recover history, to give voices to the silenced, and to carefully hear their words. It has affirmed woman as a full and equal bearer of Jewish cultural memory, a transmitter of religious legacy. In Jewish feminist theology, women are participants, intellectual contributors, and leaders of the conversation. Jewish feminist theology—its explorations into legal and liturgical texts—moves us toward Jewish living in which the Source of Life listens carefully to both the private and public voices of all, male and female.

NOTES

1. Rosemary Radford Ruether, *Sexism and God-Talk: Toward a Feminist Theology* (Boston: Beacon, 1983). A tenth anniversary edition, with a new introduction, was published by Beacon in 1993.

2. Judith Plaskow, *Standing Again at Sinai: Judaism from a Feminist Perspective* (San Francisco: Harper and Row, 1990). Parts of chapter 2 appeared in condensed and earlier versions in *Tikkun* 1, no. 2 (1986): 28–34, and *Melton Journal* 22 (Fall 1987): 3–5, 25. Part of chapter 5 appeared in a different form in Christie Balka and Andy Rose, eds., *Twice Blessed* (Boston: Beacon, 1989).

3. Tamar Ross, *Expanding the Palace of Torah: Orthodoxy and Feminism* (Hanover, NH: Brandeis University Press, 2004), xv.

4. See Pamela S. Nadell, *Women Who Would Be Rabbis: A History of Women's Ordination, 1889–1985* (Boston: Beacon, 1998). Four chapters focus on the Reform movement, with one chapter each given to the struggles within the Conservative and Orthodox denominations. See also Simon Greenberg, ed., *The Ordination of Women as Rabbis: Studies and Responsa* (New York: Jewish Theological Seminary, 1988).

5. An early apologetic tract is Moshe Meiselman's *Jewish Woman in Jewish Law* (New York: Ktav and Yeshiva University Press, 1978). The urgency can be marked by the tactics resorted to by some representatives of rabbinic leadership even of presumably middle-of-the-road Orthodoxy. See http://www.torahweb.org for a diatribe by Rabbi Herschel Schachter titled "Can Women Be Rabbis?" Some responses have been posted on the Listserv for the Women's Tefillah Network at wtn@shamash.org. In the July 30, 2004, edition of both the *Jewish Week* and *Forward,* editorials and/or news articles appeared about the Schachter piece.

6. Saul Berman, "The Status of Women in Halakhic Judaism," *Tradition: A Journal of Orthodox Thought* 14, no. 2 (1973): 2–30.

7. See Elizabeth Koltun, ed., *The Jewish Woman: New Perspectives* (New York: Schocken, 1976), and Susannah Heschel, ed., *On Being a Jewish Feminist: A Reader* (New York: Schocken, 1983). *Half the Kingdom* was produced in 1989 by Kol Ishah Productions in conjunction with the Canadian National Film Board and was directed by Roushell Goldstein and Francine Zuckerman. Regarding traditional ritual celebrations, see Micah D. Halpern and Chana Safrai, eds., *Jewish Legal Writings by Women* (Jerusalem: Urim, 1998/5758). See also Tamar El-Or, *Next Year I Will Know More: Literacy and Identity among Young Orthodox Women in Israel,* trans. Haim Watzman (Detroit: Wayne State University Press, 2002), and Rochelle L. Millen, *Women, Birth, and Death in Jewish Law and Practice* (Hanover, NH: Brandeis University Press, 2004).

8. See Elisabeth Schussler Fiorenza, *Bread Not Stone: The Challenge of Feminist Biblical Interpretation* (Boston: Beacon, 1984), 15–20. Fiorenza distinguishes between the hermeneutics of remembrance, which assumes that biblical texts and their interpretations are androcentric and bolster a patriarchal social structure, and the hermeneutics of suspicion, which nonetheless use "suspicious" sources to reconstruct women's history. See also Mary Daly's groundbreaking work, *Beyond God the Father: Toward a Philosophy of Women's Liberation* (Boston: Beacon, 1973).

9. Plaskow, Standing Again at Sinai, 23.

10. Plaskow states, "In this passage, the Otherness of women finds its way into the very center of Jewish experience" (*Standing Again at Sinai,* 25).

11. Plaskow recognizes the creative contributions of those who have worked to formulate liturgies that include the matriarchs and feminine conceptions of God. This effort is wonderfully articulated in a book published after Plaskow's volume by Marcia Falk. The first edition of *The Book of Blessings: A New Prayer Book for the Weekdays, the Sabbath, and the New Moon* (San Francisco: Harper Collins, 1996) includes original prayers, Hebrew and Yiddish poems by Jewish women translated into English, and explanatory essays.

12. Plaskow, *Standing Again at Sinai,* 72.

13. Ibid., 72–73.

14. Cynthia Ozick, "Notes toward Finding the Right Question," in *On Being a Jewish Feminist,* ed. Susannah Heschel (1983; repr., New York: Schocken, 1995).

15. Judith Plaskow, "The Right Question Is Theological," in *On Being a Jewish Feminist,* ed. Susannah Heschel (1983; repr., New York: Schocken, 1995).

16. Plaskow, *Standing Again at Sinai,* 61.

17. Carol Gilligan, *In a Different Voice: Psychological Theory and Women's Development* (Cambridge, MA: Harvard University Press, 1982).

18. Plaskow, *Standing Again at Sinai,* 64.

19. Ibid., 68.

20. For example, see Amos 5:21–24.

> I loathe, I spurn your festivals; I am not appeased by your solemn assemblies;
> I will pay no heed

To your gifts of fatlings; Spare Me the sound of your hymns
But let justice well up like water,
righteousness like an unfailing stream. (JPS translation)

21. Plaskow writes, "Observance of the law can then come to substitute for the original relation, with 'God's law' replacing God in a system that is self-enclosed and self-perpetuating" (*Standing Again at Sinai,* 69).

22. Ibid., 71.

23. Ibid., 72.

24. See Ellen Umansky, "What Are the Sources of My Theology?" *Journal of Feminist Studies in Religion* 1 (Spring 1985): 126. Some more recent Reform discussions on issues related to feminism and feminist theology are collected in Walter Jacob and Moshe Zemer, eds., *Gender Issues in Jewish Law: Essays and Responsa* (New York: Berghahn, 2001).

25. Plaskow, *Standing Again at Sinai,* 96–107.

26. These epistemological questions are discussed in Elizabeth Kamarck Minnich, *Transforming Knowledge,* 2nd ed. (Philadelphia: Temple University Press, 2005), and Hava Tirosh-Samuelson, ed., *Women and Gender in Jewish Philosophy* (Bloomington: Indiana University Press, 2004).

27. Plaskow, *Standing Again at Sinai,* 164.

28. Marcia Falk, *The Book of Blessings* (Boston: Beacon Press, 1999), 169.

29. Rachel Adler, Rebecca Alpert, Aryeh Cohen, Judith Plaskow, and Marcia Falk, "Panel Discussion of Marcia Falk's *Book of Blessings,*" *Textual Reasoning* 6, no. 3 (1997): 23. My thanks to Suzanne Smailes, technical services librarian at Wittenberg University, for bringing this article to my attention, as well as for her careful reading of a draft of this essay.

30. The comments of these theologians constituted the panel discussion written up in *Textual Reasoning* 6, no. 3 (1997): 23.

31. Edah is an organization that gives voice to the ideology and values of Modern Orthodoxy. Edah and JOFA alternate in sponsoring a conference on women and Orthodoxy every other year, usually in New York.

32. Tamar Ross, "Can the Call for Change in the Status of Women Be Halakhically Legitimated?" *Judaism* 42, no. 4 (1993): 478–92.

33. Tamar Ross, "Modern Orthodoxy and the Challenge of Feminism" in *Jews and Gender: The Challenge to Hierarchy,* ed. Jonathan Frankel (New York: Oxford University Press, 2000), 3–38. This quote is from p. 30, n. 3.

34. Ross, *Expanding the Palace of Torah.*

35. Ross, "Modern Orthodoxy," 4.

36. Ibid., 4–5.

37. Ibid., 5.

38. We can cite many sources in support of this view, but what comes to mind are the words of Samson Raphael Hirsch and Cynthia Ozick's lament in an essay written in the early 1980s. Hirsch, the late nineteenth-century Modern Orthodox leader, focused on philology in his extensive biblical commentary, written in German. Discussing a verse that uses the terms *zachar* (male) and *nikavah* (female), he

says the following: the word for male, *zachar,* is derived from the root *z ch r* (*zayin, het, resh*), meaning "to remember." His very linguistic designation calls the male to be the bearer of the tradition's cultural memory; the male represents Judaism in both knowledge and deed. Similarly, the term for female signifies the primary female function. The root *n k v,* meaning "opening" or "cavity," indicates the physical structure of the female body, alluding to its reproductive capacity and the woman attaching herself to man, thereby accepting his calling. Ozick writes that the place she feels least a Jew is often in her own synagogue—after all, if God wears *tefillin,* "like all Jews," in the words of her rabbi, where does that leave her? Femaleness has excluded her from the representative metaphor. See Hirsch, "The Jewish Woman," in *Judaism Eternal* (London: Soncino Press, 1959), 2:51, and Ozick, "Notes toward Finding the Right Question," 125. Ross also comments on Hirsch in *Expanding the Palace of Torah,* 36, noting how woman, described as mired in nature rather than culture, becomes spiritually superior in Hirsch's apologetics. Cf. Schachter, "Can Women Be Rabbis?"

39. Ross, "Modern Orthodoxy," 6.

40. The Women's Tefillah Network (WTN) Listserv of June 11, 2003, includes an excerpt of Ross's recent book, which discusses this issue.

41. The structure of the kahal, also termed *kehila,* is described and analyzed in Jacob Katz, *Tradition and Crisis: Jewish Society at the End of the Middle Ages,* trans. Bernard Dov Cooperman (New York: New York University Press, 1993).

42. Ross, *Expanding the Palace of Torah,* 136.

43. Ibid., 137.

44. Some relevant cases in U.S. law are *Planned Parenthood v. Casey,* 505 U.S. 833 (1992); *Riggs v. Palmer,* 115 N.Y. 506, 22 N.E. 188 (1889); and *McGowan v. Maryland,* 366 U.S. 420 (1961). My thanks to Janyce Katz, assistant attorney general, taxation section, state of Ohio, for locating these sources and discussing them with me.

45. Quoted in Ross, "Modern Orthodoxy," 14.

46. Moshe Feinstein, *Iggrot Moshe, Orakh Haim,* 4:49.

47. See Rochelle L. Millen, "The Female Voice of Kaddish," in *Jewish Legal Writings by Women,* ed. Micah D. Halpern and Chana Safrai (Jerusalem: Urim, 1998), 179–201, and Millen, *Women, Birth, and Death in Jewish Law and Practice* (Hanover, NH: Brandeis University Press, 2004), chap. 5.

48. See Joel B. Wolowelsky, *Women, Jewish Law, and Modernity: New Opportunities in a Post-Feminist Age* (Jersey City, NJ: Ktav, 1997), 56–70.

49. See Yehuda Henkin, *Equality Lost: Essays in Torah Commentary, Halacha, and Jewish Thought* (Jerusalem: Urim, 1999), 54–65. Also Aryeh Frimer, "Women's Megilla Readings," in *Traditions and Celebrations for the Bat Mitzvah,* ed. Ora Wiskind Elper (Jerusalem: Urim, 2003), 281–304.

50. Ross, "Modern Orthodoxy," 15. See, for example, n. 6 above and Aharon Feldman's critique of the volume, *Jewish Legal Writings by Women,* in his review essay, "Halakhic Feminism or Feminist Halakha," *Tradition: A Journal of Orthodox Thought* 33, no. 2 (1999): 61–79.

51. See Millen, "The Female Voice of Kaddish," esp. the responsum of Rabbi

Blair quoted on p. 193. Rabbi Blair states, "The kaddish brings many male Jews to the synagogue and causes them to become more involved in Judaism. This will occur also with female Jews; we would bring them closer to Jewish life and to our holy Torah." A similar view is expressed in Aaron Soloveitchik, *Od Yisrael Yosef beni hai* 100, n. 32 (Chicago: Yeshivat Brisk, 1993), 100.

52. See the appropriate entries in Uri Dasberg and Joshua Hutner, eds., *Encyclopedia Talmudit* (Jerusalem: Encyclopedia Talmudit, 1984).

53. Ross, "Modern Orthodoxy," 16.

54. Ibid.

55. Ross, "Modern Orthodoxy," 19.

56. Ibid., 21.

57. Glueckel of Hameln was a Jewish woman living in late seventeenth-century Europe. Born in Hamburg in 1646, she recorded her history in *The Memoirs of Glueckel of Hameln,* trans. Marvin Lowenthal (New York: Schocken, 1977).

58. Rayna Batya lived in nineteenth-century eastern Europe, part of the renowned and learned Epstein family. See Don Seeman, "The Silence of Rayna Batya: Torah Suffering and Rabbi Barukh Epstein's 'Wisdom of Women,'" *Torah U-Madda Journal* 6 (1996): 91–128.

59. See Mishneh Torah (Hebrew), *Hilkhot Melakhim,* 11:1. Cf. *Guide to the Perplexed,* 3:32.

60. Ozick writes, "Where is The Commandment that will say, from the beginning of history until now, *Thou shalt not lessen the humanity of women*?" ("Notes toward Finding the Right Question," 150).

61. Ross, "Modern Orthodoxy," 24.

62. Ibid., 26.

63. Ross, *Expanding the Palace of Torah,* 137.

64. An excellent study of this conflict within the Lutheran Church Missouri Synod (LCMS), the more right-wing Lutheran group in the United States, is Mary Todd's *Authority Vested* (Grand Rapids, MI: Eerdmans, 1999). Todd uses ministry of women as a case study to show how the LCMS has continually refined its concept of authority in order to maintain its own historical identity. Essays on the Missouri Synod by Donald Huber, Meuser Professor of Church History and Dean of Academic Affairs at Trinity Lutheran Seminary, also explore the dialectic between absolute revelation and historicism. With regard to Jewish tradition, a classic study is the essay by Gershom Scholem, "Revelation and Tradition as Religious Categories in Judaism," in *The Messianic Idea in Judaism and Other Essays on Jewish Spirituality* (New York: Schocken, 1971), 282–304.

65. Ross, "Modern Orthodoxy," 28.

66. Weinberg, *Seridei esh* [Hebrew], v. 3, responsum 105, p. 322. Source given in Ross, "Modern Orthodoxy," 38n107, quoted on 29. Also see Zvi Zohar, "Traditional Flexibility and Modern Strictness: Two Halakhic Positions on Women's Suffrage," in *Sephardi and Middle Eastern Jewries: History and Culture in the Modern Era,* ed. Harvey E. Goldberg (Bloomington: Indiana University Press, 1996), 119–33.

67. Ross, *Expanding the Palace of Torah,* 199.

68. For a critique of Buber's notion of revelation and his concept of "moment God," see "Martin Buber's Epistemology: A Critical Appraisal" in *Post-Holocaust Dialogues: Critical Issues in Modern Jewish Thought,* ed. Steven T. Katz (New York: New York University Press, 1983), 1–51, esp. 41–46.

69. Ross, *Expanding the Palace of Torah,* 188.

70. Plaskow, *Standing Again at Sinai,* 33.

71. Ross, *Expanding the Palace of Torah,* 201.

72. See Emil Fackenheim, *The Religious Dimension of Hegel's Thought* (Boston: Beacon, 1970).

73. Ross, *Expanding the Palace of Torah,* 205.

74. Plaskow, *Standing Again at Sinai,* 72.

75. Rachel Adler, *Engendering Judaism: An Inclusive Theology and Ethics* (Philadelphia: Jewish Publication Society, 1998).

76. Ibid., 47.

77. Ibid., xxii.

78. A fascinating explication of this principle, articulated within the rights versus obligation legal theory context, is found in an essay by Robert Cover, "Obligation: A Jewish Jurisprudence of the Social Order," in *Narrative, Violence, and the Law: The Essays of Robert Cover,* ed. Martha Minow, Michael Ryan, and Austin Sarat (Ann Arbor: University of Michigan Press, 1995), 239–49.

79. Adler, *Engendering Judaism,* xv.

80. Ibid., 34.

81. Ibid., 35.

82. Ibid.

83. See Robert Cover, "Nomos as Narrative," in *Narrative, Violence, and the Law,* ed. Martha Minow, Michael Ryan, and Austin Sarat (Ann Arbor: University of Michigan Press, 1995), 95–173.

84. An excellent discussion of minhag can be found in Daniel Sperber, *Minhagei Yisrael: Mekorot Vetoladot* (Hebrew) (Jerusalem: Mossad Harav Kook, 1990).

85. Arlene Pianko, "Women and the Shofar," *Tradition: A Journal of Orthodox Thought* 14, no. 4 (1974): 53–63.

86. Ross analyzes Adler's use of Cover's theory in *Embracing the Palace of Torah,* 149–56.

87. Ibid., 158.

88. See Judith Romney Wegner, *Chattel or Person? The Status of Women in the Mishnah* (New York: Oxford University Press, 1998).

89. Adler, *Engendering Judaism,* 176.

90. See Michael Satlow, *Jewish Marriage in Antiquity* (Princeton: Princeton University Press, 2001).

91. Adler, *Engendering Judaism,* 192.

CHAPTER TWO

MEANINGS OF SHEKHINAH IN THE "JEWISH RENEWAL" MOVEMENT

CHAVA WEISSLER

Jewish Renewal is Hasidism meets feminism.
—Rabbi David Wolfe-Blank

Renewal is a well-spring of women's energy.
—Nan Fink Geffen

God is coming through the women this time.
—Barbara Breitman

Encountering a feminist conception of God can transform a life. In Los Angeles during the 1980s, Joy Krauthammer encountered feminism through the Los Angeles Jewish Feminist Center, with such Jewish Renewal teachers as Savina Teubal and Sue Elwell, and later with Judith Halevy: "Feminism gave me the ability to worship a God who isn't the Lord. . . . I can pray to the Source of All Blessings."[1] Not long after, Krauthammer began to attend the ALEPH Kallah (the biennial weeklong gathering of Renewal Jews) and Elat Chayyim (the Jewish Spiritual Retreat Center), where she learned how to shape her spiritual practice to her new understanding of divinity: "I start the morning by greeting the sun . . . I go out in my bare feet and dance in the garden as the sun is coming up, and say the *Modah ʾani* ["I acknowledge"; a prayer said on awakening]. I learned it from Shefa Gold[2] at the Kallah in 1993. I learned that I could be free and liberated to express myself in ways I didn't know I *could*." A spiritual seeker for most of her adult life, as well as a musician, photographer, and artist, this woman, coming from a secular Jewish background and married to an Orthodox man, had been involved in both Hare Krishna and Chabad (Lubavitch Hasidism) before settling into Jewish Renewal in the early

1990s. While she still maintains connections with the Orthodox and Chabad communities, Krauthammer is so identified with the Jewish Renewal movement that she introduced herself to me by saying, "I *am* Renewal!" In addition to her work with women teachers, Krauthammer formed deep connections with such male Renewal leaders as Zalman Schachter-Shalomi, Shlomo Carlebach, David Zeller, and Stan Levy.[3]

How does one speak of (or pray to) "a God who isn't the Lord," as Krauthammer phrases it? This essay, after giving some background information on ALEPH: Alliance for Jewish Renewal, will discuss the use of God-language in Renewal and explore how it is implicated in the competing versions of feminism expressed and created by women such as Krauthammer. Although the theological meanings of God-language are important, the focus here will be on its social meanings, that is, on the implications of this mode of constructing gender for the lives of women and men in the Jewish Renewal movement. Renewal Jews insist that God cannot be comprehended in human language, and must be addressed in multiple images. However, one of the most revolutionary moves they make is their reshaping of the mythological figure of the Shekhinah, the feminine divine of kabbalah. Jewish Renewal's understanding of Shekhinah will be compared to the figure of Shekhinah in classical kabbalah and to other forms of God-language in Renewal. Further, I will argue that the Shekhinah of Jewish Renewal can only be understood if we take into account Renewal's emphasis on artistic avenues for spiritual expression.

This essay is part of a larger study of the religious world of the Jewish Renewal movement. My primary research methodology is ethnographic, including participant observation at a variety of events ranging from synagogue services to national conferences, and interviews with Renewal members and leaders.[4] I have also read a good deal of the literature, both print and electronic, produced by Renewal Jews. Of central importance to the present essay was participant observation at the sixth annual conference of the Association of Rabbis for Jewish Renewal (known as OHaLaH), held in January 2004. That year, the conference was titled "Tachat Kanfei Hashechinah! (Under the Wings of the Shechinah)," and it was devoted to an exploration of the feminine divine in Jewish Renewal. Because those who attend this event are the rabbis, and thus the leaders, of the movement, they are in a position to shape the understanding of Shekhinah for others. Both the formal sessions and informal conversations provided rich material for understanding the meanings of Shekhinah for Renewal Jews.

THE ORIGINS AND STRUCTURE OF ALEPH: ALLIANCE FOR JEWISH RENEWAL

Although many aspects of American Judaism might be characterized as "renewal" in some form, my study is more narrowly focused and confined to organizations and people closely associated with ALEPH. I have been studying ALEPH since 1999, and I have discussed its characteristics at length elsewhere.[5] According to one self-description, Jewish Renewal is rooted in a kind of neo-Hasidism, as well as in the counterculture of the 1960s, the ecological and feminist movements, and "Eastern Influences."[6] Like the Havurah movement,[7] another founding influence, Jewish Renewal is one of several alternative forms of Judaism that have flourished over the last thirty years in North America, Europe, South America, and Israel. Two rabbis, both originating from Lubavitch Hasidism, can be regarded as the founders of Jewish Renewal: Zalman Schachter-Shalomi and the late Shlomo Carlebach. Carlebach was the inspiration for the founding of the House of Love and Prayer in San Francisco in 1967.[8] Many of those associated with it later joined the Aquarian Minyan in Berkeley, inspired by Schachter-Shalomi, which was founded in 1974.[9] Schachter-Shalomi himself had founded the B'nai Or ("Sons of Light") Religious Fellowship, a precursor of ALEPH, in 1962, and incorporated it in 1978; around 1980, the name was unofficially changed to P'nai Or ("Faces of Light") to avoid the apparent sexism of the earlier title. ALEPH, the umbrella organization for the movement, was founded in 1993 from an amalgamation of P'nai Or and the policy-oriented Shalom Center, founded by Rabbi Arthur Waskow in 1982. In the summer of 2005, ALEPH and the Shalom Center decided to part ways but maintain amicable cooperation.

Currently, the organization is headed by a paid executive staff of three members—Executive Director Debra Kolodny, Chief Operating Officer Susan Saxe, and Director of Spiritual Resources Rabbi Daniel Siegel—and by a rotating board of at least twelve people, drawn from active members, with a chair, cochair, secretary, treasurer, and legal counsel. The administrative offices are in Philadelphia, but only the chief operating officer actually lives in the city; business is conducted by phone and e-mail.[10] There is also a Spiritual Advisory Council consisting of eight people who rotate every two years. They are rabbis, cantors, artists, and healers, all associated with the movement.

ALEPH's Web site describes Jewish Renewal as "a worldwide, transdenominational movement grounded in Judaism's prophetic and mystical traditions."[11] Note the term "trans-denominational." Jewish Renewal aspires not to be a new denomination—in addition to the established four: Reform, Reconstructionist, Conservative, and Orthodox—but rather to spread spirituality to all of them.[12] Sometimes members refer to Renewal as the "R & D [Research and Development]" arm of contemporary Judaism. Rabbis ordained in each of the four movements, and some who have received private ordination, are associated with Jewish Renewal. Over one hundred rabbis have completed the ALEPH Rabbinical Program. While there are thirty-seven "ALEPH-Affiliated Communities" in North America (and three abroad), affiliation need not be exclusive, but may be combined with affiliation with one of the major denominations.[13] Only about two-thirds of those who pay dues to ALEPH are also members of an affiliated congregation; one-third are either members of other sorts of congregations or not affiliated with a congregation at all.[14] ALEPH has a rabbinical ordination program and a rabbinical association, a newsletter and other publications, a biennial weeklong gathering called the Kallah, as well as a number of other programs. No longer formally affiliated, but still closely allied, is Elat Chayyim, a Jewish Spiritual Retreat Center in the Catskill Mountains of New York.[15] Several other retreat centers are found in the western and southwestern United States.

CHARACTERISTICS OF THE JEWISH RENEWAL MOVEMENT

The Jewish Renewal movement emphasizes spirituality as an approach to Judaism. The quest for an experiential relationship with the divine is absolutely central to Jewish Renewal. ALEPH sees itself as neo-Hasidic, drawing flexibly on traditional—especially Hasidic and mystical—Jewish texts and practices, as well as on other spiritual traditions, such as Buddhist meditation and yoga. Like Hasidism, Renewal emphasizes artistic spiritual expression through music, storytelling, and dance. Charismatic leadership has been central to the movement, and Schachter-Shalomi has functioned as the movement's rebbe, or spiritual head. Members recognize the importance of charismatic leadership, of Schachter-Shalomi and many other teachers (male and female), in achieving spiritual exaltation; however, there is also some recognition of the dangers of such leadership as well as ambivalence about its future role in the movement.[16] In addition, Renewal Jews are committed to "Tikkun olam" (mending the world), especially by means of ecological, peace, and social justice activism, and what they call "Tikkun ha-lev" (mending the heart), which encompasses the values of American psychotherapeutic culture. Finally, ALEPH is explicitly feminist, and explicitly welcoming to lesbian, gay, bisexual, and transgendered Jews.

THE MEMBERSHIP OF ALEPH

Although there are no statistics available on the breakdown by age, gender, or economic status of the approximately three thousand members of ALEPH, I gained some impressions in this regard from my participant observation at numerous Renewal events. In general, two-thirds to three-quarters of the participants, and about half the leaders, are women.[17] The majority of the participants are baby boomers, but some are as young as their twenties and others are in their seventies and eighties. Singles, couples (both heterosexual and homosexual), and families ("traditional" and "nontraditional") are all important segments of the membership. Many members of Renewal are married to non-Jews, have a non-Jewish parent, or have some other complexities in their religious affiliation.

Many people active in Renewal have already been involved in various other alternative spiritualities, from Hare Krishna to Chabad, and some combine Jewish Renewal with Buddhist mindfulness meditation, Native American–style shamanism, or other spiritual practices. As already mentioned above, there are those who combine Renewal with other branches of Judaism. For many, the question may be not whether they are Renewal Jews but what part Jewish Renewal plays in their spiritual economy. As one young woman told me in an interview, she thinks about God from a Reconstructionist perspective, *davens* (prays) like a Renewal Jew, "and then there's that little bit of Buddhism."[18]

A great many of the people, especially of the women, most attracted to Renewal are artists: painters, weavers, potters, writers, photographers, musicians, dancers. (There are more men among the musicians than in any other artistic field.) Some are professional artists; for others art is an avocation with an important place in their lives. Another sizable occupational group for both women and men is the "helping professions," primarily psychotherapists but also physicians, nurses, teachers, massage therapists, chiropractors, and physical and occupational therapists; except for medicine, these are, of course, professions that are dominated by women. Finally, some people are attracted to Jewish Renewal's left-wing politics; many in this group work in or consult for socially conscious nonprofit organizations. As may be deduced from this list of professions, the members of ALEPH are culturally middle class, but many are hardly well-to-do. A

"Rain of Tears." ALEPH: Alliance for Jewish Renewal used this image on Yom Kippur cards to express the importance of acting as "holy stewards of creation" and responding to the crisis in the environment. The painting (originally in color) captures the importance of the environment and nature, often portrayed as female, to Renewal and offers visual images of women and men at prayer. Used with the permission of Barbara Siegel, http://www.barbsiegel.com.

minority of ALEPH members work in the corporate world or in other more highly compensated occupations (law, information technology, and so forth).

This essay quotes numerous rabbis. Some members of OHaLaH, the Association of Rabbis for Jewish Renewal, work full time as congregational rabbis (only a few of the larger Renewal congregations are able to pay a full-time rabbi). Depending, in part, on where they were ordained, they have pulpits in Renewal, Reconstructionist, and Reform congregations, often in small or out-of-the-way communities.[19] Some rabbis combine congregational work with a variety of other occupations, and many of them have received ordination but work in other ways. They may be certified therapists or spiritual directors, work for Jewish or other nonprofit organizations, teach in universities or other schools, act as hospital, geriatric, or military chaplains, run their own nonprofit retreat, study, or policy centers, lead retreats or teach courses, give concerts, or sell their art or writing. Indeed, many Renewal rabbis do no paid congregational work but cobble together a living in entrepreneurial fashion.

JEWISH RENEWAL AND FEMINISM

Since its inception, ALEPH has been committed to incorporating the talents, insights, and experiences of women into Jewish life. Two of the eighteen "Statements of Principle" from ALEPH's Web site are germane here. First, "women and men are full and equal partners in every aspect of our communal Jewish life."[20] This speaks to the acceptance of women as rabbis, teachers, leaders, and members of a minyan. Beyond this, it implies the creation of new ways to fill these roles, informed by women's perspectives and experiences. As one Renewal rabbi remarked to me, "We didn't want to just dress up in suits and go to shul like men."[21] Another distinguished between what she called "egalitarianism, in which women get to do what men always did," and "feminism," which is "changing the map."[22] Indeed, Renewal is a wellspring of women's energy and has been characterized by one leader as "Hasidism meets feminism."[23] But Hasidism, like all "traditional" Judaism, sharply distinguishes between male and female spirituality, roles, and responsibilities. In the twentieth century, Chabad Hasidism, the school in which some of the most influential Renewal leaders were formed, in fact articulated a feminine spiritual role.[24] With this background, Renewal feminism is perhaps more likely to understand women and men as essentially different, if spiritually equal.

Second, Renewal's feminism cannot be understood simply as the full participation of women at the practical level; it extends to the theological realm as well: "We intend to open ourselves to the transformation of consciousness and action that is resulting from our living in a time when the Feminine is emerging." If the heart of Jewish Renewal is the search for an experiential connection with the divine, for Renewal Jews, feminism entails the recognition of the feminine aspect of divinity. Thus, they turn to the figure of Shekhinah, God's immanent Presence, usually symbolized as female in Jewish mysticism. "All of the dimensions of Shechina, [t]he name, the concept, the manifestation of HaShem that is intimate, that is immanent, are core to the theology of Jewish renewal," explains Debra Kolodny, executive director of ALEPH.[25] The kabbalistic myth of the exile of the Shekhinah also speaks to Renewal Jews. For the cosmos to be whole, the Shekhinah, the female aspect of the divine, must be redeemed from exile and reunited with the Holy One, Blessed be He, a masculine aspect of the godhead. This myth formed part of the original motivation of Zalman Schachter-Shalomi, and perhaps other Renewal leaders from Hasidic backgrounds, such as Shlomo Carlebach and David Wolfe-Blank, to invite women into full participation. They saw the emergence of women's voices as the expression of the divine feminine, and they held that only women could call the Shekhinah home from her exile.[26] Yet theirs was not the only view of Shekhinah that came to be expressed in Renewal, nor is Shekhinah the only way that Renewal Jews speak of and to God.

One issue that emerges from this identification of women with the feminine divine is that of "essentialist" feminism (sometimes also called "cultural" or "difference" feminism). As the theologian Rachel Adler explains,

> In an early phase of contemporary feminism's development, many feminists enthusiastically embraced [the] idea of an essential feminine nature. . . . On the basis of women's shared biological characteristics and history of patriarchal oppression, they postulated a universal women's culture whose common experiences transcended historical context, cultural difference, class and politics. . . . For Jewish women, cultural feminism provided ways to affirm the holiness of bodies that do not have "the covenant sealed in our flesh," bodies that menstruate, bodies that lactate. . . . Cultural feminism offered rich and readily accessible sources for feminine imagery.[27]

Thus, on the one hand there is "essentialist," or "complementary," feminism and on the other, social constructivist or "egalitarian" feminism. The first position is that men and women are "essentially" different in important ways. The way to achieve a just society—or to heal Judaism of its sexism—is to revalue the feminine to incorporate women's nurturing qualities and sensitivities to nature and relationships into a renewed society or a renewed Judaism. The second position is that although men and women do indeed differ biologically, most gender roles are social constructions and do not express innate or "essential" qualities of the sexes. According to this view, the way to achieve a just society—or to heal Judaism of its sexism—is to reveal the constructed, rather than natural, character of gender roles, thus freeing women and men to participate on an equal footing, in whatever ways they choose, without prejudging what masculine and feminine spirituality—or other qualities—might be. Most Renewal Jews, when asked, say that they fall somewhere in between these two approaches.

Adler is critical of essentialist feminism: "What is clear is that, because essentialist imagery reinforces gender stereotypes, it confines rather than throws open the significations of what it means to be a woman." This is true for depictions of women and for imagery of the feminine aspects of God: "[R]estricting femininity to images of parenting and domestic concern—the nursing mother, the nesting bird, the midwife, the busy *hausfrau*—limits both God and women." Most important for our topic, Adler asks, "Is it possible to extricate Shekhinah from the essentialist meanings with which it was endowed in Jewish mysticism?"[28] One question we will explore is the degree to which the myth of Shekhinah as adapted by Renewal expresses an essentialist view of women. To further this discussion, we need to look at the kabbalistic myth on which Renewal's version of Shekhinah is based and at other forms of God-language in Renewal.

SHEKHINAH IN KABBALAH

In a move that is both subtle and complex, Renewal explicitly recognizes and articulates the importance of the Shekhinah, the feminine divine of classical Jewish mysticism. An important part of the meaning of Shekhinah for people in Jewish Renewal is precisely that the concept comes from kabbalah, that is, from a *Jewish* source. Renewal Jews seek ways to express their spiritual instincts and experiences in Jewish terms, and thus they seek resources from within Judaism. Further, Shekhinah is not only "Jewish, but also "mystical," close to Renewal's emphasis on spiritual experience and to its turn toward the "mythical" rather than the "cognitive" resources from the Jewish past. To understand how Renewal has adapted the figure of Shekhinah, we'll look at the classical version of this myth, especially at the notions of gender embedded in the kabbalistic concepts of Shekhinah.

The topic of Shekhinah in classical kabbalah is vast and varied, and only a brief summary can be offered here.[29] According to kabbalistic teachings, Divinity is truly Infinite and Unknowable. This aspect of the godhead, called Ein Sof (Infinity), manifests and reveals Itself in the ten *sefirot,* or attributes, known by such names as Wisdom and Understanding, Loving-kindness and Stern Judgment. Two of these are seen in particular as having feminine qualities. The tenth and last *sefirah,* and the one most consistently imaged as feminine, is Shekhinah, the divine presence and immanence in the world. Like the moon, but unlike the other sefirot, Shekhinah has no light of her own but receives divine light and abundance from the sefirot about her and she reflects and channels them to the lower worlds.

A central myth of the kabbalah is that the brokenness of this world, the fact that we live with exile, evil, pain, and death, is an expression of the exile or eclipse of Shekhinah, her separation from the rest of the sefirot, especially from her divine spouse, Tiferet (Beauty), often referred to as Ha-Qadosh Barukh Hu (the Holy One, Blessed be He) and identified with the sun. This exile began with the sin of Adam and Eve in the garden, according to earlier kabbalah, and will end in the messianic era. Another image used by the kabbalah for the state of Shekhinah is the waxing and waning of the moon, and the very fact that the moon's light is lesser than and reflected from that of the sun. A midrash teaches that at Creation, the moon's light was as bright as the sun, and in the messianic era, her light will be restored to its primordial brilliance.[30]

In classical kabbalah, the Shekhinah is an ambivalent figure: while in exile, she is in the power of the forces of evil and can be turned to their ends. This speaks to our experience of life as painful and unpredictable. But it also reflects the ambivalence male kabbalists felt about women. Shekhinah in kabbalah encodes well-known gender stereotypes: the feminine is passive and receptive, receiving and transmitting the power of the masculine. Shekhinah can be seen as a beckoning princess or a comforting mother, but also as a stern and punitive disciplinarian.

For kabbalists, the myth of Shekhinah's exile is in part about the fate of the people of Israel; for Hasidim, it is about the life of the soul; for both, it is about the redemption and healing of the cosmos. As we have seen, Renewal Jews have adapted this myth as a way to frame gender issues. The exile or eclipse of the Shekhinah refers to the absence of women's voices and feminine spirituality from Judaism,[31] while Shekhinah herself symbolizes women's presence and power. While Renewal's Shekhinah differs from the kabbalistic Shekhinah in certain ways, it, too, is founded on gender difference. More than that, as we shall see, Renewal's version of the Shekhinah valorizes certain "feminine" qualities.

"Das Ewig-Weibliche zieht uns hinan," intoned Zalman Schachter-Shalomi, speaking at the conference of Jewish Renewal rabbis held in January 2004. He was quoting the ending of Goethe's *Faust:* "The Eternal Feminine draws us upward." Moreover, he warned, "Don't try to schlep the Shekinah into the cognitive realm. The word Shekhinah has the same *gematria* [numerical value] as *ha-ʿarafel* [the fog]. We must be comfortable in 'endarkenment' as well as in enlightenment."[32] Clearly, for Schachter-Shalomi, there *is* an "eternal feminine"; he understands Shekhinah as a mythical figure, expressing a feminine essence that is noncognitive and mysterious. Not all Renewal Jews share this view, but we shall see that some of them understand women as possessing intuitive knowledge and a connection to the natural cycles that are also bound up with their connection to Shekhinah.

SHEKHINAH AND GOD-LANGUAGE IN JEWISH RENEWAL

Rabbi Geela Rayzel Raphael offered a course titled Feminine God-Language at the Bux-Mont Jewish Community Center outside Philadelphia. The announcement for the course reads as follows: "In the last two decades God has been transformed. The King of the universe has been exploring his feminine side. Come and greet the bride, the Queen, and meet the writings of Jewish feminists who have transformed tradition."

Raphael, who considers it her mission to bring Jewish Renewal to the women of the suburbs, takes a lighthearted approach here, but the questions she raises are quite serious. To understand the meanings of Shekhinah—and her relationship to the King of the Universe—one must briefly consider the range of terms and images for God used in Renewal, and the tension between "mythical" divine images—God with personality, so to speak—and more abstract images that eschew anthropomorphism.

Recognizing that all images for God are human and limited and that the purpose of such images is to enable a connection with the divine, Renewal explicitly encourages the use of multiple names for God. A song by Rabbi Hanna Tiferet, a well-known Renewal leader and recording artist, glorifies the multiplicity of God's names:

> When I sing the name of God my spirit rises
> from the depths she soars to the light
> Shaddai Shekhina Adonai Tzevaʾot

Havaya M'kor Hayyim
Tzur Makom Eyl Elyon
Yah Ruah Elohim.[33]

Renewal worship puts this multiplicity into practice, as we read, for example, in the introduction to the prayer book used by Kehilla in Berkeley, California.

> We hope and pray that this siddur might be a vehicle to help you connect the deepest part of your being with the Holy Mystery that we call God. . . . May your experience here this Shabbat morning breathe new life into you, into this kahal, this holy gathering, and into the world.
>
> You are encouraged to use the language which is most meaningful to you in addressing the Divine Mystery and Presence. . . . [T]he traditional and unpronounceable name of God . . . has no gender and is a name of Being-Becoming. Adonai, Shechina, and Yah are some of the ways we refer to the Name without pronouncing it.[34]

Despite this pluralistic approach, some of the "traditional," overwhelmingly masculine ways of imagining God used in the Torah and the prayer book, the Talmud and the midrash, seem difficult or offensive to members of Jewish Renewal. Jewish feminist thinkers argue, and Renewal Jews agree, that God-language and social structure are intimately intertwined.[35] Powerful, gendered images of God are understood to stand for and support the power of the corresponding gender in humans. God was called "King" in biblical times because kings were the most honored and powerful members of society; "Lord," because lords command; "Father," because fathers are the heads of the household. Kings, lords, and fathers are men, and so this terminology symbolizes and reinforces the dominance of men over women and conveys the perception that maleness is somehow closer to divinity than femaleness. Both the sexism and the hierarchy embodied in these images go against Renewal's deepest principles. As Rabbi Phyllis Berman told me, "'Lord' feels so unfriendly, so external to the self and to the world. And with regard to Melekh ha-ʿolam [King of the Universe], on the simplest level, as a citizen of a democracy, I have no internal resonance with 'King.' And also . . . it doesn't help any of us to see God as this male figure. . . . My sense of God is limited neither by human gender, nor by being so far away from me. I'm no more satisfied by Malkat ha-ʿolam [Queen of the Universe]."[36] Berman's remarks express the push that motivates some participants in the Jewish Renewal movement to get beyond anthropomorphic or mythological ways of imagining the divine, and the preference for immanence rather than transcendence in Renewal conceptions of God.

Nonetheless, precisely because these masculine, transcendent images for God have been so central to Jewish liturgy in the past, there have been attempts to reinterpret and recuperate them. An effort to grapple with the masculine imagery for God appeared in the program for the 2003 Kallah. Rabbi Ruth Gan Kagan offered a class called King, Warrior, Father, Lover: Reclaiming the Masculine Face of God. Part of the description for the course reads,

> In the 80s, spiritual feminism brought to the surface our struggle with hierarchal, patriarchal Judaism; *Shechinah* was invited back from her exile into the language of our prayers and blessings, and the King was sent to his chambers. All is well. Or is it? To re-explore the masculine face of God, our approach will be deeply personal, blending ancient wisdom with new teachings. . . . Jewish tradition offers a magnificent epic of the holy dance of divine feminine and masculine within each human being. Come wrestle (or maybe dance!) with old ideas and new.

Kagan, in a Jungian move, internalizes the masculine and feminine, pointing out the balance between the two within individual souls. However, this approach did not seem to resonate with most Renewal Jews; registration for this class was too low for the course to be offered.[37]

Another exploration of the possible meanings of "King" and kindred terms has stemmed from the symbolism of Hebrew letters. This technique dissolves the literal meaning of the words by looking at their individual letters. For example, Rabbi Marcia Prager, rabbi of P'nai Or Religious Fellowships in Philadelphia and Princeton, and dean of the ALEPH Rabbinic Program, reinterprets *melekh* (king) as being made of up of the meanings of its constituent letters: "When we bring *mem* and *lamed* together with *khaf* we can read *Melekh* in this way: the maternal waters, source of creativity from which all life issues forth (*mem*), are channeled and guided (*lamed*), toward the hand/vessel that is open to receive and give (*khaf*). *Melekh* takes us from source through channel to ourselves as receivers and givers."[38] However, some Renewal Jews find this reinterpretation forced or hard to keep in mind while praying.[39] The word *ʾAdonai* has also received a reinterpretation in Renewal sources, as based on the Hebrew word *ʾeden* (אדן), "doorsill," so that ʾAdonai becomes a doorway rather than a Lord.[40] And Marcia Prager correctly points out that ʾAdonai, spelled אדני (as opposed to the Tetragrammaton), is one of the mystical names for Shekhinah.[41]

Neither of these attempts to bring back God as Father and Lord has been very successful in Jewish Renewal, and we must ask why. It may be because the balance of power in Judaism is still seen by many Renewal Jews to be very much on the side of men and the masculine. As Arlene Goldbard, vice chair of the ALEPH board of directors, put it in a post to the ALEPH Listserv in 2004,

> In virtually all davvenen [prayer] and study contexts, I must have my simultaneous gender translator engaged at all times: we can drash [interpret] away till the cows come home, but the primary texts are still the primary texts. . . . Believe me, this requires a stretch and that stretch is only slightly ameliorated by having one or two Shekhinah-centered prayers on Shabbos. . . . I'm willing to tote my simultaneous gender translator and make the stretch so far, but if the little we have done toward correcting a humongous imbalance were truly deemed having strayed too far from the male-centered tradition, having cost men too much, I think my flexibility would soon run out of steam.[42]

While Goldbard is not referring specifically to recovering male God-language here, she makes it clear that the "humongous imbalance" is still a problem in need of correction. Another post to the same Listserv reads, "I have always been drawn to rituals involving the feminine. . . . Sometimes a shift to the other side is needed to correct imbalances of the past to bring them back into balance. I don't see a move back to center at this time."[43]

More common than the effort to rehabilitate the masculine mythical images is the use of nonanthropomorphic terms for God. Joy Krauthammer uses the term "Source of All Blessings." Barbara Breitman speaks of God as Being, Life, and "a Process that is larger than ourselves."[44] God may be referred to as ʿEin ha-ḥayyim (the Source of Life, drawing on the liturgical work of Marcia Falk, who is not, herself, associated with Renewal[45]) or Ruaḥ ha-ʿolam ("Life Spirit of the Universe," instead of Melekh ha-ʿolam, "King of the Universe"). All of these terms express the immanence of the divine presence in the world and eschew both hierarchy and gender imagery. Perhaps the most widely used term is the biblical Yah, a shortened form of the Tetragrammaton, the four-letter Name of God. Despite Zalman Schachter-Shalomi's interpretation of Yah as expressing the complementarity of the masculine and the feminine,[46] others see it as akin to the Buddhist meditation of following the breath. Some Renewal Jews pronounce Yah in such as way as to recall the "breath of life" by exhaling vigorously as they speak it; Phyllis Berman translated it as "Breathing Spirit of the Universe."[47] A prayer such as the shema, although it is taken directly from a biblical text, may be recited using Yah as the divine name,[48] and readers may use Yah as they chant from the Torah. Some Renewal Jews also (erroneously, from the point of view of Hebraic tradition) take this name to be grammatically feminine and give it feminine adjectives and verbs.

Moving in the direction that also leads to Shekhinah, others create new feminine images for God. This can take the form of a simple, and rather mechanical, substitution of feminine for masculine terms: ʾImenu Malkatenu (our Mother our Queen) instead of ʾAvinu Malkenu (our Father our King), or rendering a blessing as Berukhah ʾat Yah Shekinah, ʾElohatenu Ruaḥ ha-ʿolam (Blessed are you, Yah Shekhinah, our Goddess, Spirit of the World). More creative are two related terms incorporating reḥem (womb): Raḥamema (Oh Holy Rachamema, Compassionate Womb-Mother)[49] or Raḥamima (Compassionate Mother of All).[50] Raḥamima may intend to incorporate Raḥamim, an alternative name for Tiferet (the Holy One, Blessed be He), the (masculine) sixth sefirah, into a feminine form of the divine. Note the importance of the Motherhood of God. The feminine divine is identified in these images with the capacity to bear children; birth is a symbol of creation. Such imagery shades over into the way Shekhinah is used by Renewal Jews.

WHAT'S AT STAKE: SHEKHINAH AND GENDER POLITICS

Marcia Prager states, "In the Renewal Community, the Shekinah is ascendant. Women's skills are valued, celebrated, and nourished."[51] Thus, Prager sees the Shekhinah as connected to women's empowerment. Debra Kolodny points out that "[t]he *k'vod* [honor] given to the Divine feminine has ramifications . . . in how we treat one another, in how we pray, in how we respect and honor women and intuition and nurturing, in endless ways that make up a theology that is egalitarian and womanist."[52] And according to Geela Rayzel Raphael, Shekhinah conveys to women that they are made in God's image, that they are full beings in relationship to divinity. She sees Shekhinah and other female God-language as rectifying an imbalance, restoring full spiritual power to women and raising the consciousness of men.

Abigail Weinberg, a woman in her thirties who grew up with both Renewal and Reconstructionism, gave the following analysis:

> When Zalman [Schachter-Shalomi] brought this all to everybody's attention—the idea . . . that there is a masculine and a feminine in God and

> in Judaism—which I imagine he got from your basic kabbalah and Chabad literature—people got it because it really reflects our reality. What that did was, it brought the feminine to be as important as the masculine. In a way, since the masculine had been the only thing that people had seen for a thousand years, we're rushing to catch up with the feminine and blow up the feminine. . . . Men have created the Jewish God, and now women are helping to create God.[53]

Thus, women—and men—in Renewal understand the attention paid to Shekhinah as an expression of the power of women within the movement. Both women and men function as charismatic leaders and teachers, shaping new forms of Judaism and new ways of thinking about God, and as administrators and managers of Renewal organizations and projects. The original core institutions of Renewal (P'nai Or and the Shalom Center), as well as Elat Chayyim, were created by men; however, more recently, women have created retreat centers and other programs. And there are distinguishable male and female styles of leadership, especially among those who lead services, teach courses, and create new forms of ritual, artistic, and musical expression.[54] A delicate balance, not always articulated fully, reigns between the needs and desires of men and women in the movement. One reflection of the tensions that have emerged in this regard is the constant lament that Renewal is unsuccessful in attracting a sufficient number of men, leaving them a minority of the membership.

Another manifestation of this tension is that Shekhinah seems to be seen in Renewal as primarily a "woman's God." Although Shekhinah is important to Schachter-Shalomi and some other male leaders,[55] my sense is that most men in Renewal see Shekhinah as irrelevant to themselves most of the time. For example, one man told me that he was surprised to find himself turning to Shekhinah; the only time this happened was when he was working through some issues regarding his feelings about his deceased mother. It is curious that Shekhinah, as imagined in Renewal, lacks the heterosexual erotic quality that one finds in the classical kabbalah: the hidden, beckoning princess, the exiled and longed-for spouse.[56] Along the same lines, the Shekhinah of Jewish Renewal tends to lack the "dark side," the harshness, found in kabbalistic sources.[57] Renewal's Shekhinah is motherly, not erotic or punitive.

Noting the nature of Shekhinah in classical kabbalah as an "ambiguous male projection of what woman can be," the feminist theologian Judith Plaskow remarks that the "Shekhinah is a usable image for feminists only if it is partly wrenched free from its original context, so that the tradition becomes a starting point for an imaginative process that moves beyond and transforms it."[58] This is precisely Renewal's project,[59] but its version of Shekhinah nonetheless reinscribes gender difference. Geela Rayzel Raphael teaches about Shekhinah in classes, sings to her in musical compositions, and represents her in fabric art; she stresses the difference between "the receptive receptacle of the Kabbalists, waiting to be mounted" by the male sefirot, and the "Shekhinah Queen Goddess," the transvaluation of the traditional myth. But while Raphael rejects the passivity of the kabbalistic Shekhinah, she emphatically highlights Shekhinah's feminine qualities, describing her as a sympathetic, compassionate earth mother. She connects this with her understanding of gender difference, seeing it as part of her mission "to help Jewish women . . . come to understand the feminine nature of their soul and psyche."[60]

Renewal teachers who speak of Shekhinah affirm women's power and the holiness of qualities identified with the feminine. A song titled "The Ways of a Woman" by Hanna Tiferet expresses the identification of women and Shekhinah through the characteristics often identified as feminine by "cultural" feminists.

> The ways of a woman a man cannot know,
> He does not understand
> The cycles, the seasons, the ebb and the flow
> The prayers of the earth are the secrets women know
> We sing the song of Shekhina, bringing us all home,
> Lifting us on wings of light to a place we've always known.
> We sing the song of Shekhina, waiting to be heard.
> The ways of a woman are the ways of life.
> There's power in our words.[61]

Note the intertwining of God as Shekhinah with a view of women that connects them with natural cycles and the earth. The ways of women are mysterious to men, according to Tiferet. The song ends with a warning and an invitation: "Don't stop the women from singing their song. . . . Just sing along." Men should not suppress women's spirituality, but neither are they to be excluded from this women's world.

Taking this further, there are those who emphasize that Shekhinah is both important and only part of the picture. According to Debra Kolodny, "[H]aving a whole relationship with the Divine requires a relationship with the feminine manifestation of the Divine." However, she also insists that "[a]ll of us [in Jewish Renewal] are attentive to the truth that Ha Shem

[God] is both male and female and neither male nor female." This has both theological and sociological consequences.

> [A] core theology of Jewish renewal is the obligation to achieve an internal balance of the Divine feminine and masculine. In order for us to live fully into our birthright, *b'tzelem Elohim* [in the image of God], we must strive for that balance. And, in order for the world to regain its external balance, we must strive to create systems and structures and opportunities that allow people to do this holy work, that honors and supports them, that provides role models of integrated people, that affirms and rewards success in this realm. . . . Because social constructs, along with expectations, mores, norms . . . often conflict with that obligation, our work is difficult, but it is still mandatory.[62]

Interestingly, in an interview, Kolodny highlighted gender difference: "We have different hormones. Let me tell you, they affect how we behave. . . . I say Hallelujah to those differences, because it creates . . . a dialectic that allows for some juice. . . . We're going to elevate and fully honor women in our wisdom and our different ways of knowing, and integrate women into what ha[ve] been traditionally male bastions of knowing and learning. I guess I would say that's the project, merging . . . essentialist and social-constructionist feminist theory."[63] Like many I interviewed, Kolodny insisted that she is neither an essentialist nor a social constructionist feminist, but she could see the importance of both approaches.

At a plenary session of the conference of Jewish Renewal rabbis in 2004, Rabbi Leah Novick[64] presented a view of Shekhinah as the Divine Presence/Mother who has accompanied the Jewish people throughout the ages, from biblical times to the present. She spoke of Shekhinah as the feminine Divine Presence who inspired both men and women. She distributed a handout distinguishing the "stages of Shekinah consciousness" roughly paralleling Jewish history, beginning with the "Great Mother, Earth Mother: in creation of the cosmos and in the birth and renewal of all creatures," and including, among others, the "Ethical Mother: Teachings of the Talmudic sages," the "Romantic Mother: . . . Shabbos Queen, of the Kabbalah . . . Holy apple orchard, Princess, Bride," and the "Absent Mother" of the rational process, enlightenment movement. She concludes with the "Goddess Re-awakening: Contemporary, feminist, ecological." These stages of consciousness are a schematic presentation of insights she conveys in a poem titled "Shekhinah," which she also distributed at the session. While most of the poem speaks of the way Shekhinah inspired the male sages throughout the history of Judaism, the final two verses read,

> To our diaspora Foremothers, she was the Divine Presence
> as the Compassionate Source
> the one they called out to in childbirth, illness and death
> and celebrated on the New Moon
>
> And to us contemporary seekers, she is the Divine Presence
> In the voices of women, representing the Shekhinah re-awakening
> Who is calling to us from the earth . . .
> Save the planet, stop the nuclear madness, clear the air,
> heal the sick, respect the elders, care for the children.[65]

It is only in these two final verses that Novick locates the Shekhinah in the context of women's lives. Despite her emphasis on Shekhinah as an aspect of God for all Jewish people, she affirms the special role of women in calling forth Shekhinah in the present day. She believes that the Divine Presence rests on everyone and everything, from rocks to humans: "Throughout our history, Jewish women have had a special relationship with Shekinah, but that does not preclude men and children." Note also the similarity of her language with the terms of ecological feminism. Her vision of Shekhinah is similar to Gaia, Mother Earth; for Novick, Shekhinah calls for ecological activism.[66]

At one breakout session of the conference of the Association of Rabbis for Jewish Renewal, people spoke of their understandings of Shekhinah. One topic of debate that emerged was how closely Shekhinah should be identified with women. One of the participants in the discussion said that she wanted to "decouple" Shekhinah from women, while another objected to this, saying that she very much wanted to keep that connection, especially as she was dealing with infertility issues. Another woman, known for conducting powerful rituals and study sessions, said, "All I am is about Shekinah. If she doesn't show up, I'm nothing." One of the men present spoke of how he wanted more of the "Shekhinah side" for himself: instead of the hard-driving, busy, competitive male life, he wanted a softer and gentler way to live. Although the participants had different ideas about Shekhinah, they seemed to identify her with *characteristics* understood culturally (perhaps even stereotypically) as feminine, even if they did not necessarily want to identify her with *women.*

For some men in Renewal, Shekhinah can also express men's *disempowerment.* One male in this breakout group—I hesitate to call him a participant—simply sat silently and looked bored throughout the discussion. He clearly felt compelled to be present and wished he were elsewhere. Near the end of the discussion, another man asked if "the pendulum was still swinging farther, or if it was starting to come back." It turned out that he was tremendously resentful of the ALEPH sexual ethics policy that forbids sexual contact between teacher and student, in that he felt it was directed, punitively, at men. He said that when he tried to raise the issue at teachers' meetings, other men literally pulled him back down into his seat and told him that men just could not raise this question. Although his remarks seemed "off topic" in a narrow sense, he saw, correctly, that the rise in feminine God-language was connected with the rise of female power.

Among those I have quoted, there is a range of views on how closely Shekhinah is connected with women. For some, the "song of Shekhinah" is the song of women in touch with the cycles of nature and with intuitive knowledge. For others, Shekhinah represents the feminine half of an inner psychological balance. For still others, Shekhinah is a motherly aspect of divinity that inspires both women and men. All agree, however, on two points: the very fact that Renewal Jews call upon Shekhinah expresses the empowerment of women, and that Shekhinah is tied to the qualities identified as feminine in our culture (soft, warm, motherly, nurturing). None of those quoted appears to question this construction of the feminine or worry that it could reinforce the very stereotyping of women it is meant to counteract.

SHEKHINAH SKEPTICS

Rhonda Shapiro-Rieser, a rabbinical student and spiritual director, heatedly dissented from some views expressed at the 2004 rabbinical conference: "Sometimes we forget that [Shekhinah] is a metaphor. If it's not a metaphor, it's the same problem all over again." She continued, "I don't know what 'feminine energy' is. There's been an imbalance [in Judaism], and I'm willing to go along with [correcting the imbalance], but it's a metaphor!" That is, in her view, Shekhinah, "feminine energy," and the "Eternal Feminine" are metaphors, not "real," and reifying the metaphor leads to essentialism.[67] Feminist theorists have made it clear that mythological feminine figures, if they are thought to express the essential qualities of femaleness, can be politically problematic; they may lead to the same kind of gender stereotypes that were prevalent in patriarchal culture, even if the valence seems to be reversed.[68] "Essentialist feminism is bullshit," Arlene Goldbard said in an interview. "And I tend to close my eyes to its presence in Renewal."[69]

Others, while perhaps not conscious of the dilemmas of essentialism, still find Shekhinah problematic in one way or another, though they do not reject the term entirely. Marcia Brooks, executive director of Kehilla in Berkeley for ten years beginning in the mid-1990s and active in many other Renewal groups, told me,

> I don't like to say "Shekhinah." That's just like leaving Adonai on the other side to me. It's almost this goddess thing, which is not interesting to me, although there are some prayers where Shekhinah fits very well. I especially love using feminist language, feminine God-language and feminine power relationship to God-language in the Torah service, because the Torah has always been a Tree of Life, and she has always been held near, and . . . I love saying the blessings in the feminine.[70]

Clearly, in most contexts, Brooks is not interested in any sort of goddess figure, nor does she want either a feminine or a masculine divinity. She does, however, find certain liturgical contexts appropriate for feminine imagery.

When I asked Phyllis Berman about Shekhinah, there was a long pause. Then she said that she does not feel drawn to the term "Shekhinah": "It sets up in my mind a duality about God: Adonai feels masculine and Shekhinah feels feminine. And I want unification." Here Berman is speaking particularly about addressing God in prayer; in other contexts, "Shekhinah" can be a meaningful term to her. She understands "Shekhinah-energy," for example, to express the energetic creativity of Jewish women.[71]

There are those in Renewal who simply do not find Shekhinah a terribly important figure. When Abigail Weinberg made it clear that she prefers nonanthropomorphic images for God, such as "ocean," I asked her specifically about Shekhinah. Weinberg said,

> [In Renewal] there are so many ways of saying . . . "Adonai" and "God" and "Shekhinah." The Shekhinah: Shabbos, white, embracing. If I want to get into a Shekhinah mood . . . I don't use the word a lot, but it's all about a toolbox. Jewish Renewal has just blown that toolbox up so it's much bigger and you can make a lot more things with it. So if I was

> leading Friday night services Jewish Renewal–style, I might refer to this idea of the Shekhinah, of the embracing, soft, warm God. . . . It's not that crucial to me, I guess.[72]

For Weinberg, Shekhinah does hold "feminine" qualities, appropriate for Friday night, when Jews welcome the Sabbath Queen. But Weinberg is more interested in Renewal's "toolbox," the expanded vocabulary of symbols and rituals that enables one to step out of the box of traditional liturgy.

Like Shapiro-Rieser, Weinberg recognizes Shekhinah as a metaphor, one among many. Thus there is, within Renewal, a critique of the myth of Shekhinah as expressing essential feminine qualities. In the same conversation at the rabbinical conference, Shapiro-Rieser expressed distress that essentialists are in the majority in Renewal. She objected to the stereotypical warm nurturing qualities associated with Shekhinah among Renewal Jews. "For me," she said, "the 'feminine' is Xena the warrior princess."

CONCLUSION

Let me now suggest another way of thinking about these questions. Perhaps the important distinction is less between those who take an essentialist or a social-constructionist position—after all, few members of Renewal are systematic thinkers—and more between those who are mythological or artistic thinkers, and those with a more cognitive style. For example, the sixth annual meeting of the Association of Rabbis for Jewish Renewal was judged a great success by most of those who participated. Some remarked that it was the theme of Shekhinah—and the presence of women, Shekhinah's representatives, on the planning committee—that had created the warm, open, restful atmosphere of the conference. Others said that the atmosphere had been created by excellent programming, careful setup, and attention to detail.

This striking gap between "mythological" and "cognitive" thinkers expresses the varied meanings of Shekhinah and other God-language in Jewish Renewal. Those for whom Shekhinah is a fully mythic figure, expressing essential qualities of femininity, appear to be in the majority. Even some of those who prefer nonanthropomorphic terms for God may feel that women's biology is crucial for their spirituality. Despite her insistence that God is beyond gender, for example, Phyllis Berman told me that women's capacity to bear children endows their spirituality with distinctive womanly qualities.[73] And some of those for whom Shekhinah resonates as a metaphor are resolutely anti-essentialist.[74] Thus, one cannot make a neat equivalence between types of God-language and essentialist or social-constructionist views of women.

Let me also suggest that we misunderstand the meanings of Shekhinah for Renewal Jews if we fail to attend to the artistic and the experiential dimensions. Jewish Renewal attracts a great many people with artistic talent and sensibilities, and fosters artistic expression of spirituality. The draw of Jewish Renewal for such people is that it is an opening to the imaginal dimension, to creativity, and to the mythic. There is clearly a difference between making an argument and creating a painting, a song, or a ritual. Leah Novick concludes her poem on Shekhinah, discussed above, as follows: "And to Her, we respond—we are ready to create a dwelling place for the divine here on earth, to Her we answer in music and meditation, in politics and poetry, in dance and drama, to Her we respond, 'Hineynu' yes, we are here!" It is through the arts (as well as political activism) that one creates a dwelling place for the Shekhinah.

For the artists of Jewish Renewal, Shekhinah is far more than a metaphor. This essay began with the words of Joy Krauthammer, a spiritual seeker who is an artist and a musician. For the past four years, among her other activities, Krauthammer has been the percussionist at Lev Eisha (Heart of a Woman), the Los Angeles Women's Minyan, meeting monthly "with about 150 ruach-filled, singing, Miriyahm dancing, praying, learning, sharing women." Moreover, as Rabbi Geela Rayzel Raphael showed me her silk paintings on Shekhinah themes, she talked about how doing art puts her into a meditative state. Dream language is symbols, she told me, soul language is symbols, art is symbols: "When I do the inner work, a feminine figure comes out of my consciousness. . . . Dreams and symbols: the Indwelling, the Inner—that's the Shekhinah."

NOTES

The research for this essay was conducted with funding from the National Endowment for the Humanities, and some of the writing was supported by a fellowship at the Center for Advanced Judaic Studies at the University of Pennsylvania. I would like to thank Elliot Ginsburg, Norman Girardot, Boaz Huss, Judith Lasker, Laura Levitt, Jody Myers, Ruth Setton, Jeffrey Shandler, Laurence Silberstein, and the anonymous reviewer and editorial staff of *Nashim* for their helpful comments on earlier drafts of this work.

A note on romanization of Hebrew and Yiddish words: Throughout the chapter, when quoting written materials, including e-mails, I have used the forms of romanization found in the texts quoted. This necessarily leads to inconsistencies.

1. "I am grateful to the Source of all Blessings, as Rabbi David Wolfe-Blank zt˒l [of blessed memory] taught me to call the Holy One." Joy Krauthammer, résumé, e-mail message to the author, January 24, 2003.

2. Rabbi Shefa Gold, a graduate of the Reconstructionist Rabbinical College, is a composer, musical performer, retreat leader, and teacher in Renewal circles, and director of the Center for Devotional Energy and Ecstatic Practice (C-DEEP). Shefa Gold's melody for *Modah ˒ani* is found on her audiocassette "Tzuri/My Rock" (B˒emet Productions, 1991), where it opens a "morning chanting service." As found in prayer books, the prayer means: "I gratefully acknowledge You, living and enduring King, for mercifully returning my soul to me; great is your faithfulness." In Gold's version, there are some slight but significant changes in wording: from *modeh ˒ani* (m.) to *modeh ˒ani* (f.) "I acknowledge," and from *Melekh ḥai ve-qayyam* (living and enduring King) to *ruaḥ ḥai ve-qayyam* (living and enduring Spirit), translated by Gold on the liner notes as "Spirit lives and endures." The significance of the shift from melekh to *ruaḥ* will become clear below.

3. Joy Krauthammer, telephone interview by the author, Los Angeles, January 23, 2003, amplified by e-mail message to the author, January 16, 2005. In that e-mail, Krauthammer further remarks that every day, she "studies Orthodox and Chabad," and "davvens [prays] Renewal." Krauthammer's husband died in 2006, after the original publication of this essay.

4. I began ethnographic fieldwork on the Jewish Renewal movement in 1999. Since then, I have attended five weekend retreats at the Jewish Renewal Life Center in Philadelphia, approximately fifteen retreats at Elat Chayyim, the Jewish Spiritual Retreat Center in the Catskills associated with Renewal, the ALEPH Kallah in 2003 and 2005, and four conferences (one regional and three national) sponsored in whole or in part by Jewish Renewal organizations on various topics such as Jewish meditation or Jewish education. I have attended services many times at P˒nai Or Philadelphia, as well as a single Sabbath service each at Makom Ohr Shalom in the Los Angeles area, the Malibu Jewish Center and Synagogue, and Beit Tikkun in San Francisco. I have attended two services at Kehilla in Berkeley, and three at Eitz Or in Seattle. I have conducted approximately forty face-to-face interviews with present and former Renewal Jews, on the east and west coasts, and about ten telephone interviews. Sometimes I follow up face-to-face interviews on the telephone or by e-mail, and sometimes I follow up telephone interviews with e-mail. I use snowballing to recruit interviewees.

5. Chava Weissler, "Jewish Renewal in the American Spiritual Marketplace," "Gender and Jewish Renewal," and "The Four Worlds and Kabbalah" (unpublished lectures delivered at the University of Washington, May 2003), available at http://jsis.artsci.washington.edu/programs/jewish/stroumlectures.html. Only a few scholarly articles about Renewal have been published. See especially the work of Shaul Magid: "Jewish Renewal Movement," in *Encyclopedia of Religion,* 2nd ed. (Detroit: Thompson Gale, 2005), 7:4868–74; "Rainbow Hasidism in America—The Maturation of Jewish Renewal," *The Reconstructionist* 68, no. 2 (2004): 34–60; "Jewish Renewal: Toward a 'New' American Judaism," *Tikkun* 21, no. 1 (2006):

57–60; "Jewish Renewal and the Holocaust: A Theological Response," *Tikkun* 21, no. 2 (2006): 59–62, 68; "Jewish Renewal and American Spirituality," *Tikkun* 21, no. 3 (2006): 58–60, 65–66. See also David Roper, "The Turbulent Marriage of Ethnicity and Spirituality: Rabbi Theodore Falcon, Makom Ohr Shalom and Jewish Mysticism in the Western United States, 1969–1993," *Journal of Contemporary Religion* 18, no. 2 (2003): 169–84; Cia Sautter, "*Chochmat:* Rhymes with Spirit Rock," *Journal of Religion and Popular Culture* 1 (Spring 2002), available at http://www.usaak.ca/relst/jrpc/article-chocmat.html. For a discussion of gender questions in particular, see Reena Sigman Friedman, "Women in Jewish Renewal," in *Encyclopedia of Women and Religion in North America,* ed. Rosemary Skinner Keller and Rosemary Radford Ruether (Bloomington: Indiana University Press, 2006), and Aviva Goldberg, "Re-Awakening Deborah: Locating the Feminist in the Liturgy, Ritual, and Theology of Contemporary Jewish Renewal" (Ph.D. diss., York University, Toronto, 2002).

6. "Thumbnail Origins of the Jewish Renewal Movement," a diagram in *Shabbat Morning Siddur,* comp. and ed. Rabbi Marcia Prager (Philadelphia: P'nai Or Religious Fellowship, n.d. [1990s]), 75, attributed in the second edition of the prayer book to David Wolfe-Blank. According to this diagram, the immediate influences on the Jewish Renewal movement are: Hasidism, Jewish Feminism, the Self-Actualization movement, the Ecological movement, the Havurah movement, Eastern Influences, and Latest Science. More distant ancestors include the School of Safed: Luria, Spinoza, Sabbatianism, the Emancipation, the Enlightenment, and the Holocaust, among others.

7. On the Havurah movement, see Riv-Ellen Prell, *Prayer and Community: The Havurah in American Judaism* (Detroit: Wayne State University Press, 1989), and Chava Weissler, *Making Judaism Meaningful: Ambivalence and Tradition in a Havurah Community* (New York: AMS Press, 1989).

8. On Carlebach's role, see Yaakov Ariel, "Hasidism in the Age of Aquarius: 'The House of Love and Prayer' in San Francisco, 1967–1977," *Religion and American Culture* 13, no. 2 (2003): 139–65. My study has focused on the aspects of Jewish Renewal influenced by Zalman Schachter-Shalomi. Many of Shlomo Carlebach's followers are Orthodox, and are not affiliated with ALEPH.

9. See Victor Gross et al., eds., *Ancient Roots, Radical Practices, and Contemporary Visions: The Aquarian Minyan 25th Anniversary Festschrift* (Berkeley: Aquarian Minyan, 1999). Aryae Coopersmith, originally a member of the House of Love and Prayer, told me that joining the Aquarian Minyan meant a shift from Carlebach to Schachter-Shalomi as primary teacher and inspiration (personal conversation, June 13, 2005).

10. http://www.ALEPH.org/contact.html, accessed June 21, 2005.

11. ALEPH: Alliance for Jewish Renewal, Statement of Principles, available at http://www.ALEPH.org/html/ALEPH.html.

12. On this, see Magid, "Jewish Renewal Movement," 7:4872–73.

13. "It is important to note that ALEPH/Jewish Renewal is not attempting to compete with or become a denomination of Judaism. In fact, dual affiliation is

both welcome and encouraged." This statement is from a guide for communities considering affiliation with ALEPH titled "How to Get Started," downloaded from the ALEPH Web site on June 21, 2005.

14. Debra Kolodny, e-mail message to the author, June 23, 2006; Kolodny, telephone conversation with the author, June 9, 2005; http://www.ALEPH.org/locate.html, accessed June 21, 2005. According to Kolodny, the congregational structure changed around 2003. There had been fifty congregational members of the "Network of Jewish Renewal Communities," but they did not pay congregational membership dues to ALEPH. When congregational affiliation required paying dues ($36 per congregational member) to ALEPH, which also includes members' individual memberships, as well as meeting certain organizational and religious criteria, not all of these communities chose to affiliate. As for geographical spread, California is way ahead of other states, with ten affiliated communities; other states (Arizona, Colorado, Connecticut, District of Columbia, Florida, Georgia, Illinois, Maryland, Massachusetts, Michigan, Minnesota, New Jersey, New Mexico, Oregon, Pennsylvania, Virginia, Washington, and Wisconsin) have only one or two each. There is one community each in Canada, England, the Netherlands, Spain, Mexico, and Brazil, and two in Israel. However, there are a number of other groups in Israel that exhibit features of Jewish Renewal but do not affiliate with ALEPH, although there are personal contacts between members and leaders on both continents.

15. Elat Chayyim closed its doors at the end of the summer season 2006 and moved its programs to the Isabella Freedman Jewish Retreat Center in the Connecticut Berkshires.

16. In May 2006 the movement was prompted to serious discussion about the potential for abuse of charismatic leadership by the scandal surrounding revelations of sexual abuse by Mordecai Gafni, a well-known figure in Renewal circles both in Israel and in the United States, who had served on the ALEPH Spiritual Advisory Council. Because of suspicions about Gafni's behavior, ALEPH had limited his influence and supervised his activities since 2003. After charges were pressed against Gafni in Israel, ALEPH severed all ties with him. In May 2006, Zalman Schachter-Shalomi revoked the rabbinical ordination he had earlier given him. See Jennifer Siegel, "Rabbi Fired over Sex Claims, Defenders Offer Mea Culpa," *Forward,* May 19, 2006 (http://www.forward.com/articles/7809, accessed June 23, 2006); and e-mails from Linda Jo Doctor, chair, ALEPH board of directors, May 15, 2006, Susan Saxe, chief operating officer, May 15 and 26, 2006, and Zalman Schachter-Shalomi, May 26, 2006, all sent out by Susan Saxe in her official capacity.

17. The predominance of women participants has been typical in American religious life for at least two centuries. See Ann Braude, "Women's History *Is* American Religious History," in *Retelling U.S. Religious History,* ed. Thomas A. Tweed (Berkeley: University of California Press, 1997), 87–107. It is even more characteristic of alternative spiritualities.

18. Abigail Weinberg, interview by the author, February 18, 2003.

19. Some rabbis of Renewal congregations were ordained at the Jewish Theo-

logical Seminary (for example, Burt Jacobson at Kehilla in Berkeley, Debra Orenstein at Makom Ohr Shalom in Los Angeles). David Wolfe-Blank, who died in 1999 after being the rabbi of several Renewal congregations, including Eitz Or in Seattle and the Aquarian Minyan in Berkeley, had Orthodox (Lubavitch) ordination.

20. http://www.ALEPH.org, accessed March 26, 2005.

21. Rabbi Andrea Cohen-Kiener, personal communication with the author.

22. Rabbi Phyllis Berman, interview by the author, March 27, 2005. But see the comment by another rabbi on the ALEPH-P'nai Or Listserv: "As a woman rabbi, I am not trying to promote 'the feminine.' In fact, I want to be seen as a rabbi, not a 'woman rabbi.' I am just trying to be a full-fledged, equal adult Jew who is titled to develop my leadership potential. . . . I am of the school of 'egalitarianism.'" February 26, 2004, digest 2680.

23. Ascribed to Rabbi David Wolfe-Blank by Arlene Goldbard, then vice chair of the ALEPH board of directors, in an interview on March 6, 2003.

24. On this topic, see, for example, Jody Elizabeth Myers, "The Myth of Matriarchy in Recent Writings on Jewish Women's Spirituality," *Jewish Social Studies* 4 (1997): 1–27; and Vanessa L. Ochs, "Waiting for the Messiah, a Tambourine in Her Hand," *Nashim* 9, no. 2 (2005): 144–69.

25. Both quotes in this paragraph are from Debra Kolodny, e-mail correspondence, April 13, 2005.

26. "Kabbalah teaches us that it is the feminine that will bring the messianic age. One of the signs of the emerging messianic age is that the curse of Eve will be lifted. The power, the wisdom, the voice of the feminine will once again be heard and it will be the feminine that will lead the way." Mindy Ribner, who studied with Shlomo Carlebach, in an e-mail message sent to her students on March 10, 2005, announcing a gathering for Rosh Chodesh Adar Sheni (New Moon of the Month of Second Adar).

27. Rachel Adler, *Engendering Judaism: An Inclusive Theology and Ethics* (Philadelphia: Jewish Publication Society, 1998), 98.

28. Adler, *Engendering Judaism,* 99–100.

29. There are numerous treatments of this topic in the scholarly literature. For discussions readily available in English, see, for example, Gershom Scholem, "Shekhinah: The Feminine Element in Divinity," in *On the Mystical Shape of the Godhead* (New York: Schocken, 1991), 140–96; Isaiah Tishby, "Shekhinah," in *The Wisdom of the Zohar* (Oxford: Oxford University Press, 1989), 1:371–422; Peter Schäffer, *Mirror of His Beauty* (Princeton: Princeton University Press, 2002); Arthur Green, "Shekhinah, the Virgin Mary, and the Song of Songs," *AJS Review* 26 (2002): 1–52; Sharon Koren, "Mystical Rationales for the Laws of *Niddah,*" in *Women and Water: Menstruation in Jewish Life and Law,* ed. Rahel S. Wasserfall (Hanover, NH: University Press of New England, 1999), 101–21. Elliot Wolfson argues that Shekhinah is best understood as covertly male. See his *Circle in the Square* (Albany: State University of New York Press, 1995), and his comprehensive discussion of gender issues in kabbalah in *Language, Eros, Being* (New York: Fordham University Press, 2005).

30. See B. T. Ḥullin 60b, Pirqei de Rabbi ʾEliʿezer, 6, 8.

31. Mordecai Gafni, formerly a leader of Jewish Renewal in Israel, inscribed a copy of one of his books to me as follows: "To Reb Chavah, a Rebbe and a scholar—a holy voice of the Shechinah in our generation—May G-d bless you to participate fully in the fixing of the moon, *beḥinnat tiqqun ha-nuqva, beḥinnat tiqqun ha-yareaḥ, ve-khen yehi raṣon.*" He addressed me this way in recognition of my research on the *tkhines* (women's prayers in Yiddish); note how he subsumes me to the Renewal paradigm. As noted above, because of legal charges of serious misconduct, Gafni was ousted from all leadership positions in ALEPH and at Bayit Hadash in Israel.

32. My colleague Norman Girardot points out that "fog" and "dark" are feminine symbols in Taoism.

33. Lyrics to the song "In the Light" by Hanna Tiferet Siegel on her audiocassette album *A Voice Calls,* © 1998. The names of God, for which no translation appears on the liner notes, can be translated as: Almighty, Immanent Presence, Lord of Hosts, Being, Source of Life, Rock, Place, Supernal God, Yah, Spirit, God. On the name "Yah," see below in the text. The Reconstructionist movement embraces multiple translations of the Name of God; see the series of prayer books titled *Kol Ha-neshamah.*

34. Kehilla is one of the largest Renewal congregations in North America with about four hundred families. The introduction also locates Kehilla within the Renewal movement, and defines the movement.

> Kehilla Community Synagogue is part of Jewish Renewal, a world-wide phenomenon whose influence is reverb[er]ating in all the other heterodox movements of Judaism. Those reverberations are evidenced in several ways: through the reclaiming of women's voices and experiences through new liturgy and midrashim—interpretations of biblical texts from the perspective of women; through the incorporation of movement, meditation and contemplation in our davenning, or praying; through more con[s]cious efforts toward Tikkun olam—healing and repair—in our relations with one another, with our communities and with our world.

I attended services at Kehilla on March 1 and 8, 2003. In the course of the prayers, I heard members of the congregation use different terms for God.

35. On these questions, see Judith Plaskow, *Standing Again at Sinai: Judaism from a Feminist Perspective* (San Francisco: Harper and Row, 1990), chap. 4, and Adler, *Engendering Judaism,* chap. 3.

36. Berman interview.

37. Rabbi Ruth Gan Kagan, e-mail message to the author, March 7, 2005.

38. Marcia Prager, *The Path of Blessing* (New York: Bell Tower, 1998), 123. Prager also points out that Melekh (*malkhut*) is connected to Shekhinah in kabbalistic terminology. Much of her book is devoted to explicating and interpreting the divine names found in the blessing formula of Hebrew liturgy.

39. Arthur Waskow, interview by the author, February 17, 2003.

40. I heard this interpretation orally at Elat Chayyim, and it is found, attributed to Jonathan Omer-man, with a footnote to a source in the writings of the Spanish

kabbalist Joseph Gikatilla, in Rodger Kamenetz, *Stalking Elijah* (San Francisco: Harper, 1997), 225, 339n9.

41. Prager, *Path,* 97–106.

42. ALEPH-P'nai Or Listserv, digest 2674, posted February 20, 2004, accessed February 27, 2004. See also, as part of the same debate, the following post, by a man, to digest 2673, February 19, 2004: "It has always been my opinion/feeling that for Renewal to do what is really necessary, the challenge to parts of the tradition, the 'sources' and halacha [Jewish law] must go deeper. . . . The commitment to halachah creates a situation in which men's ownership will always trump truly creative renewal. . . . I think renewal must equal revolution! The old books need to be locked away for a hundred years."

43. Post by a woman to digest 2674, February 20, 2004.

44. Barbara Breitman, telephone interview by the author, March 16, 2003. Breitman, a psychotherapist and spiritual director, is one of the directors of Lev Shomea, a Jewish Renewal Spiritual Direction program.

45. Marcia Falk, *Book of Blessings: A New Prayer Book for the Weekdays, the Sabbath, and the New Moon* (San Francisco: Harper Collins, 1996). Falk is a poet and translator, has connections with the Havurah movement, and is a member of B'not Esh ("Daughters of Fire"), a Jewish feminist collective that meets once a year to explore theological and liturgical issues. Her work is widely read by those interested in creative and/or feminist Jewish liturgy, among them, participants in Jewish Renewal.

46. See B. T. Erubin 18b, where this two-letter name is considered appropriate for the era after the destruction of the Temple. Zalman Schachter-Shalomi points out that the name expresses sexual complementarity: The *Yod* stands for the male, and the *Heh* stands for the female; see Zalman Schachter-Shalomi and Ruth Gan Kagan, "Meshal ha-Qadmoni" (unpublished ms. [Hebrew]).

47. Berman interview. This recalls Gen. 2:7: "The Lord God formed man from the dust of the earth. He blew into his nostrils the breath of life, and man became a living being" (JPS translation). It was Arthur Waskow who began pronouncing *Yah* with an out-rush of breath; the inspiration came to him in 1982 (e-mail message to the author, July 8, 2005).

48. See, for example, the rendition of the shema composed by Shefa Gold on her audiocassette *Chants Encounter,* 1994, track 5.

49. "Rachamema" is found in Geela Rayzel Raphael, "Techinah for Infertility," no. 2 in her "Techinot" (unpublished paper submitted to the Reconstructionist Rabbinical College, 1993).

50. "Raḥamima" appears in a brief ritual to bestow the title "Eshet Ḥazon" (Woman of Vision) on "Julie," March 21, 2003, by Hanna Tiferet and Daniel Siegel (unpublished manuscript). This ceremony also speaks of "Shaddai, Malkat Olam, Queen of the Eternal Presence." The very fact that the Eshet Ḥazon ceremony recognizes a special gift of feminine leadership, also termed "midwife of the soul," shows the way gender distinctions are constructed in Renewal. Hanna Tiferet was herself the first Eshet Ḥazon, honored as such in a newly created ceremony during a Shavuot celebration of Pacific Northwest havurot in 1982. See Shonna Husband-

Hankin, "Eshet Chazon: Woman of Vision," *New Menorah* 4 (April–May 1983): 4, and Hanna Tiferet Siegel, "Eshet Hazon: A Woman of Vision," in *A Ceremonies Sampler,* ed. Elizabeth Resnick Levine (San Diego: Woman's Institute for Continuing Jewish Education, 1991), 107–10.

51. Quoted in Friedman, "Women."

52. Debra Kolodny, e-mail message to the author, April 13, 2005.

53. Weinberg interview.

54. I hope to deal with this more fully in future writing.

55. Elliot Ginsburg (personal communication with the author, July 30, 2005) and David Zaslow (personal communication with the author, July 31, 2005), both influential Renewal rabbis, told me that Shekhinah is important in their devotional lives. Zaslow also insisted, "Shekhinah consciousness is not just to liberate girls to have a God-image that's female, but to redeem men from historical and biological sexism." On the other hand, when I asked Rabbi Victor Gross what Shekhinah means to men in Jewish Renewal, he replied, "Whatever it *was,* the women have absconded with it" (personal communication with the author, July 31, 2005).

56. I have seen no evidence that Shekhinah has developed any tinge of lesbian erotic devotion in Renewal.

57. When I asked Rabbi Geela Rayzel Raphael about the dark side of Shekhinah, she mentioned the Hindu goddess Kali. But she added, "If Shekhinah is standing as a symbol of female empowerment, as the earth mother, sympathetic, compassionate, you don't want to give her bad press." Geela Rayzel Raphael, interview by the author, February 27, 2005. However, this is not true of all Renewal Jews. Recall Schachter-Shalomi's mention of "endarkenment." Rabbi Laura Duhan Kaplan told me over lunch at the conference about her study of a "nasty *derash*" in the Zohar in which Shekhinah is the withholding mother. In the breakout session described above, the leader said that the "dark side of the Shekhinah cannot be done in words" but rather in visions. Interestingly, David Zaslow (above, note 56) describes Shekhinah as "fickle."

58. Plaskow, *Standing Again at Sinai,* 140.

59. A male participant in a Jewish Renewal Life Center retreat remarked to me when I pointed out some of the darker qualities of the Shekhinah of kabbalah, "Aren't we beyond that? Can't we make Shekhinah into what we want?"

60. Raphael interview.

61. Hanna Tiferet, "The Ways of a Woman," song copyright 1995, on *A Voice Calls* (audiocassette) by Hanna Tiferet. Album copyright 1998 by Hanna Tiferet Siegel.

62. Kolodny e-mail, April 13, 2005.

63. Kolodny interview.

64. According to her bio, "Rabbi Leah Novick is a spiritual teacher and counselor whose work focuses on the Divine Feminine. Rabbi Leah's healing and ritual work is grounded in experiencing the Shekhina in meditative states. An ALEPH Pathfinder, Leah lives on the Central Coast of CA and leads retreats and workshops in the U.S., Europe and Israel." Elat Chayyim: A Jewish Spiritual Retreat Center, *Retreat Guide 2000/5760* (Accord, NY: Elat Chayyim, 2000), 22. Novick writes, "I

am known as an inveterate feminist whose road to Shekhinah was paved by my involvement in the women's movement and my study of Goddess cultures." She also mentions additional biographical landmarks: "Feminist candidate for NY State Legislature 1970; founder and chair of Connecticut Women's Political Caucus; Chief Aide to Congresswoman Bella S. Abzug; Coordinator Intl. Women's Year Conference; Exec. Dir. California Commission on Status of Women; taught Women's Studies at UC Berkeley" (e-mail message to the author, June 25, 2006).

65. The handout states, "This poem was first published in Gnosis Magazine and has been reprinted in a variety of other publications and prayer books." Ellipses in original text. *Gnosis Magazine* 13 (Fall 1989): 47. Quoted with permission of Leah Novick.

66. Leah Novick, e-mail message to the author, June 25, 2006. This is made more explicit in Leah Novick, "Shechinah Theology of the Future," available at http://www.ohalah.org./novick.htm (accessed April 27, 2005): "In the present era Shekhinah is clearly planetary Gaia . . . [who calls for] widespread experience of the holiness in all the earth (Gaia) which would make it impossible to pollute, destroy or to exploit this planet or others."

67. Rhonda Shapiro-Rieser, personal communication with the author, January 2004.

68. See especially Cynthia Eller, *The Myth of Matriarchal Prehistory* (Boston: Beacon, 2000), chap. 4. With regard to the problems of essentialism in the adoption and understanding of Shekhinah in contemporary Chabad women, and participants in Rosh Hodesh groups, see Myers, "The Myth of Matriarchy," esp. 7–13.

69. Goldbard interview. She said further, "I don't think more women think that women, blood, earth, motherhood, blah, blah, in Jewish Renewal than they do every place else in Berkeley."

70. Marcia Brooks, interview by the author, March 2, 2003.

71. Berman interview.

72. Weinberg interview. In the course of her interview, Weinberg also forcefully expressed an anti-essentialist point of view. By contrast, Debra Kolodny wrote to me, "Most of us [in the Jewish Renewal movement] pray to Shechina, much more often than just Erev Shabbat when we welcome the Sabbath Bride" (e-mail message, April 13, 2005).

73. Berman interview.

74. See the above-quoted remarks of Arlene Goldbard: "[H]aving one or two Shekhinah-centered prayers on Shabbos" is a slight amelioration of women's position within Judaism, and "Essentialist feminism is bullshit."

CHAPTER THREE

A TENT OF ONE'S OWN

Feminist Biblical Scholarship, a Popular Novel, and the Fate of the Biblical Text

ADRIANE B. LEVEEN

The virtual absence of the female voice from biblical texts has drawn the sustained attention and ire of feminist scholars of the Bible for the better part of the past three decades.[1] In response, feminist scholars seek biblical women in the "margins" of scripture. Others go even further, aiming to expose "the androcentric bias or oppressive intention operative within a text, to show the text to be unalterably patriarchal and therefore, without authority or value."[2] The most important feminist opponent of such a wholesale rejection of the text is Phyllis Trible, the pioneering non-Jewish feminist scholar of the Bible. In a passionate 1973 essay Trible proposes "another way: to reread (not rewrite) the Bible without blinders of Israelite men or of Paul, Barth, Bonhoeffer, and a host of others."[3] Trible does not reject the biblical text but engages it as a feminist. Others join her in refusing to discard the biblical text by arguing "that the patriarchal framework . . . is a historical fact but is not theologically necessary."[4] These scholars excavate the female characters present in biblical prose and poetry, allowing them to emerge by reading against the grain.

This essay will examine recent trends in feminist interpretation of the biblical past, with a special interest in the results when feminists determinedly engage the biblical text rather than reject it. Wary of charges of lack of evidence and of invention, these feminists rely on the rules and methods of biblical scholarship to carefully excavate and reconstruct the ancient biblical past of women. In spite of the fragmentary nature of the evidence for female experience, by reading against the grain these scholars have done nothing less than reintroduce the biblical texts—and biblical women—in all their richly layered, multivocal complexity to a contemporary audience. They allow us to encounter the Bible in a fresh and compelling way.

To support this claim I will identify the types of questions being asked, some of the methods deployed, and the surprising results.

At the same time, feminist scholars of the Bible do not work in isolation but within a larger nonacademic community in which a parallel interest in the lives of biblical women has never been stronger. Testimony to widespread, popular interest in biblical women can be found in the astounding success of the "breakthrough feministic novel of biblical times," Anita Diamant's *The Red Tent.*[5] Such success justifies a singular focus on Diamant's fictional account as a paramount example of an inventive, imaginative approach to biblical women. As a novelist she is under no obligation to the biblical texts that provide the basis for *The Red Tent.* Instead, she can enjoy a creative freedom and even celebrate a distinct distance from the biblical text. For the purposes of this essay, Diamant's book creates an opportunity to assess feminist interpretation of the past on a continuum between two poles—that of excavation and reconstruction on the one hand and invention and imagination on the other.

The status of the text as a source becomes the key factor that divides the scholars that I survey from the novelist. This divide is not necessarily between a scholarly approach and a popular one.[6] Plenty of popular writers on the Bible are immersed in its narratives. The divide exists between those engaged in the text, even if highly critical or skeptical of it, and those who are not, either through indifference or outright rejection. By explicitly distancing herself from the Bible, Diamant joins the biblical scholars cited above who choose to reject the biblical text. The repercussions of her stance can be traced in the enormous popular response to *The Red Tent* among its readers, a response that is easily accessible thanks to the many individual reviews of the book found on the Internet. Popular reception gives us a window into the sharp hunger among readers for a female community of meaning in the present. These readers seek a precedent and legitimacy for such a community in the distant past, even if invented. I will examine what kind of role the Bible plays, if at all, in this popular encounter with the past.

Finally, after having described what I consider to be two distinct feminist projects—excavation versus invention—I conclude by considering how they interact. Somewhat unexpectedly, *The Red Tent* ends up subverting the possibilities for an unmediated and potentially rewarding encounter with biblical texts.

FEMINIST BIBLICAL CRITICISM

Contemporary feminist scholars of the Bible are quite open about their agenda. They aim to recover as much as possible of the lost lives of biblical women. To do so, they rely on the tools and methodologies of contemporary biblical scholarship in general, but they use those tools and methodologies to ask rather different questions, insistently seeking evidence for the actual lives of Israelite women and/or their portrayals in biblical texts. Methodological approaches include attention to the Ancient Near Eastern historical and cultural context, including the languages of other Semitic peoples. But feminist scholars might pay special attention to the roles of goddesses in epic narratives or to the laws governing women in those other cultures and their connections or traces in the biblical texts. Feminist scholars continue to be interested in archeological data from the biblical period but might pay greater interest to the evidence for such figures as Asherah, a possible consort of YHWH, or to the strikingly large number of female figurines found in domestic settings throughout Canaan.[7] Feminist scholars have also turned to critical theory and rhetorical analyses to identify issues of ideology, authority, and gender at play within a literary work. Finally, there have been numerous close literary readings of the biblical texts that shift our gaze to the female figures in the narrative and to their characterization, speeches, actions, and interactions with the male protagonists.[8] These feminist scholars share an interest in the women of the biblical period and unapologetically make that interest explicit. They reject as unrepresentative any study if focused exclusively on men.[9]

Feminist scholars generally make two crucial assumptions, now rather obvious thanks to the last thirty years of feminist research. First, they posit that the culture in which ancient Israelites lived and out of which they wrote their texts was unremittingly patriarchal. Patriarchy is the biggest obstacle to recovering the female voice since it either suppresses or marginalizes that voice. Second, perhaps paradoxically, feminist scholars also assume that women's lives are recoverable in spite of patriarchy. They confidently highlight aspects of female experience and amplify female voices that are present in the text. In moving from the patriarchal surface of the text to its more complicated layers beneath, feminists end up deconstructing the text in order to rebuild it. After a brief discussion of each move in turn, I will delineate some of the interesting consequences and implications of such work for our understanding of the biblical text today.

Few would dispute the claim that the Bible is androcentric. The text clearly focuses on men in far more detail than on women. As a consequence, its portrait of female characters is truncated, biased, and objectified. Such texts emerge out of and mirror a patriarchal society in which women were subordinate to men.[10] Therefore, most feminist scholars begin their work by delineating and vigorously criticizing the patriarchy out of which the Bible emerges and which it reflects, assuming that the narratives of biblical women were shaped by patriarchal views and motives. They have done readers of the Bible a great service by exposing the extent to which ancient Israelite culture was dominated by men, a domination legitimated and reinforced by legal codes devised by men in a legal system enforced by men. Males also dominated public religious life. Women simply were not part of the "great public hierarchies" (such as the priesthood).[11] A strong economic component also existed. Women were economically dependent on their fathers and husbands and therefore had to conform to their wishes.[12] Finally, patriarchal control extended to the personal lives of women "governed by their fathers before marriage and by their husbands after marriage . . . intimate aspects of women's lives really have to do with relations between men."[13] Such intimate aspects of life included a woman's sexuality, over which men exerted continuous control from childhood on.[14]

As a brief example of reading a biblical narrative in the light of such a pervasive patriarchal context, let us consider the rape of Dinah in Genesis 34. It has been described as a "political story about the struggles of males . . . for power."[15] In fact, Tikva Frymer-Kensky reads the story of Dinah as a quintessential story about male control: "Dinah's destiny cannot be allowed to rest in her hands. The brothers reestablish the control over her that they lost."[16] This patriarchal story comes to highlight the struggles between Jacob's family and the outside world as represented by the local ruler: "The story is told from the viewpoint of the family and society from which Dinah went out. From their perspective, an unmarried girl's consent does not make sex a permissible act. She has, after all, no right of consent. . . . [I]f she is a willing participant, the shame is compounded."[17] Frymer-Kensky ruefully reminds us that we will not know Dinah's feelings because "they are not the story's concern."[18] She is not condoning that fact but with a sober realism is making apparent both the workings of patriarchy and its harsh reach into biblical narrative.

Once the workings of patriarchy have been rigorously identified, the next, more pressing—and, I might add, more interesting—task of feminist biblical scholarship can occur—the retrieval and recovery of the female voice in spite of such patriarchy. Feminist scholars search for "aspects of the . . . past of women that were hidden, unnoticed, or devalued yet available for retrieval if the right questions were asked and the right sources uncovered."[19] A focus on the female voice in the text has led to extraordinarily innovative and exciting work. That work has reintroduced contemporary readers to the rich possibilities of the biblical text by stressing its multivocality.

Such work has contributed to, and is aided by, two relatively recent and interrelated factors within biblical scholarship. First, a growing understanding of the Bible as an ideological and polemical document, aimed at reforming, or even revolutionizing, ancient Israelite religious practice leads to a certain critical distance from the text.[20] Second, a consensus that biblical texts have been compiled over hundreds of years leads to a recognition of the Bible as a rich catalog of multiple traditions. Assuming that one can approach biblical narrative suspiciously and that it is made up of multiple, sometimes competing, traditions, Ilana Pardes defines the Bible as a "heteroglot text."[21] In taking such a stance Pardes reflects on what can be discovered: "Broken pieces, scattered histories, condensed naming-speeches, obscure traces of premonotheistic pasts, remnants of dreams, fragments of forgotten pursuits. . . . [W]e can reconstruct, if only partially, a fascinating array of counter female voices, without falling into the trap of idealizing the past or endorsing highly speculative and problematic myths, such as the myth of matriarchy."[22] Pardes's discoveries emerge from her intense engagement with the layers of the biblical text, an engagement that bears intriguing fruit in such a close reader.

Yet even if one does not dig deeply to excavate the layers of text but simply turns a scholarly eye and the reader's attention to the female in the plot, that shift readily expands one's perspective. For instance, one notes that Eve reaches for enlightenment and sets civilization in motion. Hagar is the first female theologian, rebelling against harsh treatment only to immediately encounter God. In a sign of her intimacy with God, Hagar even gives God a name that is unique to her experience—El Roi. Rebecca has a direct line to YHWH but apparently Isaac does not. Meanwhile Tamar takes her future into her own hands. Refusing to be locked away in her father's house she crosses the threshold and forces Judah to acknowledge his responsibility to her. Neither the life of Moses nor the rule of David would have even begun, let alone flourished, without the timely interventions, wisdom, and rhetoric of a series of remarkable women.[23]

Once we turn our attention to women in the text, observations of other roles that they might play within biblical narrative become possible. For instance, the fate of women in the book of Judges becomes a barometer for the fate of early Israelite society. When we witness the brutal rape and dismemberment of an unprotected woman in Judges 19, we recognize the extent to which the Israelite society at large is vulnerable to self-destruction and disintegration.[24] Frymer-Kensky claims an even larger role for woman as representative of Israel writ large in her wonderfully alliterative categories of women as victors and victims, virgins and voices.[25]

Simultaneously, in addition to such close literary and paradigmatic readings, a careful window into women's religious and political lives is opening ever wider. Scholars can now identify distinct forms of worship particular to women, possible forms of public leadership, and female powers in the private realm.[26] For instance, evidence within the text points to the worship of Asherah and/or the Queen of Heaven and suggests that the female figure of Wisdom in Proverbs is a divine consort.[27] Most intriguing, the retrieval of the feminine within the biblical text even includes attention to female imagery applied directly to the God of Israel. Two examples come to mind. In Genesis 49:25 the structuring force of biblical poetic parallelism leads to the naming of God as both El and Shaddai and of describing God's blessings as those of "the breast and womb."[28] Isaiah offers several remarkable images of God as woman: panting in labor (42:14); bearing a child (45:10); caring for a baby, a child of her womb (49:15); and as a mother comforting her son (66:13). Thus the female side of God emerges, however briefly, in rich poetic form. But it will only emerge if we put aside suppositions about the exclusive maleness of Israel's God.[29]

In other words, through their efforts at scholarly recovery and excavation scholars have discovered layers of female experience and agency within the biblical text. Remarkably, they have produced such results without resorting to invention. Their work has significant and far-reaching implications, not only for contemporary women but for anyone interested in a better understanding of the Bible, of its historical and cultural context, and of later exegetical traditions. The recognition that the text contains overlooked fragments and traces of other traditions makes it a richer, even more intriguing text than we had supposed.[30] Furthermore, simply shifting our gaze to the women in the text enhances the complexity of our readings of character, perspective, and plot. Such complexity has always been present but dormant within the biblical text because of our inattention. If one adds these new perspectives, fragments, and traces to the more familiar perspectives of the male writers of the Bible, then we have a more accurate picture of the diversity, richness, and even astuteness of biblical narrative along with the rather shrewd, even at times ironic, views of the biblical writers on the human condition, including the complications and subtleties of male-female relations.

Our understanding not only of the biblical text but of ancient Israelite history is expanded. How could it be otherwise? Studying only half a population produces half a story. Piecing together a picture of the whole produces a far more accurate reconstruction of the past. For instance, the institutions of ancient Israel are better understood if we consider the monarchy in light of the role played by the Queen Mother or reflect on prophecy in light of such prophetic figures as Deborah and Huldah.[31] And as already suggested, even our understanding of the biblical God can be deepened by paying attention to *all* of the images and tropes—feminine as well as masculine—that describe God.

Inevitably, feminist interest in the past leads to a heightened scrutiny of how those texts were interpreted by their later readers. Men were for centuries the primary readers of and commentators on the earliest texts of Judaism. That history of interpretation, in which women were marginalized and ignored, has become the object of feminist scrutiny and critique.[32] Thanks to such feminist analyses, we are exposed to possibilities in the text that its exclusively male interpreters have denied us. This point and its profound consequences are further developed by Frymer-Kensky: "[T]he biblical text itself, read with nonpatriarchal eyes, is much less injurious to women than the traditional readings of Western civilization. There is much to recover in the Bible that is not patriarchal, even beyond hitherto neglected stories of strong heroines. The enterprise of liberating biblical text from its biblical overlay [is] called depatriarchalizing."[33] Once we shift our gaze, it is difficult to return biblical women to the margins. It is even possible "to read women in the Jewish tradition in ways that are finally recuperative, empowering, and redemptive if we move outside the classification systems."[34] Indeed, reading the text through the lens and insights of feminist scholars can be an exhilarating process. It is also rather bittersweet since in its results it illustrates the losses and distortions incurred through the centuries when the text was read largely through the lens of its male interpreters.

To what extent can one consider such feminist scholarship part of Jewish studies?[35] Though most of the scholars I have cited are Jewish, the term "depatriarchalizing" originates with Phyllis Trible. I also referred to Trible, a pioneer in feminist biblical scholarship, in my introduction to demonstrate that the field embraces both Jewish and non-Jewish scholars who share many of the same aims, read many of the same texts, and raise many of the same issues. Principally they share a "hermeneutics of suspicion" that leads them to reassess and challenge some of the givens in a field that until recently has been dominated by men.[36] Both Jewish and Christian women are interested in the women of the Hebrew Bible. And some feminist scholars extend that interest to problematic interpretations of such New Testament figures as Mary Magdalene.

Yet what makes a feminist biblical scholar trained in Jewish studies distinct from her counterparts who hold other scholarly approaches? In the

"Women at Study Tambourine" portrays women engaged in Torah study as a norm of Jewish life. The women and their library are superimposed over an image of Jerusalem as a holy city. The tambourine visualizes what feminist Bible scholarship does—it brings women out of the margins. Used with the permission of Betsy Teutsch, http://www.kavanahcards.com/tambourines. Photo credit: Benj Kamm.

new *Jewish Study Bible* Adele Reinhartz attempts to answer that query by identifying "the extent to which they relate in some way to classical Jewish sources . . . incorporating Jewish sensibilities or experiences, however these may be defined, into their scholarship and writing."[37] Therefore, a Jewish feminist reading of the biblical text, grounded in the history of Jewish commentary, is a different reading than that of an interpreter who might be grounded in Christian commentary. Obviously those engaged in biblical studies from a Jewish studies perspective will not read a text such as Isaiah as an anticipation or prediction of Christianity. However, most feminist scholars do not rely on Jewish exegetical sources but on the modern fields of biblical, archaeological, literary, and cultural studies as described above. I would like to propose an additional possibility. When a feminist biblical scholar treats the Hebrew Bible (rather than the Old Testament) as a multivocal and figurative text, rather than a monolithic and literal one, she is aligning the text, even if she is unaware of it, with recent work that understands the multiple perspectives and disagreements within the Hebrew Bible as anticipatory of the spirit of lively debate and dissent found in the Talmud and midrashic collections.[38] In contrast to the early rabbinic commentators, contemporary feminist interpreters keep their focus on biblical women. But in common with the rabbis, such feminist interpretations contribute to an extensive written tradition of Jewish commentary that is *itself rife* with dialogue and argument.

Finally, what makes the readings of biblical scholars "feminist"? First, I would argue that the explicit agenda defined above—the exposure of patriarchy and a sustained attention to the women of the biblical text—must take place to consider a piece of biblical scholarship as engaged in the feminist project. Second, engagement in such a project, with its aim of exposure, critique, and recovery, breaks down the barrier between a supposedly neutral or objective stance, studying a topic for the topic's sake, and a stance that seeks to discover or reclaim some ignored aspect of the past. The second possibility recognizes the extent to which every study has implications that might impact contemporary life, for good or ill. Such engagement is often accompanied by a willingness on the part of the feminist scholar to introduce her own presuppositions in the project. As an example, Frymer-Kensky spells out her presuppositions at the end of her fine introduction to *Reading the Women of the Bible:* "I am also a feminist. . . . Gradually, like other people, I became aware of androcentricity and patriarchy and how they affect all elements of life. I began to see how patriarchy has distorted monotheism itself, how it has impoverished our religious traditions and perverted biblical ideas. . . . When my scholarship presents alternative readings, I choose those readings that I believe will prove most beneficial to people."[39] Her comment conveys an unapologetic recognition that feminist scholarship has serious implications for our lives. Reviewers of *Reading the Women of the Bible* excitedly embrace those implications. For instance, a reviewer in the *Journal of Hebrew Scriptures* notes that Frymer-Kensky "provide[s] hope and healing for women and men in the contemporary world."[40] David Noel Freedman writes that "Frymer-Kensky has applied her expertise in the culture and traditions of the ancient Near East to the Hebrew Bible. . . . This book has much to say about and to women of every era and age, but its spirit, scope and breadth go beyond any generic limits: men—perhaps even more than women—can and should learn much from it, both about the Bible and the women in it."[41] One last comment will suffice to make the point: "Here is biblical interpretation that eliminates much of the distance between the text and the reader. These stories illuminate the themes and dangers, hopes and fears, that are characteristic of human life anywhere and at any time."[42] As these reviews suggest, the work of a feminist biblical scholar may break down the clear demarcations between scholarly and practical relevance in interesting and even moving ways as she places the biblical text in front of the reader in a new light.

Let us take stock of the key developments just surveyed. Feminist biblical scholarship is an engaged scholarship that follows scholarly rules and methodology but asks a series of original and innovative questions of the biblical period and its texts. This approach has ingeniously recovered the female voice in the text, thereby illustrating the text's multivocality. Thus we are introduced to a new way of reading that allows us to reengage the biblical text with a fresh perspective.

With this in mind, what happens if we leave behind the scholarly world and move along the continuum of feminist interpretation of the Bible to the popular novel, from fidelity to the biblical text to imaginative renderings of the biblical world, from one end of the continuum to its opposite? Since no work on the Hebrew Bible has been more popular in recent years than *The Red Tent,* it is an obvious choice for scrutiny. On the one hand Diamant is motivated by the same drive as other feminists have been to recover the female past in the biblical period. On the other hand, the novelist uses techniques that appear distinct from, or even alien to, that of feminist biblical scholars. Thus her results are strikingly different. That is to be expected. However, that the very success of Diamant's novel raises serious questions about the role and status of the biblical text among contemporary readers is less expected. Their fidelity to *The Red Tent* noticeably outweighs their interest in the original text. Such consequences will be made apparent through a brief analysis of the novel and its reception.

THE RED TENT

Diamant's novel clearly contributes to feminist critical discourse on the limits of a patriarchy that silences the voices of biblical women. Like other feminists, Diamant seeks to reconstruct obscure female experience.

However, in contrast to the scholarly work described above, Diamant imagines the lives and words of the matriarchs while ignoring the actual narrative, however fragmented, found in the biblical text.[43] As I shall argue below, it is this distance from the biblical text that raises the most provocative questions concerning the content and reception of her novel.

Many of the scenes in *The Red Tent* take place in intimate settings inhabited only by women as the female characters undergo rituals of healing and celebration. Through these scenes the novel offers readers ancient female traditions in which they can delight. Above all else, they can be privy to the transmission of female experience from one generation to the next: "In the ruddy shade of the red tent, the menstrual tent, they ran their fingers through my curls, repeating the escapades of their youths, the sagas of their childbirths. Their stories were like offerings of hope and strength poured out before the Queen of Heaven, only these gifts were not for any god or goddess—but for me."[44] Diamant is successful in drawing an imagined and highly evocative female past, especially in the first section of her book, "My Mother's Stories." Dinah provides us with many tales of her mothers and aunts as well as other women she encounters in order to fulfill her promise of preserving female memory. Female physical experience dominates—not only menstruation but infertility and miscarriage, dark hints of incest, sexually satisfying encounters, and an extraordinary numbers of birth scenes (both Rachel and Dinah are midwives).[45] A female articulation of these experiences is central to the story. Dinah describes what menstruation means in rather idyllic terms: "I will idle with my mothers and my sisters in the ruddy shade of the red tent for three days and three nights, until first sight of the crescent goddess. My blood will flow into the fresh straw, filling the air with the salt smell of women."[46]

A friendship between Dinah and an Egyptian woman named Meryt exemplifies the centralization of the female in this tale in striking contradistinction to her position within biblical narrative. Diamant succeeds because the observing eye, the one who defines the female here, is herself a woman. Meryt describes Dinah: "I have never seen nor heard tell of a more skilled midwife. She has Isis's hands, and with the goddess's love of children, shows the compassion of heaven for mothers and babies . . . she is an oracle too, my dears. Her dreams are powerful and her anger is to be feared for I have seen her blast an evil man out of the prime of his life for harming a young mother."[47] Thus Diamant has taken feminist criticism of the Bible to heart. We do not have to hunt for biblical women in the margins of the narrative; they are front and center. We see women as other women describe them and learn about their experiences in their own words.

In common with feminist scholars, Diamant seeks to expose the patriarchy that ultimately controls biblical women. But in her reading, patriarchy is equated with uncontrolled violence. In *The Red Tent* Dinah's brothers are greedy, self-serving murderers. They are depicted this way as a result of another move that I consider quite problematic both as a feminist and as a scholar of the Bible. Diamant turns the rape of Dinah into a love story. Thus the rapist of the biblical text becomes a hapless lover, himself a victim to the murderous rage of Dinah's Israelite brothers. What is at stake in such a move? Feminists have long argued for a heightened attention to rape and its ramifications, including a sustained critique of the general treatment of victims of rape. A victim of rape often fears that her story will be minimized or denied and/or she will be blamed for inviting the violent assault.[48] But in Diamant's novel Dinah willingly engages in sex with Shechem. Does Diamant inadvertently fall into the trap of denying and minimizing a terrible ordeal and of shifting our focus away from the perpetrator? When asked why she changed the rape to a love affair, Diamant explained,

> I could never reconcile the story of Genesis 34 with a rape, because the prince does not behave like a rapist! After the prince is said to have "forced" her (a determination made by the brothers, not by Dinah) he falls in love with her, asks his father to get Jacob's permission to marry her, and then agrees to the extraordinary, even grotesque demand that he and all the men of his community submit to circumcision. . . .
>
> Furthermore I wanted Dinah and all of the women in my story to be active agents in their own lives, not passive pawns or victims.[49]

Diamant's interest in Shechem and his behavior as well as her reference to the brothers is curious. If one follows the majority of commentaries and translations of Genesis 34:2, it is the narrator, not the brothers, who first informs us, in typically laconic fashion, that Shechem "lay with her by force." In addition, in her desire to have Dinah become an independent agent, Diamant confuses the issues of exploitation, brute force, and power inherent in a violent act such as rape with issues of female sexual desire and choice.

Finally, and perhaps most curiously, in her imaginative recounting of the incident, Diamant rescues Shechem from an infamous act. Yet in contrast, she graphically, even vociferously, condemns Dinah's brothers. Diamant attributes the most venal of motives to Simon and Levi. They act out of sheer personal calculation and greed because they are worried over their diminishing status and position within the tribe. They are willing to ruthlessly exploit others, including their sister, for their own gain. They commit murder with abandon: "My brothers' knives worked until the dawn revealed the abomination wrought by the sons of Jacob. They murdered every man they found alive."[50] As noted by Rabbi Benjamin Edidin Scolnic, "[A]n act of vengeance for a rape becomes an act of cold-blooded murder for personal gain and other evil reasons."[51]

There is no doubt that this is a highly troubling story in the Bible, open to many different types of reading, including one that condemns the brothers. But I would like to point out that the Bible itself has something to say about this episode through an inner biblical critique of the episode that Diamant briefly mentions. On his deathbed Jacob condemns the violent actions of the brothers: "Simeon and Levi, the brothers—weapons of outrage their trade. . . . Cursed be their fury so fierce, and their wrath so remorseless!" (Gen. 49:5, 7). Such criticism of the brothers *within* the biblical text, an act of self-correction, offers the beginning of a response to the tragedy of Dinah's rape and the violent consequences. But this act of textual self-correction is ignored in Diamant's reading. In the novel, as he lays dying, Jacob passes over the events of Genesis 34.[52]

THE HOLY BOOK

The most striking difference between Diamant and the feminist biblical scholars cited above is the novelist's explicit distance from the biblical text. On her Web site she straightforwardly reports that she "did not study the Bible or rabbinic sources."[53] Perhaps Diamant's Dinah provides an explanation for the decision to move away from the actual biblical text as a source. Dinah criticizes the possibilities for discovering female experience within the pages of the Bible. Her testimony intends to fill in the gaps men created by ignoring the stories of women, stories left out of the Bible. Referring to the biblical text as "*your* holy book," Dinah seeks to replace its incomplete tales with female memory: "I wish I had more to tell of my grandmothers. It is terrible how much has been forgotten, which is why, I suppose, remembering seems a holy thing."[54] Thus the holy book is replaced with the holiness of female memory. The Bible cannot serve as a resource for the recovery of a female past.

Yet a novel that so explicitly re-creates the ancient setting and bases itself on the broad contours of the biblical story (the binding of Isaac, the rivalry between Leah and Rachel, and the story of Esau and Jacob are just a few of the biblical themes that color her story) does invite a consideration of its connections to the original source. After all, part of the novel's widespread appeal derives from its biblical setting and promise of enlightenment concerning the lives of biblical women. As we have begun to see, as she reconstructs the story of Dinah, Diamant's disengagement from the biblical text leads to some of the more troubling aspects of the novel. To understand both the novel's appeal and its ability to disturb, one must consider the connections between the original text and the novel in the mind of the readers of *The Red Tent.*

READING IN THE RED TENT

As a scholar of the Bible I am equally fascinated by the huge success of *The Red Tent* and by what drives its readers. No one factor on its own produces a best-seller. In the case of *The Red Tent* the combination of Jewish cyberspace, the recent flourishing of book clubs, and, above all, a paperback novel that would attract that most desired and strategically targeted of readers—a woman—have all contributed to its success.[55] And it is a success. According to Darin Keesler, marketing director of Picador Press, as of February 2005, "The trade paperback edition of *The Red Tent* has sold over 2.5 million copies . . . and it continues to sell briskly. The hardcover edition has sold over 70,000 copies."[56] I am also interested in who buys and reads the novel. In particular, to what extent are the readers of *The Red Tent* interested in the biblical source of the work? To what extent does that matter? What do the readers tell us?

We can best get to the heart of what readers of *The Red Tent* find evocative and meaningful by looking directly at their comments rather than at more formal criticism.[57] To access the comments of the reading audience, especially its relation to the biblical text, I turn to cyberspace and the online reviews of books by the "average reader." The reader responses I survey should not be considered comprehensive and all-inclusive. The amount of material on the Web alone makes that kind of catalog beyond the parameters of this essay. I elucidate only a mere handful of comments, identifying themes that emerge repeatedly, though from a limited sample. Since the Internet is my source, I know little about these readers—their age, economic class, or religious denomination. All I know is that they report that they are women and that they are moved to record their responses to *The Red Tent* publicly on the Web. I have chosen to use four Web sites that range from general to self-described as "spiritual." They are the following: bookclique@tcpl.lib.in.us, a discussion group from November 9, 2001, through December 8, 2001, sponsored by a local library with prompts from a facilitator; http://half.ebay.com/products/customer_reviews, an online consumer site that contains a wide range of views of the book; http://www.newvision-psychic.com/bookshelf/RedTent.htm, a site that focuses on books about female spirituality; and http://amywelborn.typepad.com/openbook/2004/05, an individual's Web site. This last site exhibits explicitly Christian images, such as Mary and Jesus in the manger. I tried to avoid using more than one comment from any individual reader. Many of the reviews originate on ebay since it has the widest variety of responses from which to draw. Note that a citation to the specific Web site accompanies each response.

I will highlight several themes that readers identify as significant. These include praise for the book's ability to create a world in which the lives of biblical women are developed in greater detail, thereby offering contemporary women a legacy from the past. At the same time there is clear delight in Diamant's passionate description of female experience regardless of historical period or biblical accuracy, thereby creating a timeless celebration of what it means to be a woman. Readers especially react to Diamant's vision of a deeply connected female community. Taken together, the responses of the readers convey not only a range of emotional reactions to Diamant's work but a range of reactions to the novelist's relationship to the biblical source material for *The Red Tent.* The intensity of these latter responses appears determined by one's prior knowledge of the actual biblical text.

Interestingly, the bonds between the female characters are mirrored in the identities of those who gave the book to the reader and those with whom the reader plans to share the book—female family members and women in general: "After receiving this book from my mother-in-law, I couldn't read it fast enough. . . . I recommend it to women from all walks of life."[58] Another reader comments, "[I]t is a book I will want to read over and over, and give to my daughter when she is older."[59]

Actual familial connections are joined to cries of metaphoric sisterhood. One reader announces, "I believe that every woman should read this book!"[60] Another reader advises us, "This is a book that you will want to pass around to all of the important women in your life."[61] The presence of meaningful female connection and the longing for its continuation throughout one's life are woven through many of the comments. Perhaps paradoxically the community revealed in these comments is composed of both immediate family with their intimate ties and all women, though they have no apparent ties in common. Strangers become "sisters" as the bonds between women are forged through the shared reading of *The Red Tent.*

A second type of comment appreciates Diamant's ability to capture what it means to be a woman. In a poignant and heartfelt reflection, one reader writes, "I cherish this book because it has told me some of what being a woman is about, something that only a woman knows deep inside, and our damaged mothers have lost the ability to help shed light upon. Books like these are what guide me along, unafraid, into womanhood."[62] The tone of the comment captures the intensity and passion present in many of those who are deeply moved by Diamant's attempt to identify the core attributes of female experience. Taken together these comments suggest that Diamant becomes an intermediary between an impoverished present and a more satisfying past. Readers hungry for contemporary female communities of meaning are looking to a past that Diamant gives them. Other considerations, such as the accuracy of Diamant's reconstruction of that past or her mischaracterizations of biblical characters and episodes, are far less important.

My last sampling illustrates a surprisingly broad array of responses in those who do address the biblical context of *The Red Tent.* Attitudes range from a reader who does not know the Bible and does not care whether the novel is accurate, to others who assume that *The Red Tent* is conveying biblical women's experience, to a third group who are incensed by the inaccuracies of the novel. An example of the first response advises future readers, "You don't have to be a biblical scholar or even BELIEVE in the bible to enjoy this book."[63] After admitting she did not know the Bible, another reader said the book inspired her to return to the original biblical narrative: "My knowledge of the Bible's version of the events was extremely limited. . . . I just enjoyed the story, without worrying about what was real and what wasn't. . . . After enjoying the book so much, I did go back to my Bible and read up. . . . Having read *The Red Tent* made the bible passages SO real."[64] More commonly, readers commented on experiencing the biblical world of women firsthand thanks to *The Red Tent* almost as if they were watching a movie or a live performance. One reader describes the book simply as bringing Dinah's "story to life." Another notes that "this vivid novel truly brought alive the biblical times from a woman's perspective."[65] For many *The Red Tent* simply replaces the biblical narrative.

There were plenty of dissenting voices among readers as well. One reader bemoans the inaccuracies of the novel vis-à-vis the Bible. Another confesses, "I couldn't get past the second chapter, as it was so horribly against the truth of the Bible. There was such a great opportunity to reach so many women who may not know the Bible, but the opportunity was wasted."[66]

The treatment of Dinah's brothers also comes in for criticism. A female reader objects, "I wish Diamant hadn't made all of them [Dinah's brothers] quite so cartoonish and one-dimensional. Perhaps they had one or two redeeming characteristics. . . . I applaud shedding light on the women, but couldn't that have been done without darkening the memories of the men?"[67]

EXITING THE RED TENT

Diamant's work marvelously avoids equating the history of "male" experience with "female" experience.[68] Instead, *The Red Tent* conjures up the missing part of the record, even if fictional. And Diamant has had remarkable success in introducing the issues of feminist interpretation of the past to a popular audience. Her work has found a devoted and passionate readership. Yet the comments of her readers suggest an exodus from the biblical text. As the *Boston Globe* proclaimed, "It is tempting to say that *The Red Tent* is what the Bible would be like if it had been written by women."[69] This quote, placed on the back cover of *The Red Tent,* adds to the conflation of the novel and biblical narrative. Yet *The Red Tent* is not the Bible "if written by women"—far from it. Ironically, the novel's very success as a feminist portrayal of the biblical era precludes a direct engagement with the far more complex (and subtle) original.

Placing Diamant's novel on the continuum of feminist interpretation creates the opportunity to assess the results of her approach to the Bible vis-à-vis those who choose to more directly engage the biblical text. The contrast is stark. By choosing to rely on the original texts in only limited fashion, I would argue that Diamant's popularized version of biblical characters and their stories misses what is most exciting and compelling in the more sustained scholarly and popular readings that directly engage biblical narratives.

Such a substitution is a loss because feminist criticism that remains engaged with the text has produced extraordinary results. Feminist criticism has succeeded in recovering a female voice, muffled by centuries of male disinterest, for a receptive reader. Such criticism joins a venerable tradition in which new questions and concerns have been continually brought to bear on the biblical text and its interpretations. Before the modern period it is incontestable that such interpretation rested predominantly in the hands of male Jews who commented on, studied, and fought over the text. But in our period women have decisively joined in and contributed to that engagement. Female interpreters can bring their own questions and concerns to the text and in so doing have the potential of transforming its stories *yet again*.[70]

In fact feminist criticism has given us a Bible that is intriguingly complex. This type of approach has influenced, joined, and strengthened a trend in recent years that approaches the Bible as a compilation of collective memories over a period of time, memories that reveal a full panoply of voices, competing ideologies, and political points of view.[71] In light of that work, feminist scholars are able to recognize the imprints of countless generations, including women and their influence, as preserved and embedded in the layers of textual traditions. The resulting tapestry of Torah is increasingly seen as a "Divine Symphony."[72] As such, the Bible's underlying patriarchy is apparent, but its compositional development over hundreds of years, its multiple and contradictory traditions, resists and subverts that patriarchy. In other words, rather than turning away from the Bible, recent approaches to the original text offer the possibilities for innovative discoveries *within* the textual world not only for scholars but for popular readers as well. Such approaches positively contribute to the study of the Bible today. We are reintroduced to a more satisfying and complete text, one that manages to preserve the enduring insights of a people whose speculations and passions, uncertainties and longings, and tentative encounters with each other and with God can perhaps even now illuminate our own experiences. Reading against the grain, the Bible's ambiguity and wonderfully laconic narrative voice invite the reader to wrestle with the text to make sense of it and ourselves. At times in such wrestling one may even glimpse its sacred core.

Of course the "God-wrestler" par excellence of the Bible is Jacob, the one who greedily grasps after a birthright and a blessing, who changes over time in fits and starts, but never completely, and who repeatedly encounters God in profoundly mysterious and enigmatic ways.[73] Yet according to Diamant, Jacob renames himself Isra'El "so that people would not remember him as the butcher of Shechem."[74] Why would a novelist flatten such an artistically accomplished and complex portrayal, distilling the multifaceted character who came to represent the people Israel into a murderous butcher? She has replaced the wonderful ambiguity of the original text with a rather crude, simplistic caricature. On the premise that she is empowering women, Diamant's feminist reading of Dinah's story flattens and simplifies an immensely subtle original text. Her reading becomes increasingly hostile to other key Jewish meanings in the text that are as significant for a feminist reader as for any other.[75]

In the end one's engagement with or distance from the text matters enormously. What gets preserved and what gets lost in the process may enrich us or impoverish us. *It may also impoverish the text.* For it is in encounter that both the reader and the text are continually transformed. Feminists engrossed in the narratives of biblical women have learned to wrestle with the biblical text and, as a result, take their place in our time as those who have reintroduced it to us in its complexity and enigma. I would call the fruits of such wrestling an ongoing blessing.

NOTES

I would like to thank Sharon Gillerman and Riv-Ellen Prell for their helpful comments. I would also like to acknowledge the following people with whom I have conversed about various aspects of this essay: Isa Aron, Ellen Bob, Arnie Eisen, David Ellenson, Carla Fenves, Jacqueline Hantgan, Patricia Karlin Neumann, David Kaufman, Gideon Lewis-Kraus, Susan Lippe, Barbara Pitkin, and Amy Sapowith.

1. For a concise history of feminist scholarship on the Bible, see Ilana Pardes, *Countertraditions in the Bible* (Cambridge, MA: Harvard University Press, 1992), 13–38. For an excellent bibliography of such scholarship, see Alice Bach, *Women in the Hebrew Bible* (New York: Routledge, 1999). Most recently, see Carol Meyers, *Households and Holiness: The Religious Culture of Israelite Women* (Minneapolis: Fortress, 2005), for both a brief history of scholarly interest in biblical women and for some of the methodological missteps Meyers identifies.

2. Quoted in Naomi Graetz, "Dinah the Daughter," in *A Feminist Companion to Genesis,* ed. Athalya Brenner (Sheffield: Sheffield Academic Press, 1993), 315.

3. Phyllis Trible, "Depatriarchalizing in Biblical Interpretation," *Journal of the American Academy of Religion* 41, no. 1 (1973): 30–48 [31]. Trible is referring to the Apostle Paul and the twentieth-century Protestant scholars Karl Barth and Dietrich Bonhoeffer.

4. Anne E. Carr, "The New Vision of Feminist Theology," in *Freeing Theology,* ed. Catherine LaCugna (San Francisco: HarperCollins, 1993), 12.

5. Deborah Fineblum Raub, "Profile: Anita Diamant," *Hadassah Magazine* 83 (March 2002), available at http://www.hadassh.org.

6. As examples of work geared toward a popular audience while remaining quite close to the biblical text, see, in order of publication, Judith A. Kates and Gail Twersky Reimer, eds., *Reading Ruth* (New York: Ballantine Books, 1996); Ellen Frankel, *The Five Books of Miriam* (San Francisco: HarperCollins, 1998); and Vanessa Ochs, *Sarah Laughed: Modern Lessons from the Wisdom and Stories of Biblical Women* (New York: McGraw-Hill, 2005).

7. Meyers, *Households and Holiness,* 27–35, discusses the possible meaning of the female figurines at length while rejecting a focus on female deities as the path toward understanding Israelite women's religion: "It assumes that goddesses are

linked mainly to female worshipers, when in fact people of both genders apparently participated in cultic practices directed toward deities of either gender" (6). Meyers would also object to my suggestion that feminist scholars use contemporary biblical methodologies to ask different questions. Meyers attacks what she calls "masculinized approaches" and calls for feminist scholars to break away from Western models of scholarship. For her full discussion, see 4–11. In spite of that note of caution, I would cite two male scholars that I find extraordinarily useful in helping us move away from a reality as defined only by the biblical text to a reality based on textual evidence combined with archeological discoveries. They are William G. Dever, *What Did the Biblical Writers Know and When Did They Know It?* (Grand Rapids, MI: Eerdmans, 2001), 174–98; Dever, *Did God Have a Wife? Archeology and Folk Religion in Ancient Israel* (Grand Rapids, MI: Eerdmans, 2005); and Mark S. Smith, *The Memoirs of God* (Minneapolis: Fortress, 2004), 54–55, 111–12, 114–16. The degree of reciprocity and mutual influence between these scholars and more explicitly feminist scholars is worthy of further study but beyond the confines of this essay.

8. The work of Mieke Bal provides ample evidence of this kind of literary and cultural approach. See *Lethal Love* (Bloomington: Indiana University Press, 1987), *Murder and Difference* (Bloomington: Indiana University Press, 1988), and *Death and Dissymmetry* (Chicago: University of Chicago Press, 1988). Tamara Eskenazi shows an astute sensitivity to cultural and ideological issues in "Torah as Narrative and Narrative as Torah," in *Old Testament Interpretation,* ed. James Luther Mays, David L. Petersen, and Kent Harold Richards (Nashville: Abingdon, 1995). Also note the surveys done of feminist biblical scholarship by Adele Reinhartz: "Midrash She Wrote: Jewish Women's Writing on the Bible," *Shofar* 16, no. 4 (1998): 6–27, and "Jewish Women's Scholarly Writings on the Bible," in *The Jewish Study Bible,* ed. Adele Berlin and Marc Brettler (Oxford: Oxford University Press, 2004). For a recent example of literary readings of biblical women, see Tikva Frymer-Kensky, *Reading the Women of the Bible* (New York: Schocken, 2002).

9. For instance, Athalya Brenner admits "a bias toward the neglected areas of female lives in ancient Israel and the Hebrew bible rather than a more naïve interest in male lives as representative of human life, a subject which has been interpreted as gender inclusive for centuries." See Brenner, *The Intercourse of Knowledge* (New York: Brill, 1997), 4.

10. Reinhartz describes how the biblical text "mirrors a patriarchal society, that is, a society in which women have a secondary role" ("Midrash She Wrote," 8).

11. Tikva Frymer-Kensky, *Studies in Bible and Feminist Criticism* (Philadelphia: Jewish Publication Society, 2006), 160. Meyers, *Households and Holiness,* 13–26, argues that the religious practices of women generally took place within the realm of the household.

12. Frymer-Kensky, *Reading the Women of the Bible,* xiii.

13. Susan Niditch, "Portrayals of Women in the Hebrew Bible," in *Jewish Women in Historical Perspective,* ed. Judith R. Baskin (Detroit: Wayne State University Press, 1998), 29.

14. Frymer-Kensky, *Studies in Bible and Feminist Criticism,* 160.

15. Brenner, *The Intercourse of Knowledge,* 139.

16. Frymer-Kensky, *Reading the Women of the Bible,* 194.

17. Ibid., 183, 188. Frymer-Kensky argues that when Dinah went out unprotected and/or had sex with Shechem, either action would be considered problematic enough that it would motivate the brothers' actions against Shechem and his town whether or not a rape had occurred (182–83). Her reading supports Anita Diament's move to turn the rape into a love story, a move I criticize below. In spite of Frymer-Kensky's reading, most readers of the English translation of Dinah's story would encounter an English translation that stated that Shechem took Dinah "with force" or strongly implied that a rape occurred.

18. Ibid., 182.

19. Carr, "The New Vision," 10. There are times when the Bible needs to be combined with other approaches. See, for example, Meyers, *Households and Holiness,* on the religious culture of Israelite women in which she relies on anthropology and archeology as well as the biblical text.

20. In particular see the fine essay by Stephen Geller, "The Religion of the Bible," in *The Jewish Study Bible,* ed. Adele Berlin and Marc Brettler (Oxford: Oxford University Press, 2004), 2021–40.

21. Pardes, *Countertraditions in the Bible,* 4. Similarly, Niditch emphasizes and relies on the heterogeneity of biblical texts ("Portrayals of Women in the Hebrew Bible," 27).

22. Pardes, *Countertraditions in the Bible,* 144. Note her discussion of the influence of Bakhtin on her work on pp. 3–4.

23. For this reading of Eve, see, among many feminist works, the interesting argument of Israel Knohl, *The Divine Symphony* (Philadelphia: Jewish Publication Society, 2003), 39–40. On Hagar, see the work of Phyllis Trible, "Hagar: The Desolation of Rejection," in *Texts of Terror* (Philadelphia: Fortress, 1984), and, in general, her close readings of a series of biblical women in *God and the Rhetoric of Sexuality* (Philadelphia: Fortress, 1978). I wrote on Hagar vis-à-vis Abraham in "Reading the Seams," *Journal for the Study of the Old Testament* 29 (March 2005): 259–87 [278–81].

24. A point convincingly argued by Tammi J. Schneider, *Judges* (Minnesota: Liturgical Press, 2000).

25. Frymer-Kensky, *Reading the Women of the Bible,* xvii–xxii.

26. Niditch, "Portrayals of Women in the Hebrew Bible," 34. See also Meyers, *Households and Holiness.*

27. For a recent discussion of the evidence for goddess worship in ancient Israel, see Mark Smith, *The Memoirs of God* (Minneapolis: Fortress, 2004). For a discussion of Wisdom, see Claudia Camp, *Wisdom and the Feminine in the Book of Proverbs* (Decatur, GA: Almond Press, 1985).

28. I want to thank my former rabbinical student Ricki Kosovske for pointing this out to me in her highly original and creative reading of labor and birth imagery in biblical narrative. Mark Smith suggests that female imagery for God probably originated in polytheistic practices, testifying to a great familiarity with Asherah among the early Israelites. See Smith, *The Memoirs of God,* 26. Diamant depicts

female worship of goddesses, particularly the Queen of Heaven, Asherah, and Ishtar. What she does not show are biblical women involved with Yahweh or an awareness of the images of the feminine in Yahweh (as pointed out to me by Micah Citrin, another former rabbinical student). Nor are her characters curious about Jacob's God, El. In fact El is a terrifying god of "thunder, high places, and awful sacrifice. . . . This was a hard, strange god, alien and cold." Anita Diamant, *The Red Tent* (New York: Picador, 1997), 13.

29. Phyllis Trible labels the language of Isaiah *gynomorphic* in "Depatriarchalizing in Biblical Interpretation," 32–34.

30. This is illustrated in the work of Ilana Pardes, who "sketch[es] the ways in which antithetical female voices intermingle with other repressed elements such as polytheism." This description of Pardes's work can be found in Reinhartz, "Midrash She Wrote," 16.

31. Frymer-Kensky, *Studies in Bible and Feminist Criticism,* 166.

32. Reinhartz, "Midrash She Wrote," 15, identifies the significance of such a focus in the work of Brenner.

33. Frymer-Kensky, *Studies in Bible and Feminist Criticism,* 167.

34. Quoted in Reinhartz, "Midrash She Wrote," 18.

35. Or, as put by Reinhartz, how do contemporary biblical scholars "negotiate the challenges raised by the feminist movement and its Jewish permutations?" ("Midrash She Wrote," 7).

36. Reinhartz notes the commonalities between Jewish and Christian feminist scholars in "Jewish Women's Scholarly Writings on the Bible," in *The Jewish Study Bible,* ed. Adele Berlin and Marc Brettler (Oxford: Oxford University Press, 2004), 2005.

37. Ibid., 2004.

38. This is an insight I owe to Knohl, *The Divine Symphony.* To call the Hebrew Bible the Old Testament is to adapt a Christian perspective, which understands it as completed or properly viewed only through the lens of the Christian Bible.

39. Frymer-Kensky, *Reading the Women of the Bible,* xxvi.

40. Susan Graham, review of *Reading the Women of the Bible, Journal of Hebrew Scriptures* 4 (2002–3), available at http://www.arts.ualberta.ca/JHS/reviews/review097.htm.

41. David Noel Freedman, review of *Reading the Women of the Bible, Library Journal,* available at http://www.libraryjournal.com.

42. Walter Harrelson, review of *Reading the Women of the Bible, Library Journal,* available at http://www.libraryjournal.com.

43. Diamant explains this on her Web site, http://www.anitadiamant.com/faqs redtent.html.

44. Diamant, *The Red Tent,* 3.

45. Carol Meyers's description of the religious culture of Israelite women points to a widespread interest in the topics emphasized by Diamant—fertility, reproduction, and midwifery. See *Households and Holiness,* 62–70.

46. Diamant, *The Red Tent,* 170.

47. Ibid., 266.

48. Two very succinct summaries of the issues involved for a victim of rape when she tells others what has happened include *Surviving Sexual Assault,* ed. Rachel Grossman (New York: Congdon and Weed, 1983), and *The Rape Crisis Intervention Handbook,* ed. Sharon L. McCombie (New York: Plenum, 1980). Nancy Venable Raine, a writer and victim of rape explains why she finally broke her silence: "But silence has the rusty taste of shame. The words *shut up* are the most terrible words I know. . . . The man who raped me spat these words out over and over during the hours of my attack. . . . It seemed to me that for seven years—until at last I spoke—these words had sunk into my soul and become prophecy. And it seems to me now that these words, the brutish message of tyrants . . . preserve the darkness that still covers this pervasive crime. The real shame, as I have learned, is to consent to them." Raine, *After Silence* (New York: Crown Publishers, 1998), 6.

49. Anita Diamant, http://www.anitadiamant.com/faqsredtent.html. Rabbi Susan Lippe raised the issue of rape in the novel in a personal communication. Critical of the imagined reciprocity between Dinah and Shechem, Rabbi Lippe pointed out that Diamant replaced the biblical assault with another sexual violation of Dinah. She was even drugged in the process when her mothers took a wide-mouthed frog "with spread-eagled legs and used it ceremonially [to] break the hymen of initiates to the red tent." For this description, see Keri James, *The Chronicle,* available at http://www.powells.com/cgi-bin/bibkio. See Diamant, *The Red Tent,* 170–73, for the scene in question.

50. Diamant, The Red Tent, 204.

51. Rabbi Benjamin Edidin Scolnic, e-mail excerpt, January 27, 2005. For printed essay, see Scolnic, "When Does Feminist Biblical Interpretation Become Anti-Semitic?" *Conservative Judaism and the Faces of God's Words* (Lanham, MD: University Press of America, 2005), 83–85.

52. I used the new translation of Robert Alter, *The Five Books of Moses* (New York: Norton, 2004). For Diamant's treatment of Jacob's deathbed scene, see *The Red Tent,* 311–12. Diamant has her characters recount her invented version of the events of Genesis 34 on pp. 316–17 of the novel.

53. Diamant, http://www.anitadiamant.com/faqsredtent.html.

54. Diamant, *The Red Tent,* 3.

55. The marketing strategies for *The Red Tent* deserve a separate essay. For enlightening descriptions of such strategies that include the targeting of a female audience, a Jewish audience, and a "spiritual" audience, and for the flourishing of book clubs that reinforce such a market, see the following: Janice A. Radway, *Reading the Romance: Women, Patriarchy and Popular Literature* (Chapel Hill: University of North Carolina Press, 1984); Bonny V. Fetterman, "Significant Jewish Books," *Reform Judaism Magazine* 5, no. 99, available at http://www.reformjudaismmag.org; Patricia Holt, "The Red Tide, Anatomy of a Best-seller," *Ms. Magazine,* October/November 2001, available at http://www.msmagazine.com/oct01/redtent.html; Marcia Ford, "Beyond Handselling," *Publishers Weekly,* September 23, 2002, available at http://www.publishers weekly.com; Deborah Fineblum Raub, "Profile:

Anita Diamant," *Hadassah Magazine* 83, no. 7 (March 2002), available at http://www.hadassah.org; and Jonathan Franzen, *How to Be Alone* (New York: Farrar, Straus and Giroux-Picador, 2003).

56. Darin Keesler, e-mail message to the author, February 2005.

57. As convincingly argued by Radway, *Reading the Romance.*

58. scottydog_1, December 10, 2004, http://www.half.ebay.com/products/customer_reviews.

59. queenofprussia, July 30, 2001, http://www.half.ebay.com/products/customer_reviews.

60. jar93, September 20, 2004, http://www.half.ebay.com/products/customer_reviews.

61. carmodycampbell, August 9, 2002, http://www.half.ebay.com/products/customer_reviews.

62. Danielle, June 18, 2001, http://www.newvision-psychic.com/bookshelf/RedTent.html.

63. bearmom1, December 28, 2002, http://www.half.ebay.com/products/customer_reviews.

64. Anonymous, November 12, 2001, bookclique@tcpl.lib.in.us.

65. hapahappiness, July 21, 2002, lillianbreeze, June 18, 2003, http://www.half.ebay.com/products/customer_reviews.

66. mamaardra, November 19, 2003, http://www.half.ebay.com/products/customer_reviews.

67. Ellen, March 1, 2000, http://www.newvision-psychic.com/bookshelf/RedTent.html.

68. See note 9 above.

69. Excerpted from the *Boston Globe* on http://www.powells.com/cgi-bin/bibkio, a site of synopses and reviews.

70. We ignore the continuing influence of biblical narratives within contemporary cultural discourse, including issues crucial to women's experience and freedoms, at our own peril.

71. In a list of recent work, I would include two I have cited frequently in the present essay: Smith, *The Memoirs of God,* and Knohl, *The Divine Symphony.* I would also include the recent work of Ronald Hendel, *Remembering Abraham* (Oxford: Oxford University Press, 2005), and Ilana Pardes, *The Biography of Ancient Israel* (Berkeley: University of California Press, 2000).

72. The reference is to the title of Knohl's *The Divine Symphony.*

73. For a reading that emphasizes the enigma of the scene, see Stephen A. Geller, "The Struggle at the Jabbok: The Uses of Enigma in a Biblical Narrative," *JANES* 14 (1984): 37–60. Arthur I. Waskow popularizes the term in *Godwrestling* (New York: Knopf, 1987).

74. Diamant, *The Red Tent,* 208.

75. Riv-Ellen Prell, personal communication with the author, March 2005.

PART TWO

REDEFINING JUDAISM

CHAPTER FOUR

WOMEN IN REFORM JUDAISM

Between Rhetoric and Reality

KARLA GOLDMAN

Leaders of American Reform Judaism have often celebrated their movement's role as a champion of women's equality within a religious tradition known for the restrictions it places on women's ability to participate in and lead public worship. Indeed, changing roles and expectations for women have played a steady role in shaping the emergence and evolution of Reform Judaism in the United States. Chief among Reform Judaism's liberating innovations were the abolition of a separate women's gallery within the synagogue in the 1850s and the ordination of the first American woman rabbi in 1972. Despite the real impact of these institutional changes, the American Reform movement has always struggled to match women's realities within the movement to its leaders' rhetorical commitment to gender equity. In recent decades, this has meant coming to terms with the realities of female religious and lay leadership and the recasting of women's congregational work in a post-feminist era. As in American Judaism generally, the impact of women's changing roles on the Reform movement has been most evident over the last twenty to thirty years. It is important to recognize and remember, however, that efforts to adapt Judaism to society's evolving expectations for women have shaped American Reform Judaism throughout its history.

The beginnings of American Reform in part reflected the ideology and efforts of nineteenth-century German Jewish Reformers who sought to adapt traditional Jewish worship to the perceived demands for rational religious practice brought by the Enlightenment. Although mid-nineteenth-century immigrant rabbis from German-speaking lands played a major role in shaping the American movement, American Reform Judaism found a distinct expression that was both more radical and broader than German Reform in terms of actual practice.[1] This distinctiveness emerged most clearly in redefinitions of women's place in the synagogue. Although mid-nineteenth-century German Reform leaders made the case for women's equality in Judaism and sought to abolish "anachronistic" laws and customs that stifled the public expression of women's religiosity, it was only in the United States that practical innovations adopted by the Reform movement actively restructured the nature of women's participation in public worship.[2]

CHANGING PLACES: WOMEN IN EARLY AMERICAN REFORM SYNAGOGUES

Even before the emergence of a distinctive Reform movement, American synagogue practice and design displayed sensitivity to American understandings of female religious agency. Early generations of American Jewish women quickly seemed to realize that American culture demanded women's presence at public worship, and colonial-era American synagogue builders did away with the partition barriers that kept women out of sight in traditional women's galleries. By the 1850s, many American synagogues boasted mixed male and female choirs, confirmation ceremonies that recognized the religious education of both boys and girls, and women's galleries that offered tiered rows of seats, carefully affording a clear view of, and to, the many women who took their place at regular worship services.[3]

The departure that most clearly heralded the arrival of a Reform style of worship and that definitively separated that style from traditional Jewish practice was the introduction of family pews. Introduced first in Albany in 1851 and then in New York City's Temple Emanu-El in 1854, family pews appeared as part of an array of liturgical and ritual reforms introduced into these two congregations when each moved into a former church building. Rather than add a central reader's desk and a balcony for women in accord with standard American synagogue design, these congregations adopted the existing church layout that arrayed the worshipers, men and women together, in rows facing a pulpit at the front of the auditorium. Most of the reforms introduced in these and other early American Reform congregations, including the pulpit at the front of the sanctuary, found parallels in German Reform efforts. Family pews in the synagogue, however, remained an exclusively American innovation well into the twentieth century.[4]

It does not appear that family pews were introduced out of concerns for women's equality. More relevant seemed to be the desire to construct a worship environment that comported with evolving notions of respectability and aesthetics. Early nineteenth-century American synagogues displayed much in the way of chaotic, unorganized, and unharmonious behavior by and between those in attendance that had little to do with the "elevation" and "devotion" that synagogue leaders associated with properly cultured and prosperous religious assemblies. Segregated into galleries, women were difficult to integrate into efforts to homogenize and refine the behavior of individual worshipers. Most disturbingly, separation seemed to isolate the women as an exotic and sexualized Oriental other, rather than as the respectable Occidental ladies they were meant to be.[5]

The opulent Reform Jewish temples that arose in urban centers from San Francisco to New York City in the years after the Civil War testified to the prosperity, achievement, and refinement of American Jews. The family pews that filled their sanctuaries were a critical component of the civilized sensibility that these synagogues were meant to display. Offered a place in the sanctuary, Jewish women occupied the family pews of these magnificent temples in force, continuing a trend that had marked early nineteenth-century American synagogues. In a departure from the traditional pattern of synagogue worship, but in keeping with the attendance patterns of most American Christian denominations, women quickly came to dominate attendance at weekly Sabbath services as men increasingly attended to business concerns on the Jewish day of rest.[6]

"EMANCIPATION"

With the introduction of family pews, Reform leaders began to celebrate their movement for its "emancipation" of Jewish women. Yet the second half of the nineteenth century brought mixed results in forwarding the public position of women in America's Reform congregations. Women in many communities worked actively to raise money for their congregations—they pushed for the building of synagogues and paid congregational debts.[7] They also took important teaching roles in congregational schools that offered girls a supplementary religious education equivalent to that of boys. Many nineteenth-century Reform congregations rejected the exclusively male bar mitzvah, adopting the confirmation ritual observed on the festival of Shavuot (in May or June) as the primary adolescent rite of passage, a practice that incorporated equality for girls in religious education.[8] But if much of the religious behavior and identity of women in American Reform Judaism had been transformed from traditional patterns, they lacked the institutional structures that could give them a sustained collective voice or authority.

The gap between nineteenth-century rhetoric and realities about women's place in the American movement is captured in the words and actions of Rabbi Isaac Mayer Wise. Wise is regarded as the great builder of American Reform Judaism because of his instrumental role in the founding of the movement's central institutions, the Union of American Hebrew Congregations (UAHC) in 1873, Hebrew Union College (HUC) in 1875, and the Central Conference of American Rabbis (CCAR) in 1889. Wise was the rabbi at the Albany synagogue in which family pews were first introduced in 1851, and he later celebrated his role in thus beginning woman's "emancipation" within Judaism. Wise failed to point out, however, that although he arrived in Cincinnati in 1854, his congregation there neglected to introduce family pews until 1866 when they built a grand new temple incorporating the innovation. When Wise was seeking support for the creation of a rabbinical college, he also advocated the need for a female theological seminary counterpart. No such institution was ever created—a few female students did enroll in the early Hebrew Union College, but none advanced very far in her studies.[9]

Most tellingly, Wise argued strenuously in 1876 that women should be given "a voice and a vote." Reform would not be "complete," he declared, until women were considered members of their congregations and allowed to serve on congregational governing boards both "for the sake of the principle and to rouse in them an interest for congregational affairs." He announced himself "ready to appear before any congregation" to plead the cause "of any woman wishing to become a member."[10] These were strong statements, but we should note that Wise's own congregation—over which he had a great deal of influence—never even discussed the possibility of such a reform during his lifetime.

NEW ROLES

In the late 1880s new structures began to emerge that would absorb the latent energies and expand the agency of women within Reform congregations. The first Jewish Sisterhood of Personal Service in New York City provided a prototype that was quickly emulated in Jewish congregations throughout the country. These groups of Americanized Jewish women first focused their energies on the impoverished eastern European Jewish multitudes that had begun arriving in the United States. The new sisterhoods formed in many of New York's uptown synagogues, ranging from Reform to Orthodox, cooperated in dividing responsibility for care of the city's immigrant districts. Members engaged in a broad range of social welfare work directed toward aiding newly arrived immigrants. There was a great emphasis on "friendly visiting" and the dispensing of material aid to "worthy" recipients, but sisterhoods of personal service in New York and San Francisco, and similar groups in other cities, also offered vocational schools, classes, and clubs for working girls, child day care and kindergartens, and employment bureaus. Acculturated Jewish women throughout the country created religious schools that attempted to expose immigrant children to an Americanized form of Judaism. Although the work of these organizations was outwardly directed, it brought a measure of shared purpose and community to the women of these congregations.[11] The advent around the turn of the century of "professionalized" Jewish social service organizations (staffed by men) to address the needs of new immigrants ultimately marginalized the benevolent activities of these organizations, but the sisterhood workers were not ready to return to their homes.[12]

ACTIVISM IN AND BEYOND THE SYNAGOGUE

The activation of women's energies that had arisen to meet the needs of new immigrants had inspired a general awakening of organized activism among acculturated Jewish women at both the local and national level that began to match the intensity of Christian women's commitments to causes like temperance and missionary work. Much of this energy found its expression within synagogues. Instead of gathering as they had often previously done as ad hoc groups to advance particular and limited congregational projects, women in many Reform synagogues around the country during the 1890s started to approach their responsibilities on a permanent organized basis. Congregations, in turn, began to depend on synagogue women's groups to take responsibility for the physical, charitable, and social needs of the community. This activation of female energy for the benefit of the congregation intersected with efforts by graduates of Hebrew Union College to expand the institutional work of Reform congregations beyond the narrow scope of worship. Women's groups offered services in whatever ways congregations would allow them to participate. In some communities this meant that they became more involved in addressing the needs of religious school children or in furnishing and decorating their temple buildings. In other synagogues, women's participation became the key to sparking a general expansion of congregational cultural and charitable activities. The emergence of synagogue auxiliary associations offered women, for the first time, positions on various committees devoted to congregational work, and opportunities to be officially recognized for their communal contributions. A wave of temple building in the 1890s and early twentieth century became necessary to encompass the expanding and variegated institutional life made possible by women's emerging activism.[13]

Carrie Obendorfer Simon, born in 1872, became the leading figure in the movement to channel these temple groups and their energies into a national organization. Simon's mother had been a founder of the Cincinnati section of the National Council of Jewish Women (NCJW), and Carrie had served as the section's secretary. After marrying a young rabbi, Simon traveled with him first to Sacramento then to Omaha where she carried on NCJW work. As the council, the first national Jewish women's membership organization, struggled to reconcile the varied religious approaches of its diverse membership, however, Simon, like many other women, turned her attention to local congregational work.

When the Simons moved to the nation's capital, Carrie founded the Ladies Auxiliary Society of Washington Hebrew Congregation in 1905 for the purpose of "congregational work, pure and simple, and to endeavor to establish a more congenial and social congregational spirit."[14] In 1913 the male leadership of the UAHC issued a call "to all ladies' organizations connected with congregations belonging to the Union" to send delegates to a meeting to be convened in Cincinnati "for the purpose of organizing a Federation of Temple Sisterhoods." The meeting, held in conjunction with the national UAHC convention, was attended by 156 delegates (mainly the wives of UAHC delegates) from fifty-two congregations. Carrie Simon was elected as the organization's founding president.[15]

A NEW ERA: THE IMPACT OF THE NATIONAL FEDERATION OF TEMPLE SISTERHOOD (NFTS)

The creation of a national framework for women's work in Reform congregations helped transform the identity and work of Reform Jewish women at a local level. With the founding of NFTS, many local congregations that had not previously had women's membership organizations created sisterhoods, and the work of many existing women's organizations was transformed by the advent of a national organization. The energy engendered by the creation of NFTS encouraged tens of thousands of women to focus their energies on congregational life and on the broader efforts of American Reform Judaism.[16]

The contributions of both new and reconfigured sisterhoods to the educational, material, and social life of American Reform congregations were transformative. Sisterhood groups moved boldly to take on a vast range of responsibilities within their communities. Often responding to suggestions from the national leadership, sisterhoods across the country took on a staggering list of concerns and activities in the service of their communities. Religious schools were transformed by an infusion of new elements that included holiday entertainments and treats, libraries, and extracurricular activities. Synagogue design was reenvisioned and gifts of organs, carpeting, furniture, and building wings proliferated. The social experience of congregational life was reinvented with food provided at the end of worship services and annual meetings reimagined as elaborate congregational dinners complete with entertainment and dancing.[17]

On a national level, early initiatives that have become longtime traditions included the production of an annual art calendar and the support of rabbinic education and HUC, through funds for student scholarships. A national campaign raised money for the school's Sisterhood Dormitory that opened in Cincinnati in 1925 as a residence for rabbinical students. Another central and continuing effort was introduced with the founding of the Jewish Braille Institute in 1931.[18]

The impetus and legitimacy given to practical synagogue work by the creation of a national Jewish women's organization helped transform women's political status within their congregations. The impact of their national and local contributions led to growing expectations that women should be recognized as full participants in the work of Reform Judaism. As women expanded their auxiliary work, congregations began to depend increasingly on their contributions. One reflection of women's growing integration into the community can be seen in the number of congregations that acted to redefine their membership categories so that women who were neither single nor widowed could become "associate" members of their congregations.[19]

The founding and impact of the NFTS engendered even higher expectations for the recognition of women as full participants in synagogue life. Already in 1916, National Council of Jewish Women leader Rebekah Kohut, who was active in the sisterhood of New York's Temple Emanu-El, felt free to question "who would dare to say that a woman, as the President of the congregation, or women on the Board of Trustees, could not guide the destinies of the synagogue as successfully as men!" Unlike earlier expressions of such sentiments within the Reform movement, Kohut's words were more than rhetorical. By 1915 a number of Reform congregations across the country not only were inviting women to attend annual congregational meetings but had also asked local sisterhoods to send representatives to attend synagogue board meetings. The incorporation of women into previously all-male boards of trustees solidified the contributions and status of women leaders within the congregational world.[20]

In NFTS rhetoric, "religious equality" became synonymous with recognition of women's political status as voting members and potential leaders within their congregations. The passage of the women's suffrage amendment to the U.S. Constitution in 1920 pushed most Reform congregations across the country to assign formal and full membership to all women within their communities. In most places, this also meant that women were offered regular representation, chiefly through sisterhood officers, on congregational boards of trustees. The founding of NFTS brought in its wake a profound reconceptualization of the possibilities for women's authority in Jewish public life. At the organization's founding convention, the only speakers to address the assembled delegates had been rabbis and prominent Jewish men, lending their seal of credibility to the women's gathering. Sisterhood women came to understand, however, that their practical work, their changing status within congregational governance structures, and their contributions to the national Reform movement carried an authority of its own. When Stella Freiberg, as president of an organization that now claimed 50,000 members, addressed the NFTS national convention in 1925, she emphasized that sisterhood women no longer needed men to validate their efforts: "I don't know how the rabbis will feel about it, but we have not called upon them to invoke us with their blessing. Our own women are doing it."[21]

QUESTIONS OF LEADERSHIP

Inevitably, the growth of a cadre of local and national sisterhood leaders, together with the logic implicit in the women's suffrage amendment, confronted male Reform leaders not only with the challenge of accommodating new roles for women in lay governance but with the question of female religious leadership. In 1920 Martha Neumark, a student at HUC and the daughter of an HUC professor, requested that she be allowed, like her male classmates, to serve a high holy day pulpit as a student rabbi. Faced with the possibility that Neumark might present herself as a candidate for ordination, the college's board of governors and faculty and the Reform movement's federation of rabbis, the Central Conference of American Rabbis (CCAR), all took up the question of whether to approve, in principle, the ordination of women rabbis.

Some traditionalist-leaning members of the faculty expressed misgivings as to whether the Reform movement, in ordaining women, would irreparably sunder itself from the other movements in Judaism. Nonetheless, the faculty unanimously agreed that this innovation was consistent with the inclusive and progressive tenets of the Reform movement and equivalent to other major breaks with tradition accepted by the movement. Consideration of the issue at the 1922 CCAR convention was especially noteworthy for the decision of the delegates to invite female members of the audience—wives of the rabbis in attendance—to take part in the discussion. Although the faculty and the CCAR both voted to support the proposed change, HUC's board of governors, which had to make the final decision, ultimately rejected the proposal.[22]

A number of women continued to pursue studies within the Reform rabbinical institutions. Three women engaged in substantive study at New York's Jewish Institute of Religion (JIR), founded in 1922 by Rabbi Stephen S. Wise, during the 1920s and 1930s. Although the faculty accepted them as students, it does not appear that they ever expected these women to become rabbis. In fact, when Helen Levinthal actually completed the JIR curricular requirements for ordination in 1939, the faculty chose to award her a bachelor of Hebrew letters degree rather than rabbinical ordination.[23]

But even as the question of whether women should serve as rabbis lay dormant, sisterhood women in Reform synagogues continued to push, in less radical fashion, against limitations on Jewish women's religious identity. The "Sisterhood Sabbath" emerged in the early 1920s as a way to honor congregational sisterhoods for their manifold contributions to their communities. In 1922 the NFTS leadership promoted the Sisterhood Sabbath, the goal of which was to create an occasion that would encourage greater synagogue attendance and prompt rabbis to acknowledge the work of women within their communities. Some sisterhoods, reporting on their observance in the early 1920s, described the sermons that their rabbis prepared for these occasions, but, intriguingly, many more reported on sermons that were delivered by their own members. The Sisterhood Sabbath quickly developed into an unusual opportunity for women's public religious expression. In addition to delivering sermons, sisterhood women often led all or part of the Sisterhood Sabbath services themselves, or at least participated in guiding some of the readings. A 1923 NFTS report noted the widespread phenomenon of sisterhood women conducting these services, "sermon and all." Although limited to once a year, the annual practice helped change expectations about the possibilities of women's participation within public worship. Many sisterhoods also took responsibility for leading worship services during the summer when rabbis went on vacation and attendance was smaller.[24]

MAKING A DIFFERENCE

Throughout the interwar years, the energy and creativity of women within the Reform movement provided their communities with a rich congregational life. The appointment of Jane Evans in 1933 as the organization's first executive director secured the organization's seriousness of purpose and effectiveness in action. With tireless devotion, even after her retirement in 1976, Evans worked to sustain individual sisterhoods across the country and provided the national organization with a consistent and broad vision. Evans never let NFTS retreat from its commitment to supporting women's advancement within their congregations and within Judaism, to responding to the social and political challenges of the contemporary life, and to the firm conviction that NFTS could make a difference in the lives of its members and the world.[25]

During World War II, as had been the case during World War I, many women looked to their sisterhoods to formalize their contribution to the war effort. They knitted, crocheted, baked cookies, organized blood banks, sold bonds, conducted first-aid classes, and resettled Jewish refugees, all under the auspices of their congregational sisterhoods. Continued postwar growth in synagogue activity reflected a nationwide return to religion that enlivened both churches and synagogues through the 1950s. As synagogue organizational life flourished, sisterhoods were critical in sustaining synagogue life in older congregations and in creating new frameworks for community as old and new congregations found their way to the suburbs.

The child-centered focus of these congregations in building religious schools and creating congregational holiday events provided a meaningful and demanding focus for sisterhood efforts. Before the war, NFTS created a national network that encouraged women in Reform congregations to offer local college students opportunities to sustain their Jewish identities. After the war, sisterhood leaders were instrumental in assisting the National Federation of Temple Youth as it became a central and dynamic force in the Reform movement. Another critical postwar innovation guided by local sisterhoods was the introduction of synagogue gift shops. Not only did the sale of Judaica within the temple foster Jewish ritual practice within the home, a recurrent concern for NFTS, it also helped provide a steady source of income for the local groups.[26]

TOWARD EQUALITY?

The confirmation service with its egalitarian commitment to Jewish education for both boys and girls had been an early aspect of the Reform movement's agenda. As the bar mitzvah ceremony regained popularity in Reform congregations after World War I, however, confirmation ceremonies became increasingly a province for girls alone. The feminization of the group confirmation service, together with the bar mitzvah ceremony's emphasis on individual Jewish ritual skills and obligations, highlighted the gender inequity within Jewish worship that confirmation was meant to neutralize. Mordecai Kaplan, founder of the Reconstructionist movement, introduced the first bat mitzvah ceremony as a female counterpart to the bar mitzvah for his own daughter in 1922. The bat mitzvah ceremony gradually took root within the Conservative movement in the 1930s and 1940s. The Reform movement's commitment to the confirmation rite, however, slowed acceptance of the bat mitzvah in Reform temples.

Bat mitzvah ceremonies began to appear in Reform congregations in the 1950s and made more general progress in the 1960s. Varying in format, a Reform bat mitzvah often involved having a girl read or chant the weekly reading from the prophetic books of the Bible and give some kind of talk during the Friday evening service. By contrast, the bar mitzvah ceremony for boys took place on Saturday morning, with the prophetic reading in its traditional place following the traditional weekly Torah reading drawn from the Pentateuch. With the rise of the feminist movement, the idea of sustaining distinctive rituals to mark the religious obligations and duties of boys and girls, or of men and women, within Judaism became increasingly untenable. By the mid-1970s, a Saturday morning bat mitzvah service identical in its requirements to the ceremony held for boys was in place in most Reform congregations.[27]

Progress toward incorporating increasing equality for women at the level of Reform lay and religious leadership moved in fits and starts through the 1950s and 1960s, as the rhetoric of gender egalitarianism and equality of opportunity became more familiar in the broader culture. Male Reform leaders did not actively support, but did not prevent, a decision by the Reform congregation in Meridian, Mississippi, to appoint Paula Ackerman, the widow of their deceased rabbi, to serve as the community's spiritual leader from 1951 to 1953. Neither did the movement prevent other Reform congregations in Trinidad, Colorado, and Akron, Ohio, from turning to qualified women when they needed someone to lead services and provide spiritual leadership. When CCAR president Rabbi Barnett Brickner asked the conference to declare a commitment to the principle of female ordination in 1956, he may have been prompted by these cases, by changing societal expectations for women as professionals, and by the leadership already shown by rebbetzins (rabbis' wives) like his own highly able and educated wife, Rebecca Brickner. Although his proposal received general approval, the question was "laid on the table" until those with opposing views could present their case—or, as it turned out, indefinitely.[28]

At the same time that the movement's male leadership failed to move forward in affirming their approval of the concept of women's religious leadership, Reform Jewish women continued to build a case for recognition of their abilities through their ongoing, assiduous work on behalf of their congregations and the movement. NFTS had long proved a training ground in communal leadership, offering those involved in its work opportunities to guide their own organizations and to participate in the deliberations of local congregations and the national Reform movement.

In a few instances, women were able to find recognition as leaders outside the framework of women's organizations. Jeanette Weinberg began a sixteen-year term as president of her congregation in Frederick, Maryland, in 1943. Natalie Lansing Hodes served as the founding president of her Philadelphia congregation in 1952. Most significantly perhaps, Helen Dalsheimer, national president of NFTS, became the president of Baltimore Hebrew Congregation in 1956, thus becoming the first woman to lead one of the Reform movement's largest congregations.[29]

Women's service in these roles helped keep questions of women's leadership within the Reform movement alive. Jane Evans, NFTS executive director, was particularly committed to pushing the movement on this issue. She initiated a broad consideration of the question of women's ordination in the organization, culminating in a general discussion at the group's 1963 convention. Reflecting shifting cultural currents and renewed attention to questions of women's equality, the delegates determined to request a meeting of all Reform Judaism's governing bodies to take up the question of women's ordination.[30]

RABBIS

No such conference ever took place. In fact, the issue was ultimately resolved without any grand pronouncements from the movement's organizing bodies. By the mid-1960s, HUC-JIR (two institutions that merged in 1950) president Nelson Glueck was making it clear that he would ordain a female candidate when the opportunity arose, moving the question from abstract commitment to practical reality. Sally Priesand had come to Cincinnati from Cleveland in 1964 with every intention of becoming a rabbi. Along with a few other women, she entered the school's joint undergraduate program with the University of Cincinnati. As she continued her studies past the college level, it soon became clear that Priesand would be the one to create the opportunity that Glueck had been seeking. After Glueck died in 1971, Alfred Gottschalk followed through on his predecessor's commitment, ordaining Priesand as the first American woman rabbi in 1972. Barbara Ostfeld Horowitz was invested at HUC-JIR's New York campus as the first seminary-trained female cantor in 1975.[31]

These pioneering steps in allowing women to take on the most prominent roles of Jewish religious leadership have had profound symbolic and practical implications both within the Reform movement and beyond. The presence of women clergy has reconfigured expectations of what women should be allowed and encouraged to do in a wide variety of Jewish settings. Many see the ordination of Sally Priesand, and of the more than four hundred Reform women rabbis who have followed her, as the ultimate realization of women's religious equality by the Reform movement. Indeed, the embrace of equality for women at every level of leadership and life emerged as an unshakable core tenet of Reform Judaism during the last quarter of the twentieth century. Yet, inevitably perhaps, institutional realities within the Reform movement during this period often failed to match the movement's commitment to its ideal of gender equality.

TENSION

Although women, individually and collectively, had been prime shapers of Reform Judaism since it first emerged, the movement's central institutional and leadership structures had always been exclusively male. Accordingly, as in many arenas of American society, the Reform movement during the last quarter of the twentieth century became a setting for both the tension and the energy that so often accompany challenges to long-established patterns of gender order. Many women who found themselves in positions of status and authority within the Reform movement that had previously been occupied exclusively by men struggled to obtain respect and job security. At the same time, many found themselves in a position to meet a hunger for the new perspectives and new questions that women rabbis could bring to the Reform religious framework.

Not surprisingly, many early women rabbis encountered hostility as they took on this new role. Moreover, little thought had gone into preparing Reform communities to accept women rabbis or into anticipating unfamiliar practical issues, such as the question of building maternity leaves into rabbinic contracts. In response, in 1976, when there were only three women Reform rabbis, the CCAR created the Task Force on Women in the Rab-

Women's Rabbinic Network, March 2, 1982, HUC-JIR, New York, on the tenth anniversary of the ordination of the first woman rabbi. Used with the permission of the Jacob Rader Marcus Center of the American Jewish Archive.

binate, chaired initially by Sally Priesand, which was intended to work toward the successful integration of women into the profession. Another significant force in shaping the place of women rabbis in the Reform movement arose with the creation of the Women's Rabbinic Network (WRN) in 1980. The WRN displaced an earlier organization, the Women's Rabbinic Association, which had brought together Reform and Reconstructionist women rabbis.[32]

As a constituent organization of the movement's CCAR, the WRN serves dual purposes. Through newsletters and biennial meetings, it has reduced the isolation of individual members and offered forums to address common issues. In addition, the WRN has been extremely effective as an advocate for the issues faced by women and (like the NFTS before it) in opening formerly all-male hierarchies to female participation. One significant contribution has been offering women rabbis a broader context in which to understand the struggles they face in their individual rabbinates. Entering a professional culture based on the premise that one's wife could take care of family and life responsibilities, many women rabbis have struggled to accommodate their desire to meld family and personal lives with their career. The network has been an important agent in contesting a professional model that has become increasingly problematic for both men and women.

Despite the WRN and the fact that, by the early 1980s, the number of female HUC-JIR students began to approach parity with that of their male classmates, women rabbis continued to face distinctive challenges. A 1980 survey of congregations by the WRN reported diverse fears that women rabbis would be too soft-spoken, too weak, too emotional, too challenged by the effort of balancing family and career, and too unfamiliar. A 1994 survey of 103 Reform women rabbis showed that half of the respondents had experienced some form of sexual harassment in their professional roles.[33]

ENERGY

Even as women rabbis faced persistent challenges, they also began to reshape Reform congregations and American Judaism in profound ways. As women assumed formal leadership in Jewish worship and ritual, many began to view Jewish ceremonies, liturgies, texts, and traditions in a new light; they became more aware of the relevance and significance of their own experience. Rabbi Laura Geller, ordained in 1976, was among the first to point out that women rabbis, as they broke down the traditional exclusivity of Jewish leadership, could offer congregants a sense of greater access to the sacred and help them think more critically about their concept of God. She was also a pioneer in formulating Jewish traditions that address the many stages of women's lives that had been overlooked by a male-centered tradition. She and her many colleagues have created ceremonies to mark baby namings, gay unions, weaning, the beginning and end of menstruation, miscarriages, abortion, and divorce, among other significant life events.[34] Reform women rabbis have also been important participants in the creation of feminist midrash, reexaminations of biblical texts often from the perspectives of female participants, and in emerging critiques of traditional Jewish liturgy.

The most radical of recent efforts to accommodate Jewish practice and liturgy to evolving gender concerns have occurred for the most part outside the Reform movement.[35] Reform liturgical efforts geared toward introducing gender-inclusive language have been slowed by worries about preserving the familiarity of traditional texts for congregants with weak Jewish educations and by differing perceptions of the extent to which the language of traditional Jewish prayer should be seen as a male expression of religiosity. In 1993 the movement published a "gender-sensitive" liturgy meant to supplement the 1975 Reform prayer book, *Gates of Prayer*. The sensitive edition avoids male pronouns in referring to God in its English prayers and translations. Changes in the Hebrew text are limited to adding the names of the matriarchs to liturgical references to the patriarchs.[36] The long and extended process toward creating the movement's new siddur to be published in 2007 has reflected, in part, a discomfort with more challenging liturgical revisions that some see as too awkward and some see as too radical.

Other reflections of the impact of women's changing roles within Reform congregations include the elaboration of Jewish prayers and worship services directed toward physical and spiritual healing. The work of singer/songwriter Debbie Friedman, whose music has been embraced by the Reform youth movement and Reform congregations, has been critical to this trend as has the work of rabbis like Nancy Flam, who has been active in creating and directing a number of Jewish healing centers in California. The popular emergence of bat and bar mitzvah ceremonies for adults represents a general trend toward greater access to textual knowledge and authority among Reform congregants. Women, many of whom felt that their earlier Jewish educations were limited because of their gender, have been the most active in taking advantage of this innovation and in moving generally toward greater participation in congregational ritual and life. Many within the movement, in fact, have begun to express concern about a growing absence of men engaged in congregational participation and leadership.

WOMEN OF REFORM JUDAISM IN A CHANGING WORLD

In the current communal context, where women can claim full access to religious and lay leadership, and as women have taken on professional roles both within and outside Judaism, some question the continued relevance of gender-segregated congregational organizations. Although many sisterhoods continue to attend to the fundamental social, spiritual, and material needs of their communities, other congregations have seen a waning of energy within their sisterhood organizations. With so many women taking on professional responsibilities outside the home, congregational leaders can no longer draw freely on the energy and time of a cadre of talented female volunteers. As a result, much of the responsibility for sustaining a more limited range of congregational activities is increasingly undertaken by paid (male and female) staff members.

Meanwhile, many women now become involved in synagogue life and governance without first rising through a congregational women's organization. As women take on lay leadership roles that were once monopolized by men, many have become wary of the subsidiary role often ascribed to sisterhood groups. This concern was reflected in the NFTS's 1993 decision to change its name to Women of Reform Judaism, the Federation of Temple Sisterhoods (WRJ). The name change reflected a desire to be seen not merely as an auxiliary service group but as an organization that puts its members and their interests at the center of the Reform movement. The national WRJ remains a strong institutional entity, but it, too, has struggled to adapt to a changing social and religious context.

In many ways WRJ continues to fulfill NFTS's traditional role within the movement, including its longstanding support of Reform youth activities and rabbinical education both for American-born students and for rabbinical students from around the world. WRJ sustained the focus on social justice issues pioneered by its first executive director, Jane Evans, throughout the twentieth century. Now, in the first decade of the twentieth-first century, the organization appears to have turned to engaging with the difficulties of sustaining a vibrant women's organization in the post-feminist era. Recent national gatherings have focused on how to secure organizational strength and on fostering appreciation for the unique contributions and experience of a Jewish women's organization. This sense of the meaning WRJ can provide to its members and their communities is reflected in its recently adopted tagline: "Women of Reform Judaism: Stronger Together."

WRJ has also attempted to incorporate changing expectations for the content of women's relationship to Judaism by creating major national projects that focus on Torah as the center of Jewish life. In 2001 WRJ celebrated the completion of a "Women's Torah," to be used at significant WRJ gatherings, written by a professional male scribe but, symbolically, by all the women of Reform Judaism. The other major Torah project embarked on by WRJ is an ambitious women's Torah commentary. Scheduled for publication in late 2007, it will offer historical and textual annotation and essays that illuminate the biblical text from the perspective of women's experience and scholarship. Through these projects, WRJ seeks to demonstrate the commitment of Reform Jewish women to claiming and redefining the tradition and texts of Jewish life.[37]

REALIZING POSSIBILITIES

As the WRJ's Torah commentary project suggests, women's voices and religious authority have come to play central roles in the continuing effort to interpret an ancient tradition for a contemporary world. Female leadership, whether rabbinic or lay, has indeed become an unquestioned feature of American Reform Jewish life. However, enduring differentials in male and female rabbinical salaries indicate that limits to equality remain. Even though women rabbis have now been in the field long enough to qualify for positions requiring seniority, a review of rabbinical posts at large congregations, of faculty positions at HUC-JIR campuses, and of leadership roles within the movement reveals strikingly few women in the central roles that determine the future of the movement.[38]

Evidence from the early years of the twenty-first century points both to the entrenched male-centered institutional culture of Reform Judaism and to the authentic possibility of meaningful shifts in this pattern. Although most major Reform leadership positions are still held by men, the current general portrait of the influence of women in the American Reform movement is one of great promise. In the early 1990s, the different HUC-JIR campuses had appointed only a few isolated women to their faculties. A few more were hired over the course of that decade. Since 2000 new appointments, especially on the New York and Los Angeles campuses, have multiplied the number of women on the HUC-JIR faculty many times over. At the institutional level, in 1992 Rabbi Julie Spitzer became the first woman to serve as a director of one of the UAHC's fourteen regional offices that offer assistance and support to congregations within their geographical area. In 2003, five women held similar positions, although only two fill these posts in 2006. In the late 1990s, a few women were hired for the first time as senior rabbis at some of the movement's largest congregations, positions that have traditionally been associated with the highest stature within the Reform rabbinate. Their number is slowly growing. From 2003 to 2005, Rabbi Janet Marder served as president of CCAR. Marder's accession to the CCAR presidency represented the first time that a woman held one of the posts generally considered to constitute the core leadership of the Reform movement. (The male-held posts of HUC-JIR president and Union of Reform Judaism president are open-ended appointments with no specific time limits.)[39]

Most significantly perhaps, the CCAR's central liturgical endeavors have been assigned, for the first time, to women. A new Reform Haggadah for Passover, the first in twenty-six years, edited by Rabbi Sue Levi Elwell, appeared in 2002. Meanwhile, the first new daily and weekly Reform prayer book in more than thirty years, *Mishkan T'filah* (A dwelling place for prayer), edited by Rabbi Elyse Frishman is scheduled for publication in 2007. Elwell in particular has been associated with feminist challenges to the patriarchal texts and traditions of Jewish culture. She had already coedited a feminist Haggadah and is coeditor of a book titled *Lesbian Rabbis.* Frishman has seen part of her charge in editing the new prayer book to be to incorporate the feminist critique of Jewish prayer into the mainstream liturgy of the Reform movement. Future Reform congregations and households will thus encounter Jewish ritual shaped by women who have been a part of the feminist liturgical ferment that has energized liberal Judaism's recent relationship to its ancient patriarchal texts.[40]

There was more evidence of the growing power of women rabbis to shape the course of Reform Judaism in the role of the WRN in pushing the CCAR to take a public stand on the religious validation of same-gender marriages or commitment ceremonies. Although the CCAR had passed a resolution indicating its approval of gay civil marriage in 1997, the intention of considering the question of religious officiation at such unions during the 1998 CCAR conference was deflected at the last moment for fear of introducing a debate that would be too controversial and destructive of unity within the movement. All indications were that the organization would try to avoid this issue as long as possible. In 2000, however, pushed by the WRN to place a vote on the CCAR conference agenda approving rabbinic officiation, the Reform rabbis made headlines with their resolution declaring that "we support the decision of those who choose to officiate at rituals of union for same-gender couples, and we support the decision of those who do not."[41] The final, cautiously worded resolution represented a compromise that nonetheless signified the acceptance of religious sanction for gay unions by a mainstream religious organization.

ENDURING QUESTIONS

Sally Priesand, the first woman ordained by a rabbinical seminary, retired in 2006 after thirty-four years in the rabbinate. With this symbolic marker of the end of the beginning of the era of women rabbis, it is clear that the impact of female spiritual leadership is being felt at the core of the Reform movement. Given the way that Priesand and her successors have helped reshape the Reform movement and American Judaism, it is tempting to present their story as one of transformation and triumph. Challenges, however, remain. The Reform movement has not conducted a study like the 2004 Conservative survey that found women's total absence from positions of leadership in the largest Conservative congregations and disturbing disparities reflected in the extent to which Conservative male rabbis were more likely to have higher pay, a spouse, and children than their female counterparts.[42] It is likely that Reform women rabbis find a greater level of acceptance than do their Conservative colleagues, and the WRN has done important work in addressing many shared difficulties. Still, the differences with the Conservative experience are a matter of degree than of kind. There were only twelve Reform women rabbis in 2006 leading congregations with more than six hundred families, and women's salaries continue to trail those of men.[43]

Moreover, there are frequent instances of women finding that their placement or renewal in clergy positions is complicated by concerns about their marital status, childcare responsibilities, sexual orientation, wardrobe, personal appearance, or inability to get along with male supervisors. Unfortunately, given the very small world of the Reform rabbinate, negative stories about past experiences can be the most difficult to share when future employment opportunities are at stake. Ironically, women who become victims of gender-based employment issues may suddenly find themselves battling the Reform's movement's loud rhetorical commitment to gender equality, facing almost reflexive denials that gender bias could have played any role in their experience. Although the faculty on some campuses of the

HUC-JIR now feature a strong female presence, progress has been neither rapid nor smooth.[44] None of these difficulties negates the overall and symbolic progress that women have found within the Reform movement, but they should remind those both inside and outside the movement that the journey is not over.

In the effort to create a religion with which acculturating American Jews could feel comfortable, American Reform Judaism has always been at the forefront of challenging traditional limits on women's roles in Jewish life. From family pews to women rabbis and cantors, the particular adaptations necessary for realizing the principle of religious equality for men and women have evolved along with the broader society's often confusing mix of expectations for proper gender roles. In whatever era, gendered transformation within Reform Judaism has brought forth possibility, ambivalence, and the suggestion of future innovations. The achievement of true gender equality within American Jewish culture, as within American society, may always remain elusive. The recognition, however, that a vibrant and relevant Judaism must respond to the challenges raised by the position of women in contemporary life derives from the earliest days and concerns of American Judaism's Reform movement.

NOTES

1. On Reform Judaism, see Michael A. Meyer, *Response to Modernity: A History of the Reform Movement in Judaism* (New York: Oxford University Press, 1988). Additional reflections on the relationship between American and German Reform can be found in Leon A. Jick, *The Americanization of the Synagogue, 1820–1870* (Hanover, NH: University Press of New England, 1976); Naomi W. Cohen, *Encounter with Emancipation: The German Jews in the United States, 1830–1914* (Philadelphia: Jewish Publication Society, 1984), 164–66; *American Jewish History* 90, no. 1 (2002), especially articles by Mark K. Bauman, Karla Goldman, and Pamela S. Nadell; and Tobias Brinkmann, *Von der Gemeinde zur "Community": Jüdische Einwanderer in Chicago 1840–1900* (Osnabrück: Univ.-Verl. Rasch, 2002).

2. See Karla Goldman, *Beyond the Synagogue Gallery: Finding a Place for Women in American Judaism* (Cambridge, MA: Harvard University Press, 2000).

3. Goldman, *Beyond the Synagogue Gallery*, 42–54, 80–99, 103–5, 83–92; David Philipson, "Confirmation in the Synagogue," *Central Conference of American Rabbis Yearbook* 1 (1889): 43–58.

4. See Goldman, *Beyond the Synagogue Gallery*, 93–99, 106–7, 121–26, 129–33, and Jonathan D. Sarna, "The Debate over Mixed Seating in the American Synagogue," in *The American Synagogue: A Sanctuary Transformed*, ed. Jack Wertheimer (Cambridge: Cambridge University Press, 1987), 363–94.

5. Goldman, *Beyond the Synagogue Gallery*, 78–83, 100–120.

6. Ibid., 129–33.

7. Ibid., 137–50. On nineteenth-century Jewish women's organizational life, see Idana Goldberg, "Gender, Religion and the Jewish Public Sphere in Mid-Nineteenth Century America," (Ph.D. diss., University of Pennsylvania, 2004), 27–112.

8. Goldman, *Beyond the Synagogue Gallery,* 150; Meyer, *Response to Modernity,* 285; Philipson, "Confirmation in the Synagogue."

9. Isaac Mayer Wise, *Reminiscences,* ed. David Philipson (Cincinnati: Leo Wise, 1901), 212; Meyer, *Response to Modernity,* 260–63; Goldman, *Beyond the Synagogue Gallery,* 148; Isaac Mayer Wise, "What Should Be Done," *Israelite,* August 4, 1854; *Proceedings of the Union of American Hebrew Congregations,* vol. 1 (1873–79) (Cincinnati: Bloch, 1879), 228.

10. Isaac Mayer Wise, "Woman in the Synagogue," *American Israelite,* September 8, 1876, 4.

11. Felicia Herman, "From Priestess to Hostess: Sisterhoods of Personal Service in New York City, 1887–1936," in *Women and American Judaism: Historical Perspectives,* ed. Pamela S. Nadell and Jonathan D. Sarna (Hanover, NH: Brandeis University Press, 2001), 148–81; Goldman, *Beyond the Synagogue Gallery,* 175–79; see also Jenna Weissman Joselit, "The Special Sphere of the Middle-Class American Jewish Woman: The Synagogue Sisterhood, 1890–1940," in *The American Synagogue: A Sanctuary Transformed,* ed. Jack Wertheimer (Cambridge: Cambridge University Press), 206–30.

12. Herman, "From Priestess to Hostess," 167–68; Joselit, "Middle-Class American Jewish Woman," 210.

13. Goldman, *Beyond the Synagogue Gallery,* 181–85, 188–92; David Kaufman, *Shul with a Pool: The "Synagogue-Center"* in *American Jewish History* (Hanover, NH: Brandeis University Press, 1999), 32–35.

14. See Mark I. Greenberg, "Carrie Obendorfer Simon," in *Jewish Women in America: An Historical Encyclopedia,* ed. Paula E. Hyman and Deborah Dash Moore (New York: Routledge, 1997), 1260–61; Pamela S. Nadell and Rita J. Simon, "Ladies of the Sisterhood: Women in the American Reform Synagogue, 1900–1930," in *Active Voices: Women in Jewish Culture,* ed. Maurie Sacks (Urbana: University of Illinois Press, 1995), 65.

15. Deborah Levine Lefton, "Women's Equality in the Synagogue: The National Federation of Temple Sisterhood's Search for Autonomy, 1913–1930" (Rabbinic thesis, Hebrew Union College–Jewish Institute of Religion, Cincinnati, 2001), 17–18.

16. Ibid., 27.

17. Goldman, *Beyond the Synagogue Gallery,* 206–8; Karla Goldman, "The Public Religious Lives of Cincinnati's Jewish Women," in *Women and American Judaism: Historical Perspectives,* ed. Pamela S. Nadell and Jonathan D. Sarna (Hanover, NH: Brandeis University Press, 2001), 122; Pamela S. Nadell, "National Federation of Temple Sisterhoods," in *Jewish Women in America: An Historical Encyclopedia,* ed. Paula E. Hyman and Deborah Dash Moore (New York: Rout-

ledge, 1997), 980; Nadell and Simon, "Ladies of the Sisterhood," 66–67; Lefton, "Women's Equality," 32–38.

18. National Federation of Temple Sisterhoods, "The Days of Our Years, Service through Sisterhood, 1913–1963" (National Federation of Temple Sisterhoods, 1963); Nadell, "National Federation of Temple Sisterhoods," 980; Lefton, "Women's Equality," 74–78.

19. Goldman, *Beyond the Synagogue Gallery,* 192–96.

20. Quoted in Lefton, "Women's Equality," 39–57.

21. Goldman, *Beyond the Synagogue Gallery,* 210–11; Freiberg quoted in Lefton, "Women's Equality," 44–46.

22. See Pamela S. Nadell, *Women Who Would Be Rabbis: A History of Women's Ordination, 1889–1985* (Boston: Beacon, 1998), 62–72; Ellen M. Umansky, "Women's Journey toward Rabbinic Ordination," in *Women Rabbis: Exploration and Celebration,* ed. Gary P. Zola (Cincinnati: HUC-JIR Rabbinic Alumni Association Press, 1996), 27–42; *Central Conference of American Rabbis Yearbook* 32 (1922): 156–77.

23. Nadell, *Women Who Would Be Rabbis,* 72–85.

24. Lefton, "Women's Equality," 80–88.

25. Nadell, "National Federation of Temple Sisterhoods," 981–82.

26. National Federation of Temple Sisterhoods, "The Days of Our Years"; Joellyn Wallen Zollman, "Shopping for a Future: A History of the American Synagogue Gift Shop" (Ph.D. diss., Brandeis University, 2002).

27. Paula E. Hyman, "Bat Mitzvah," in *Jewish Women in America: An Historical Encyclopedia,* ed. Paula E. Hyman and Deborah Dash Moore (New York: Routledge, 1997), 126–28; Regina Stein, "The Road to Bat Mitzvah in America," in *Women and American Judaism: Historical Perspectives,* ed. Pamela S. Nadell and Jonathan D. Sarna (Hanover, NH: Brandeis University Press, 2001), 223–34.

28. Nadell, *Women Who Would Be Rabbis,* 120–27, 130–31; on rebbetzins, see Shuly Rubin Schwartz, *The Rabbi's Wife: The Rebbetzin in American Jewish Life* (New York: New York University Press, 2006).

29. Nadell, *Women Who Would Be Rabbis,* 129.

30. Ibid., 132–38.

31. Ibid., 148–57, 163–69.

32. Carole B. Balin, "From Periphery to Center: A History of the Women's Rabbinic Network," *CCAR Journal: "Wisdom You Are My Sister": 25 Years of Women in the Rabbinate* 44 (Summer 1997): 1–12.

33. Janet B. Liss, "Sexual Harassment and Discrimination in the Rabbinate," *CCAR Journal: "Wisdom You Are My Sister": 25 Years of Women in the Rabbinate* 44 (Summer 1997): 53–61.

34. Laura Geller, "Reactions to a Woman Rabbi," in *On Being a Jewish Feminist,* ed. Susannah Heschel (New York: Schocken, 1983), 210–13; Geller, "Encountering the Divine Presence," in *Four Centuries of Jewish Women's Spirituality: A Sourcebook,* ed. Ellen Umansky and Dianne Ashton (Boston: Beacon, 1992), 242–47.

35. See, for example, Marcia Falk, *The Book of Blessings A New Prayer Book for the Weekdays, the Sabbath, and the New Moon* (San Francisco: HarperCollins, 1996); Havurat Shalom Siddur Project, *Birkat Shalom* (Somerville, MA: Havurat Shalom Siddur Project, 1991).

36. Chaim Stern, ed., *Gates of Prayer for Shabbat: A Gender Sensitive Prayerbook* (New York: Central Conference of American Rabbis, 1992); Stern, ed., *Gates of Prayer for Shabbat and Weekdays: A Gender Sensitive Prayerbook* (New York: Central Conference of American Rabbis, 1994).

37. See WRJ's Web site: http://urj.org/wrj/ (accessed August 15, 2003, July 1, 2006).

38. Laura Geller, "From Equality to Transformation," in *Gender and Judaism,* ed. T. M. Rudavsky (New York: New York University Press, 1995), 246–51; Karla Goldman, "A Worthier Place: Women, Reform Judaism, and the Presidents of Hebrew Union College," in *Contemporary Debates in American Reform Judaism: Conflicting Visions,* ed. Dana Evan Kapla (New York: Routledge, 2001), 176–77.

39. Jean Bloch Rosensaft, "The Women Faculty of HUC-JIR," Hebrew Union College-Jewish Institute of Religion *Chronicle* 61 (2003): 6–10, 30–31, notes that of the twenty-four women introduced by this article as the "women faculty of HUC-JIR," fifteen actually have tenure or tenure-track faculty appointments. Janet Marder's installation speech, "Kos Y'shuat Esa: I Will Lift Up the Cup of Salvation," is on the CCAR Web site at http//www.ccarnet.org/marder.html (accessed August 15, 2003). For Web sites of regional UAHC offices, see http://uahc.org/offices.shtml (accessed August 15, 2003) and http://urj.org/offices (accessed July 6, 2006).

40. Sue Levi Elwell, ed., *The Open Door: A Passover Haggadah* (New York: CCAR Press, 2002); Tamara R. Cohen, Sue Levi Elwell, Debbie Friedman, and Ronnie M. Horn, eds., *The Journey Continues: Ma'yan Passover Haggadah* (New York: Ma'yan, 1997); Rebecca T. Alpert, Sue Levi Elwell, and Shirley Idelson, eds., *Lesbian Rabbis: The First Generation* (New Brunswick: Rutgers University Press, 2001); Elyse D. Frishman, "Entering Mishkan T'filah," *CCAR Journal* 51 (Fall 2004): 57, 58, 62, 66.

41. CCAR resolutions are available at http://ccarnet.org/reso/ (accessed August 15, 2003). Listserv discussions before the vote reflected resentment over the CCAR's role and questions about the necessity or propriety of still having a separate organization for women rabbis.

42. See Steven M. Cohen and Judith Schor, "Gender Variation in the Careers of Conservative Rabbis: A Survey of Rabbis Ordained since 1981," 2004, available at http://www.jtsa.edu/rabbinical/women/ras.pdf (accessed July 1, 2006).

43. "Religion Journal; Pioneering Rabbi Who Softly Made Her Way," *New York Times,* May 20, 1906.

44. The forced resignation of Rabbi Sheldon Zimmerman as president of HUC-JIR after he was censured by the CCAR in 2000 for past breaches of ethical sexual conduct suggests that the presence of women rabbis on the CCAR's ethics committee had enabled the Reform movement to address a type of abuse of power that had often been ignored or swept under the rug by the Reform establishment. Inter-

estingly, many of Zimmerman's Reform colleagues, asked to comment on the situation, made a point of emphasizing Zimmerman's commitment to women's equality within the rabbinate. In response, Dartmouth professor Susannah Heschel countered that the revelations of Zimmerman's past behavior inevitably raised questions about how well the school's historically male culture had been able to respond to women's needs and experience. Her letter refers to the fact that the only HUC-JIR faculty members not to receive tenure in recent decades were two professors who were each the first women to be hired to the faculty of their respective campuses. "Zimmerman Quits as HUC President, Alleged Ethics Violations Cited," *Cincinnati Enquirer,* December 6, 2000; "Suspended Rabbi Quits Seminary Presidency," *New York Times,* December 7, 2000, 22A; Susannah Heschel, "The Glass Ceiling at Hebrew Union College," letter to the editor, *Forward,* January 19, 2001, 8.

CHAPTER FIVE

MITZVAH, GENDER, AND RECONSTRUCTIONIST JUDAISM

DEBORAH DASH MOORE AND ANDREW BUSH

"Even though some of us no longer regard the traditional practices as commanded by God," Mordecai M. Kaplan confesses in *Judaism as a Civilization* (1934), "we may still refer to them as" mitzvot. Usually translated as commandments, mitzvot refer to an entire system of Jewish religious practice codified in law or halakhah. Kaplan's almost off-handed challenge to the idea of commandments handed down by God includes the equally provocative notion that Jews could retain the concept of mitzvot even while rejecting their foundation in revelation. But after this reassuring gesture that includes himself, a rebellious rabbi among the skeptics, Kaplan immediately turns a polemical edge against this key term, mitzvot, seeing in its usage a dangerous terminological inertia that obstructs a thoroughgoing reconstruction of American Jewish life. So he continues the sentence: "provided we avowedly use that term in a metaphorical sense, in the sense that they [mitzvot] arouse in us the religious mood."[1] Mitzvah as metaphor, not commandment. And then, as though deliberately to disrupt that religious mood he had just offered in a gesture of compromise, Kaplan asserts that the proper term for these *uncommanded* commands that impose no obligation and carry no sanction is "folkways."[2]

With this deft reinterpretation of a category central to Jewish religion, Kaplan, the founder of Reconstructionist Judaism, reveals his implicit appreciation of the significance of gender to any modern effort to reimagine Jewish life. Kaplan understood the traditional relationship of mitzvah to halakhah and how it girded a gendered legal system that rejected women as whole Jews. He did not want to jettison Judaism's legal tradition but he did want it to change to reflect new realities of American Jewish life.[3] "Nowadays, it is almost axiomatic," he explained, that as human circumstances "change and shift, any law that remains fixed works harm rather than good, and a law that does harm to human life cannot be a just law."[4] Hence he turned to folkways for their inherent flexibility and responsiveness.

Kaplan struggled for several decades to develop an alternative to Modern Orthodox, Reform, and Conservative Judaism that he saw emerging in New York City in the first decades of the twentieth century. Born in Lithuania in 1881, the son of a rabbi, Mordecai Menachem Kaplan arrived in New York City in 1889 as a child of nine. His father's decision to join Rabbi Jacob Joseph, who had been invited to serve as chief rabbi for a group of Orthodox congregations on the Lower East Side, brought the family to the immigrant neighborhood. But the experiment in communal organization soon collapsed as the congregations quarreled amid charges of fraud and corruption. Mel Scult, in his definitive biography of Kaplan, titles his opening chapter "From Motl to Maurice to Mordecai," suggesting through name changes the passages Kaplan traversed before arriving in the United States. In New York, he attended the fledgling Yeshiva Etz Chaim while continuing his studies with his father. The Orthodox intellectual household encouraged questioning of established verities, a penchant Kaplan retained throughout his subsequent studies at public high school, City College, the newly established Jewish Theological Seminary (JTS) of America, and Columbia University. Earning a B.A. from City College, a diploma from JTS, an M.A. from Columbia, and *smikhah* from the highly respected Rabbi Isaac Jacob Reines in Europe, Kaplan received the best education of both Jewish and American worlds. His education positioned him to understand and interpret dilemmas facing his rapidly secularizing Jewish contemporaries in the United States. In addition to his intellectual trajectory, his extensive institutional involvement with Jewish education, religious groups, and communal organizations provided the experiential background for the radical proposals he would ultimately formulate in his magnum opus, *Judaism as a Civilization: Toward a Reconstruction of American-Jewish Life*.[5]

Kaplan recognized that he was living during a time of crisis for American Jews and that any search for conciliation among competing Jewish ideologies required boldness. Where others found stark, even irreconcilable differences between Orthodoxy and the liberal movements, Kaplan argued that in fact Reform and neo-Orthodoxy shared the same conception of religion and of Judaism as a religion, conceptions that he believed to be a deadening influence on American Jewish life. Both movements saw "no purpose to ritual observance other than the promulgation of the two main principles, the unity of God and the brotherhood of man," Kaplan argued. "The only difference," he averred, "is that the Reformists find only a limited number of religious precepts capable of serving that purpose, while the Neo-orthodox claim that every religious precept can be shown to convey some moral or spiritual truth."[6]

Kaplan's translation challenged such truth claims, since "folkways" derive from folks, from humanity, and not from God. His move obviated the debate between Reformists and neo-Orthodox; folkways do not have the binding authority of law. Through this displacement from the singular revelation of God to the ongoing evolution of Jewish civilization, multiple in its many locales, Kaplan opened American Judaism to gender equality. Law may restrict suffrage or set other distinctive privileges and obligations. But a civilization is comprised of all of its constituents, women and men.

Unlike Reform Judaism, then, Kaplan did not want to place ethical monotheism at the center of Jewish life; unlike Orthodox Judaism, he did not want to identify Torah as the first among equals. Rather, like Conservative Judaism with which he was formally aligned until the institutionalization of the Reconstructionist movement, Kaplan thought that the people Israel should occupy the heart and soul of Judaism and that belief in God and observance of Torah needed to find their rationale in the Jewish people's ideas and actions. Somehow, he was convinced, a living people would find a way to express its core values as long as it was given an opportunity to relate imaginatively to its traditions, to practice its festivals and holy days, to incorporate its own lived experiences into Judaism. That was one reason Kaplan continued to teach homiletics at the Jewish Theological Seminary of America and to direct its Teacher's Institute. He hoped that a new generation born in the democratic United States would find its voice and its perspective and he sought to influence them.

Yet Kaplan was also impatient. He did not feel that he could wait for change to occur. He was married; he had four daughters; he prayed daily. He needed a community that would share his point of view and sustain him in his efforts to move Judaism toward an indigenous American form of practice and belief. So he experimented. First he convinced a group of wealthy garment manufacturers willing to take a risk to invest in a new type of synagogue that would combine prayer, study, and recreation.[7] The Jewish Center opened on West 86th Street in New York City in 1918. A twelve-story building, it contained a spacious synagogue on the second floor, a small sanctuary on the ground floor, classrooms and a library on the upper floors, a large hall for dining and festive events and a kosher restaurant to cater them, a gymnasium in the basement, and, in its most innovative feature, a pool located above the streets of Manhattan. The Jewish Center transformed into reality Kaplan's ideas about a synagogue that was a center for neighborhood activities. Unlike traditional synagogues, it offered something for the entire family, women as well as men, girls as well as boys. But Kaplan soon fell out with his supporters. Although they found his sermons spellbinding, they were unwilling to accommodate his proposals for radical changes within the sanctuary itself. So Kaplan left.[8]

But he still had to pray somewhere and since a group of loyal followers left with him, they soon incorporated the Society for the Advancement of Judaism (SAJ). Kaplan modeled the SAJ on the Ethical Culture Society founded by Felix Adler, who had been his teacher at Columbia University. Kaplan admired him but he also thought Adler had gone too far. Why, Kaplan wondered, must you leave Judaism if you cannot stand before the ark and say in good conscience, "[T]his is the Torah that God gave to Moses"? Why not just change the words to say what you mean and what you think your ancestors really meant when they uttered the prayer?[9] Kaplan proceeded to introduce such changes. He tried to say what he believed and to relate his convictions to what he thought Jews had believed in the past. He called this process of transvaluation the finding of functional equivalents for traditional ideals and institutions.[10] His goal was to have the Jewish past become a living reality for Jews in the present. Sometimes things went smoothly, but other times the familiar words, despite their objectionable meaning, proved resistant to change. Kaplan found the Kol Nidre prayer ridiculous, for example, its disavowal of vows distressing, its placement at the start of the Sabbath of Sabbaths that was Yom Kippur uninspiring. So he proposed substituting Psalm 130, a beautiful expression of spiritual yearning, set to the same melodious chant. His followers went along for a year or two, but then they rebelled. Kaplan retreated.[11]

But Kaplan refused to retreat when gender was the issue. Instead, he took a decisive step forward. In March 1922 his brilliant and precocious oldest daughter, Judith, was approaching her thirteenth birthday. Two years earlier American women across the United States had gone to the polls to vote for the first time. The status of women was changing, moving toward legal equality. Kaplan wanted to mark his daughter's coming-of-age in an analogous way that Judaism would have recognized had Judith been a boy. So he improvised. "The Friday night before the service my father decided what I was to do," Judith Kaplan Eisenstein later recalled. "I was to recite the blessings, read a portion of the Torah *sidra* in Hebrew and in English and conclude with the blessings." That was it. "No thunder sounded. No lightning struck," she remarked with a touch of irreverence. Even though she read from a printed Humash and not from a Torah scroll, even though she read after the completion of the regular Torah service, that first bat mitzvah in the United States "was enough to shock a lot of people," including her own pious Orthodox grandparents and aunts and uncles.[12]

The reconstruction of mitzvot as folkways—"Bar and Bat Folkway"—was crucial to the groundbreaking step toward gender equality of that first bat mitzvah. Most simply, conceived as law, Kaplan would have had no authority to legislate his daughter's way to the bimah—but there she was, turning thirteen with no time to convene rabbinical courts or await learned response. Nor would this have been merely another case of impatience: she was turning thirteen alongside all the Jewish daughters of a United States that had just granted suffrage to women. However, at a more fundamental level for Judaism, Kaplan was recognizing that the bar mitzvah, chopped liver swans and other innovations of caterers aside, represented the very institution of halakhic gender discrimination, since the call to the Torah scroll for the honor of reading a portion for the first time was the public induction of the thirteen-year-old male into the all-male precinct of the minyan, the acknowledgment that he had fulfilled the legal condition—statutory male adulthood—required to take on the responsibility of the mitzvot in his own person. Understood as commandment under legal sanction, not only the bar mitzvah but also mitzvot more generally reaffirmed this legal discrimination.

Kaplan did not set out to overthrow halakhic authority, but his attention to civilization made him aware that American Jews had already effectively done so, for, as he observed, sanctions no longer held sway with the majority, and without the power of sanctions there was no law. Jews in America were attracted, and in Kaplan's own case, deeply committed to America's democratic ideals. The alternative conception of folkways gave these egalitarian impulses a theoretical articulation with far-reaching implications. Halakhah, after all, had always been subject to some qualification by *minhag* (traditional customs), but the distinction between the two was maintained, and law took precedence. Folkways subsume halakhah under minhag, as it were, but the very use of the nontraditional term suggests that innovative customs were no less authorized than longstanding usage in Kaplan's view.

Kaplan's choice of "folkways" as his key term is, in fact, a programmatic decision to speak in an American idiom. Its adoption can be traced to his explication of a characteristically blunt assertion in *Judaism as a Civilization:* "[T]here is little at present in Jewish life that offers a field for self-expression to the average man and woman who is not engaged either as rabbi, educator, or social worker. If one does not have a taste for praying three times a day and studying the Bible and rabbinic writings, there is nothing in any of the current versions of Judaism to hold one's interest as a Jew."[13]

The gender balance in which the average woman stands alongside the average man is likewise characteristic and a cornerstone of the theoretical edifice he will build in his proposed solution to this dilemma, namely, "to accept Judaism . . . as a social . . . heritage. It is a social heritage," Kaplan writes, "because it is the sum of characteristic usages, ideas, standards and codes by which the Jewish people is differentiated and individualized in character from the other peoples."[14] Then comes a footnote. "This definition of a civilization is a paraphrase of the definition of ethos" in William Graham Sumner's *Folkways.*[15] Here may be found the germ of the idea behind transposing mitzvot into folkways, one that points to its integral relationship to Kaplan's fundamental definition of Judaism as a civilization.

William Graham Sumner began his career in the Episcopal ministry, a man known for his dynamic sermons, but left for Yale University and the chance to teach in the new field of the Science of Society, as sociology was called in the late nineteenth century. Sumner was a towering but curmudgeonly figure, and his concepts of ethnocentrism, of in-group and out-group, entered common language.[16] Kaplan refers to Sumner's own magnum opus, *Folkways: A Study of the Sociological Importance of Usages, Manners, Customs, Mores, and Morals,* published in 1906, four years before his death, a work that decisively influenced the direction of American sociology. Sumner argues that the foundation of the ethos of a people is its folkways, which arise in response to the physiological needs of the individual. While these are to be distinguished from mores, the product of a later stage of social development, "[t]he process of making folkways is never superseded or changed," Sumner explains. "It goes on now just as it did at the beginning of civilization." Everyday usage and custom "exert their force on all men always. They produce familiarity, and mass acts become unconscious."[17]

The individualistic etiology of the folkways is given explicitly social scope in mores, according to Sumner: "When the elements of truth and right"—that is, the unconscious assumption that the characteristic behaviors learned by individuals and transmitted to the group are simply natural and hence universal—"are developed into doctrines of welfare, the folkways are raised to another plane. They then become capable of producing inferences, developing into new forms, and extending their constructive influence over men and society. Then," Sumner explains, "we call them the mores. The mores are the folkways, including the philosophical and ethical generalizations as to societal welfare which are suggested by them, and inherent in them, as they grow."[18]

This latter term, "mores," appears only fleetingly in *Judaism as a Civilization;*[19] instead Kaplan employs Sumner's term "folkways" while giving it the strong societal orientation reserved by Sumner for "mores." The shift, however, is not merely lexical but ideological. "Sumner, the most outspoken disciple of Herbert Spencer in America," writes the radical sociologist Lewis Coser, "combined evolutionism, laissez-faire, and Malthusian pessimism with the ardor of a great Puritan divine."[20] In short, Sumner's work in sociological theory supported conservative social views.[21]

Kaplan would reverse the political valence and use "folkways" to articulate his own progressive stance. Since Sumner has long since lost currency, one need not dwell on his ideological stance. More important, then, is that Kaplan reversed Sumner's ends and means. Sumner's social groups share folkways; they develop mores to achieve the goal of greater communal welfare. Kaplan, on the other hand, considered communal welfare a means to achieve the end of establishing Jews as a social group in the United States, where the ethos of European Jewry was rapidly dissolving.

Yet Sumner's conceptualization remains crucial for Kaplan: "Ethics, having lost its connection with the ethos of a people," Sumner argues, "is an attempt to systematize the current notions of right and wrong upon some basic principle, generally with the purpose of establishing morals on an absolute doctrine, so that it shall be universal, absolute and everlasting."[22] But this is only to assert, as Sumner himself declares in a formulation with a strikingly contemporary ring, that such claims to absolute truth as Kaplan found in contemporary Reformists and neo-Orthodox are inevitably "historical, institutional, and empirical."[23] Kaplan went beyond sociology, however, when he moved from observation and conceptualization to the outline and promotion of a concrete set of proposals intended not merely to understand the Jewish people in the present but also to maintain them as a people in the future.

This pragmatism, with its own American heritage in the writings of John Dewey with which Kaplan became acquainted in his studies at Columbia University, has Jewish roots as well. Indeed, Kaplan's appreciation of a Jewish distinctiveness provides a final contrast to Sumner. Kaplan cites one of the relatively sparse references to Jews in *Folkways,* where they appear as one example among many in support of Sumner's assertion that the idea of *chosenness* was widespread in antiquity and indeed generally characteristic of all peoples, even in modern times. Sumner develops the observation to account for contemporary prejudice—though no longer in relation to

Jews. Kaplan instead moves from the recognition of the commonality of each people's sense of election by their gods to a Jewish difference "*in having carried common values to pragmatic conclusions never dreamt of by other peoples.*"[24] As concerns gender, Kaplan's pragmatic conclusions had not been dreamt of by his own people either.

More generally, as Kaplan notes in the preface to the postwar edition of the book, "Judaism as a civilization" was "not intended as a slogan to abet laxity in ritual observance or indifference to religion," as some of its critics claimed. Rather it was a call to American Jews first of all "to re-affirm Jewish peoplehood" and then to "revitalize Jewish religion."[25] Once Jews accepted the "civilization" concept, they could shift their concern from negative observances, which traditionally outnumber positive ones, to performing and developing new folkways, which are the expression of an American ethos for Jews. An America where Jewish women could vote but not *daven* called out for a formal acknowledgment of the entrance of women into their majority in the Jewish community. The *Bet din* was not hearing the case in 1922 and the Reformists had turned their attention from ethos to ethics. So where law did not avail, Kaplan came to treat the mitzvot "as religious poetry in action,"[26] that is, to reconceptualize commandment as folkway. The creation of bat mitzvah was his poetry.

Kaplan had a thoroughly democratic zeal for pluralism. Successful experiments would catch on and spread; unsuccessful efforts to integrate nonindigenous practices into Judaism would fall by the wayside. "Diversity is a danger when we are dealing with law," he wrote. "But, on the assumption that Jews would accept the *misvot* not as laws, but as folkways, spontaneity would not only help to foster the *misvot* but would also give rise to an unforced uniformity which would be all the more valuable because it was not prescribed."[27]

Kaplan introduced a number of examples of what might happen were Jews to think of mitzvot as folkways. For instance, he rejects the defense of the mitzvot related to kashrut on physiological grounds, and not only because modern conditions obviate any particular concern for the ills of pig meat. Instead he reasons that the goal of traditional mitzvot, newly reconstructed as folkways, is not to improve the welfare of the group known as Jews but to help the Jews recognize themselves and each other as a group. Were one to argue for a kosher diet for the sake of better hygiene, even if it would make Jews healthy, it would not make them Jews. But to argue that only those who maintain a kosher diet are Jews, true Jews, would be to divide a community into the minority of those who believed in sanctions from the majority of those who did not. Between the two arguments—the one eschewing the "*accumulated momentum and emotional drive*" of tradition in the name of modernity, the other rejecting modernity altogether in the name of tradition—Kaplan poses the bridge of folkways. To recognize a specifically Jewish diet as a folkway is to acknowledge tradition as a cohesive force while undermining its normative value. Thus, when Kaplan urges, "*There need not be the feeling of sin in case of occasional remissness nor the self-complacency which results from scrupulous observance,*" he does far more than make concessions to assimilation.[28] He contests the position of mitzvot as an evaluative fulcrum upon which inclusion in the Jewish community must be balanced, for his premise of the preeminence of peoplehood makes the "feeling of sin" equivalent to the feeling of divorce from the community. There need be no feeling of having departed from—or having been excluded from—the Jewish people on the basis of laxity with regard to halakhah. To contravene the laws of God would be a sin against the covenant, but to adapt traditions to modern times is only to be true to the social origins and consequently the ever-changing nature of folkways. Yet even here Kaplan articulates his position as an echo of tradition, since he makes the point of strict observance double-edged: those who are remiss are given a place among the people, but those who are scrupulous to the degree of self-complacency are reminded of the questioning of the primacy of cult over ethics in the prophetic books.

By eliminating the notion of command, Kaplan makes folkways a matter of choice. Although he did not explicitly anticipate the current diversity of kashrut practices in the United States, ranging from extreme stringency to specialized *glatt* kosher dairy products (despite the oxymoron) to "kosher style" delicatessen to vegetarian and eco-kosher, he probably would not have been surprised. He expected diversity and thought it was a good thing. What all of these forms of kashrut have in common, he might have argued, is their implicit recognition of an important Jewish folkway—and a recognition that it is a folkway. Though many of the varieties of kosher experience are entirely consistent with halakhah, it is as a willful participation in the Jewish people that the conceptual shift to folkways helps to explain Jewish practices sociologically and to support as a Jewish choice in American life. Had kashrut remained a mitzvah, rather than a folkway, patterns of settlement in the second and succeeding generations of immigrants might well have presaged the demise of Jewish life in America that has in fact not come. To leave behind the Jewish enclave with its kosher butchers and bakers, its *mikvah* and shul within walking distance, as of course most American Jews did in a country with ingrained habits of geographical and social mobility far different than those in Europe, would have all but meant to forfeit one's place in the Jewish people, for want of the means to observe many mitzvot.[29] The portability of folkways following folk practices ensured that not only kashrut but also mikvah and shul would survive. Moreover the conception of folkways had important implications for gender, to which Kaplan was sensitive. Since a full-time kitchen manager is needed to meet the demands of the mitzvot associated with kashrut, for instance, where domestic labor is the lot of women, as it certainly was in Kaplan's America, the argument for folkways is linked to the enlargement of women's opportunities. Choices with respect to the maintenance of folkways in the kitchen enable choices for women in their work and life outside the home.[30]

What motivates the choice of kashrut, even in traditional practice, in Kaplan's revised understanding, is the desire to participate as Jews in a collective endeavor and to gain access to spiritual experience and meaning. His conception of folkways set practice free from the burden of truth. Understood as folkways, kashrut aroused a religious mood. When coupled with Kaplan's suggestion of prayer before and after meals, it transformed a meal in a Jewish home into "a social and spiritual act."[31] No doubt it was the American in him that equated self-consciousness, self-expression, and self-fulfillment with freedom of choice. Free choice replaced chosenness as a keystone of American-Jewish life in Kaplan's view, and folkways were integral to that freedom. Kaplan was confident that American Jews would inevitably choose to be American; Jewish folkways, he hoped, would make it possible for them to choose to be Jews as well.

Some folkways, Kaplan readily admits, are more important than others. One could categorize folkways as religious or cultural, although "in actual life both cultural and religious elements are interwoven in the same folkway."[32] Kaplan offers as examples of the latter the wearing of tallit at services, the Jewish calendar, and the Hebrew language. But, again, once accepted as folkways, rather than mitzvot, legal distinctions no longer apply to practice and, thus, there is no obstruction to women donning a tallit to pray—and designing it, too. Not all of Kaplan's suggestions had such a direct feminist import as the invention of bat mitzvah, though he frequently gave sermons on women's political emancipation and cited biblical sources to support his arguments. Nor, it should be recalled, have all feminist responses to gender inequality in Judaism been consonant with Kaplan's reconstructions. Yet his critique of hierarchy was essential to subsequent feminist Jewish theology. Reconstructionism could not imagine going back to stand again at Sinai, as Judith Plaskow would later argue with much brilliance; nor could it consider engendering Judaism through alternative narratives, as Rachel Adler has persuasively maintained.[33] Rather, Reconstructionism took its stand among American Jews as their indigenous version of Judaism, one grounded in the primacy of democratic experience, of pluralism, of individualism, and of women's fundamental equality with men. And though Plaskow and Adler do not cite Kaplan directly, his displacement of the authority of law and the male privilege that it has sustained remains an important forerunner to their feminist positions within Judaism.

While many innovations that Kaplan introduced into Jewish religious practice subsequently became institutionalized in the Reconstructionist movement and especially its prayer books, beginning with *The New Haggadah* in 1941, the latter is especially illustrative of the implications of the folkways concept for gender issues. "No folkway could be more beautiful," Kaplan wrote about Pesah, "and at the same time so saturated with the ideal of self-realization through freedom. And the *seder* night—one has to seek far among the civilizations of the world," he effused, "to find a folkway so compact of pathos, wistfulness and mystic yearning, yet one that is human and simple enough to be loved by the youngest child, about whom the entire observance is centered."[34] In this spirit, Kaplan and his coeditors eliminated the Ten Plagues and added historical sections on Moses; they changed the language of the kiddush to remove references to Jews as a chosen people, and they added paragraphs detailing the modern meaning of the Exodus. In short, they treated the Haggadah as a folkway, amenable to interpretation.[35] "It has a message that is fraught with power and beauty," the editors wrote. "It needs only to be transposed into a new key—into the key of modern thought, modern experiences, and modern idiom. The language and concepts of the ancient rite need to be revised so that they go straight to the minds and hearts of the men and women of today."[36] Aside from the inclusion of women, no less than men, among those who have minds as well as hearts, this new key does not sound a distinctly feminist note. Yet *The New Haggadah*—which, by clear implication renders the familiar one "Old," and thus superseded—shocked many of Kaplan's colleagues at the Jewish Theological Seminary. That shock would grow, incidentally, when the Reconstructionists published their controversial Sabbath Prayer Book in 1945. It so provoked Orthodox Jews that the Union of Orthodox Rabbis of the United States and Canada convened a Bet din to excommunicate Kaplan and burn the siddur.[37] Despite this bitter attack, which affected his entire family, who were shunned along with their father (his daughter Selma remembers that she could no longer purchase hallah and cake at a local bakery on 86th Street), Kaplan refused to retreat.[38]

Nevertheless, with regard to the Haggadah, if not perhaps also the siddur and *makhzor,* retrospect declares that Kaplan carried the day. In the wake of *The New Haggadah,* one now finds dozens of new Haggadahs published every year in the United States, some of which are explicitly feminist.[39] The vitality represented by this abundance and the diversity speak in Kaplan's favor. For if traditional Passover mitzvot are contested by their pluralism, they are contributing to the formation of an American Jewish ethos in which, significantly for women, the principal religious folkway is enacted not in the traditionally male domain of the synagogue service but in the home. In this gendered space tales of *bubbe's* gefilte fish are as likely to be transmitted as a full account of the Exodus from Egypt.

As the Reconstructionist rabbi Rebecca Alpert points out, Kaplan recognized in 1936 that equality ultimately could come about only through women's "own efforts and initiative. Whatever liberal-minded men do" would largely remain in the realm of "a futile and meaningless gesture. The Jewish woman must demand the equality due her as a right to which she is fully entitled."[40] To those efforts and initiatives Kaplan's reconstructed folkways contributed a conceptual grounding for dramatically reconceiving the relationship of Jews to God and Torah, because now the category "Jew," separated from the discriminations of the law, included both men and women. Self-consciousness, self-expression, self-fulfillment: these are not gender-specific ways but simply modern, simply human. Kaplan's commitment to contemporary American ideals of equality, pluralism, and diversity implied by the "self" of that consciousness, expression, and fulfillment resulted in an enduring legacy that continues to influence the direction of Jewish life in the twenty-first century.

What features of this legacy are particularly salient for gender equality? First, equal education for boys and girls. Kaplan understood education to involve goals for adulthood. If Jewish boys and girls were ideally to grow up into separate spheres then they would require different types of education. But if boys and girls were to grow up to become Jewish adults, sharing both the private sphere of the Jewish home and the public spheres of Jewish communal life, then they needed the same education. That meant they both needed to learn Hebrew and to study sacred texts; they both needed to learn democratic practices and how to be good citizens; they both needed to learn skills to earn a livelihood; and they both needed to gain appreciation for the arts.

Second, equal responsibility for the future of Jewish life. Kaplan expected leadership to come from women and as well as men. He anticipated that women would create their own organizations (indeed, his lifetime coexisted with the heyday of Jewish women's organizations in the United States) where they would set their own priorities that would improve Jewish life in the United States and Israel. Kaplan did not imagine a glass ceiling that would keep women from achieving the top positions of leadership.

Third, ritual innovation to express women's equality. Kaplan is most known for initiating bat mitzvah as an expression of a Jewish girl's equality within the synagogue, something he did with his oldest daughter, Judith. But the spirit behind the first bat mitzvah would animate other changes in Jewish religious practice. Kaplan could create a bat mitzvah because he imagined Judaism as an evolving religious civilization, flexible and creative, responsive to Jews in each era. Since he was living in an age that recognized women's equality, Judaism could respond to that with imagination. The bat mitzvah would be only the first step in a variety of changes, from allowing women to receive *ʾaliyot* to the Torah to counting women in the minyan. More recent rituals, such as baby-naming ceremonies for Jewish girls to parallel the bris for boys, have followed naturally from these assumptions. They represent Kaplan's legacy for new generations.

Fourth, legal decisions to rectify mistreatment of Jewish women and their abuse. Kaplan called for changes in halakhah regarding the execution of divorce among Jews. He did not want to cede marriage and divorce to secular authorities. He felt that both belonged as expressions of communal and individual identity. Therefore, Jewish law and practice had to change to reflect women's inherent equality with men. This remains a matter of unfinished business for American Jews, in part because less attention has been paid to creating new instruments of halakhah than to congregationally based change.

Fifth, language of prayer to reflect one's beliefs. Kaplan never shied away from tackling the sanctity of the prayer book when it no longer expressed what was true. Thus he eliminated the prayer praising God as one who resurrects the dead as well as the more central affirmation that Jews were God's chosen people. Although Kaplan did not change the siddur to speak of matriarchs as well as patriarchs, such contemporary modifications reflect his feminist legacy. Kaplan emboldened American Jews to articulate their deepest convictions through their prayer book, to couch their understandings of equality within the framework of tradition. These guidelines have inspired feminists to wrestle with the language of liturgy, a process that continues.

For many years Kaplan opposed the establishment of a separate denomination of Reconstructionism. He did not fear controversy but he valued unity and hated to exacerbate divisiveness among American Jews. But his son-in-law, Rabbi Ira Eisenstein (Judith's husband), gradually took on the mantel of leadership after World War II. Like his father-in-law, he was impatient. Although he edited *The Reconstructionist,* a biweekly journal of ideas, Eisenstein wanted to move beyond ideas to institutions. In the 1950s he spurred efforts to form a loosely knit federation of congregations and *havurot.* Eisenstein took these initial steps toward denominationalism even as such Reconstructionist innovations as bat mitzvah acquired increasing popularity first among Conservative congregations and then within the Reform movement.[41]

In 1968 the Reconstructionist Rabbinical College opened its doors in Philadelphia. The following year it admitted its first woman student, Sandy Eisenberg (Sasso), who received ordination in 1974.[42] There were no lengthy debates on the issue because of Kaplan's position on mitzvot.[43] Kaplan came to the ceremony of dedication and hammered the mezuzah onto the doorframe. The establishment of the college under Eisenstein's leadership, the creation of a civilization-based five-year curriculum, and the ordination of Reconstructionist rabbis reflected a commitment to create an alternative Jewish religious movement in the United States. Reconstructionism would put Kaplan's ideas into practice and continue to extend them to meet new circumstances. But behind Reconstructionist practices, including, of course, the decision to admit women to the rabbinate after the college opened as well as the willingness to hire women as full-time faculty and upper-level administrators, lay a gendered understanding and critique of Judaism that can be seen most clearly in the rethinking of mitzvot as folkways. That change bore an intimate relationship to Kaplan's, and subsequently Reconstructionism's, basic thesis that Judaism was not a religion but a civilization.

The last quarter of the twentieth century witnessed the rapid growth of Reconstructionism as a movement. Despite its growth, it remained the smallest denomination in Judaism. It was also institutionally far less complete than the other movements, lacking many of the age- and gender-segregated forms of organization characteristic of religious life in the United States. In 1970 the social scientist Charles Liebman acknowledged the new movement's existence in a penetrating article. Liebman doubted that Reconstructionism would ever amount to much. Although in the essay he contends that its ideas of Judaism reflected the views of most American Jews, he thought that these attitudes may have made good sociology but did not, in fact, make for a viable religion. Reconstructionism was also far more willing to jettison practices that retained their emotional hold on American Jews.[44] In the past three decades since that first assessment,

Reconstructionism's easy egalitarianism, participatory congregations, and openness to experimentation often attracted American Jews who were disaffected with Jewish religious life. Reconstructionism has also continued to influence the much larger Reform, Conservative, and Orthodox movements in Judaism, serving as a source of pragmatic innovation. For example, a number of its rabbis have become leaders advocating the inclusion of gay and lesbian Jews as full, active members of congregations.

Kaplan left a daunting legacy to American Jews in the twenty-first century. It includes the following challenges: reaffirming Jewish peoplehood in its diversity and pluralism; revitalizing Jewish religion; recognizing Judaism as a civilization, which means a form of life not a form of truth; and thus accepting that Jewish folkways, not mitzvot, are the proper terms for interpreting Jewish spiritual and social practices, unless, of course, one wishes to speak metaphorically.

NOTES

1. Mordecai M. Kaplan, *Judaism as a Civilization: Toward a Reconstruction of American-Jewish Life* (1934; repr., New York: Schocken, 1967), 431.

2. By the time he sat down to write *Judaism as a Civilization,* he had published versions of his manifesto in the *Menorah Journal,* experimented in creating institutional alternatives to the synagogue, and introduced ritual innovations in religious worship. See Mordecai M. Kaplan, "A Program for the Reconstruction of Judaism," *Menorah Journal* 6, no. 4 (1920): 181–96; Kaplan, "Toward a Reconstruction of Judaism," *Menorah Journal* 13, no. 2 (1927): 113–30; Kaplan, "Judaism as a Civilization: Religion's Place in It," *Menorah Journal* 15, no. 6 (1928): 501–11.

3. "Judaism as a civilization must be anything but antinomian," he wrote in 1927. "No permanent social structure is conceivable without law." Kaplan, "Toward a Reconstruction of Judaism," 126.

4. Kaplan, *Judaism as a Civilization,* 45.

5. The best biography of Mordecai M. Kaplan is Mel Scult's *Judaism Faces the Twentieth Century: A Biography of Mordecai Kaplan* (Detroit: Wayne State University Press, 1993).

6. Kaplan, *Judaism as a Civilization,* 434.

7. For an alternative reading that emphasizes the role of Joseph Cohen, see David Kaufman, *Shul with a Pool: The "Synagogue-Center" in American Jewish History* (Hanover, NH: University Press of New England, 1999), 228–41.

8. Jeffrey S. Gurock and Jacob J. Schacter, *A Modern Heretic and a Traditional Community: Mordecai M. Kaplan, Orthodoxy and American Judaism* (New York: Columbia University Press, 1997), 88–134.

9. "Although Kaplan had contempt for Adler because he had left the Jewish fold when he established Ethical Culture, he was drawn to Adler's thought, both in the classroom and through his publications. Adler emphasized a religion of

obligation that is realistically related to the experience of those professing it." Mel Scult, introduction to *Communings of the Spirit: The Journals of Mordecai M. Kaplan, Volume I: 1913–1934* (Philadelphia: Reconstructionist Press; Detroit: Wayne State University Press, 2001), 47.

10. Kaplan wrote,

> The task of reinterpretation consists first in selecting from among the ideational and practical consequences of the traditional values those which are spiritually significant for our day, and then in turning those consequences into motives of thought and conduct. Functional interpretation, therefore, implies a knowledge of the background of the teaching or institution interpreted, of the various contexts in which that teaching or institution occurs, and most of all a knowledge of human nature as it functions in society and in the individual. Reinterpretation is the process of finding equivalents in the civilization to which we belong for values of a past stage of that or another civilization. (*Judaism as a Civilization,* 389)

11. See Scult, *Judaism Faces the Twentieth Century,* 280–327, esp. 286–91. Even his mother "got into the act. Writing to her son on the occasion of his daughter Selma's bas mitzvah, Anna Kaplan wished the family all the best and then proceeded to mention an article in the *SAJ Review* that she did not like. Taking this tack led her to think of other things she did not like, including the *Kol Nidre.* 'You are destroying Judaism,' she wrote. 'Do you understand what you are doing to yourself? I will not tell you what you are doing to me and maybe to your father in his grave. . . . I am too weak now I cannot write more. Be well and happy with your family. [signed] Your mother'" (288–89).

12. Quoted in Paula E. Hyman, "Bat Mitzvah," in *Jewish Women in America: An Historical Encyclopedia,* ed. Paula E. Hyman and Deborah Dash Moore (New York: Routledge, 1997), 126–27.

13. Kaplan, *Judaism as a Civilization,* 178.

14. Ibid., 179.

15. Ibid., 535.

16. Lewis A. Coser, "American Trends," in *A History of Sociological Analysis,* ed. Tom Bottomore and Robert Nisbet (New York: Basic Books, 1978), 297. Coser, a democratic socialist and activist, was himself a major figure in the field of sociology in the United States and taught for many years at Brandeis University.

17. William Graham Sumner, *Folkways: A Study of the Sociological Importance of Usages, Manners, Customs, Mores, and Morals* (1906; repr., New York: New American Library, 1940), 46.

18. Ibid., 42.

19. Kaplan, *Judaism as a Civilization,* 218.

20. Coser, "American Trends," 294.

21. Alfred Kazin, for instance, distinguishes clearly between a conservative intellectual group at the turn of the twentieth century, in which he includes Sumner, and the Progressives, in which he places John Dewey, and surely would have placed

Kaplan, had he taken notice of him in *On Native Grounds: An Interpretation of Modern American Prose Literature* (1942; repr., Garden City, NY: Anchor, 1956).

22. Sumner, *Folkways,* 48.

23. Ibid., 41.

24. Kaplan, *Judaism as a Civilization,* 256. Emphasis in the original. The passage in Sumner reads in part,

> The Jews divided all mankind into themselves and Gentiles. They were the "chosen people." The Greeks and Romans called all outsiders "barbarians." Each state now regards itself as the leader of civilization, the best, the freest, and the wisest, and all other nations as inferior. Within a few years our own man-on-the-curbstone has learned to class all foreigners of the Latin peoples as "dagos," and "dago" has become an epithet of contempt. These are all cases of ethnocentrism. (29)

25. Kaplan, *Judaism as a Civilization,* x.

26. Ibid., 434.

27. Ibid., 439.

28. Ibid., 441. Emphasis in the original.

29. See the discussion of the community center in Andrew Bush and Deborah Dash Moore, "Kaplan's Key: A Dynamo 'in de middle' of the Neighborhood," in *Key Texts in American Jewish Culture,* ed. Jack Kugelmass (New Brunswick: Rutgers University Press, 2003), 249–53.

30. Recent restrictions on Jewish women's authority, for example in scrutinizing the kashrut of vegetables or water, serve to emphasize this point.

31. Kaplan, *Judaism as a Civilization,* 443.

32. Ibid., 433.

33. Judith Plaskow, *Standing Again at Sinai: Judaism from a Feminist Perspective* (San Francisco: HarperCollins, 1990); Rachel Adler, *Engendering Judaism: An Inclusive Theology and Ethics* (Philadelphia: Jewish Publication Society, 1998).

34. Kaplan, *Judaism as a Civilization,* 450.

35. Scult, introduction, 53–54.

36. *The New Haggadah* (New York: Behrman House, 1941), vi.

37. "Orthodox Rabbis 'Excommunicate' Author of Prayer Book Though He Is Not a Member," *New York Times,* June 15, 1945, 11. For a good discussion of the issues around the excommunication, see Zachary James Silver, "The Excommunication of Mordecai Kaplan: How an Act of Intolerance Paved the Way toward Cultural Pluralism in Post-war America" (senior honors thesis, University of Pennsylvania, 2005).

38. Selma Kaplan Goldman, interview by Marilyn Price, Reconstructionist Rabbinical College Oral History Project, 2003.

39. See, for example, *The Santa Cruz Haggadah* (Capitola, CA: Hineni Consciousness Press, 1992); *The Journey Continues: The Ma'ayan Passover Haggadah* (New York: Ma'yan, 2002); *An Open Door: A Passover Haggadah,* ed. Sue Levi Elwell (New York: Central Conference of American Rabbis, 2002).

40. See Rebecca T. Alpert's trenchant entry on Reconstructionist Judaism in *Jewish Women in America: An Historical Encyclopedia,* ed. Paula E. Hyman and Deborah Dash Moore (New York: Routledge, 1997), 1132–35, quote on 1132.

41. Eventually, a version of bat mitzvah spread to Orthodox congregations and even to Israel.

42. Sally Priesand, the first woman rabbi in the United States, was ordained at Hebrew Union College-Jewish Institute of Religion in 1972.

43. Alpert, *Jewish Women in America,* 1134.

44. Charles Liebman, "Reconstructionism in American Jewish Life," *American Jewish Year Book* 71 (1970): 3–99.

CHAPTER SIX

THE TENSIONS THAT MERIT OUR ATTENTION

Women in Conservative Judaism

SHULY RUBIN SCHWARTZ

> When change is justified and inescapable, we must have the integrity and the daring to change.
>
> —Andre Ungar, in "Here's What I Think"

> What happens, for example, if a woman is called to participate in a minyan at a time when she must nurse her baby?
>
> —Louis Linn, response

These remarks encapsulate both the nuances of the Conservative movement's commitment to tradition and change and the extent to which these competing values have often coalesced around gender issues. The latter question assumes a commitment to halakha that includes praying with a minyan (quorum of ten necessary for public prayer). It also reflects societal values that place a mother's obligation to her nursing infant above obligations to self or community. At the same time, the former statement assumes a commitment to creating a just society, a commitment that obligates Jews to effect changes that will hasten that outcome.

Conservative Judaism, the spiritual heir of the Positive Historical School of Judaism founded by Zechariah Frankel in mid-nineteenth-century Germany, first emerged in the United States as a traditional response to the radical path blazed by Reform Judaism. This conservative group coalesced around the founding of the Jewish Theological Seminary (JTS) in 1886 and then developed further under Solomon Schechter, president of the reorganized Jewish Theological Seminary (1902–15). Throughout the twentieth century—particularly in its second half—the movement attempted to apply these often contradictory principles to contemporary life. And women's rights issues were always at the core of these struggles. Because of this, if one examines the movement's approach to women's issues, one gains a vivid view of the evolution of the movement itself.

CHANGE THROUGH TRADITIONAL GENDER ROLES

Up through the post–World War II period, the Conservative movement expressed its regard for women primarily by upholding traditional societal views about gender. It celebrated the Jewish homemaker by praising her indispensability to the preservation of Judaism. Both Solomon Schechter and his wife, Mathilde, strongly believed that women who saturated their homes with Jewish content and spirit would successfully capture the loyalties of the next generation of Jews. To help women reach these goals, Mathilde Schechter founded Women's League in 1918 as the women's division of the United Synagogue of America, the lay organization of Conservative Judaism. Mathilde understood her institution-building achievement as an expansion of the homemaker role in which she took so much pride. By rationalizing her accomplishments in this way, Schechter epitomized the Conservative movement's approach to tradition and change for its early twentieth-century women.[1]

Similarly, during the period of rapid growth of the Conservative movement in the interwar and post–World War II periods, women took on leadership roles in their local Conservative synagogues. But they generally did so in stereotypically feminine spheres. They often took responsibility for assisting in Sunday and religious schools, and they played an instrumental role in organizing classes for mothers in Jewish living and observance. Women maintained synagogue kitchens by serving as cooks and hostesses for the collations, luncheons, and dinners that were essential to the success of synagogue activities. Synagogue women also introduced and staffed synagogue gift shops, and, in this way, they introduced Jewish ceremonial objects as well as Jewish books and artwork into the homes of Conservative Jews.[2]

Women's League provided national leadership for women's roles in Conservative Judaism. For example, Betty Greenberg and Althea Osber Silverman shared their views on the beauty and spirituality of the Jewish home in "The Jewish Home Beautiful," a pageant first presented in the Temple of Religion of the World's Fair in 1940 and then published as a popular book by Women's League in 1941. The book included descriptions and illustrations of table settings, traditional recipes, and music, all of which demonstrated the potential for creating a stylish Jewish home filled with beauty, spirituality, and the latest style.

Silverman, author of *Habibi and Yow,* and Sadie Rose Weilerstein, author of the *K'tonton* series, became noted children's authors. They helped mothers enrich their children's Jewish upbringing by providing adventurous, age-appropriate stories on Jewish customs and festivals. They demonstrated that one could concurrently embrace American culture and transmit Jewish tradition to one's children; traditional Jewish living was compatible with the aspirations of upwardly mobile American women.[3]

Similarly, the "Judaism-in-the-home" project, introduced in the 1950s and chaired by Rose Goldstein and Anna Bear Brevis, produced instructional materials to teach a new generation of sisterhood women the meaning of Jewish holidays and rituals in order to promote family-based observances. A series of ʿOneg Shabbat (Sabbath celebration) programs based on the weekly Torah portions were developed under the leadership of Education Department Chairmen Evelyn Garfiel, Rose Goldstein, and Adina Katzoff. In 1952, the newly created Ceremonial Objects and Gift Shop Department made Jewish ritual objects and other ceremonial items, including New Year cards, accessible to all sisterhoods. In all of these achievements, Women's League succeeded in large measure by focusing its efforts on areas that reinforced traditional gender expectations and strengthened traditional Jewish female roles. All the while, Women's League greatly expanded the arena of women's influence and involvement in Jewish life.[4]

NEW ROLES

Along with this growth of Women's League as the champion of women's leadership in traditionally gendered spheres there was also a growing commitment on the part of the movement to enhance opportunities for women in new arenas. Solomon Schechter himself permitted one woman—Henrietta Szold—to attend classes with rabbinical students,[5] and, in 1909, he created the Teachers Institute, which "opened the portals of the Seminary to women students" and offered Jewish higher education to men and women on an equal basis. From 1915 on, the Teachers Institute also offered a professional teacher-training curriculum that enabled women not only to obtain superior Jewish learning but also to prepare for careers in Jewish education.[6] Schechter also argued for the extension of religious education not only to advanced students but to Jewish women at large.[7]

This commitment to the education of women continued with the University of Judaism, founded as the West Coast branch of JTS in 1947.

Women filled its extension classes, which were held in locations around Los Angeles. To a large degree, the university's strength rested in its mission as a school designed to cultivate an educated lay female leadership.[8] Up until this point, gender expectations prevailed, however, since this intensive Jewish education still precluded studying for ordination.

The path that led women from the periphery to the center of synagogue life began with the introduction of mixed seating in prayer services, a pattern that took hold in Conservative synagogues during the interwar period. By 1955, mixed seating characterized the overwhelming majority of Conservative congregations and served as a yardstick to differentiate them from their Orthodox counterparts. This development gained momentum in the movement because it conformed to modern American views about women's place in worship services. Moreover, given women's central role in the postwar synagogue, restricting them proved impractical.[9]

A more progressive view of women's place in synagogue life also led to the virtually universal acceptance of bat mitzvah in the Conservative movement in the postwar period. Introduced in 1922 by Mordecai M. Kaplan for his own daughter, Judith, bat mitzvah became a crucial incentive for recruiting and retaining girls in the same supplementary religious school educational setting as boys. The ceremony itself also provided a public forum in which to mark the religious coming-of-age for Jewish girls. However, bat mitzvah did not initially signal the full embrace of egalitarianism, for the ceremony generally marked the end of a girl's inclusion in public synagogue rites rather than the beginning of lifelong involvement in the religious life of the congregation.[10]

HALAKHA AND WOMEN IN CONSERVATIVE JUDAISM

All of these developments with regard to women were understood by the movement to be accommodations to modernity within the framework of halakha. Yet resolving the plight of the *agunah,* a woman unable to remarry because her husband refused to give her a *get* (Jewish divorce), proved more difficult to resolve within those parameters. Thus, it is with this issue that the movement first tested the limits of its commitment both to women and to Jewish law. So critical has this issue been for the movement that David Golinkin, president of the Schechter Institute of Jewish Studies in Jerusalem, quipped that the movement "was obsessed with this dilemma from 1930 until 1970."[11]

In 1930, Louis Epstein, an acknowledged expert in the legal issues concerning Jewish marriage and divorce, proposed that the Rabbinical Assembly append to the marriage contract a document stipulating that should the marriage dissolve, the husband would authorize his wife to act as his agent to write her own *get* under rabbinical supervision. Colleagues praised the solution as "an example of the kind of *halakhic* modernization that the Conservative rabbinate was meant to handle," because it created a mechanism within halakha to resolve it. Yet the proposal ultimately failed because of opposition by Orthodox rabbis and by even some members of the Jewish Theological Seminary faculty.[12]

During World War II, the unique circumstances of war increased pressure on the Conservative movement to find a workable solution. In response, the Rabbinical Assembly, under the expertise of renowned JTS professor Louis Ginzberg, prepared a special get that granted a divorce to women whose husbands had not returned three years after demobilization. When this emergency provision lapsed after the war, the National Women's League petitioned the Rabbinical Assembly for a permanent solution to the agunah issue. In 1953, another notable JTS Talmud professor, Saul Lieberman, formulated a clause to insert in the marriage contract. This clause addressed the problem by stating that both husband and wife agreed that should the marriage end, the wife would be entitled to force her husband to come to a Jewish court, and, if necessary, to civil court, for arbitration. At the time, Lieberman attempted to establish a *Bet din* (court of Jewish law) with prominent Orthodox rabbis, including Joseph Soloveitchik, to jointly adjudicate such matters of personal status. Had he succeeded, Lieberman—through his resolution of the agunah issue—would have aligned Conservative Judaism with the other halakhic movement, Orthodoxy. This would have securely anchored Conservative Judaism among the branches of Judaism committed to halakha.[13]

Though the joint Bet din plan never materialized, apparently because of opposition by right-wing Orthodox leaders, the Joint JTS-Rabbinical Assembly Law Committee adopted Lieberman's takkanah (rabbinical enactment), and it became widely used throughout the movement. It seemed to perfectly demonstrate the movement's dual allegiance to halakha and to addressing pressing concerns of the day; to preserving tradition and to protecting both women and the Jewish family. Unlike its Reform counterpart, Conservative Judaism did not resolve the issue by declaring that a civil divorce would suffice to end marriage. Nor did the movement offer an egalitarian takkanah that would have empowered women to initiate divorce equally with men. Lieberman's effort best captured the way the movement understood its tradition-and-change mandate in mid-twentieth-century America.

By the mid-1970s that understanding no longer satisfied many Conservative Jews, and, again, it was an issue of gender that forced the movement to reassess its commitment to slow-paced evolutionary change. Within ten years, the movement voted to ordain women. Within another decade, a majority of congregations had endorsed women's equality in synagogue ritual. The movement's embrace of egalitarianism tipped the balance toward a commitment to change.

CHALLENGING THE TRADITION-AND-CHANGE RATIO

The Conservative movement began its inexorable move toward egalitarianism in the 1950s. The Committee on Jewish Law and Standards in 1955 permitted women to be called up for *ʾaliyot* (Torah honors). The author of the responsum, Aaron H. Blumenthal, explained that "the time has come for someone to reverse the direction in which the halachah has been moving for centuries." He reviewed the halakhic literature on the topic and argued that since the prohibition was based more on longstanding custom than on law, he could permit the change without undermining halakha.[14] Although at that time only a few synagogues in the Minneapolis area called women to the Torah, the precedent had been established. Presciently, Isaac Klein's dissenting opinion predicted that this decision would lead to egalitarianism. Klein warned ominously about the slippery slope: "If you want to carry things to the logical conclusion you should say that women put on *tefillin* every morning."[15]

In the early 1950s at the Conservative movement's summer camp Ramah, girls routinely took on limited ritual roles. They led grace after meals and read from the book of Lamentations on the Ninth of Av, but the responsum permitting women to receive ʾaliyot had little impact on camp practices. By the late 1960s, the pace of change accelerated. After the Rabbinical Assembly's Committee on Jewish Law and Standards 1970 decision that egalitarian congregations did not violate their "essential loyalty" to Jewish traditions, advocates of egalitarianism pressed for an immediate enhancement of ritual roles for girls at camp. After a period of study, JTS chancellor Gerson D. Cohen approved calling up girls to the Torah as of the summer of 1974. Within ten years, all the Ramah camps adopted an egalitarian approach to prayer, with provisions made for dissenters.[16]

In 1973, the Committee on Jewish Law and Standards passed a takkanah allowing women to count equally with men in the minyan. The author, Philip Sigal, noted that he was influenced in his thinking by changing realities: "We live in a radically changing world, and foremost among those transformations taking place is that of the status of women. The equalization of women with men had been progressing at an accelerating pace in recent years in various phases of the socio-economic context of society, as well as in new attitudes toward women in the sexual-moral sphere."[17] Like the Lieberman clause, the change was effected not through reinterpretations of existing laws but through a new enactment. In this case, though, the takkanah was adopted not to resolve a specific hardship but rather for sociological reasons, that is, to keep pace with a "radically changing world" and "new attitudes." Additional resolutions further expanded women's roles in other areas of ritual, including serving as prayer leaders. In that same year, the United Synagogue of America also resolved to permit women to participate in synagogue rituals and to promote equal opportunity for women in positions of leadership, authority, and responsibility in congregational life. From 1972 to 1976, the number of Conservative congregations giving ʾaliyot to women increased from 7 percent to 50 percent. By 1986, 83 percent of congregations counted women in the minyan.[18]

These more rapid and more radical changes came about in response to grassroots pressure for equality in synagogue ritual life, pressure that did not exist in critical numbers before this period. In 1972, Ezrat Nashim, a group of young, well-educated women, most of whom were products of the camps and schools of the movement, presented to the Rabbinical Assembly a call for the public affirmation of women's equality in all aspects of Jewish life. The group demanded that women be granted membership in synagogues, be counted in a minyan, be allowed full participation in religious observances, be recognized as witnesses in Jewish law, be allowed to initiate divorce, be permitted and encouraged to attend rabbinical and cantorial school and perform as rabbis and cantors in synagogues, be encouraged to assume positions of leadership in the community, and be considered bound to fulfill all the commandments equally with men. Ezrat Nashim stopped just short of demanding rabbinical ordination and investiture as *hazzanim* (cantors) for women.[19]

After a decade of debate, deliberation, and agitation, the JTS faculty voted in 1983 to admit women to its Rabbinical School. Both Pamela Nadell and Beth Wenger[20] have ably traced the month-by-month developments of the ordination struggle during these years. They recount the arguments of the stakeholders, including members of the Rabbinical Assembly, the

JTS faculty and Ezrat Nashim. Each author also documents the process through which women's ordination finally gained approval. They demonstrate the way in which the struggle forced the movement's leaders to articulate where they stood on the continuum of tradition and change when it came to gender issues. For example, Saul Lieberman—the author of the clause resolving the agunah question—opposed women's ordination on halakhic grounds. And, as we have seen, he considered halakhic concerns to be paramount. In contrast, Gershon Cohen changed his views and came to support ordination for reasons similar to those that motivated Sigal. After listening to the views of Conservative Jews, Cohen became convinced that such a change was imperative. He saw its potential as a magnet for his growing conviction that Conservative Judaism assert itself as the "militant center."[21] Reinforcing that perspective, Wenger notes that the politics of ordination relied little on the experiences of actual women and that the decision to ordain women had more to do with the larger agendas of male religious leaders than with women themselves. Yet a generation later, Cohen's successor, JTS chancellor Ismar Schorsch, reasoned that the vote passed because in the intervening years, a preponderant majority favoring women's ordination had coalesced with the Conservative Jewish community.[22] How did a majority of the Conservative movement's laity and rabbis grow to embrace the implications of women's equality in the span of little more than a decade? And what role did gender concerns and women's voices play in this evolution?

Since, as Wenger notes, Conservative Jewish women's views and experiences were not central to the decision to ordain women, one must look elsewhere to try to discover their views on the issue. The richest written source is the monthly publication of Women's League, *Outlook* magazine, which had served as a lively forum for Conservative Jewish women since 1930. Women stood to gain—or lose—the most from the outcome of these debates. And while they played little role in the halakhic responsa that were written, women propelled the community to embrace egalitarianism. A focus on their attitudes seems particularly relevant to better clarify how so many of the laity came to support women's equality in religious life. Similarly, one can learn a great deal about the evolving views of Conservative rabbis by reviewing how they address the issue of women's equality in the Rabbinical Assembly's publication, *Conservative Judaism.* Rabbis played an instrumental role in effecting change within their congregations. Thus, an examination of their shifting attitudes is also essential to understanding how the movement came to endorse women's rights in synagogue life by the mid-1980s in a way that relied more on a commitment to addressing contemporary realities than on loyalty to halakha. While not an exhaustive assessment of all movement publications and of the mind-set of laity and rabbis, a review of how *Outlook* and *Conservative Judaism* covered the question of women's roles in Judaism from 1972 to 1986 reveals the many ways, both overt and subtle, that the opinions of Conservative Jewish women and rabbis developed over time.

THE WOMEN'S ISSUE IN *OUTLOOK* MAGAZINE

Through the pages of *Outlook* one learns that Women's League grappled with egalitarianism by raising questions about the women's movement as a whole and reflecting openly on the potential impact of feminism on its readers. *Outlook* also continued to focus on the organization's core commitments: strengthening Jewish knowledge and fostering Jewish observance. This dual-pronged approach enabled the magazine to build consensus slowly, giving readers time to work through their hesitancies concerning women's equality and its place in a movement devoted to tradition as well as change.

In the fall 1972 issue, in response to a query asking readers how they felt about the status of women in Jewish life, *Outlook* included a range of responses, from "human dignity demands that each human being shall decide for him-/herself what his/her obligations in religious life must be" to the doomsday prediction that "to offer women 'total equality' with men naturally reduces their own womanliness and further emasculates the manliness of men. A shading of the sexual ensues, and this is the beginning of the end of civilization and Jewish living."[23]

In the next issue, *Outlook* reported on the debate on women's rights that took place at its recent National Women's League convention. The article diplomatically reviewed the opinions expressed, and both advocates of women's equality and naysayers found voice within its pages. In keeping with the spirit of the movement, the article ended with Conservative rabbi Israel Silverman's plea for evolutionary, not revolutionary, change.[24]

In 1973, Gerson Cohen chose to take the issue of women's rights in synagogue ritual directly to the movement's women by writing an article for *Outlook* that reaffirmed the status quo. At that time, he explained that ordaining women "would hardly reflect the consensus of the Conservative Movement, whether of its laity or its professional leadership." Reiterating the movement's commitment to tradition and change—with the implication that this principle overrode that of egalitarianism—he warned that "development and change" must be "carefully governed by the principles of Judaism itself."[25]

Though not openly contradicting the seminary's chancellor, *Outlook* included—in the same issue—an article by another rabbi that promoted gender equality, albeit it on a less controversial matter. David Aronson urged that the "mother be given equal recognition with the father in the identity of their child, and that her name be used together with the father's in all religious records." Explaining that a resolution to this effect had been introduced at the last Rabbinical Assembly convention, he hoped that the Committee on Jewish Law and Standards would recommend the change.[26] The juxtaposition of Aronson's proposal with Cohen's statement suggests a desire to emphasize that though the movement might not be ready to ordain women rabbis, other avenues of equality could and should be pursued.

Many articles appeared throughout the next decade arguing both for and against equal rights for women in Judaism. Women authored most of them, though halakhic matters were usually discussed by (male) rabbis. For example, Harold M. Kamsler, in "Menstrual Taboos, Jewish Law and 'Kovod Tsibbur,'" debunks a popular line of reasoning against women's rights by maintaining that "the argument that women are not to be called to the Torah because of menstrual flow is patently a specious one."[27]

Letters in reaction to Cohen's article were mostly critical of his conservative stance. But *Outlook* signified its awareness of the complexity of the issue by featuring responses from a (male) rabbi who disapproved and a rebbetzin who supported Cohen's position. Congregational rabbi Andre Ungar authored the first epigraph to this chapter, that "when change is justified and inescapable, we must have the integrity and the daring to change." He concluded that "if, in fact—as Dr. Cohen rightly suggests—education is something our women should be involved in, why not follow this to the logical conclusion, and offer ordination—not grudgingly, but as a right, as a blessing to us all?" In contrast, Tziporah Heckelman, a Jewishly knowledgeable educator and rabbi's wife, claimed that though she had liberated herself "from the tea-pouring, fund-raising stereotype of my mother's generation," she feared that erasing role distinctions would only aggravate competitiveness between men and women. Heckelman brooded about whether "vicarious fulfillment and taking turns [had a] . . . place in 20th century human relationships." Subsequent letters, including one by the members of Ezrat Nashim, vehemently disagreed with Cohen's assumptions and conclusions. But by including diverse perspectives, *Outlook* acknowledged the validity of maintaining divergent points of view.[28]

Outlook continued to print articles that discussed both the implications of the women's movement on the lives of its readers and the narrower question of women's rights in synagogue life. These articles reflect the growing awareness of how profoundly the feminist revolution affected all areas of life and how difficult it was to adopt black-and-white positions on any issue. For example, in an article on zero population growth, one woman stresses the unique challenges it posed to concerned Jews, for "Z.P.G., the freezing of the population level, makes no adjustment to replace the loss of six million Jews in the Holocaust."[29] Similarly, Marcia Baltimore Cohen, in "How to Be a Jewish Working Mother," writes about the importance of juggling work, household chores, and mothering. Despite painting a progressive picture, she presents a fairly traditional view of women's obligations, including shopping, cooking, and maintaining the home. She advises that "priority-wise, the responsibilities of the Jewish working mother as wife should probably come first."[30]

A year later, *Outlook* reported on a dialogue with Betty Friedan and Willard Gaylin about the impact of feminism on the Jewish woman. Friedan trumpeted the feminist revolution and applauded its gains. But she also declared that the pro-family goals of second stage of feminism were equally important. Feminism and family must not be viewed as conflicting with one another. As Friedan put it, "[A] woman needs to 'be for herself' in order to 'be for her family.'" That same issue noted proudly that at the 1980 Women's League Convention, for the very first time, each woman called to the Torah read her own portion.[31]

Outlook continued to raise concerns over the impact of new opportunities for women. In "Can a Jewish Mother Survive in the Eighties?" Cindy Daniels writes of the challenges of relating to a working or Gentile daughter-in-law. She notes wistfully that "life was simpler when mothers remained in sheltered homes, caring for their plants, their husbands, their kids, and the class turtle which turned rusty in the coffee can. But we are confident that, supported by the traditions and strength of our heritage, the 'Jewish Mother' will meet the challenges of today and of tomorrow and solve them as she has done in every yesterday." The reader wonders whether the author is trying too hard to convince herself as well as her readers that all will turn out well. On a more sanguine note, Rela Geffen Monson writes about the opportunity feminism afforded to remake fatherhood so that both spouses could work together to raise Jewish children.[32]

The spring 1980 issue included a second article by Gerson Cohen in which he explains why he had reversed his position and come to believe that the ordination of women "had become an ethical imperative." Cohen acknowledges the halakhic arguments evident in the debates on both sides of the issue but then concedes that "the Jewish community could ill afford to forego the services of one half its committed members." He ends by calling for the "creation of a genuinely Conservative laity," a goal that he believes takes "precedence over a study of the status of women in Jewish law."[33] Even when speaking forcefully for women's ordination, Cohen carefully anchors his views in the movement's age-old commitment to tradition and change. Yet despite the consistent rhetoric, the emphasis had shifted. Ethical imperatives now loomed larger than halakhic fealty.

Outlook devoted its entire spring 1984 issue to a "Progress Report" on the Jewish woman. It clearly viewed the moment—after the historic 1983 vote to admit women to JTS's rabbinical school—as a milestone of sorts. Yet here, too, the magazine reflects lingering ambivalence. On the one hand, *Outlook* reports optimistically on all that had been accomplished in a decade. Articles by three accomplished women—congregational rabbi Sandy Sasso, Talmud professor Judith Hauptman, and New York state senator Carol Berman—celebrate how far women had come.[34] On the other hand, different articles emphasize how much still remained to be done to help older women achieve personal growth, to meet the needs of younger women and their families, and to strengthen the Jewish home.[35]

In this brief span of a dozen years, then, *Outlook* had given Conservative Jewish women a forum for exploring the implications of the women's movement that proved neither too provocative nor too reactionary. In this way, the magazine enabled readers gradually to integrate egalitarianism into their longstanding commitment to Conservative Judaism. But the ground rules had been transformed. Women now framed the terms of the debate, and their needs and goals now more forcefully influenced the movement's halakhic choices.

RABBINIC REFLECTIONS

As the journal of the Rabbinical Assembly, *Conservative Judaism* served a function similar to that of *Outlook* but for the movement's rabbis. Like *Outlook*, it, too, grappled with the women's movement by devoting articles over the years to a wide range of views. And just as *Outlook* provided a comfortable forum for *Conservative Jewish* women to come to terms with egalitarianism, *Conservative Judaism* gave rabbis the opportunity to do the same. Yet Conservative Judaism chose a more dramatic way to introduce this issue. In this journal written primarily by (male) rabbis for (male) rabbis, the publication of two lead articles by women on women's rights signaled the unprecedented nature of the challenge.

These clarion calls for equality by Ezrat Nashim members Paula E. Hyman and Judith Hauptman appeared in the summer 1972 issue. Both authors tried to reassure the journal's largely male rabbinic readership that, as Hyman explains, "Jewish feminists have not rejected Judaism; we are struggling with it in our desire to find a way to fulfill ourselves as Jews and as women." Similarly, Hauptman soothingly portrays her views of change as a continuation of the age-old halakhic process to which Conservative Jews were dedicated. She expresses the hope that "we will soon see a re-institution of the processes so admirably evolved and applied by the earlier Rabbis." But despite these reassurances, the radical nature of Hyman and Hauptman's arguments is evident. The editor tempered these articles by including in the same issue a response by a right-wing member of the Rabbinical Assembly, David M. Feldman, who bluntly questions whether "the ultimate demand of *Ezrat Nashim* [could] be met, that 'women be considered as bound to fulfill all mitzvot equally with men.'"[36]

Two years later, and one year after Gerson Cohen's arguments against ordination appeared in *Outlook, Conservative Judaism* published a paper by Mortimer Ostow, chairman of the department of pastoral psychiatry at JTS and a close personal friend of Cohen, which delineates the psychological arguments against women's ordination. Stephen C. Lerner, the journal's editor at the time, later explained that its publication did not signify the journal's retreat from a commitment to women's equality. Rather, it reflected the widely disparate and volatile views within the movement. As editor, he routinely published articles by JTS faculty members, and Ostow's paper had been delivered at a JTS conference. In his recollection, Ostow's oppositionist view represented the majority perspective among seminary faculty at that time.[37]

According to Ostow's grim assessment, egalitarianism would precipitate male impotence, erotic fantasies in the synagogue, and antinomianism. He especially frowned on practices that made "the sexes look alike; for example, the use of a *tallit* for women." Ostow acknowledges the injustice in asking women to surrender their self-esteem in deference to insecure men, yet he concludes that it would be worth the sacrifice, for "the society whose men have little self-respect and who are unreliable sexual partners is one which holds little gratification."[38]

Reponses to Ostow's article, written mostly by men, ran the gamut.

Seymour Siegel, JTS professor of theology and chairperson of the Rabbinical Assembly Committee on Jewish Law and Standards, took offense at Ostow's one-sided concern with men's psyches. As he explains,

> We should consider the effect that the deprivation of opportunity has had upon the psyche of women. It is not fair to consider only the effect upon men. It is true that the emotional health of men is a great factor in the social and emotional well-being of women. But the reverse is also true: women's claim that the ritual deprivations which they have suffered in the past have caused them anguish and pain should be taken seriously.[39]

Similarly, David Graubart, a member of the Rabbinical Assembly Committee on Jewish Law and Standards, found Ostow's remarks insulting to both sexes. Louis Linn, a colleague in the Department of Pastoral Psychiatry, admitted that Ostow had overestimated the "'role of genitality' in the issues before us." Yet he also warns against the possibly dire consequences of egalitarianism on Jewish family life. Linn queries fearfully, "What happens to family life if women accept ritual obligations on an equal footing with men? What happens, for example, if a woman is called to participate in a minyan at a time when she must nurse her baby?"[40]

Conservative Judaism strengthened its support for egalitarianism by publishing two articles on women in the same issue: Ellen F. Schiff's "Hannah, Jessica, Bessie—and Me?" combs the Bible, Western literature, and Jewish culture for Jewish role models of female achievement. Chaim Listfield, in "Women and the Commandments," reviews traditional sources to demonstrate the halakhic validity of one of the linchpin arguments for granting women religious equality: "women have the option to accept for themselves the performance of positively stated time-bound mitzvot as an obligation."[41]

The journal also continued the debate on Ostow's views by printing additional letters to the editor in a subsequent issue. Most excoriated Ostow for his views. Arthur Green expressed "shock and horror." Linda Switkin, a clinical psychologist, was "appalled by the one-sidedness of the mental health point of view represented." Dana Charry, a psychiatrist, criticized JTS for asking "a psychiatrist to give a professional opinion on an issue which is essentially religious and political." *Conservative Judaism* also solicited Ostow's response. In it, he reiterates his initial views, insisting that precluding women from serving as rabbis or assuming identical functions and identical religious garb to men would not "constitute serious discrimination against women."[42]

With the battle lines sharply drawn, *Conservative Judaism,* slowly made the case for women's equality over the next few years. Given its largely rabbinic subscribers, it is not surprising that most articles continued to be written by men and that they explored the halakhic justifications more than the sociological or communal ones. After all, the rabbinic arm of the movement was the one most closely tied to halakha. Blumenthal, author of the 1955 responsum on ʾaliyot, appraised the decisions made by the law committee in the postwar period. Beginning with his belief that the rabbis of the Talmud, "in a variety of ways and with a variety of proof texts . . . declared that men and women are equal before the law," Blumenthal sought to demonstrate that the recent debate over women's equality was part of a long continuum of halakhic decision making. He highlights the many steps the committee had already taken in the last twenty-five years to expand women's opportunities. For example, the committee had proposed formulas for women to recite at wedding ceremonies, encouraged women to say the mourner's kaddish for deceased relatives, and allowed women to participate with men in the three-person quorum required to publicly lead grace after meals. Yet Blumenthal acknowledges other issues, such as women's ability to serve as witnesses, rabbis, and cantors, which had not yet been resolved in favor of women's equality.[43]

The two responses to Blumenthal's review offered a more conservative position. By cleverly leading with a critique by a woman, *Conservative Judaism,* like *Outlook,* demonstrated the complexity of views within the movement. Miriam Shapiro pleaded for respect "for what I am as a woman" not for "how well I can fulfill a man's image of what status is." She challenged the law committee to write papers on "bringing back this [feminine] aspect of Rosh Hodesh, or the aspect of Hanukkah which honors women." Chaim Pearl was more receptive to Blumenthal's position. He endorsed the basic impulse of the law committee in giving women a more equal place in Jewish ritual at the marriage ceremony, but he drew the line at halakhic change. He expressed fears about marriage "in an age when the standards of domestic life are at a dangerously low ebb," implying that egalitarianism would exacerbate contemporary problems.[44]

Appealing to Conservative rabbis' understanding of their roots in historical Judaism, *Conservative Judaism* also included articles that explored the issue of women's equality from a historical perspective. Leonard Swidler wrote "Women and Torah in Talmudic Judaism," explaining that "since questions concerning the role of women in contemporary Judaism are being raised more and more frequently, it is essential that the historical roots of these questions be laid bare in the formative Talmudic period."[45] Alan Silverstein studied the evolution of Ezrat Nashim, giving the newly formed organization and its views both credibility and visibility.[46] Shaye J. D. Cohen concludes in "Women in the Synagogues of Antiquity" that women had assumed leadership roles in the synagogues long ago. He slyly admits that the existence of six women who served as real heads of synagogues in the ancient world did not truly aid the contemporary "cause of those who seek the ordination of women," but he nevertheless happily greeted "Rufina, Theopempte and Sophia . . . as the first women 'rabbis.'"[47] Myra Shoub introduced the field of Jewish women's history to the readers of *Conservative Judaism,* explaining that "these sources and methodologies are required to direct our study toward the often neglected half of the community, the Jewish women."[48] Finally, Sidney H. Schwarz's reviewed the movement's efforts to address the agunah issue.[49]

Each of these scholarly articles attempted to sway rabbis' opinions in favor of women's rights. Like *Outlook,* however, *Conservative Judaism* also included articles that exposed readers to other areas of Jewish life touched by the women's movement. For example, it tackled the implications of the women's movement for Jewish family life in George Johnson's "The Lifestyle of Low Fertility: The Changing Needs of Jewish Women." Johnson warned that "new work values of the seventies do not mesh well with the suburban ecology" and that two-career families inevitably result in more conflicted young women. Echoing the plaints of Women's League leaders, he predicted that "if increasing numbers of our most energetic women turn from the volunteer world to the professional one, many Jewish organizations may be in trouble."[50] At the same time, *Conservative Judaism* also introduced readers to creative midrash. Lynn Gottlieb gave expression to "female voices of the past" and the necessity of receiving "them into our present" as a way of filling the gaps in the tradition caused by the absence of women's voices.[51]

Like *Outlook* then, *Conservative Judaism* included a variety of perspectives. Over the span of a dozen years, it, too, gradually drew its readers toward endorsing the feminist position by subsuming halakhic arguments under broader concerns. In the case of *Conservative Judaism,* that expansive perspective culminated in a special 1986 issue devoted not only to women and halakha but to all aspects of Jewish women's studies, though as before, most articles were written by men.[52] Articles reviewed the impact of feminism on Bible study, midrash, Jewish history, Jewish ritual, sociology, and

Ordination of Rabbi Amy Eilberg with other students at the Jewish Theological Seminary, 1985. Used with the permission of the Jewish Theological Seminary.

egalitarianism. Benjamin Skolnic advocated for the legitimacy of feminist Bible interpretation, while David Kraemer offered a developmental perspective on the laws of family purity. Esther Altshul Helfgott examined one congregation's process of study and change with regard to women's ritual roles. Nahum M. Waldman suggested that the marriage contract eliminate what he considered to be "judgmental" distinctions concerning the bride's status as virgin, widow, or divorcée. Albert S. Axelrad went farthest, raising his commitment to egalitarianism to the level of halakhic imperative. As he explains, "I will not compromise my egalitarian commitment, because it is a religious 'principle,' not a 'preference.'"[53]

One sees, then, in *Conservative Judaism* as in *Outlook,* that the halakhic justifications came to play a role secondary to the urgent need to address the needs of contemporary women. In contrast to the agunah issue, which affected fewer women and whose resolution in the 1950s did not stem from a broad societal mandate, the decision to embrace equality for women in the 1970s and 1980s grew out of the larger American cultural groundswell for women's rights that swept up Conservative Jews as well. Because of this, the movement came to endorse a view that shifted its emphasis from a commitment to halakha and gradual change toward an endorsement of egalitarianism as an ethical imperative.

Ironically, this shift also helped address the agunah issue more completely. Over time it had become apparent that the Lieberman clause had not fully resolved the agunah problem. Many rabbinic authorities hesitated to bring Jewish legal matters to civil courts, and civil courts were reluctant to decide religious questions. This proved true even in states like New York with laws prohibiting one spouse from impeding the remarriage of the other. As commitment to women's equality increased and as the movement took a stance more independent of Orthodoxy, the joint *Bet din* of the Conservative movement became more aggressive in dealing with this problem. In the 1980s, it certified Conservative rabbis to write *gittin* (bills of divorce) and began to utilize *hafkaat kiddushin* (annulment of the marriage) more frequently as a tool against extreme recalcitrance. These measures enabled the movement to aide women far beyond what the Lieberman clause accomplished without abandoning its core commitment to Jewish law.[54]

THE OTHER HALF OF THE JEWISH FEMINIST STRUGGLE

Soon after the movement reached consensus for egalitarianism it began to face new challenges. These, too, found expression within National Women's League and its magazine, *Outlook.* Authors began to question whether egalitarianism precluded maintaining a separate sphere—and organization—for women. The spring 1984 *Outlook* progress report carried an article by Nina Cardin titled "Let Me In; Let Me Out," in which she argues that "equal obligation, equal access and equal representation are only half the Jewish feminist struggle." The other half consists of a search for prayers and rituals unique to women and often outside the world of halakha. Cardin claims that both aspects of feminism are necessary to fully humanize Judaism, a view that goaded the movement to clarify how one might harmonize fidelity to women's equality with new commitments to women's spirituality and difference.[55]

At the same time, Women's League also experienced challenges to its viability, for the success of the women's movement precipitated a decline in the organization's membership. As more and more younger women gained the advanced education and career preparation that the organization lauded, they entered the workforce and declined to involve themselves in sisterhood. Many did not appreciate why they ought to give of their severely limited volunteer hours to a separate women's organization.[56]

Working on several fronts to address these challenges, Women's League created several subdivisions to attract younger members. These include Z'havah, which generates leadership for women forty-five and under and "gives younger members a point of focus and connection with the larger organization." WLCJNet is an online discussion group for all members of Women's League, which provides yet another way to appeal to a younger, computer-savvy audience.[57]

In addition to launching these subgroups, Women's League embraced Cardin's views. It published Cardin's Simhat Bat Kit, a collection of ceremonies for welcoming infant girls[58] and issued *Under the Wings of the Sh'khinah: A Jewish Healing Service.* Both emphasize new rituals and prayers, and though they do not contradict halakha they favor innovation and creativity over tradition. They also reflect renewed appreciation of feminine qualities.[59] Similarly, a recently issued pamphlet on the mitzvah of Bikkur Holim (visiting the sick) explains that women are especially suited to performing this mitzvah for "many people believe that women are endowed with a unique nurturing spirit. When women visit those who have breast cancer, or have suffered a miscarriage or given birth to a stillborn child, they can relate with a special compassion."[60] Despite its ironclad commitment to equal rights for women, the organization has begun to reaffirm its belief in the indispensability of gendered attributes for a flourishing Jewish life.

Riv-Ellen Prell, in her study of two Conservative synagogues in the 1990s, finds that this ambivalence between achieving equality and celebrating difference permeates synagogue practice. On the one hand, opening the doors to women's participation brought new vitality to Jewish observance for women: "Women reflected on their Jewish practice in a self-conscious way that men did not. No man in this study mentioned wearing a tallit as a choice or decision. . . . For women, by contrast, whether to wear a tallit was a question. When a woman chose to wear a tallit, it became a personal statement and a ritual act that more consciously linked her to Jewish practice."[61]

On the other hand, this very equality paved the way for a new appreciation of difference. Thus, while some women chose to wear the traditional wool tallit (prayer shawl) with its black and white stripes, others opted for "feminine" colors, fabrics and shapes that emphasize the femaleness of the wearer. Similarly, though some women wore *kippot* (skullcaps), other women chose creative head coverings that more readily conform to their hairstyles. Also, women rarely don *tefillin* (phylacteries), leading to the anomalous role of the woman rabbi in many communities as the sole woman wearing tefillin at the morning minyan. This unresolved issue of equality versus difference remains alive in rabbinical training as well. JTS specifically requires women candidates "to accept equality of obligation for the mitzvot from which women have been traditionally exempted, including tallit, tefillin and tefillah [prayer]." The Ziegler School for Rabbinic Studies at the University of Judaism acknowledges that "some women in the Ziegler community wear tefillin, while others choose not to." This new openness to female difference threatens the movement's commitment to an egalitarianism in which rituals remain steady with the only difference being the equality of obligation for men and women.[62]

This ambivalence manifests itself among children as well. Barry A. Kosmin, reporting on his study of Conservative bar and bat mitzvah age children, found that in 1995–96, 78 percent of the synagogues that he studied reported that "they treated bar and bat mitzvah students exactly alike in both ritual and training." Eighty-three percent of synagogues count women in the minyan, 79 percent permit women to lead prayer services, and in 88 percent of synagogues, women can read from the Torah. But Kosmin also found that underlying this consensus in favor of egalitarianism, only 36 percent of the girls reported receiving instruction on how to put on tefillinim compared with 76 percent of the boys. (This may help explain why so few women have taken on this mitzvah.) He also learned that "since their bar/bat mitzvah, 64 percent of those asked to make up a Minyan by their synagogue were boys." Kosmin did not ask whether the girls took on the mitzvah of tallit equally with boys or whether they wore a head covering as their male counterparts surely did. Some congregations now require both boys and girls to wear tallitot, head coverings, and tefillinim, but most do not. An ambiguous stance means that girls still can (and do) opt out just as readily as they opt in. A Jewish boy does not have such a choice.[63]

Similar unresolved issues concerning the goals and limits of egalitarianism have surfaced among women rabbis. On the positive side, some believe that they have expanded the traditional views of rabbinic work and have succeeded more easily than men have in nontraditional rabbinic roles, such as chaplaincy or outreach work, where individuals do not have a preconceived vision of male success. Women rabbis also believe that they have had more freedom to experiment religiously, because congregants already perceive them as different. But some women rabbis feel that their sex is a liability in their careers, because equality in principle does not translate into true equality in the job market. They are convinced that simply because of their gender they are automatically less desirable candidates for a job, despite their qualifications and experience.

A recent study issued by the Rabbinical Assembly confirms this view. It found that women rabbis are more likely to be employed part time, serve smaller congregations, and earn less than their male counterparts. They are more likely to experience unfair treatment and report lower levels of professional satisfaction. Recently ordained women rabbis of the class of 2004 found themselves negotiating contentiously with congregations over maternity leave, while their older married colleagues find it difficult to balance the demands of the congregational rabbinate with family life. Single women rabbis fear that their career choice has limited their opportunities to marry and have children. All of this demonstrates the extent to which equal opportunity falls short of full egalitarianism. Such tensions are to be expected within the movement, for society at large has not yet fully resolved them. When the movement eventually comes to terms with these inconsistencies, yet another realignment of the movement's commitment to tradition and change will emerge.[64]

Another source of growing tension is the conclusion by some that embracing egalitarianism requires a renunciation of the pluralism that underlies the movement's commitment to both tradition and change. The movement has always prided itself on including individuals and congregations on both ends of the religious spectrum. Yet for those who have embraced equality as an ethical imperative, there is little tolerance for others in the movement who disagree. As Nina Cardin explains,

> [F]or some, the coupling of egalitarianism and pluralism within the movement is indeed a strained co-habiting. To these thinkers, egalitarianism is the opposite of pluralism: Pluralism embraces non-egalitarian principles, egalitarianism shuns them. How, the egalitarians argue, can we accept that which violates our principles, that which denies us? How, the pluralists respond in kind, can a movement based on an ideology of pluralism and hence inclusion of a wide variety of views, confer hegemony upon the interpretation of women's status?[65]

Individuals committed to egalitarianism feel marginalized by the continued legitimacy of nonegalitarian options in the movement that they find particularly demoralizing to women rabbis. According to Andrea Merow, egalitarianism ought to be fully embraced as part of the movement's pursuit of justice in all areas of life. Most recently, some have extended this ethical imperative a step further, arguing that a commitment to equality must include equal rights—including ordination—for gay and lesbian Jews.[66] We can certainly marvel at how far Conservative Judaism has evolved. The movement today looks completely different for its women than it did fifty years ago. We can also appreciate the process of change, for Conservative Judaism succeeded in embracing equal rights for women first by tackling the agunah issue—the symbol of women's inequality—and then by promoting broader change by giving voice to its constituents over time and allowing consensus to build. New challenges have come to the fore, however, as individuals recognize the inconsistencies of their commitments. As the movement and Conservative women evolve, they will further deepen their understanding of what true egalitarianism entails, how best to achieve it, and at what cost. The tensions that merit our attention at the beginning of this new century reflect the continuing vitality of a movement constantly struggling to maintain conflicting allegiances to Jewish law, egalitarianism, pluralism, and difference.

NOTES

1. David Golinkin, "The Influence of Seminary Professors on Halakha in the Conservative Movement: 1902–1968," in *Tradition Renewed: A History of the Jewish Theological Seminary of America,* ed. Jack Wertheimer (New York: Jewish Theological Seminary, 1997), 2:450; *They Dared to Dream: A History of National Women's League 1918–68* (New York: National Women's League of the United Synagogue of America, 1967), 10–11; Mrs. Solomon (Mathilde) Schechter, "Address," 1919, *The United Synagogue of America and the Women's League Annual Reports* (New York: n.p., [1920]), 108–9, box 1 (1919–50), Women's League Archives, New York; "A Valorous Woman" (editorial), *Outlook* 2 (September 1930): 2; Mrs. Jacob S. (Fanny) Minkin, "Mrs. Solomon Schechter: An Anniversary Appreciation," *Outlook* 2 (December 1931): 2.

2. Deborah Dash Moore, *To the Golden Cities: Pursuing the American Jewish Dream in Miami and L.A.* (New York: Free Press, 1994), 100–109; Joellyn W. Zollman, "Shopping for Our Future: The Synagogue Gift Shop as Jewish Women's History" (Ph.D. diss., Brandeis University, 2002).

3. Betty D. Greenberg and Althea O. Silverman, *The Jewish Home Beautiful* (New York: National Women's League of the United Synagogue of America, 1941); *They Dared to Dream,* 56–58; Jenna Weissman Joselit, "'A Set Table': Jewish Domestic Culture in the New World, 1880–1950," in *Getting Comfortable in New York: The American Jewish Home, 1880–1950,* ed. Susan L. Braunstein and Jenna Weissman Joselit (New York: Jewish Museum, 1990), 51–53; Althea Osber Silverman, *Habibi and Yow* (New York: Bloch, 1946); Silverman, *Habibi's Adventures in the Land of Israel* (New York: Bloch, 1951); Sadie Rose Weilerstein, *The Adventures of K'tonton: A Little Jewish Tom Thumb* (New York: Women's League for Conservative Judaism, 1964); Weilerstein, *K'tonton in the Circus* (Philadelphia: Jewish Publication Society, 1981); Weilerstein, *K'tonton in Israel* (New York: National Women's League of the United Synagogue of America, 1964); Weilerstein, *K'tonton on an Island in the Sea* (Philadelphia: Jewish Publication Society, 1976); Weil-

erstein, *K'tonton's Yom Kippur Kitten* (Philadelphia: Jewish Publication Society, 1995).

4. *They Dared to Dream,* 66–79.

5. Ismar Schorsch, "Schechter's Seminary: Polarities in Balance," *Conservative Judaism* 55 (Winter 2003): 12–13; *Jewish Women in America,* s.v. "Szold, Henrietta"; Baila Round Shargel, *Lost Love: The Untold Story of Henrietta Szold* (Philadelphia: Jewish Publication Society, 1997), 8.

6. Schorsch, "Schechter's Seminary," 12; David Kaufman, "Jewish Education as a Civilization: A History of the Teachers Institute," in *Tradition Renewed: A History of the Jewish Theological Seminary of America,* ed. Jack Wertheimer (New York: Jewish Theological Seminary, 1997), 1:567–79.

7. Schorsch, "Schechter's Seminary," 13.

8. Deborah Dash Moore, "Another Glowing Chapter: The University of Judaism," in *Tradition Renewed: A History of the Jewish Theological Seminary of America,* ed. Jack Wertheimer (New York: Jewish Theological Seminary, 1997), 1:805–6.

9. Marshall Sklare, *Conservative Judaism* (1955; repr., Lanham, MD: University Press of America, 1985), 85–90. This issue had already been resolved in Reform a century earlier. See Jonathan D. Sarna, "The Debate over Mixed Seating in the American Synagogue," in *The American Synagogue: A Sanctuary Transformed,* ed. Jack Wertheimer (Hanover, NH: Brandeis University Press, 1987), 363–94; Karla Goldman, *Beyond the Synagogue Gallery: Finding a Place for Women in American Judaism* (Cambridge, MA: Harvard University Press, 2000), 93–99.

10. Paula E. Hyman, "The Introduction of Bat Mitzvah in Conservative Judaism in Postwar America," *YIVO Annual* 19 (1990): 133–46; Regina Stein, "The Road to Bat Mitzvah in America," in *Women and American Judaism,* ed. Pamela S. Nadell and Jonathan D. Sarna (Hanover, NH: Brandeis University Press, 2001), 223–34; Stein, "The Boundaries of Gender: The Role of Gender Issues in Forming American Jewish Denominational Identity, 1913–1963" (Ph.D. diss., Jewish Theological Seminary, 1998), 94–95, 101–4; Jenna Weissman Joselit, "An Engendered Judaism," *Conservative Judaism* 48 (Fall 1995): 52.

11. Golinkin, "The Influence of Seminary Professors," 2:474n41.

12. Louis M. Epstein, "Adjustment of the Jewish Marriage Laws to Present-Day Conditions," *Proceedings of the Rabbinical Assembly* 5 (1935–36): 232; Pamela S. Nadell, *Conservative Judaism in America: A Biographical Dictionary and Sourcebook* (New York: Greenwood, 1998), 272–321; Sidney H. Schwarz, "Conservative Judaism and the Agunah," *Conservative Judaism* 36 (Fall 1982): 37–44.

13. Jules Harlow, ed., *A Rabbi's Manual* (New York: Rabbinical Assembly, 1965), 37–38; Stein, "Boundaries of Gender," 272–321; Schwarz, "Conservative Judaism and the Agunah," 37–44; Golinkin, "The Influence of Seminary Professors," 2:450–52, 474n41; Marsha L. Rozenblit, "The Seminary during the Holocaust Years," in *Tradition Renewed: A History of the Jewish Theological Seminary of America,* ed. Jack Wertheimer (New York: Jewish Theological Seminary, 1997), 2:293; Harvey E. Goldberg, "Becoming History: Perspectives on the Seminary Faculty at Mid-Century," in *Tradition Renewed: A History of the Jewish Theological Seminary*

of America, ed. Jack Wertheimer (New York: Jewish Theological Seminary, 1997), 1:370.

14. Seymour Siegel, ed., *Conservative Judaism and Jewish Law* (New York: Rabbinical Assembly/Ktav, 1977), 279.

15. Quoted in Stein, "Boundaries of Gender," 118.

16. Michael Brown, "It's Off to Camp We Go: Ramah, LTF, and the Seminary in the Finkelstein," in *Tradition Renewed: A History of the Jewish Theological Seminary of America,* ed. Jack Wertheimer (New York: Jewish Theological Seminary, 1997), 1:844–45; Jack Wertheimer, "JTS and the Conservative Movement," in *Tradition Renewed: A History of the Jewish Theological Seminary of America,* ed. Jack Wertheimer (New York: Jewish Theological Seminary, 1997), 2:430.

17. Siegel, *Conservative Judaism and Jewish Law,* 282.

18. Jack Wertheimer, ed., *Conservative Synagogues and Their Members: Highlights of the North American Study of 1995–96* (New York: Jewish Theological Seminary, 1996), 16.

19. Jacob R. Marcus, *American Jewish Woman: A Documentary History* (New York: Ktav, 1981), 894–96; Alan Silverstein, "The Evolution of Ezrat Nashim," *Conservative Judaism* 30 (Fall 1975): 41–51; Pamela S. Nadell, *Women Who Would Be Rabbis: A History of Women's Ordination, 1889–1985* (Boston: Beacon, 1998), 170–71.

20. Nadell, *Women Who Would Be Rabbis,* 170–214; Beth S. Wenger, "The Politics of Women's Ordination," in *Tradition Renewed: A History of the Jewish Theological Seminary of America,* ed. Jack Wertheimer (New York: Jewish Theological Seminary, 1997), 2:485–523.

21. Gerson D. Cohen, "The Conservative Movement in Our Tenth Decade," *Proceedings of the Rabbinical Assembly* 41 (1977): 42, quoted in Paula E. Hyman, "The Unfinished Symphony: The Gerson Cohen Years," in *Tradition Renewed: A History of the Jewish Theological Seminary of America,* ed. Jack Wertheimer (New York: Jewish Theological Seminary, 1997), 1:261.

22. Wenger, "Politics of Women's Ordination," 516.

23. "Our Readers React . . . to 'Two Worlds,'" *Outlook* 43 (Fall 1972): 8–9, 30.

24. Betty F. Maskewitz, "Women's Rights—The Debate Continues," *Outlook* 43 (Winter 1972): 17–18.

25. Gerson D. Cohen, "Women in the Conservative Movement: 1973," *Outlook* 44 (Winter 1973): 5–6.

26. David Aronson, "And Her Name Shall Be Called in Israel," *Outlook* 44 (Winter 1973): 7, 28.

27. Harold M. Kamsler, "Menstrual Taboos, Jewish Law and 'Kovod Tsibbur,'" *Outlook* 44 (Fall 1973): 12–13, 30.

28. "Here's What I Think: Readers React to Gerson D. Cohen's Article in the December Issue of Outlook," *Outlook* 44 (Summer 1974): 10–11, 27–30.

29. Etta Kamsler, "We Women," *Outlook* 45 (Winter 1974): 22, 34.

30. Marcia Baltimore Cohen, "How to Be a Jewish Working Mother," *Outlook* 50 (Winter 1979): 5, 18–19.

31. Jan Shulman, "The Impact of Feminism on the Jewish Woman: A Dia-

logue," *Outlook* 51 (Winter 1980): 7, 20; Fran Silver, "Reflections on Tefillot," *Outlook* 51 (Winter 1980): 6.

32. Cindy Daniels, "Can a Jewish Mother Survive in the Eighties?" *Outlook* 51 (Spring 1981): 9, 19; Rela Geffen Monson, "Jewish Macho in the '80s," *Outlook* 52 (Spring 1982): 7, 20.

33. Gerson D. Cohen, "On the Question of Ordination of Women," *Outlook* 50 (Spring 1980): 5, 22.

34. Sandy Eisenberg Sasso, "Women in the Pulpit," Judith Hauptman, "Talmud Pioneer," and Carol Berman, "A Minority of the Minority: The Jewish Woman on the Political Scene," *Outlook* 54 (Spring 1984): 6–8, 20–22.

35. Selma Weintraub, "Our President Speaks: Open Minds, Open Doors, Open Hearts," Ellen Ashkenazy Ufberg, "So What's Left for Me?" and Ruth Perry, "The Editor's Perspective: Altered and Altared States," *Outlook* 54 (Spring 1984): 4, 9, 10, 19, 21.

36. Only Hyman is identified as a member of Ezrat Nashim here. Paula E. Hyman, "The Other Half: Women in the Jewish Tradition," Judith Hauptman, "Women's Liberation in the Talmudic Period: As Assessment," and David M. Feldman, "Woman's Role and Jewish Law," *Conservative Judaism* 26 (Summer 1972): 14–21, 22–28, 29–39.

37. Stephen C. Lerner, telephone conversation with the author, April 20, 2003.

38. Mortimer Ostow, "Women and Change in Jewish Law," *Conservative Judaism* 29 (Fall 1974): 11.

39. Seymour Siegel, response, *Conservative Judaism* 29 (Fall 1974): 14–15.

40. Louis Linn, response, *Conservative Judaism* 29 (Fall 1974): 16.

41. Ellen F. Schiff, "Hannah, Jessica, Bessie—and Me?" *Conservative Judaism* 29 (Fall 1974): 36–41; Chaim Listfield, "Women and the Commandments," *Conservative Judaism* 29 (Fall 1974): 42–50.

42. Arthur E. Green, Linda R. Switkin, Dana Charry, and Mortimer Ostow, "Women and Change in Jewish Law: Responses to the Fall 1974 Symposium," *Conservative Judaism* 29 (Fall 1974): 37, 43, 46, 54.

43. Aaron H. Blumenthal, "The Status of Women in Jewish Law," *Conservative Judaism* 31 (Spring 1977): 24–40.

44. Miriam Shapiro and Chaim H. Pearl, "The Woman's Role: A Continuing Discussion," *Conservative Judaism* 32 (Fall 1978): 63–70.

45. Leonard Swidler, "Women and Torah in Talmudic Judaism," *Conservative Judaism* 30 (Fall 1975): 21–40.

46. Silverstein, "The Evolution of Ezrat Nashim," 41–51.

47. Shaye J. D. Cohen, "Women in the Synagogues of Antiquity," *Conservative Judaism* 34 (November–December 1980): 23–29.

48. Myra Shoub, "Jewish Women's History: Development of a Critical Methodology," *Conservative Judaism* 35 (Winter 1982): 33–46.

49. Schwarz, "Conservative Judaism and the Agunah," 37–44.

50. George E. Johnson, "The Lifestyle of Low Fertility: The Changing Needs of Jewish Women," *Conservative Judaism* 31 (Spring 1977): 16–20.

51. Lynn Gottleib, "The Secret Jew: An Oral Tradition of Women," *Conservative Judaism* 30 (Spring 1976): 59–62.

52. Benjamin E. Skolnic, "The Validity of Feminist Bible Interpretation," Burton L. Visotzky, "Midrash Eishet Hayil," David C. Kraemer, "A Developmental Perspective on the Laws of Niddah," Ivan G. Marcus, "Mothers, Martyrs, and Moneymakers: Some Jewish Women in Medieval Europe," Emily Taitz, "Kol Ishah—The Voice of Woman: Where Was It Heard in Medieval Europe?" Mayer I. Gruger, "The Jewish Goddess in an Orthodox Haggadah," Esther Altshul Helfgott, "Beth Shalom's Encounter with the Woman Question," Albert S. Axelrad, "Let Principle Encounter Principle: Conservative Judaism and Religious Egalitarianism," and Nahum M. Waldman, "The Designation of Marital Status in the Ketubah," *Conservative Judaism* 38 (Spring 1986): 10–82.

53. Waldman, "The Designation of Marital Status," 81; Axelrad, "Let Principle Encounter Principle," 78.

54. Gershon Schwartz, personal conversation with the author, April 11, 2003; Morton Leifman, "The Agunah Unbound," *Outlook* 54 (Spring 1984): 11, 18.

55. Nina Cardin, "Let Me In; Let Me Out," *Outlook* 54 (Spring 1984): 5, 18.

56. Gloria Cohen, telephone conversation with the author, April 8, 2003.

57. http://www.wlcj.org/services.html; Cohen, telephone conversation with the author.

58. Nina Beth Cardin, *Simhat Bat: Ceremonies to Welcome a Baby Girl* (New York: Women's League for Conservative Judaism, 1998).

59. *Under the Wings of the Sh'khinah: A Jewish Healing Service* (New York: Women's League for Conservative Judaism, n.d.).

60. *The Mitzvah of Bikkur Holim* (New York: Women's League for Conservative Judaism, 2000), 13.

61. Riv-Ellen Prell, "Communities of Choice and Memory: Conservative Synagogues in the Late Twentieth Century," in *Jews in the Center: Conservative Synagogues and Their Members,* ed. Jack Wertheimer (New Brunswick: Rutgers University Press, 2000), 341.

62. *Jewish Theological Seminary of America Academic Bulletin* (New York: Jewish Theological Seminary, 2002), 88; *Ziegler School of Rabbinic Studies: Hamadrikh, a Guide to the School 2002–2004* (Bel Air, CA: University of Judaism, n.d.), 20.

63. Barry A. Kosmin, "Coming of Age in the Conservative Synagogue: The Bar/Bat Mitzvah Class of 5755," in *Jews in the Center: Conservative Synagogues and Their Members,* ed. Jack Wertheimer (New Brunswick: Rutgers University Press, 2000), 250–51; Anne Lapidus Lerner, telephone conversation with the author, April 10, 2003; Stephanie Dickstein, telephone conversation with the author, April 14, 2003; Andrea Merow, telephone conversation with the author, April 30, 2003.

64. Steven M. Cohen and Judith Schor, "Gender Variation in the Careers of Conservative Rabbis: A Survey of Rabbis Ordained Since 1985," July 14, 2004 (unpublished paper); Lerner, telephone conversation; Dickstein, telephone conversation; Merow, telephone conversation; conversations with anonymous mem-

bers of the JTS rabbinical school class of 2004, May 14, 2004; Mychal Springer, "A Rabbinate on the Fringe," *Conservative Judaism* 48 (Fall 1995): 83.

65. Nina Beth Cardin, "Women in the Rabbinate: The First Ten Years," *Conservative Judaism* 48 (Fall 1995): 5.

66. Merow, telephone conversation. David M. Feldman attempts "to salvage for us the pluralism of mutual respect" in "Her Majesty's Loyal Opposition," *Conservative Judaism* 48 (Fall 1995): 42.

CHAPTER SEVEN

WOMEN IN ORTHODOXY

Conventional and Contentious

NORMA BAUMEL JOSEPH

During the twentieth century Jewish women were challenged with many opportunities and obstacles. In the context of North America, women were at times encouraged to "take their place" on the stage of American and Canadian culture. Some entered the world of business and education and did so with astounding success. But in the religious world of Orthodox Judaism and especially in the synagogue, their place was contested. As Orthodox women, they accepted the role of halakhah (Jewish law) as defining that place and were loyal to that heritage. But as daughters of modernity, educated in the Jewish legal system, some fought the limitation of their aspirations and the restrictions of roles placed upon them by medieval rabbinic constructions of gender. It is not a truism that Orthodox Judaism is fundamentally oppressive to women. Predictably, Orthodox Judaism has been characterized as degrading or subjugating its female adherents. This stereotype is inaccurate both historically and theologically. Yet there are numerous problem areas within the living tradition. Consequently, many women have challenged the community to eliminate areas of discrimination and enable women to participate more actively and completely in the practice of Judaism.

Both insiders and outsiders acknowledge that Orthodoxy does not welcome change. Particularly in terms of women's roles, the claim has been made that nothing ought to or can change. Although some Orthodox women do not experience any form of deprivation, others have refused to accept a frozen past as the ideal prototype for the future. Over the past century they have challenged the system to gain greater participatory roles. The clash between those seeking change and those upholding the unchanging nature of religious law and authority has generated increasing tension since the rise of religious feminism in the 1970s.[1] Orthodox feminists claim that despite the rhetoric of the Orthodox leadership, change and innovation are not anathema in Jewish law even in terms of women's involvement. Nonetheless, resistance to Orthodox feminism is surely based on fear of those claims for change. Especially problematic is the specter of the slippery slope. Rabbis and community leaders ask, "What will it lead to?" Fearful of major shifts and transformations, they cannot understand or agree. The divisions in Orthodoxy resonate with these questions focusing on women's role.

> Nowhere is the tension greater than with regard to the status and role of women within the Orthodox community. Nowhere has the dialogue—if it can be called that—between laity and rabbinate been less enlightening. There has been lots of heat and noise, many charges and counter charges, much name calling and too little light. Rabbis and their wives have, by and large, found satisfaction in current Orthodox practice. They appear to have no understanding that many women are not spiritually satisfied with these arrangements. Not all of the yearnings of these dissatisfied women may be satisfied. The problem is that many in the rabbinate do not appreciate their dissatisfaction. The result is a festering sore that will only get uglier if not attended to forthrightly.[2]

This essay will explore three distinct situations that illustrate the tension between Orthodox feminists and the rabbis upon whose authority they depend. First, a major transformation took place in the twentieth century in terms of educating females. It appears to have been approved quickly and then progressed slowly over a long period of time. The actual concept of democratic universal Jewish education was accepted without major clashes as the rabbinic position shifted from a talmudic polemic to one of normative acceptance. Yet the rabbis still vehemently disagree concerning the curriculum content.

Second, changes in ritual practice were often easily accommodated when perceived as signs of female piety and obedience. Increased prayer and study were applauded, as was greater attention to the legal requirements of kashrut, menstrual prohibitions, and hair covering. In this group, the motivating factors may at times have been feminist but often were not. Additionally, some holiday and many life cycle rituals were implemented without any legal dispute. The resulting shift permitted new ritual acts to take place at home and in the public realm. Notably, many of these ritual expansions were initiated at the grassroots level rather than via rabbinic directive.

Thus, in the expanding realm of ritual roles and participation, some developments took place below the gaze of rabbinic justification while the religious leadership welcomed others. However, some efforts by Orthodox women became sources of international conflict, often bringing down the censure of rabbis and rabbinical courts. In examining, as a third example, the notorious debate surrounding the women's *tefillah* (prayer) groups (WTGs), it will become apparent that while many women saw themselves as loyal and conventional Orthodox Jews, they were categorized as contentious and rebellious by much of the leadership. This persistent divergence in perception appears to be symptomatic of the controversy provoked by gender issues in Modern Orthodoxy.

Orthodox Judaism is a denomination that claims a continuous link with the past tradition.[3] Pointedly, within the movement there is a vociferous opposition to calls for change. It is, in fact, the denial of change in religious practice that particularly distinguishes this group from other Jewish movements: Orthodox Judaism emerged in the nineteenth century in opposition to those who wished to reform the tradition.[4] The challenge of change to the Orthodox sector is particularly difficult when it comes to questions of gender. Key debates have centered on the place of women's leadership, learning, and participation, particularly in ritual practice within the tradition. In fact, in the twentieth century the changes that were created by a variety of forces have allowed Orthodox women to be better educated, more ritually involved, and more communally active than previous generations had been. Nonetheless, problems remain as some Orthodox women continue to challenge the very system of traditional religious authority and practice that defines their lives. For Orthodoxy, the process of attending to these issues is complicated by a complete acceptance of and commitment to the absolute authority of halakhah. Since the law derives from an eternal God, it is deemed immutable and binding on all Jews. The rabbis, as committed scholars of the law, are charged with the responsibility for its interpretation and application. This system requires that all issues, including those related to gender, be adjudicated within the system, item by item, individual by individual, rabbi by rabbi rather than being based on ideologies of progress, public opinion, human rights, or gender equality. Further, these decisions are to be developed internally based only on legal precedents and not necessarily conforming or suited to contemporary external standards. Questions relating to gender touch on all these areas as demands for the redefinition of women's role, place, and status challenge the quest for preservation of tradition.

Given the Orthodox commitment to law and male rabbinic authority and its disdain for change, the feminist fight for equality of the 1970s did

Lilith Magazine, no. 9 (1982), cover: "Can an Orthodox Woman Champion Feminism?" Reprinted with permission from *Lilith* magazine—independent, Jewish, and frankly feminist. http://www.Lililth.org. Photo by Marilynne Herbert, http://www.Marilynne.Herbert.com.

not have the same resonance for Orthodox women. Many undertook a religious balancing act that attempted to preserve their commitment to halakhah by establishing their priorities as loyal daughters while attempting to develop an Orthodox feminism. Others refused the feminist appellation, afraid of charges of disloyalty and communal disfavor. So the tension grew between the women and the rabbinic leadership as well as between the women themselves, at times pitting the middle-aged activists (the so-called baby boomers) against the younger generation of learned women.

The dilemma facing Orthodox women is how to accommodate a commitment to halakhah and its (currently male) rabbinical hierarchical system with a personal passion for greater ritual agency; how to accept a centuries-old legal structure while pressing for change; and how to align a sense of distinctive gender roles (promoted by Jewish law) without succumbing to the disengagement or marginalization of women that has characterized Orthodox Judaism. Many Orthodox women in North America today oppose any changes in Orthodox Judaism. Others, however, are arguing that while the basic system is authentic and appropriate, there are elements that require transformation.[5] Orthodox feminists are women who are faithful to Orthodox Judaism but also challenge it defiantly. They are confident of their own commitment to Judaism and knowledgeable enough to seek precedent for innovation. They are committed to "expand[ing] the spiritual, ritual, intellectual, and political opportunities for women within the framework of *halakha*."[6] Orthodox feminists seek greater ritual responsibility and active roles as communal leaders to the full extent permitted within halakhah. They expect to be a part of the covenantal community as full members; they envision a partnership of equals. And all this is claimed with a sincere commitment to Jewish tradition and continuity.

EDUCATION

The lives of twentieth-century Orthodox Jewish women have been radically changed from those of Orthodox women of previous eras because of the development of schools for girls and young women.[7] Until the modern period, education was the preserve not only of the elite, but especially and primarily of the male members of the elite class.[8] This pattern was ruptured in the modern period with highly significant consequences. The essential context for the debate about women's place in modern Jewish society is the right of Jewish women to be educated. This advocacy came from the Orthodox world where it was initiated in Europe but took root in North America.

Sociological surveys show that in this century Jews in America have spent more time in specifically Jewish educational institutions than ever before. These schools, founded on the American concepts of democracy and public education, were, from the beginning, accessible to all Jews, even women.[9] Early on, American demands for universal public education fit well with immigrant needs to be absorbed into American culture. In order to "fit in," Jews sought access to American secular education. Orthodox leaders were consistently committed to creating specifically Jewish schools, and the value placed on education in America helped facilitate the maintenance of religious institutions. Jewish schools proliferated after World War II, which coincided with a growing American acceptance of ethnic diversity and distinctiveness. Many American Jews came to believe that some form of institutional Jewish education was a necessary condition for the survival of Judaism.[10] This democratization created a unique form of Jewish education in which not only privileged men but all Jews, including girls and women, were encouraged to learn.

The Orthodox rabbinic response to this transformation varied from reluctant approval to routine endorsement. At the beginning of the twentieth century in Russia, one woman, Sarah Schnirer, sought to establish a school to teach women about Judaism. An early advocate of combining secular and religious education for girls, Schnirer wanted to develop well-integrated graduates who would be knowledgeable about the world while also able to maintain a faithful respect for tradition and traditional authorities. Her model was so successful that by 1937 there were approximately 250 Beth Jacob schools with over 38,000 students spread all over Europe.[11]

Schnirer understood that rabbinical authorization and support were essential for her project. Lithuanian Rabbi Yisrael Meir HaKohen, known as the Hafetz Hayim, endorsed her plan, ruling that modern circumstances required formal education for girls because they could no longer learn the traditions by emulating their mothers.[12] His use of the language of obligation, of mitzvah, set a new legal standard even though his reasoning was based not on concern for the women themselves but on the fear that women would no longer be able to instruct their children properly.[13]

Following on these European legal precedents, many rabbinic leaders and institutions in America assumed girls' education to be normative.[14] Ironically, those who maintained that the law does not change first legitimated this new standard in the Orthodox world. By proclaiming continuity while denying change, the practice of universal education for female Jews became normative. The new practice was proclaimed in such a way that it was immediately accepted as part of a traditional Judaism, necessary for its survival and not perceived as a threat. Across North America, Jewish schools proliferated. Initially, most educational efforts took place in synagogue contexts. After World War II, almost equal numbers of boys and girls attended Orthodox day schools, some of which were coeducational and some of which taught the same subjects to both genders.

Thus, although radical, the inclusion of women in formal educational institutions was an evolutionary development without major recriminations. However, the discussion of curriculum, of exactly what girls may study, was intensely debated. The right-wing establishment refused to teach women Talmud. Some even rejected direct use of biblical texts. Girls were taught stories, rituals, and laws but without using the sacred texts themselves. The liberal Orthodox schools, labeled modern or centrist, were eager to include female students in all sectors of the curriculum. By the 1950s girls could receive an excellent Jewish education, especially in centrist Orthodox schools. The gender gap in education was most pronounced in right-wing Orthodox schools and in non-Orthodox supplementary education. In the 1970s Jewish postsecondary education increased. Yeshiva University, a standard-bearer of the Orthodox community, did not accept women into its seminary but established a separate school, Stern College, for women in 1954. It was there that Rabbi Joseph B. Soloveitchik inaugurated the controversial first Talmud lecture for women. Debates continue today over whether women can study and teach Talmud, with a variety of rabbinic opinions and communal practices.

Given the growth of private education in North America, the general increase in Jewish commitment to schools and the rise of feminist activism, the second half of the twentieth century exploded with opportunities for women to advance as Jewish students and scholars. Orthodox Jewish women today are far more likely than their grandmothers to have received some formal Jewish education. Some seek professional degrees and jobs, others propose only to learn, sit, and study for the love of Torah. In Israel, women can get official authorization from the chief rabbinate to act as advocates (*toanot*) in divorce law or advisors (*yoatsot*) in menstrual law. There are proliferating institutes, such as Drisha in New York and others in Israel too numerous to list, where any woman can study Jewish texts without any formal program or degree expected. Other women are entering the halls of academe, and still others have entered the beis medrash, the scene of intensive Torah study. Whether in coeducational environments, sex-segregated schools, or women-only study groups, as children or adults, women are amassing the tools and skills of Jewish scholarship. Ever so slowly the historically gender-restricted ideal of Torah study has become an egalitarian goal. Orthodox women, like their male counterparts, are advised to use their spare time studying some portion of Torah. Even though the emergence of independent knowledgeable women as leaders and potential rabbis was, in all likelihood, not anticipated by the earlier decisors, it was their decisions that unequivocally opened the path for that eventuality. And the subsequent absence of opposition is as remarkable as the rapid growth and almost universal acceptance of this educational innovation. Equally remarkable is the concurrence of this development with secular feminism. Though many pioneers in Jewish women's education disavow any connection to the current phase of feminist praxis, the surrounding culture of concern for women's participation has empowered these educational advances. Feminism both contributed to and framed these transformations. However, since the commitment to change is threatening, the conflict between feminist identification and Orthodox practice is ever present.

Orthodox women today are certainly better educated than were their mothers and grandmothers. Consequently, they are more involved both ritually and communally. For some, their current status is deemed both appropriate and acceptable. For others, many of whom are Orthodox feminists, the current absence of women in key areas and their lack of public participation is unacceptable. These women have benefited from the new educational environment. Their studies have, in fact, led them on a collision course. They want the permissible to be permitted. They know that they can retain their commitment to halakhah while demanding ever-expanding experiences within Orthodoxy.

RITUAL CELEBRATIONS

It is in the arena of ritual law that we find most conspicuous gender distinctions that have resulted in such an outcry for change in the last fifty years. The vast array of laws governing traditional Jewish ritual practices exempts women from fourteen rites.[15] Among those from which they are exempt are the recitation of the *shema* (a fundamental prayer), the donning of *tsitsit* (fringes) and *tefillot* (phylacteries), living in a *sukkah* (for festival of booths), waving a *lulav* (palm fronds), and hearing a shofar (ram's horn); among those for which they are still obligated are prayer, putting up a mezuzah (an amulet on the doorpost), and reciting the grace after meals. Over the centuries, the exemptions have been defined and refined by rabbinical decisions, and there have been shifts in women's performance. Some have become so ingrained in the ritual repertoire of pious women that memory of the exemption status is fading. For instance, women have been going to considerable lengths to hear the shofar on Rosh Hashanah for centuries. Some have argued that, based on the behavior of women, the legal category itself has shifted from exemption to one of obligation, which creates a remarkable precedent.[16] As noted above, many Jews, particularly those in the Orthodox community, today consider the education of girls and women, which was initially an exemption, bordering on a prohibition, an obligation and a right.[17] None of these shifts appears to have caused rabbinic ire. Most were accepted as motivated by women's practice and piety. But in the latter half of the twentieth century, women's increased ritual praxis was at times perceived as threatening, emanating from external feminist agendas.

Nonetheless, along with their increasing participation in traditional "male" rituals, women continued to create and participate in their own new rituals. Although this is true in all the denominational movements within the Jewish community, it is no less so within the Orthodox world. Many of these new rituals mark life cycle events, important occasions in the lives of individual women. Since the late 1960s, the birth of a baby girl is often celebrated with a *simhat ha'bat*, a "rejoicing of the daughter."[18] The bat mitzvah is an exemplar of new ritual celebration for females. Marking of the coming-of-age of twelve-year-old girls, this ritual performance enables young women to celebrate and acknowledge their Jewish commitment. Although the impetus may be the same for all denominations, the pattern that developed clearly differentiates between them. In Orthodox communities, due to legal considerations and a resistance to imitating the boy's public synagogue performance, some ceremonies are enacted in homes or schools, while others take place in synagogues when there are no formal prayer services. Some of the ceremonies are liturgical, but many use an educational format instead. An increasing number of girls celebrate their bat mitzvah at the separate women's prayer services discussed below. What is especially noteworthy is that in almost every Orthodox community today, many of whom eschew feminism, there exists some format for the recognition and celebration of a girl's initiation as an adult Jew on her twelfth birthday.[19] In addition, noticeable changes have begun appearing in weddings.[20] However, the saying of kaddish (the mourner's prayer for the dead) has forced some of the most personal confrontations between women and the rabbinate. Most modes of traditional ritual mourning included women, but there is one glaring hole: the mourner's kaddish prayer. According to many, there are no legal prohibitions against women reciting kaddish, which provides Jews in mourning with a public ritual mode for memorializing a deceased relative and expressing grief. Since the medieval custom specified male relatives, most women assumed that they could not recite it and probably were not bothered by the exemption. However, by the end of the twentieth century women increasingly opted for kaddish responsibilities, especially in the Orthodox community. The ensuing conflict created more problems than comfort. The difficulties arose from the fact that this prayer requires a "community" to respond to the mourner; in Orthodox Jewish practice this means that a quorum, or minyan, of men answer the woman reciting the prayer. Some rabbinic authorities are worried that this practice will cause women to want to be counted in the minyan and/or argue for mixed seating. Others are concerned with issues of modesty and women's place in the public arena of synagogue. However, more and more Orthodox congregations are welcoming, or at least permitting, women to say the kaddish.[21]

Orthodox women's ritual activities have also changed with regard to the holidays. As with the life cycle rituals, women are both taking on traditional "male" rituals as well as creating new ones. A few Orthodox women have voluntarily taken on the ritual obligation of wearing prayer shawls (tallitot and tsitsit) and tefillot. These women have encountered, and continue to encounter, the same type of opposition experienced by women who recite the mourner's kaddish. Again, the most contentious are those that take place in the public arena of synagogue services. Since 1971, some congregations have allowed women to dance with a Torah scroll on Simhat Torah. The battle over the Torah scrolls often was a real battle with men pulling the scrolls out of women's hands. There is no legal reason why women should be denied the joy of dancing with the Torah but it appeared to be symbolic of feminist unrest and was therefore deemed unacceptable. These public ritual activities were also grassroots developments but were not perceived as emanating out of piety; they were seen as directly challenging rabbinic authority. Yet many of these changes in holiday celebrations predate feminist concerns, deriving from a very traditional desire to participate and assume mitzvot (obligations). Consistent with this path of increased ritual activity is the growing custom of young married women covering their hair. Although by the middle of the twentieth century there was a significant movement among Orthodox women to move away from this custom, the 1970s witnessed an unexpected reversal, and today increasing numbers of Orthodox women are once again covering their hair upon marriage. Thus, although increased ritual activity would appear to fit with a feminist agenda, head covering challenges this impression. Perhaps, as some argue, increased ritual activity has nothing to do with feminist protest but is defined by careful attention to the rule of law in Orthodoxy. Or perhaps hair covering is linked to feminist causes as argued by some Muslim feminists.[22] Fundamentally, one would have to argue that not all of the increase in ritual activity is linked to feminism. Most cogently, the rise of Jewish education has both caused and been the result of the increase of praxis and commitment, predating and presupposing feminist concerns.

Orthodoxy values ritual obligation but historically enjoins women's exemption from a series of ritual practices. The cumulative result had been the absence of women from several key public positions and experiences. The above ritual innovations, while still maintaining a distinctive role and identity for Orthodox women, have begun to challenge and change that image. They developed a sense of female ritual activity in the public sphere that is normal and acceptable. They explored the limits of rabbinic authority and pushed the envelope of women's obedience, piety, and spiritual motivation.

PRAYER

Along with the new attitude toward education, American Orthodox Jews also, and even more overtly, developed new ideas regarding synagogue and prayer. Women praying is not a new phenomenon; some women even held leadership roles in this realm. But their presence in synagogue was mostly hidden. In fact, many texts equate the men's section with the synagogue exclusively and the women's section is treated as another constellation.[23] Certainly, men's prayers and synagogue activities were the central focus of all historic descriptions of communal synagogue life.[24]

Despite the conventional wisdom that women historically did not attend synagogue regularly, texts indicate the opposite.[25] In talmudic times, women were great synagogue goers; Tractate Sofrim (18:4) mentions that it was a duty (for men) to translate the biblical and prophetic portion of the week for the women. Texts from the rabbinic period indicate women's presence and activity during prayer, and the physical structures of European medieval synagogues clearly indicate that women attended services.[26] Some women, such as thirteenth-century Urania and Richenza, were eulogized as synagogue singers.[27] Because they were often unable to participate or even hear the main service, women relied on knowledgeable female elders, wise women known as *zogerin,* to direct them in separate prayers. Sometimes working at their own pace and level of understanding, often substituting Yiddish prayers known as *tkhines,* following their own female leaders, these women prayed publicly and communally as well as privately and individually.[28]

Through the study of these texts we can see that women did have a religious life that was prayer based, over which they had control and which frequently led them to a female-centered form of worship in the synagogue. Women prayed together, in synagogue led by a woman, in their own language, addressing their own issues. We can hear intimations of their sense

The Montreal Women's Tefillah Group: This photograph was taken on the occasion of Rosh Hodesh Tammuz (the Hebrew equivalent of July), during which the group celebrated a bride's upcoming wedding. Used with the permission of Norma Baumel Joseph.

of centrality, legitimacy, assumed authority, and powerful intimacy with God and the sacred realm. Were they marginalized? The women were on the margin from all perspectives of formal synagogue architecture, ritual practice, and community standards, but they were central to their own practice and perceptions. Contemporary pious women who still follow the centuries-old traditions of their ancestors attend synagogue services not only on the Sabbath but on Mondays and Thursdays as well.[29]

However, by the twentieth century many Orthodox women no longer prayed and seldom went to synagogue, even though this violated the law that states clearly that women are exempt from reciting one prayer (the shema) but obligated to another (tefillah).[30] Although rabbinic law includes many permutations and combinations of this basic mishnaic statement, the bottom line is that women are obligated to pray every day. And, throughout history, most women in traditional communities did pray, although, even as early as the seventeenth century, Rabbi Avraham Gumbiner (known as the Magen Avraham) commented on women's inattention to this commandment. In the modern period, this inattention expanded to such a degree that many religiously observant women did not pray because they thought they were exempt from prayer.[31]

WOMEN'S PRAYER GROUPS

The growth in Jewish education for women, however, collided with this nonobservance. The increasing numbers of modern-day Jewish women knowledgeable in the language and skills of prayer formed a growing community. Currently, most Orthodox women born after World War II know how to pray in Hebrew and do so regularly. In the 1970s some of these women, not only Orthodox, began to form their own separate prayer groups to maximize their personal prayer experience.[32] These groups followed Orthodox law; they accepted the model of gender separation and did not dispense with the *mehitsa* (the partition separating men and women during prayer), nor did they constitute themselves as a minyan.[33] They also sought and obtained (male) rabbinic approval for their activities. Nevertheless, the overwhelming rabbinic backlash of the Orthodox majority was vigorous though unexpected.[34] The debate surrounding the legal status of such expressions has neither reached consensus nor eliminated the growing phenomenon.[35] Women continue to gather in small groups seeking a halakhically recognized form of public, personal, and communal prayer. Along with supportive rabbis, they contend that they can touch, read from, and dance with a Torah. More important, the women maintain that they act out of a sincere commitment to Torah law. Rather than rebelling, they are requesting that the permissible be permitted them.

Debate continues to this day even as the prayer groups continue to proliferate. For many observers the women's tefillah groups (WTGs) are symbolic of the tension between Orthodoxy and feminism: "These women's Tefilah groups are the cutting edge of the Jewish women's movement within Orthodoxy."[36] They display a commitment to halakhah while demonstrating the problems within that legal system. They highlight the conflict between women's desires for greater involvement and their acceptance of rabbinic authority. Finally, they expose the weight given to public policy as an alternative to law in determining communal standards. In discussing women's increased presence and subsequent influence in halakhic deliberations, Tamar Ross writes eloquently about women's refusal to allow public policy decisions to override halakhic flexibility and their interests.

> Equipped with their heightened critical awareness and recognition of the role that nonjuridical considerations play in the application of *halakhic* principles, women participating in *halakhic* deliberations will inevitably come to challenge the regnant scale of values governing public policy issues that affect their concerns. Firsthand familiarity with the sources promotes the understanding that although stringency is sometimes a matter of religious zeal, at other times it reflects either a fear of the unknown or ignorance of the wealth of *halakhic* considerations and avenues for flexibility. To the extent that women . . . participate in *halakhic* discussion, they will serve as a natural restraint upon any tendency of the *halakhic* establishment to fight conservative battles for communal identity on the back of women's interests.[37]

Thus, in the process of seeking new ways to experience Judaism, to celebrate their roles as active adult Jews, the women challenged the practice of Judaism while maintaining that they were not rebelling. The origins of this particular phenomenon are unclear. Some claim that WTGs emerged from women's Simhat Torah dancing.[38] Others noted that it began in 1971 with small study, ritual, or prayer groups meeting in private homes.[39] One of the focal points of the original WTGs was Rosh Hodesh, the new moon, traditionally known as a women's holiday; others were based on monthly Sabbath services.[40] Lincoln Square synagogue in New York supposedly started a group in 1972 while Harvard University's Hillel started a prayer group in the spring of 1973. A group of women in Baltimore decided to form a women's prayer group in 1974.[41] Products of modern Jewish educational institutions, these women knew how to pray but were not satisfied with their normal routine of prayer. They understood the importance of ritual participation and sought to increase their roles as practicing Jews in a new communal format. Influenced by the prevailing women's movement as well as by traditional patterns of gender separation, they resolved to pray together once a month.

Soon, in several communities, women, in conjunction with their rabbis, established prayer groups. Groups currently exist in the United States, Canada, Australia, Israel, and England.[42] By the end of the twentieth century, many WTGs gathered monthly and on special occasions such as a bat mitzvah, female baby naming, or bridal celebration. In answer to a recent query, only 11 of 47 groups responded that Rosh Hodesh is linked to their service in some way. Yet the early selection of Rosh Hodesh marked this movement from the beginning. Although today many new groups do not claim any relationship to this holiday, it linked them to a past tradition and gave them a sense of historical legitimacy. It blended the unprecedented with conventional patterns: resurrecting an ancient tradition and merging it with a feminist design. It also established unacknowledged links with other Rosh Hodesh groups that are not Orthodox or strictly prayer events. This ancient New Moon holiday was historically known as a special day for women, a gift from God to the righteous women of Israel. In its new configuration, some women gathered on Rosh Hodesh to pray in exactly the same format as men; gathering in a group, in a synagogue, leading services, reading from the sacred Torah scrolls, sometimes wearing the special garments of tsitsit and tefillot. The feminist agenda of establishing women's agency by placing them in the center was fused with traditional Jewish patterns of gender segregation and rabbinic authority. Women naively expected that their behavior would be accepted if not applauded since they were relying on past traditions and emulating past practices. Unlike Conservative and Reform Jews, they appeared to accept the ideal of separation. Consequently, they elected to pray as a group of women—only. They also wanted to act according to Orthodox norms. Thus, they asked for rabbinic approval. Submission to halakhic authority—male authority—marked this endeavor as significantly different from other feminist activities. They did not join Conservative feminists in demanding rabbinic ordination for themselves. In fact, some of their Jewish sisters mocked them for continuing to play the "good girl" submissive role. Many participants were practicing Orthodox Jews, some were newcomers (*ba'alot teshuva*), and, even though most were feminist, they continued to seek rabbinic approval, guidance, and advice. This expanding group of women was seeking new ways to pray to experience a more active form of participation and a woman-centered service without abandoning their commitment to Orthodox halakhah. In spite of everything, Orthodox praxis was their guiding standard and goal.

Operating as traditional Jews, they were dismayed by the response: rabbinic disapproval was swift and strong. Although some rabbis and congregations were supportive, the overwhelming majority of Orthodox Jews perceived this nascent movement as a rebellion, a threat to "tradition." Many of the groups were not allowed to hold their services in synagogues, few were allowed access to the Torah scroll, and some were even threatened with communal ostracism. The women thought of themselves as Orthodox, accepting certain restrictions and complying with Jewish law. The larger community labeled them disobedient. Clearly, then, there were two perceptions present in this controversy: Were they being submissive or subversive, conventional or contentious?

In first setting out to pray with women only, the women themselves were experimenting with a new experience of prayer while accepting the liturgical restrictions within the construct of rabbinic guidelines. Fealty to the law and its rabbinic interpreters is an Orthodox standard that the women continue to be committed to. Living within an Orthodox world, these women did not attempt or claim revolution. Yet the rabbis found their acts subversive. The women were forming groups outside the norm, separating from the community, pretending that their prayer format was as "kosher" as that of the regular congregation. What did they want? What would it lead to? Who were they to demand this? Why weren't the old ways good enough for them?

Given that women are exempt from public prayer, prayer at a specific time, and the wearing of certain ritual garments, accepting increased ritual obligations might appear to some as voluntarily paying more taxes. Why do it? Interestingly, some of the arguments against women's prayer groups have used this line of reasoning: women have enough to do; why increase the burden? But for many Jews, ritual has great value. Performing mitzvot, accepting God's commandments, and fulfilling obligations are all signposts of merit and devotion in Judaism. Thus, the women claimed to be following traditional Jewish values: seeking connections to God, covenant, and community. Moreover, the women asserted they were following in their female ancestors' footsteps. Women in the past increased their ritual obligations and prayed, sometimes publicly. The difference in this case revolved around issues of public performance and communal representation. Obviously, the initial thrust for increased women's rituals in the Jewish community emanated out of an equal access motivation. The women's prayer groups, like the elaboration of bat mitzvah ceremonies and baby namings, attempted to replicate male patterns of ritual participation. Although these innovations were focused on women, religion was still being defined in male normative terms. Orthodox women's prayer groups then were formed to give women a chance to act out communal prayer in imitation of the male pattern. Some see this format as an experiment, as a means to an end of greater participation in the regular integrated communal service. They appear to be seeking an egalitarian Orthodox service, exactly what the rabbis fear.[43] Others vociferously disagree with that approach and maintain a desire for a women-only experience. They declare that they would not abandon their separatist service no matter what became available to them in synagogue settings. Recently on the Women's Tefillah Network (WTN) Listserv there was a heated discussion about this, emanating out of descriptions of women's dancing with and reading of the Torah on Simhat Torah.

Despite these internal differences and other distinctions of style and purpose, they all seem to agree that they are following halakhic guidelines and norms.

In the clash between these groups and the rabbinic right, the facts of the case are as misrepresented as are the motives of both sides. Each group misunderstands and misrepresents. The opposing rabbis have continuously labeled the women's prayer groups "minyanim." The normative definition of minyan has become entrenched as ten males over the age of thirteen. In the original instance of the Baltimore group, Rabbi Shlomo Goren, chief rabbi of Israel, in a private responsum (legal decision), gave the women permission to realize minyan status and say all the prayers.[44] This controversial decision was rendered under conditions of secrecy and confidentiality. Other groups were not given nor sought such permission, and Rabbi Goren retracted his permission in 1989. Although there is legal precedent for challenging the gender restriction of the minyan concept, most other women's groups consciously avoid halakhic controversy. Hence, they do not say certain prayers and avoid the minyan format.[45] Nonetheless, they have been accused of undermining the legal categories of prayer and gender.

In 1985, the famous "Riets 5" responsum was issued.[46] It came from a respected group of Yeshiva University rabbis condemning the women's prayer groups. The main critique focused on the quorum issue. But since the groups themselves were not using that category, the criticism appears inadequate. Their next point centered on the idea of communal allegiance. If the women were praying separately, they were guilty of abandoning the community (*poresh min ha'tsibbur*). This claim was perhaps the most insulting to the women. Their efforts came as a result of feeling separated from the prayer community, neglected and shunted off to the sidelines. Again the inaccuracy of the charge is glaring. According to Jewish law, women are not obligated to be present nor were they expected at communal services. Their rabbis never gave sermons encouraging or demanding their attendance. Books on women and Judaism such as the popular one by Moshe Meiselman state that women's only and highest prayer level is the private one. For so many years, women were encouraged to pray alone at home. So why would they be considered abandoning their communal commitment by praying separately with other women? After many years of private censure, this public denunciation created a backlash of rage as well as a growing interest in it.

The women and their supporters fought back. Rabbi Avi Weiss produced a book on women and prayer as a way of explaining the legal basis of his support. Rivka Haut and others wrote letters and explanations. The WTN, founded by Haut in reaction to the rabbis, produced a newsletter enabling groups to keep in touch and share information. Early conferences focusing on women and Jewish law were framed to include material on women's prayer groups: two in New York (1983, 1988) and two in Israel (1985, 1989). Women continued to form new prayer groups. The movement was growing despite—or perhaps because of—rabbinic displeasure.

WOMEN OF THE WALL (WOW)

One major development emerged from the First International Jewish Feminist Conference in 1988, held in Israel. Some of the women who were involved in their own prayer groups in America decided to pray together at the Western Wall in Jerusalem (the Kotel). Eighty women from all denominations joined together on a Thursday morning and a new movement in Israel was born: the Women of the Wall.[47] In 1989, Israeli and diaspora women joined in an interminable ongoing legal action during which, for the first time in history, the religious rights of Jewish women were argued in a court of law. The Supreme Court asked for a response from the state, and in the interim issued an injunction against women praying out loud with a Torah at the wall. The Israeli group Women of the Wall and the North American International Coalition for the Women of the Wall have been working since that time to attain this basic religious right. On May 22, 2000, the Supreme Court unanimously upheld the right of women to pray at the wall out loud while wearing prayer shawls, but opposition both from political parties in the Knesset and from individuals at the wall gained momentum and the decision was not actualized. In October 2003, the Supreme Court reversed its decision and ruled instead that the state of Israel must provide a secure site for the women. Another location, Robinson's Arch, was chosen by the government, but this is a proposal that the Women of the Wall have consistently rejected. As of this writing the issue has not been resolved, but the legal battle is over. The government prepared Robinson's Arch in 2004 but the Women of the Wall claim the court case was only about the Kotel itself and so continue to pray there without their full Torah service, which they hold at another site.

Potentially momentous, yet in substantive ways nothing has happened; the Israeli courts and government committees have continuously avoided any operational decision or closure. By not rendering a decision, the state effectively silenced both groups of women. Yet the women maintained their allegiance to the cause and the interdenominational Israeli group has continued praying together even though political and legal issues complicate the situation: "In Israel, especially after the prayer and Torah-related activities of the Women of the Wall garnered virulent *haredi* opposition for over two decades, *tefillah* groups became more and more the symbol of Orthodox feminism and the target of antifeminist ire."[48]

More than ten years after the founding of the WTN and nine years after the first WOW experience, the Jewish Orthodox Feminist Alliance (JOFA) was founded by Blu Greenberg. Orthodox feminists had come of age with many items on their agenda including women's prayer. In 1997, the first JOFA conference was held. A few weeks before the conference, a group of rabbis from Queens banded together to denounce women's prayer groups and forbade any of their congregants or students from attending bat mitzvah ceremonies in a WTG. Again the claims and counterclaims were contradictory. The dispute dominated the Jewish media and gave a great deal of advance publicity to the JOFA conference. Instead of the expected four hundred attendees one thousand women registered. That number doubled for the next conference. Far from removing women from their community, women's prayer groups created community for many Orthodox women.

RABBINIC DECISIONS

The women and their supporters, however, have also miscalculated and misconstrued the rabbinic response. At the outset, Rabbi Goren's permission was to be kept a secret. To a certain degree the private decision was violated when it became public. Consequently, Rabbi Goren was so virulently attacked that he withdrew his original decision.

In casting about for authoritative legal resources, some relied on specific responsa as precedents. Significantly, those documents cannot be read as unqualified endorsements. Scrutinizing these ambiguous legalities, misreading, and misrepresenting is an intricate process. One of the main sources used is the decision of Rabbi Moshe Feinstein. In an unpublished but widely circulated letter written in his name by his grandson on the issue of women's prayer groups, he says,

> However, as a matter of theory alone, it is possible to state that were there a group of religiously observant women whose considerations were solely for the sake of heaven and without any contesting of God's Torah or Jewish custom, why would it be appropriate to prevent them from praying together? They could also read from the Torah scroll, but they should be careful not to do so is such a way as to cause error that this constitutes the congregational reading?[49]

This text does reveal the theoretical validity of the act, but it does not endorse actual women's prayer groups. Between the righteous and the rebellious, the distinguishing factor is motive. Strikingly, nowhere in the text do we hear the voice of the women involved.

Various contemporary decisions concerning women's ritual participation hinge on just such a determination of motive. In one responsum (*Hanashim Hashaʾananot, Iggerot Moshe, Orakh Hayim* 4:49),[50] Rabbi Feinstein articulates his position concerning women and ritual participation. He posits that since some women today are influenced by external movements, they are angry and think they can change the law. Although he notes that they are *shomrei torah* (faithful to the Torah), he calls them heretics. In wanting to change practice, he thinks that the root of their desire stems from a denial of the eternal nature of the Torah. Their motives render the requested acts forbidden.

Remarkably, in the very same paragraph, he notes that women may of course opt to perform rituals, such as shofar and lulav, from which they are officially exempted: "To be sure, permission is given to every woman to perform mitzvoth that the Torah did not command her. They are even considered to have a duty and a reward in the performance of these obligations. In fact, according to the judgment of the *Tosaphists* they are entitled [authorized] to make the appropriate blessing. As is our custom women observe the commandments of *shofar* and *lulav* and even make the appropriate blessings. Accordingly [given this, lit.], even *tsitsit*."[51]

These acts are encouraged since Rabbi Feinstein has no doubt that the motives stem from a keen desire to fulfill God's law. Women who are conscientious about these extra practices are deemed righteous. Only those who are influenced by the women's movement are called rebellious. He further clarifies this point in issuing his decision: "However, since [in our case] it is not for this purpose, rather the desire comes out of a rebellion against God and his Torah, it cannot be an act of mitzvah at all. On the contrary, it is a forbidden act; forbidden as a heresy that she expects a change in the laws of the Torah."[52] Given his clear statements in these two texts, it appears curious if not inappropriate for the women to use his decision as supportive. Yet their situation and conviction compels their reliance on his letter. Added to that is his theoretically permissive stance. Finally, if he condemns the act because of motive, they claim that their motives are pure and "for the sake of heaven." The debate persists with both sides using Rabbi Feinstein's words. The same confusion surrounds the position of Rabbi J. B. Soloveitchik. Since we do not have a written text of his opinion, we can rely only on oral tradition. Some of his disciples claim that he gave his tacit permission to the formation of WTGs. Thus, Rabbis Shlomo Riskin and Weiss claim to have had the crucial support of Modern Orthodoxy's key spokesman. However, Rabbis Moshe Meisleman and Mordechai Twersky claim the absolute opposite. In their reportage, Rabbi Soloveitchik was adamant in his opposition. Rabbis Aryeh and Dov Frimer claim that while the Rav (as he was known by his students) found no objections halakhically, it was due to public policy that he thought the innovation of women's prayer groups unwise and unacceptable.[53] It is ironic that the women who wish to engage in greater ritual activity out of sense of devotion to God are thought of as rebellious. The uses of tradition and law in these disparate arguments expose elements of religious boundaries, self-identities, and gender distinctions that appear to plague Modern Orthodoxy.

GROWTH OR DECLINE

Reading the negative rabbinic positions might lead one to think that there were many women's prayer groups. Despite the international spread of the groups and perhaps because of the opposition, their numbers are not large. The WTN now uses the Internet to communicate and has a list of more than sixty groups.[54] But in the scheme of Jewish demographics and organizational escalation, these numbers do not represent a significant population. Sylvia Barack Fishman found that "not a single one of the women, rabbis, and scholars interviewed for this study believes the *tefillah* groups to be the most important result of feminism and related social trends in the Orthodox community. Many women and men expressed the belief that the groups were a transient or transitional phenomenon."[55]

In another study, Ailene Nusbacher explores the growth patterns of these groups and poses some concerns over their future.[56] She found that although there were numerous groups and even new ones forming, the membership of existing groups was small and not necessarily expanding. There is a preponderance of professional workingwomen and newcomers to religion. Most of the women are in their forties and fifties. In a study conducted by Sidney Langer at Stern College for women, he found that although over 80 percent were actively engaged in daily prayer, 77 percent had never participated in a WTG.[57] More significantly, they were not interested. The majority of students either rejected separate women's prayer or were ambivalent. Interestingly, the author did not find that doubts about the halakhic status were the decisive issue. The vast majority of those who had attended went for a special occasion such as a bat mitzvah. Nusbacher notes that high school girls stopped attending because of the pressure from their peers and religious studies teachers. Nusbacher posits that text study was more attractive to the younger women than were prayer groups. Along with Rabbis Aryeh and Dov Frimer, who have written extensively on Jewish law and WTGs, she concludes pessimistically that there were serious obstacles to the growth and spread of these groups.[58]

Although Stern College students do not attend WTGs, Columbia University women do. At Columbia, there was even a daily women's prayer service begun in 1997. Clearly, the Stern faction is mostly Orthodox and the Columbia group is denominationally mixed. But the university cohort should not be overstated. There are some tefillah groups on campuses in North America but they are rare. It might be that prayer groups will always be small and that their membership will always consist of women who are older. If young girls are not joining, their mothers are. Is this possibly an age-grading phenomenon? When I asked a number of college students why they were not attending, they readily told me that they did not want to be branded "feminist" in their community. They wanted to remain within established Orthodox norms; they especially wanted to be able to marry the "right guy." Clearly, this form of worship will not satisfy all women. Whether this is a factor of preference for study, fear of being labeled, or a gender gap is yet to be determined. But it is undeniable that the movement, though small, is threatening and growing. Rivka Haut optimistically notes that although her daughter may have been one of the only young women in their WTG, her granddaughter's experience in Maryland is one of normalcy and acceptance. Thirty years, after all, is a short time. Perhaps just as the education transformation took one hundred years, it is too soon to claim a definitive position on the success and viability of these groups.

Nonetheless, there are clear accomplishments. Women who attend do so searching for meaningful prayer or a spiritual experience, and to escape a prevalent sense of exclusion. They seek ways within the Orthodox community to experiment with religious expressions and they search for knowledge that will inform their praxis. They have also learned a wide range of prayer skills not attainable in their standard prayerful lives. According to Sylvia Barack Fishman, "[T]here is no doubt that tefillah groups have played and continue to play an extremely significant role in initiating and fostering more widespread changes in other areas of Orthodox life."[59]

Given the small numbers, the rabbinic antagonism is remarkable and disproportionate. Perhaps it signals a systemic problem. More than just a small matter of once a month prayer, the reactions to this "movement" indicate a much larger series of problems within Orthodoxy. Undoubtedly the clearest example of the conflict for women within Orthodox Judaism is found in the Jewish divorce process. One could argue that the current process of Jewish divorce calls into question the validity of any claim for feminism coexisting with Orthodoxy.

Although a Jewish divorce is a halakhic requirement for all Jews, it is in the Orthodox community with its strict adherence to law that we find the most egregious problems. Many Orthodox Jews, male and female, many who are far removed from any feminist concern, will admit that one of the greatest problems facing Jewish law today is how to resolve this legal injustice. It is explicitly in divorce that all criticism of halakhah from a feminist perspective finds its cumulative or symbolic center. And it is here that the call for authentic change reaches a crescendo. The transformations listed above emanate from women's desire for increased knowledge and involvement. But with divorce the basic claims of justice in Judaism are most severely challenged. No one can argue that Jewish law treats women nobly given the current state of divorce law. Jewish divorce, like any other, can be simple or complicated; a release or a tragedy; straightforward or a swindle. It can set people free to resume or reinvent their lives, or it can embroil individuals and families in a never-ending cycle of abuse. The original intent of rabbinic Judaism was to ensure a tolerable disengagement. Regrettably, the current implementation does not ensure that minimal standard. And, although primarily an Orthodox issue, it also affects many other Jews, especially those living in Israel where all divorces are determined by Orthodox Jewish law. According to the law, it is the husband who must initiate a divorce. If he is either unable or unwilling to give her a get (Jewish divorce), she cannot remarry. The increasing number of "chained women" (*agunot*) and the proliferation of unsettled cases have prompted many individuals and organizations to propose solutions, but so far there is no consensus or universal acceptance of any of these proposals. In the meantime, women are abused by a system of law that claims to be just. The conflicts between Orthodoxy and feminism culminate with agunot. The feminist critique and call for transformation resonate within Orthodox feminism, but there is no easy partnership or negotiation here.

CONCLUSION

Orthodox feminist women see themselves as loyal and operating within the bounds of established Jewish law; rabbinical opponents see them as subversive. How shall we understand this group of American Jews? By accepting Orthodox standards, how can they be seen as destroying the system? By accepting halakhic rules, are they reinscribing that patriarchal system? Are they co-opted into the system while they struggle against it? Questions abound. Why did WTGs choose ritual and why follow the male standard for prayer? If one function of ritual is to establish community, to link the individual to a recognized group and pattern of belief and behavior, then the question arises as to what community is being established by these women's groups. Is there a new concept of Orthodoxy and of community? Are women present and representative of it? Is this what threatens the opposing rabbis?

Women's tefillah groups can be seen as the exemplars of Orthodoxy's struggles with modernity and with gender issues. Merely by meeting once a month they challenged the male face of Orthodox synagogue prayer. As with the study of Torah, they took on male ritual expertise and achieved something. Praying with women in an Orthodox setting destabilizes male hegemony even as it pays deference to it. Seeking a "kosher" way to express their spiritual yearning, they are linked to their female ancestors and to male rabbinic modes of interpretation and legal application. Their concerns put women front and center and challenge the system in the name of the system. In that sense women's prayer groups subvert an androcentrism that exclusively links male public performance with God's central covenant. Women's groups experimented with a variety of formats—study, prayer, meditation, new age ritual, personal discussion—in an attempt to address their own spiritual needs within a Jewish context. This led many women to an awareness of the lost worlds of women's different ritual practice and to a sense of historic community. Women in the past had been ritual experts.[60] They had a direct intimacy with God as well as a sense of their own empowerment. They performed and created ritual that addressed their needs with an unquestioned sense of legitimacy. Some Orthodox women continue that tradition today in a variety of ways. Blu Greenberg summarizes the significance of these events in the following way:

> Earlier, I stated that in the Orthodox community feminism is not systematically used as a hermeneutic to redefine the law. But one can easily see that it has influenced change. Everything I have described is a departure from the past yet is considered *halakhically* acceptable by some segment of the Orthodox community. . . . Taken item by item none are earth-shaking but all together they add up to something highly significant: the redefinition of women's role in the community.[61]

Women in the Orthodox world expected and accepted to defer to their male authorities and traditions. The women of these prayer groups do not deny that. Nevertheless, they broke with that tradition, asking to be included in new ways, forcing accommodation to their needs. Their resistance to rabbinic opposition is based on their own knowledge, skills, and needs and that is radical.

NOTES

I wish to thank Riv-Ellen Prell for her patience and help. Susan Sered read and commented on an earlier version of a section of this essay from a 2001 American Academy of Religion conference. Sonia Zylberberg, my research assistant, contributed to this article in her usual efficient way.

1. For a full description, see Blu Greenberg, "The Feminist Revolution in Orthodox Judaism in America," in *Divisions between Traditionalism and Liberalism in the American Jewish Community: Cleft or Chasm,* ed. Michael Shapiro (Lewiston, NY: Edwin Mellen, 1991); Sylvia Barack Fishman, *Changing Minds: Feminism in Contemporary Orthodox Jewish Life* (New York: American Jewish Committee, 2000).

2. Marc Stern, "On Constructively Harnessing Tensions between Laity and Clergy," March 2003, available at http://www.jlaw.com/Commentary/ms-Laity Clergy.html.

3. Note that Orthodoxy is not monolithic: the multifaceted Orthodox community contains a large variety of disparate positions. Ranging from "ultra" to "modern," this sector of Jews includes Hasidic groups, yeshivish Jews, Ashkenazi and Sephardi Orthodoxies, Agudah followers, Mizrahi Religious Zionists, Modern Orthodox, and many combinations thereof. No other Jewish denomination includes such a diverse and fragmented distribution of positions, especially with regard to women's roles.

4. The most notable of these was Rabbi Moses Sofer, known as the Hatam Sofer, who claimed the "the new is forbidden in the Torah."

5. Greenberg, "The Feminist Revolution in Orthodox Judaism in America," 55–78.

6. As stated in the mission statement of JOFA, the Jewish Orthodox Feminist Alliance. See http://www.jofa.org.

7. I situate a detailed explanation of this claim in "Jewish Education for Women: Rabbi Moshe Feinstein's Map of America," *American Jewish History* 83 (1995): 205–22.

8. Note that this phenomenon that was not unique to Jews; it also existed for the larger communities within which the Jews resided.

9. Jonathan Sarna, *American Judaism* (New Haven: Yale University Press, 2004); Reuven Bulka, ed., *Dimensions of Orthodox Judaism* (New York: Ktav, 1983); Lloyd P. Gartner, ed., *Jewish Education in the United States: A Documentary History* (New York: Teachers College Press, Columbia University, 1970).

10. Perhaps this has been the impetus for the prevalence of the nostalgic myth of learned ancestors.

11. See Deborah Weissman, "Bais Yaakov," in *The Jewish Woman: New Perspectives,* ed. E. Koltun (New York: Schocken, 1976), 142.

12. His plan, of course, did not extend to Talmud and other esoteric subjects still reserved for men. He also did not envision an egalitarian study hall but a system of separate schooling for male and female students.

13. Orthodox Rabbi Samson Raphael Hirsch of Frankfurt/Main also extended Torah studies to women in the late nineteenth century. Drawing on the fact that there had already been schools for girls in Germany throughout the century, albeit with very limited Jewish content, Hirsch claimed that women had always had some kind of access to study and, further, that all women were obligated to study. But his claim reified divided gender roles and different rules for women who, he stated, did not need all the mitzvot or rituals because they were constructed differently. Rabbi Samson Raphael Hirsch, *Horeb: A Philosophy of Jewish Life and Commentaries,* trans. Dr. I. Grunfeld (London: Soncino Press, 1962), vol. 2, chap. 75, sec. 494. See also his commentary on Gen. 1–3. I discuss these differing rabbinic views in "A Feminist Scenario of the Jewish Future," in *Creating the Jewish Future* (Toronto: Centre for Jewish Studies, York University, Alta Mira Press, 1998).

14. According to Rabbi Moshe Feinstein, one of the most prominent American Orthodox decisors, the education of females was a simple matter and not particularly controversial; he declared it obligatory for a father to pay for his daughter's education. Rabbi M. Feinstein, *Iggerot Moshe, Yoreh Deah* (New York, 1981), 1:137, 2:113, 3:87.

15. See Rachel Biale, *Women and Jewish Law* (New York: Schocken, 1984), for a detailed discussion of the relationship between women and the mitzvot (10–43).

16. Arlene Pianko, "Women and the Shofar," *Tradition* 14, 4 (1974): 53–62.

17. See my article "Jewish Education for Women: Rabbi Moshe Feinstein's Map of America," *American Jewish History* 83 (1995): 205–22.

18. Because there is not any established ritual there are many variations in the individual rites. Many include the *mi sheberakh* prayer that is used in the naming ceremony in the synagogue, wine and candles, and references to biblical and historically significant Jewish women as well as the compulsory naming of the baby. Mothers are active participants in the ritual, and, in rare instances, a female relative takes on the role of *sandakit,* the female counterpart to the male *sandak* who holds the baby boy at his circumcision.

19. See my article on bat mitzvah: "Ritual Law and Praxis: Bat Mitsva Celebrations," *Modern Judaism* 22, no. 3 (2002): 231–60.

20. Some involve the *Shabbat kallah,* the bride's *tish,* and the recitation of *sheva berachot* (the seven blessings to the couple under the *chupah* [wedding canopy]).

21. Rochelle L. Millen, "The Female Voice of Kaddish," in *Jewish Legal Writings of Women,* ed. Micah D. Halpern and Chana Safrai (Jerusalem: Urim, 2002). See Millen, *Women, Birth, and Death in Jewish Law and Practice* (Hanover, NH: Brandeis University Press, 2004).

22. Sajida Alvi, Homa Hoodfar, and Sheila McDonough, eds., *Muslim Veil in North America: Issues and Debates* (Toronto: Women's Press, 2003).

23. The words "beit haknesset" are consistently used for the men's section while the women's area is specifically labeled as either the "weibershul" or "Ezrat Nashim." There is even a halakhic debate over whether women can say kaddish from the women's section since if it is not part of the synagogue then they are not praying with the required male quorum.

24. Yet it is clear from Bernadette Brooten's work that we cannot assume that women were historically inactive in synagogue leadership roles. Brooten, *Women Leaders in the Ancient Synagogue* (Chico, CA: Scholars Press, 1982).

25. See various essays in Susan Grossman and Rivka Haut, eds., *Daughters of the King* (Philadelphia: Jewish Publication Society, 1992), especially Susan Grossman, "Women and the Jerusalem Temple," 15–38, and Hannah Safrai, "Women and the Ancient Synagogue," 39–49. Text references include: TB Ber. 17a, Sot. 22a, Lev. R. 9, 9, Sofrim 18:4. See also Solomon Schechter, "Women in Temple and Synagogue," *Studies in Judaism,* vol. 1 (Philadelphia: Jewish Publication Society, 1911).

26. Brooten, *Women Leaders.* Medieval European synagogues had a separate women's section, frequently called the weibershul. This area, sometimes a room or annex, was so separate that some women, called zogerin, would lead the others in prayer. The communities in Worms and Frankfort built separate buildings for the women (*Encyclopaedia Judaica,* s.v. "mehizah," 11:1235, 192, 226). The Be᾿er Hetev in his commentary on the laws of reading the *megillah* notes that some young women went to the women's synagogue, *beit ha-knesset nashim* (Shulhan Arukh, OH 689).

There are numerous sources confirming women's presence in the medieval synagogue. See Israel Abrahams, *Jewish Life in the Middle Ages* (Philadelphia: Jewish Publication Society, 1981); Emily Taitz, "Kol Ishah—The Voice of Woman: Where Was It Heard in Medieval Europe," *Conservative Judaism* 38, no. 3 (1986): 46–61; Howard Tzvi Adelman, "Italian Jewish Women at Prayer," in *Judaism in Practice: From the Middle Ages to the Early Modern Period,* ed. Lawrence Fine (Princeton: Princeton University Press, 2001). For a comprehensive annotated bibliography, see Cheryl Tallan, "Medieval Jewish Women in History, Literature, Law, and Art: A Bibliography," available at http://www.brandeis.edu/hirjw/pubs/MEDWOM_2006_bib.doc.

27. Taitz, "Kol Ishah," 54.

28. See Chava Weissler, *Voices of the Matriarchs: Listening to the Prayers of Early Modern Jewish Women* (Boston: Beacon, 1998). There are now a number of publications and collections of these Yiddish prayers translated into English.

29. Susan Sered, *Women as Ritual Experts* (New York: Oxford University Press, 1992), 112–14, describes elderly retired women who do not know how to pray but go to synagogue regularly as an expression of piety.

30. Berakhot 20b.

31. Hence the numerous articles and books published recently trying to confirm that women are obligated to pray and that historically they did so. An interesting series of articles in Judaism highlights the various readings and consequences of the level of women's obligation. See Judith Hauptman, "Women and Prayer: An

Attempt to Dispel Some Fallacies," *Judaism* 42 (1993): 94–103; Michael Broyde, Joel B. Wolowelsky, and Judith Hauptman, "Further on Women as Prayer Leaders and Their Role in Communal Prayer: An Exchange," *Judaism* 43 (1993): 387–413.

32. There are numerous descriptions and discussions of women's prayer groups. Rivka Haut, "Women's Prayer Groups and the Orthodoxy Synagogue," in *Daughters of the King,* ed. Susan Grossman and Rivka Haut (Philadelphia: Jewish Publication Society, 1992); Avraham Weiss, *Women at Prayer: A Halakhic Analysis of Women's Prayer Groups* (Jersey City, NJ: Ktav, 1990).

33. One group, the Baltimore group, claimed minyan status with rabbinic permission. See later discussion.

34. Moshe Meiselman, *Jewish Woman in Jewish Law* (Jersey City, NJ: Ktav, 1978); Abba Bronspiegel, "Minyanim Meyuhadim le-Nashim," *Hadarom* 54 (Spring 1985): 51–53; Hershel Schachter, "Ze'i Lakh be-Ikvei ha-Zon," *Beit Yizhak* 17 (1985): 118–34. These authors condemn the women's prayer groups, referring to them as "minyanim," which is the designation for a quorum that these groups have not claimed.

35. The most comprehensive presentation of the halakhic material is in Aryeh Frimer and Dov Frimer, "Women's Prayer Services: Theory and Practice," *Tradition* 32, no. 2 (1998): 5–118. Their basic conclusion is that there are no compelling halakhic grounds prohibiting women's prayer groups.

36. Rela Geffen, "Intersecting Spheres: Feminism and Orthodox Judaism," in *Jewish Sects, Religious Movements, and Political Parties: Proceedings of the Third Annual Symposium of the Philip and Ethel Klutznick Chair in Jewish Civilization,* ed. Menachem Mor (New York: Fordham University Press, 1993), 189.

37. Tamar Ross, *Expanding the Palace of Torah: Orthodoxy and Feminism* (Hanover, NH: Brandeis University Press, 2004), 235.

38. Rabbi Riskin claimed that he was the first rabbi to accommodate women's desires to read from the Torah in 1971. Susan Sapiro, "Women's Tefilah Groups: Orthodoxy, Feminism and Worship" (unpublished paper, 1996).

39. Arlene Agus, personal communication with the author, February 6, 2005.

40. Arlene Agus, "This Month Is for You," in *The Jewish Woman,* ed. Elizabeth Koltun (New York: Schocken, 1975); Sue Berrin, ed., *Celebrating the New Moon: A Rosh Hodesh Anthology* (Northvale, NJ: Jason Aronson, 1996).

41. Tovah Jane Eisen, "Baltimore Women's Minyan," Women's Tefillah Groups (paper presented at the Conference on Women, Tradition and Prayer, June 1984, Teaneck, NJ), 5.

42. In 1983, 16 groups were listed as WTGs. In 2001 there were 21; in 2005, 60 were listed on the WTN.

43. There are a few, such as Shira Hadassha in Israel.

44. He later rescinded that permission, stating he was only talking theoretically without any practical application.

45. There is one group in Portland under rabbinic supervision that does consider itself a minyan.

46. In response to a query from Rabbi Louis Bernstein, president of the Rab-

binical Council of America, this decision was signed by Rabbis Nissan Alpert, Abba Bronspiegel, Mordechai Willig, Yehuda Parnes, and Hershel Schachter and published in *HaDarom* 54 (1985): 49–50.

47. Rivka Haut and Phyllis Chesler, eds., *Women of the Wall* (Woodstock, VT: Jewish Lights, 2003).

48. Fishman, *Changing Minds,* 39.

49. Translation of letter to Rabbi Fund from Rabbi Mordecai Tendler, Sivan 4 5743.

50. For a full description and analysis, see my forthcoming "Those (Over)Confident Women: Heretical Insiders in Rabbi Moshe Feinstein's Responsa," in *Jewish Legal Writings by Women,* vol. 2, ed. C. Safrai and M. Halpern.

51. Iggerot Moshe, OH 4:49. This is my translation.

52. Ibid.

53. The various positions are described in *Tradition* 32 (Fall, Winter, and Spring 1998).

54. The e-mail address of the WTN is wtn@shamash.org.

55. Fishman, *Changing Minds,* 39.

56. Ailene Cohen Nusbacher, "Efforts at Change in a Traditional Denomination: The Case of Orthodox Women's Prayer Groups," *Nashim* 2 (1999): 95–110. Her original research was done in 1997. She then prepared a new questionnaire for the Edah conference in 2001 and reported on it in a joint session with me.

57. Sidney Langer, "Women's Prayer Groups: A Case Study in Feminism and Modern Orthodoxy," *Ten Da'at* 11 (1998): 43–48.

58. Frimer and Frimer, "Women's Prayer Service."

59. Fishman, *Changing Minds,* 39.

60. For a marvelous exploration of the religious world of elderly Kurdish women in Jerusalem, see Susan Starr Sered, *Women as Ritual Experts* (New York: Oxford University Press, 1992). This ethnographic description illuminates and illustrates the richness of women's ritual lives and their perceived centrality. Sered has opened our discourse by designating illiterate Iraqi elderly women as ritual experts. She exposes their sense of themselves as both authoritative and central. They move easily from their household base into the public domain. They treat the rabbi with respect but know what they know. Their intimacy with God, ritual mastery, and knowledge of sacred matters is not mediated by any place, person, or text. Thus, religious experience and expertise are revealed in places not previously explored for religious action.

61. Greenberg, "The Feminist Revolution in Orthodox Judaism in America," 73–74.

CHAPTER EIGHT

BRIDGES TO "A JUDAISM TRANSFORMED BY WOMEN'S WISDOM"

The First Generation of Women Rabbis

PAMELA S. NADELL

When the women who became Reform rabbis wanted to celebrate the twenty-fifth anniversary of the ordination of Sally Priesand, the first woman rabbi in America, they dedicated a special issue of the *CCAR Journal* to female voices only and called it *Wisdom You Are My Sister.* Here they shared their stories. They recounted their journeys to ordination. They described their lives as wives and mothers, lovers and partners, and how the personal intertwined with the professional. Guest editor Rabbi Donna Berman saw her colleagues "voicing their opinions, wrestling with texts, thinking about God and theology and ritual and the future of Judaism." As they did so, they conveyed the joys and the challenges of pioneering in the first generation of women rabbis. Berman read these essays as part of the deliberate recovery of women's hidden voices, the unearthing and invention of women's Torah, and her colleagues affirmed that they were indeed engaged in creating "Jewish teachings that are, at long last, the product of the whole Jewish people."[1] Yet even as these rabbis prefer to present "the many different voices of many different women rabbis,"[2] one theme stands out as paramount not only in this collection but also throughout the significant body of writing produced by the women who became rabbis—their passionate engagement with Jewish feminism.

Women Remaking American Judaism asks, how did so many of the innovations pioneered by Jewish feminists—the baby-naming ceremonies, the gender-sensitive liturgies, the women's *sedarim,* the reclaiming of *mikvah,* the Rosh Hodesh celebrations, the adult bat mitzvah, the new ceremonies for healing after rape and divorce, the feminist critique of Jewish texts, the new feminist midrashim, to name several—become mainstream so quickly in American Jewish life? One answer lies with the women who became rabbis. Their visibility in the pulpit and the impact of their writing have given them enormous influence even though they rarely invented the contours of feminist Judaism. Reform rabbi Laura Geller acknowledges that "most of the systematic work in the area of Jewish feminist theology has been done by women scholars who are not themselves rabbis and that the same holds true for much of the most creative work in prayer and liturgy."[3] Nevertheless, the women who became rabbis stood "on the front line" of Jewish feminism and were often among the first to adopt its revolutionary changes.

More important, because of who they are and where they stand, they have had the opportunity to bring Jewish feminism to America's Jews. Touched by feminist rabbis in the classroom, on the bimah, over Shabbat dinner, and often at the most vulnerable moments of their lives—as they wed, celebrated their newborns, *kvelled* at *b'nai mitzvah,* and mourned the dead—American Jewish boys and girls, men and women encountered feminist Judaism. The women who became rabbis laid the bridges over which crossed the feminist critique of Judaism to the homes, synagogues, and communities of modern America's Jews.

Whether these women are Reform, Reconstructionist, or Conservative rabbis, or were ordained through Jewish Renewal, they show themselves collectively, in their congregations, within their rabbinates, and especially through their writings, to be outspoken feminists. Even though denominational labels differentiate America's rabbis, articulating the feminist critique binds the women who became rabbis across the denominations. Ordained as rabbis, teachers, and preachers in America, committed to preserving Conservative or Reform Judaism, they obviously follow divergent practice. One adheres to the dietary laws, another does not; one observes two days of festivals, another honors but a single day. But when it comes to sanctifying the sacred in women's lives, to seeking female role models in the Jewish past, and to carving out spaces and places for women to experience the holy together within Judaism, feminism trumps the denominational divide for the women rabbis.

Almost from the start, the women who became rabbis gave voice to their feminism in print. But three years after her ordination Sally Priesand brought out *Judaism and the New Woman.* A model of the feminist critique, as it was then articulated, Priesand was angry. She wrote, "The bright spots in the biblical treatment of women . . . are few and far between." Biblical law was unjust, when it punished women, and not men, for adultery. Levirate marriage was "a disgrace to the dignity of woman." Seeking "great Jewish women" across Jewish history, she discovered new "role models" for contemporary Jewish women like the women's rights champion Ernestine Rose and the social service advocate Bertha Pappenheim. Priesand demanded gender equity within Judaism. She wanted to see daughters and sons welcomed "into the covenant of our tradition . . . with an equal ceremony," bat mitzvah the same as bar mitzvah, and women "participate in every aspect of synagogue ritual." She expected women to count in a minyan, read from the Torah, and be obligated to recite kaddish, and she hoped that the masculine language of the liturgy would soon "give way to 'humanity' and 'ancestors.'"[4]

Even as Priesand's ordination paved the way for those who would follow in her footsteps, her *Judaism and the New Woman* became but the first volume on a long shelf of books, essays, and even an occasional documentary[5] in which women rabbis have articulated the feminist critique of Judaism. This literature includes narratives of personal journeys to ordination;[6] of how they cast a feminist eye upon traditional Jewish texts and practices;[7] and of the new religious ceremonies they celebrate.[8] A few have even written specifically for children.[9]

When these women write and speak and voice their feminism, they do so with the authority none before them held—that of the education and office of rabbi. Rabbis are "symbolic exemplars," Conservative rabbi Jack H. Bloom told his colleagues in 1980, when there were not yet any women in the Conservative rabbinate. That means the "the pulpit rabbi is a symbolic leader who is set apart to function within his community as a symbol of that community and as an exemplar of that community's desire for moral perfection." The rabbi, he writes, is "larger than life," a "walking, talking, living symbol and stands for something other than himself." Symbolic exemplarhood "makes [their] words count," so that people remember who officiated at their wedding and what the rabbi said at their son's bar mitzvah, because congregants see "the rabbi in some crucial way [as] . . . a different kind of human being," "more moral, more learned." It is this perception that gives the rabbi authenticity, and that authenticity gives the rabbi "the power and ability to affect and influence others" and "to change the future of the American Jewish community."[10] Conservative rabbi Amy Eilberg captures the weight of "symbolic exemplarhood" quite succinctly: even as the thought is anathema to Jewish tradition, for many Jews, "on some level, the rabbi is regarded as a representative of God."[11]

Women rabbis intuit the power of their "symbolic exemplarhood" even if they do not use the term. As Karen Soria learned from the countless interviews she gave after she became the first woman rabbi in Australia, the title matters. Whenever she pointed out that a female rabbinical student had preceded her down under, Soria saw the effect of ordination in others eyes: "[S]he was not the first, I was."[12] Another knows: "There is a magic to the title 'rabbi.'"[13] And that magic means that as the women rabbis reiterate and deepen the feminist critique of Judaism, their voices carry the weight of their position and its power, and its "magic" brings the message home to their congregants.

FEMINISTS CRITIQUE JEWISH TRADITION

What are their messages? A small sample of the writings of women rabbis across the denominations reveals the tropes of their feminist critique. As Sally Priesand did in *Judaism and the New Woman,* the women rabbis wrestle with the sacred texts of Jewish tradition—the liturgy of the prayer book, the teachings of the Bible, the giant corpus of rabbinic literature. They decry the all too often exclusion of women's voices and visions in the texts. For example, Reform rabbi Lisa A. Edwards understood that the traditional Rosh Hashanah service ignored "women-centered themes in the liturgy" because the rabbis in the distant past were uninterested in including women. But while she could explain away inattention to women in the past, she grew angry when she found it in the present in the Reform movement's 1984 high holy day prayer book *Gates of Repentance.* Its publicity boasted its "contemporary, gender-sensitive language throughout." But its authors, perhaps out of concern for contemporary sensibilities, had excised the traditional Torah reading for the first day of Rosh Hashanah. So instead of reading each new year of how, after the birth of Isaac, Sarah compels Abraham to cast out Hagar and Ishmael, *Gates of Repentance,* according to Edwards, "dramatically reduces the presence of women . . . in the entirety of the services for Rosh Hashanah . . . creat[ing] a Rosh Hashanah observance with less interest in women than probably any in the history of Judaism."[14]

When women rabbis find women appearing in the Jewish past, they hungrily gravitate to them. Then they reinvent them and reinterpret their lives to cast them as role models and to teach lessons for Jews today, just as Priesand sought out role models in Jewish history. Reform rabbi Deborah R. Prinz analyzes how and why contemporary Jewish women have claimed the story of Lilith (Adam's first wife based on Genesis 1:27: "male and female He created them").[15] Jewish Renewal rabbi Lynn Gottlieb recasts Eve as "'everywoman' on the journey through girlhood, middle years, and old age" and imagines the matriarchs, including Hagar, as "tribal mothers" whose stories "affirm women-to-women relationships."[16] In *The Women's Torah Commentary,* women rabbis from across the denominations find ways to interject women into almost every one of the fifty-four weekly Torah portions. They explore female characters unnamed in the text, like Naamah, Noah's wife. They find lessons in minor biblical characters like Lot's wife; Rachel's maidservant, Bilhah; Joseph's wife, Asnat; and Serach bat Asher, "the only daughter mentioned of all of the progeny of Jacob's twelve sons." They use the biblical laws of kashrut to discuss Jewish women's association with holiday foods and to raise concerns about eating disorders. After God kills the sons of Aaron, they wonder how the women "connected to Aaron and his sons" responded, and ask their reader to "[i]magine if we were to witness Elisheva's reaction, to hear *her* voice."[17]

Not surprisingly, they boast of the bridge their feminist critique of the texts has paved, of the impact their teaching has had. Reform rabbi Elyse Goldstein speaks of how students approach her and say, "Now having a woman rabbi, I'm aware that there is an issue of women in the text or even an absence of women in text."[18] Amy Eilberg sees what happens as the women of the congregation come to understand their exclusion: "If humanity is created in the image of God, they muse, and God is so unmistakably male, then unavoidably, I as a woman am less like my Creator than is a man. The logic is irrefutable, and immensely painful."[19]

BECOMING RABBIS

Even as they lay bridges to the women of the Jewish past, women rabbis also open bridges to their own lives, for they know "that being a role model is always a part of what I do."[20] Understanding the weight of that responsibility, women rabbis feel compelled to tell their stories, to open windows onto their journeys.[21] Their commitment to chronicle comes "not only out of pride, but also out of a sense of duty, so that [their] children may have the role models that [they] did not have."[22] Not only do they expect that these will guide their children, their contemporaries, and the next generation who will follow in their footsteps, but they also believe that "when we make time and space for our stories to be heard, we bring healing to the world."[23]

Thus they recount their personal journeys toward ordination. Sally Priesand opens *Judaism and the New Woman* with a brief account of her path.[24] The biographies of the contributors to *The Women's Torah Commentary* include short statements about when and why each decided to become a rabbi.[25] In *Lesbian Rabbis,* eighteen women tell their stories and recount their struggles to "create systems of meaning and connections between Judaism and lesbianism and religious leadership."[26]

Some have even written book-length memoirs of their experiences. In *Life on the Fringes: A Feminist Journey toward Traditional Rabbinic Ordination,* Haviva Ner-David, who in 2006 at last received the Orthodox ordination she had long sought, unabashedly recounts her adolescent rebellion against religious observance, her bout with anorexia, her increased commitment to the commandments including ones women traditionally did not observe, and her struggles to find egalitarian positions within Jewish law.[27] In *With Roots in Heaven,* Jewish Renewal rabbi Tirzah Firestone describes a series of spiritual experiments that took her from the Orthodoxy of her youth "through years of searching for God in Benedictine monasteries and Hindu ashrams, traveling to northern Minnesota to prepare for the apocalypse, and into Universalist churches" before returning to Judaism through the movement of Jewish Renewal.[28]

As they relate the personal—that at ordination she sensed "not only was I being ordained but that the women who had been denied the title of rabbi were receiving it as well";[29] that she likes wearing a robe because it expanded when she was pregnant;[30] of the jobs lost because she is a lesbian[31]—the individual voices of this first pioneering generation of women rabbis weave the history of the "unique collective."[32] In fact, the women who became rabbis are, as Conservative rabbi Debra Reed Blank writes, "profoundly aware of history and [their] own role in it."[33] This, too, grows directly out of their feminist critique, for the reclaiming of women's history became a major thrust of the new American feminism. As Gerda Lerner conveys so brilliantly in *The Creation of Feminist Consciousness,* men with their written history benefited from knowledge transmitted from one generation to the next, but not women, who, denied knowledge of their history, had to discover anew what previous generations had already uncovered.[34] The community of women rabbis, a self-consciously pioneering generation, is aware of the importance of women's history and is determined to write their own chapter. They see that theirs is a singular history. Hence they compile lists of firsts: not only the first women ordained in each denomination—Sally Priesand in Reform Judaism in 1972, Sandy Eisenberg Sasso in Reconstructionist Judaism in 1974, and Amy Eilberg in Conservative Judaism in 1985—but also "the first woman president of the Reconstructionist Rabbinical Association, the first female rabbi to serve in Israel, the first Orthodox-trained female rabbi."[35] They narrate this history as they remember it, as Amy Eilberg does when she writes, "The Conservative movement has always figured centrally in the history of Jewish feminism."[36] To make certain that they record it before too much time passes by, the Reform women rabbis have welcomed one of their own, rabbi and historian Carole B. Balin, to chronicle the history of the Women's Rabbinic Network, the association they founded in 1980.[37]

WORKING RABBIS

Even as the women who became rabbis constitute a "unique collective," they have also joined the enormous cohort of America's working women.[38] Women who work understand that gender impacts the workplace, and women rabbis voice concern for "equality and equity" there. This, too, is part of the feminist critique they convey to their male colleagues and their congregants. In her 1991 luncheon address to the Reform movement's Central Conference of American Rabbis, surely a prestigious slot in this annual gathering, Ellen Lewis specifically pointed to barriers women rabbis sense in their professional lives. She described how they feel disadvantaged in negotiating salaries, and she exposed gendered pay inequities. She told of how the women have had to fight for family medical coverage, although male rabbis routinely get it, and of the tensions evoked by their needing maternity leave.[39]

They see gender bias broadly in the workplace. In 1987, Amy Eilberg described "an unspoken policy" that allowed Conservative movement congregations "full autonomy" in deciding whether to consider hiring a woman rabbi.[40] Reform rabbis Janet B. Liss and Debra Hachen surveyed their female colleagues and uncovered both the extent of gender discrimination in hiring rabbis and experiences with sexual harassment.[41] Reconstructionist rabbis Rebecca Alpert and Goldie Milgram found that their female colleagues were concerned about congregants trespassing physical and gender-related boundaries.[42]

All women who work, whether in factories or corporations or schools, whether they heal the sick, weld automobiles, or clean homes, negotiate the same gendered shoals of the workplace. But the women rabbis sense that, especially as they care for their families, they are judged more critically. Ellen Lewis recalled that she was once in a meeting when a male colleague rushed out to pick up his son from school. Even as those in the room said, "What a good father!" she suspected that were she to do the same, "people's reaction would be not, 'What a good mother!' but 'Is she putting her children's needs ahead of the congregation's?'"[43] The women rabbis write with

Rabbi Laura Geller, one of the first women ordained in the Reform movement, on Rosh Hashanah, Temple Emanuel, Beverly Hills, California, where she is senior rabbi. Used with the permission of Bill Aron, http://www.billaron.com.

eloquence about their striving for "balance between home and work, renegotiating, again and again, peace between . . . passions and . . . profession, between caring for . . . families and caring for the Jewish people."[44] Janet Marder reads this trope in a historical context as a deliberate response to the 1922 responsum of Jacob Lauterbach. Lauterbach, then professor of Talmud at Reform's Hebrew Union College, opposed women's ordination convinced, that women could never successfully combine the rabbinate with marriage and motherhood.[45]

But this emphasis on the personal, the autobiographical, can be read another way. It distinguishes the women who became rabbis from their male colleagues. The longing to tell their story, to view through the prism of their own lives whatever they wish to teach rarely surfaces in the writings of male rabbis as overtly or naturally as it does in the works penned by their female colleagues.[46] Male rabbis are far less likely to share their reflections—whether on prayer or study, Shabbat or the sacred days, or living a life infused by Judaism—with the sentence, "I am writing this article a few months before my forty-seventh birthday,"[47] as Reconstructionist rabbi Sheila Peltz Weinberg has. They rarely write, as Conservative rabbi Debra Cantor has, about marriage, infertility, or sexual relations.[48]

A DIFFERENT VOICE

How do we make sense of this "different voice" of the women rabbis? They refer knowingly to social psychologist Carol Gilligan's pathbreaking analysis of women's difference.[49] In this 1982 classic on female development, Gilligan calls for an understanding of female psychology tested against a standard other than that of the male. She concludes that women's lives are characterized by their "embeddedness in lives of relationship, their orientation to interdependence, [and] their subordination of achievement to care." Thus, she finds, women "make a different sense of experience, based on their knowledge of human relationships."[50] This is where women rabbis begin when they seek to teach Judaism through the prism of their own lives, families, and experiences.

This emphasis on the personal can also be read, as theorists of autobiography see it, "as devoted to the creation of personal myth, to the practice of an art of self-invention."[51] Identity is not given but is constructed, and telling a life story plays a significant role in shaping identity. Some scholars see women's autobiography as distinct from that of men for it "tests boundaries between the public and the private spheres . . . [and] exhibits a collective consciousness." It can also become "a vehicle for conveying a message about history."[52] Because this first generation of women rabbis has gone where none of their sex had gone before, incorporating autobiographical reflections into their writings enables the "self-invention" of the individual and of the group and the transmission of their history.

As women entered rabbinical school classes in the 1970s and 1980s, they came, at first as isolated individuals, to realize just how much the tradition they were determined to master ignored. For example, in the mid-1970s, as Laura Geller studied at Hebrew Union College-Jewish Institute of Religion, she heard her teacher say that "there is no important moment in the lifetime of a Jew for which there is no blessing." Perhaps generations of males had blindly accepted the claim, but she, well aware of the many moments in women's lives unhallowed by tradition, did not.[53] Just as they sought to create bridges to lead their congregants to women in Jewish texts, the women who became rabbis searched for new ways to connect women to Judaism and the Jewish community. As Priesand calls for in *Judaism and the New Woman,* they sought gender equity within Jewish ritual life.

REMAKING AMERICAN JUDAISM

Women rabbis turned a critical lens on the trajectory of women's lives asking how Judaism could signify moments of change, joy, and despair, and especially those intimately linked to the feminine. They seek to unite Judaism, through Jewish feminism, to the occasions, great and small, that rest at the core of women's lives. Laura Geller had realized that there were many moments in the lifetime of a Jewish woman "for which there is no blessing." But the women rabbis began by searing into Jewish consciousness that even where blessings and ceremonies did exist to which women might turn, they were all too often inadequate and in desperate need of transformation.

Not surprisingly, women rabbis' first ritual experiments focused on birth. As Sandy Eisenberg Sasso argued in 1973, when she was still a student at the Reconstructionist Rabbinical College, "The need to create a feminine counterpart must begin at birth by giving as much ceremonial importance to a girl's birth as to a boy's, and by considering more fully the unique emotional experiences of the mother." The conventional naming of a newborn girl during the Shabbat morning service pales beside the powerful ceremony of a boy's circumcision on the eighth day following his birth. Seeking an equally commanding rite for naming a daughter and one that would recognize that girls and women as well as boys and men share in the covenant God made with the nation Israel, Sasso wrote what may be the first published "covenantal birth ceremony for the Jewish daughter."[54] Later women rabbis followed with an array of designs for this new ritual.[55]

But while Judaism traditionally offered a space for naming a daughter, this same tradition largely ignored so many of women's other spiritual needs.[56] It took women rabbis confronting their own sexuality and fertility, and deeply conversant with "the traditions [which] were framed by men and consequently reflect male perspectives and concerns," to comprehend the glaring absence of avenues for women's spirituality. As Conservative rabbi Susan Grossman wrote, "Until I had suffered a miscarriage, I had never understood. . . . Now I understand." But at that heavy moment in her life, she discovered that the tradition in which she was "so much at home" had abandoned her: "There are no traditional prayers to recite over a miscarriage. There is no funeral or mourning ritual to follow. After suffering a miscarriage, a woman does not even routinely recite the prayer said after coming safely through a dangerous experience, *birkat ha-gomel,* something all women can do after giving birth." Seeking comfort for herself, her "Meditation after a Miscarriage" burst forth.[57]

In fact, women rabbis have published an astonishing array of prayers, readings, and ceremonies for what Conservative rabbi Debra Orenstein calls "invisible life passages":[58] prayers for going to the mikvah (the ritual bath) "to be said on the evening the couple wishes to conceive,"[59] for the first months of pregnancy and for entering the ninth month, for the onset of labor, for a Caesarean birth, and for nursing for the first time. They have also written for those grieving infertility, suffering stillbirth, seeking medical intervention, and turning to adoption. They have imagined ceremonies for the onset of menses and the completion of menopause, for healing after rape, and for remaining single, as well as "a ritual acknowledging marital separation."[60] Their remarkable creativity suggests that no event or personal milestone in the female life cycle remains untouched by this spiritual experimentation.

Women rabbis have not only sought to sanctify the private, they have also turned their attention to the public settings of Jewish life, seeking to include women and sanctify the female in new ways. They echoed Priesand as they demanded "gender-sensitive" liturgies for the Sabbaths and festivals, and each of the liberal movements of American Judaism has published them.[61] They have revisioned Passover. They lead communal women's seders. They have brought both a cup of water for Miriam to the seder table and an orange to the seder plate.[62] They have reclaimed Rosh Hodesh, the New Moon, as the women's holiday, inventing "ceremonies which draw upon the similarity between women's cycles and the moon's cycles, the capacity of both women and the moon to physically wax and wane, ebb and flow, give birth, die, and be reborn."[63]

In particular, they have reappropriated mikvah, the pool in which married women immerse for the ritual cleansing required to resume sexual relations following its proscription during and immediately after menstruation. As Elyse Goldstein explains, "The *mikvah* is a good example of taking something that women have thought of as a negative image and turning into a positive one." Mikvah becomes a place for women to celebrate Rosh Chodesh, to find solace for infertility, to mark a milestone, or to bring closure to a crisis. It becomes not a place to get "permission to go forth to men," but rather a place that offers an "inward permission to be who you are, to be fully female, to experience your own cycle."[64]

Finally, women rabbis have also opened another bridge for American Jews by extending the feminist critique to include "the challenges that face gay and lesbian people." They criticize their synagogues, their congregants, and their colleagues for "perpetuat[ing] a heterosexist message every time we ask someone if they are married or single, and offer them no more choices than that." They ask their colleagues, as Reform rabbi Stacy Offner has, "to present gay men and lesbians . . . as being a purposeful part of God's creation, and an indispensable part of our world."[65] They seek, as Haviva Ner-David does, to find a path through Jewish law, to move beyond the biblical injunction that made homosexuality "an abhorrent thing," punishable by death, to allow "for a homosexual relationship to be sanctified and for a gay couple to be together openly and unashamedly in a halachic community."[66] They lead the Jewish community in confronting "a wide range of issues of concern to gays and lesbians . . . [including] the acceptance of gay men and lesbians as Jewish teachers, cantors, and rabbis,"[67] and they have composed services for gay and lesbian ceremonies of commitment.[68]

RABBIS AND FEMINISTS

Collectively in their published writings, women rabbis prove themselves unabashedly feminist. As Reform rabbi Sue Levi Elwell explains, they devote their "professional energies toward helping realize a Judaism and Jewish life transformed by women's wisdom." They seek to "be agents of the creation of feminist Judaism, a Judaism that not only includes but integrates women and a range of women's insights, a Judaism that places women in the center." They demand that "critical thinking informed by feminist theory and scholarship *must be integrated* into every aspect of the rabbinical curriculum—and into every aspect of [their] rabbinates."[69] They seek, as Laura Geller has phrased it, "to shift the paradigm from the equality between men and women to the transformation of Judaism itself."[70]

Women rabbis have thus laid a bridge for all to the feminist critique of Judaism. Although they rarely pioneered the innovations of Jewish feminism discussed throughout the present volume, they were often the first to take its teachings to heart. Among the more than five hundred women rabbis in America today,[71] feminism has bridged the divisions their denominational distinctiveness usually demands. Standing in this first generation of women deemed worthy of the two-thousand-year-old title of rabbi, they have shared their love for Judaism and passion for its texts and teachings while simultaneously proclaiming, "I am proud to be a Jewish feminist."[72] Their writings reveal them its boldest champions, and the authority they wield as rabbis has made them its most influential teachers. Wherever they have stood—on pulpits and in classrooms, under the *huppah* and at the circumcision table—they have, sometimes just by their presence, more often by their words, helped transform American Judaism to open up new spaces for women. As they enlightened their congregants, students, and male colleagues about women and gender, they reshaped American Judaism in ways utterly unimaginable a short half century ago. The bridge to Jewish feminism that they have erected may well stand as the most lasting legacy of this pioneering generation of women rabbis.

NOTES

I would like to thank Riv-Ellen Prell for her insightful critiques of earlier versions of this essay.

1. Donna Berman, "Introduction," *CCAR Journal: "Wisdom You Are My Sister": 25 Years of Women in the Rabbinate* 44 (Summer 1997): i–iv.

2. Elyse Goldstein, introduction to *The Women's Torah Commentary: New Insights from Women Rabbis on the 54 Weekly Torah Portions,* ed. Elyse Goldstein (Woodstock, VT: Jewish Lights, 2000), 25–35, 31.

3. Laura Geller, "From Equality to Transformation: The Challenge of Women's Rabbinic Leadership," in *Gender and Judaism: The Transformation of Tradition,* ed. T. M. Rudavsky (New York: New York University Press, 1995), 243–53.

4. Sally Priesand, *Judaism and the New Woman* (New York: Behrman House, 1975), especially 6, 9, 13, 121, 27, 28. Note that the book does not indicate that it is a revision of her 1972 rabbinic thesis, "Toward a Course of Study for Reform High School Youth Dealing with the Historic and Changing Role of the Jewish Woman." On Preisand's rabbinic thesis, see Pamela S. Nadell, *Women Who Would*

Be Rabbis: A History of Women's Ordination, 1889–1985 (Boston: Beacon Press, 1998), 165–68.

5. *Half the Kingdom,* dir. Francine Zuckerman and Roushell N. Goldstein, Kol Ishah Productions, 1989. The following notes (6–9) are but a small sample of the literary output of the women rabbis.

6. Haviva Ner-David, *Life on the Fringes: A Feminist Journey toward Traditional Rabbinic Ordination* (Needham, MA: JFL Books, 2000); Tirzah Firestone, *With Roots in Heaven: One Woman's Passionate Journey into the Heart of Her Faith* (New York: Dutton, 1998).

7. Elyse Goldstein, ed., *The Women's Torah Commentary: New Insights from Women Rabbis on the 54 Weekly Torah Portions* (Woodstock, VT: Jewish Lights, 2000); Debra Orenstein and Jane Rachel Litman, eds., *Lifecycles: Jewish Women on Biblical Themes in Contemporary Life,* vol. 2 (Woodstock, VT: Jewish Lights, 1997); Debra Orenstein, *Lifecycles: Jewish Women on Life Passages and Personal Milestones,* vol. 1 (Woodstock, VT: Jewish Lights, 1998).

8. Laura Levitt and Sue Ann Wasserman, "*Mikvah* Ceremony for Laura," in *Four Centuries of Jewish Women's Spirituality,* ed. Ellen M. Umansky and Dianne Ashton (Boston: Beacon Press, 1992), 321–26; Susan Grossman, "Finding Comfort after a Miscarriage," in *Daughters of the King: Women and the Synagogue,* ed. Susan Grossman and Rivka Haut (Philadelphia: Jewish Publication Society, 1992), 284–90.

9. Mindy Avra Portnoy, *Ima on the Bima: My Mommy Is a Rabbi* (Rockville, MD: Kar-Ben Publishing, 1986); Mindy Avra Portnoy, *Mommy Never Went to Hebrew School* (Rockville, MD: Kar-Ben Publishing, 1989); Mindy Avra Portnoy, *Matzoh Ball: A Passover Story* (Rockville, MD: Kar-Ben Publishing, 1994); Sandy Eisenberg Sasso, *God's Paintbrush* (Woodstock, VT: Jewish Lights, 1993); Sasso, *In God's Name* (Woodstock, VT: Jewish Lights, 1994); *Sasso, A Prayer for the Earth: The Story of Naamah, Noah's Wife* (Woodstock, VT: Jewish Lights, 1996).

10. Jack H. Bloom, "Inner Dynamics of the Rabbinate," in *Proceedings of the Rabbinical Assembly,* ed. Jules Harlow (New York: Rabbinical Assembly, 1980), 132–37.

11. Amy Eilberg, "*Kol Isha:* A New Voice in Conservative Judaism," in *The Seminary at 100: Reflections on the Jewish Theological Seminary and the Conservative Movement,* ed. Nina Beth Cardin and David Wolf Silverman (New York: Rabbinical Assembly, 1987), 349–59, 357.

12. Karen A. Soria, "Windows onto My Journey," *CCAR Journal: "Wisdom You Are My Sister": 25 Years of Women in the Rabbinate* 44 (Summer 1997): 92–95, 93.

13. Elizabeth Weiss Stern, "Practical Realities of Religious Leadership," in *Lifecycles: Jewish Women on Biblical Themes in Contemporary Life,* ed. Debra Orenstein and Jane Rachel Litman (Woodstock, VT: Jewish Lights, 1997), 306–11, 309.

14. Lisa A. Edwards, "Lost and Found: The Presence of Women in the Observance of Rosh Hashanah," *CCAR Journal: "Wisdom You Are My Sister": 25 Years of Women in the Rabbinate* 44 (Summer 1997): 21–38, esp. 29, 21, 32; *CCAR Press, 1998 Catalog,* http://www.ccarnet.org/press/prayer.html (accessed December 6, 2002).

15. Deborah R. Prinz, "Lilith: Lust and Lore," *CCAR Journal: "Wisdom You Are My Sister": 25 Years of Women in the Rabbinate* 44 (Summer 1997): 62–69. The article that propelled Jewish feminists to claim Lilith was Aviva Cantor, "The Lilith Question," 1976, repr. in *On Being a Jewish Feminist,* ed. Susannah Heschel (New York: Schocken Books, 1983), 40–50.

16. Lynn Gottlieb, *She Who Dwells Within: A Feminist Vision of a Renewed Judaism* (New York: HarperCollins, 1995), 7–8.

17. Goldstein, *The Women's Torah Commentary,* esp. 113, 99, 223.

18. Elyse Goldstein, "Rabbi Elyse Goldstein," in *Half the Kingdom: Seven Jewish Feminists,* ed. Francine Zuckerman (Montreal: Vehicule Press, 1992), 71–88, 79.

19. Eilberg, "*Kol Isha,*" 358.

20. "Tosefta: Additional Voices," *CCAR Journal: "Wisdom You Are My Sister": 25 Years of Women in the Rabbinate* 44 (Summer 1997): 165–68, quotation, Julie Spitzer, 165.

21. See, for example, Soria, "Windows onto My Journey."

22. Goldstein, introduction, 35.

23. Sue Levi Elwell, "Transitions and Transformations: Creating Judaism for the Twenty-First Century," *CCAR Journal: "Wisdom You Are My Sister": 25 Years of Women in the Rabbinate* 44 (Summer 1997): 40. As I demonstrated in *Women Who Would Be Rabbis,* the women who sought ordination also sensed their historic importance and told the stories of their journey to the press. For example, one left a handwritten list of twenty-four of her lectures titled "Lectures of the One and Only Woman Rabbi," *Regina Jonas: The First Woman Rabbi in the World,* http://www.hagalil.com/deutschland/berlin/rabbiner/jonas.htm (accessed January 7, 2002). However, in researching this essay, I was struck by how often autobiographical elements appear in the published writings of the women rabbis, for example, most of the essays in Orenstein, *Lifecycles.* This topic merits further exploration.

24. Priesand, *Judaism and the New Woman,* xiii–xvi.

25. Goldstein, *The Women's Torah Commentary.*

26. Rebecca Alpert, Sue Levi Elwell, and Shirley Idelson, eds., *Lesbian Rabbis: The First Generation* (New Brunswick: Rutgers University Press, 2001), 1.

27. Ner-David, *Life on the Fringes;* Peggy Cidor, "For the Sake of Righteous Women," *Jerusalem Post,* May 4, 2006.

28. Firestone, *With Roots in Heaven,* 30.

29. Goldstein, "Rabbi Elyse Goldstein," 73.

30. Ellen Lewis, "Luncheon Address: CCAR Convention, 1991," *CCAR Journal: "Wisdom You Are My Sister": 25 Years of Women in the Rabbinate* 44 (Summer 1997): 13–20, 17.

31. Stacy Offner, "Toward Sharing the Dream," *CCAR Journal: "Wisdom You Are My Sister": 25 Years of Women in the Rabbinate* 44 (Summer 1997): 46–52.

32. Lewis, "Luncheon Address," 14.

33. Debra Reed Blank, "A View from the Inside: September 1986," in *The Seminary at 100: Reflections on the Jewish Theological Seminary and the Conservative*

Movement, ed. Nina Beth Cardin and David Wolf Silverman (New York: Rabbinical Assembly, 1987), 51–56.

34. Gerda Lerner, *The Creation of Feminist Consciousness: From the Middle Ages to Eighteen-Seventy* (New York: Oxford University Press, 1993), 166.

35. Goldstein, introduction, 35.

36. Eilberg, "*Kol Isha,*" 349.

37. Carole B. Balin, "From Periphery to Center: A History of the Women's Rabbinic Network," *CCAR Journal: "Wisdom You Are My Sister": 25 Years of Women in the Rabbinate* 44 (Summer 1997): 1–12.

38. In the year 2000, 58 percent of American women over the age of sixteen were in the labor force; U.S. Census Bureau, *The Percentage of Women 16 and over in the Labor Force Has Risen since 1960,* http://www.census.gov/pubinfo/www/multimedia/WHcharts.html#labor (accessed July 27, 2004).

39. Lewis, "Luncheon Address," 17–18.

40. Eilberg, "*Kol Isha,*" 351.

41. Janet B. Liss, "Sexual Harassment and Discrimination in the Rabbinate," *CCAR Journal: "Wisdom You Are My Sister": 25 Years of Women in the Rabbinate* 44 (Summer 1997): 53–61.

42. Rebecca Alpert and Goldie Milgram, "Women in the Reconstructionist Rabbinate," in *Religious Institutions and Women's Leadership: New Roles inside the Mainstream,* ed. Catherine Wessinger (Columbia: University of South Carolina Press, 1996), 291–310.

43. Lewis, "Luncheon Address," 18.

44. Elwell, "Transitions and Transformations," 40.

45. Janet R. Marder, "Are Women Changing the Rabbinate? A Reform Perspective," in *Religious Institutions and Women's Leadership: New Roles inside the Mainstream,* ed. Catherine Wessinger (Columbia: University of South Carolina Press, 1996), 271–90. For the text of Lauterbach's responsum with an introductory essay, see Pamela S. Nadell, "Ordaining Women Rabbis," in *Religions of the United States in Practice,* ed. Colleen McDannell (Princeton: Princeton University Press, 2001), 2:389–417.

46. Recent data for my observation are admittedly impressionistic. However, in *Conservative Judaism in America: A Biographical Dictionary and Sourcebook* (Westport, CT: Greenwood, 1988), I note that Conservative rabbis were extremely reticent about writing memoirs or personal history. Even though pulpit rabbis have published countless volumes of sermons, these too only occasionally reveal autobiographical information (381).

47. Sheila Peltz Weinberg, "The *Amidah* and Midlife," in *Lifecycles: Jewish Women on Life Passages and Personal Milestones,* ed. Debra Orenstein (Woodstock, VT: Jewish Lights, 1998), 286–96.

48. Debra Cantor, "On Being Married," in *Lifecycles: Jewish Women on Life Passages and Personal Milestones,* ed. Debra Orenstein (Woodstock, VT: Jewish Lights, 1998), 181–84.

49. For example, Amy Eilberg cited Carol Gilligan's work in both her senior ser-

mon and the essay "*Kol Isha.*" Amy Eilberg, "Senior Sermon: Parashat Vayakhel Pekudey," ms. in Jewish Women's Resource Center (New York, March 16, 1985); Eilberg, "*Kol Isha,*" 353–56. These are but two examples, but my wide reading in this literature shows that this work is often cited. On this point, see also Rita J. Simon and Pamela S. Nadell, "In the Same Voice or Is It Different?: Gender and the Clergy," *Sociology of Religion* 56, no. 1 (1995): 63–70.

50. Carol Gilligan, *In a Different Voice: Psychological Theory and Women's Development* (Cambridge, MA: Harvard University Press, 1982), 171–72.

51. Paul John Eakin, *Touching the World: Reference in Autobiography* (Princeton: Princeton University Press, 1992), 63.

52. Margo Culley, "What a Piece of Work Is "Woman"!: An Introduction," in *American Women's Autobiography: Fea(S)Ts of Memory,* ed. Margo Culley (Madison: University of Wisconsin Press, 1992), 3–31.

53. Laura Geller, "Encountering the Divine Presence," 1986; repr. in *Four Centuries of Jewish Women's Spirituality: A Sourcebook,* ed. Ellen M. Umansky and Dianne Ashton (Boston: Beacon Press, 1992), 243–47.

54. Sandy Eisenberg Sasso, "B'rit B'not Israel: Observations on Women and Reconstructionism," *Response: A Contemporary Jewish Review* 8 (Summer 1973): 101–5, quotation, 103.

55. This topic deserves its own history. Historical essays on women in the rabbinate refer to this frequently; see, for example, Alpert and Milgram, "Women in the Reconstructionist Rabbinate"; Sue Levi Elwell, "Women's Voices: The Challenge of Feminism to Judaism," in *Religious Institutions and Women's Leadership: New Roles inside the Mainstream,* ed. Catherine Wessinger (Columbia: University of South Carolina Press, 1996), 331–43.

56. Scholar Chava Weissler has illuminated the literature of early modern Jewish female prayers, the *tkhines;* Chava Weissler, *Voices of the Matriarchs: Listening to the Prayers of Early Modern Jewish Women* (Boston: Beacon Press, 1998). See also Nina Beth Cardin, ed., *Out of the Depths I Call to You: A Book of Prayers for the Married Jewish Woman* (Northvale, NJ: Jason Aronson, 1991).

57. Grossman and Haut, *Daughters of the King,* 285–86.

58. Orenstein, *Lifecycles,* 117. Orenstein lists an array of moments Jewish men and women should honor in their lives. They include first love, first sexual experience, weaning, finding out the biopsy is negative, becoming a grandparent, cooking a grandmother's recipe, and "discovering Jewish feminism" (119–20).

59. Nina Beth Cardin, *Tears of Sorrow, Seeds of Hope: A Jewish Spiritual Companion for Infertility and Pregnancy Loss* (Woodstock, VT: Jewish Lights, 1999), 28.

60. Orenstein, *Lifecycles;* Levitt and Wasserman, "*Mikvah* Ceremony for Laura."

61. For the new liturgies, see Chaim Stern, ed., *Gates of Prayer for Shabbat and Weekdays: A Gender Sensitive Prayerbook* (New York: Central Conference of American Rabbis, 1994); *Kol Heneshamah* (Wyncote, PA: Reconstructionist Press, 1994); Leonard S. Cahan, ed., *Siddur Sim Shalom for Shabbat and Festivals* (New York: Rabbinical Assembly/United Synagogues of Conservative Judaism, 1998).

62. Perhaps the best known of the feminist transformations for the seder is the

addition of an orange to the seder plate. Originally conceived by Susannah Heschel as symbolizing the fruitfulness that would accrue to the Jewish community by fully including gays and lesbians, an alternative story circulated that made this a response to the exclusion of women from the rabbinate. In this widely repeated version a man told Heschel that a woman belongs on the bimah as much as does an orange on the seder plate; *Orange on the Seder Plate,* http://www.ritualwell.org/Rituals/ritual.html?docid'702 (accessed July 14, 2004). Which reading of this symbol is intended by those liberal Jews who follow this new tradition is unknown.

63. Lenore Bohm, "The Feminist Theological Enterprise," *CCAR Journal: "Wisdom You Are My Sister": 25 Years of Women in the Rabbinate* 44 (Summer 1997): 70–79.

64. Goldstein, "Rabbi Elyse Goldstein," 82–83.

65. Offner, "Toward Sharing the Dream," quotations, 47–48.

66. Ner-David, *Life on the Fringes,* 119; Lev. 20:13.

67. Alpert, Elwell, and Idelson, *Lesbian Rabbis,* 11–12.

68. Leila Gal Berner and Renee Gal Primack, "Uncharted Territory: Lesbian Commitment Ceremonies," in *Lifecycles: Jewish Women on Life Passages and Personal Milestones,* ed. Debra Orenstein (Woodstock, VT: Jewish Lights, 1998), 173–77.

69. Elwell, "Transitions and Transformations."

70. Geller, "From Equality to Transformation," 251.

71. For statistics, see Deborah E. Lipstadt, "Feminism and American Judaism: Looking Back at the Turn of the Century," in *Women and American Judaism: Historical Perspectives,* ed. Pamela S. Nadell and Jonathan D. Sarna (Hanover, NH: Brandeis University Press/University Press of New England, 2001), 291–308, 305n2.

72. Eilberg, "*Kol Isha,*" 359.

PART THREE

REFRAMING JUDAISM

CHAPTER NINE

PHASING IN

Rosh Hodesh Ceremonies in American Jewish Life

JODY MYERS

One of the first ritual innovations of Jewish feminism was a new Rosh Hodesh ceremony. The Jewish feminist movement entered public awareness through its leaders' demands for radical changes in synagogue and communal life, but this new ritual produced little controversy. It was performed outside the synagogue, used no ritual objects circumscribed by Jewish law, included no prayers requiring a minyan, and involved only women. Yet, the New Moon celebration was a rich and colorful expression of Jewish women's feminist consciousness. Created in 1972, it has been one of the most widely accepted ritual expressions for Jewish women to celebrate each other and express gratitude to God for creating women.

Ritual was a natural outlet for Jewish women who were battling for equality within the religious or Jewish communal sphere. Virtually all forms of Judaism award a central place to ritual expression. Jewish feminists were seeking not only to practice the rituals from which men had excluded them but to revive those which Jewish women had done in the past and whose meanings had been lost or required reinterpretation. Revived—in contrast to new—rituals legitimize new ideas by locating them in the imagined pristine era of antiquity. Through such rituals, Jewish women assert their importance to Jewish life in the present as well as the past. Connecting women to the appearance of the new moon, the fundamental marker of sanctified time through the Jewish calendar, conveys women's central role in Jewish culture.

This essay sketches the origins and history of the modern women's Rosh Hodesh ceremony. It will highlight aspects of the ritual that help account for its popularity. The first is its built-in flexibility: it is a structure that has accommodated different kinds of feminist sensibilities. Jewish women who advocate *egalitarian feminism,* the effort to achieve parity between women and men in the exercise of religious and communal power, construct ceremonies that give voice to their ideals and enable them to practice newly acquired skills in a safe setting. Women who prefer *cultural feminism,* which deals less overtly with power relations and focuses its efforts on reshaping Jewish culture to include women's voices and experiences, also use Rosh Hodesh to affirm their unique experiences as women. Each group can create its own Rosh Hodesh ceremony, and in many cases the same gathering can serve both. Even the most politically averse gatherings have been seedbeds for broader structural changes in Judaism and for egalitarian feminism.

Second, the women's Rosh Hodesh group creates community. People who perform rituals do not always do so in order to actualize a collection of theological truth claims or to concretize abstract intellectual principles, but to express their membership in a community. Catherine Bell's observation that ritualized action is a strategy for the negotiation—or maintenance or qualification—of power relations within a society is helpful. However, her observation does not exhaust the psychological and social meanings of a communal ritual like Rosh Hodesh, nor does it explain why it emerges in a voluntary, group setting. Rosh Hodesh rituals were created for many reasons, chief among which was to enable women to feel appreciated, loved, and celebrated *as women* in a religious context. This goal was compatible with the efforts to gain equality for women *as Jews* within the synagogue and community. Different groups of women shaped their ceremonies to fit their own needs, and so the functions of the rituals vary: some provide a cathartic, emotional experience; some place the participants within the larger framework of Jewish history and the cosmos; some are vehicles for women to learn together, compare experiences, and share ideas; and some combine one or more of the above or additional elements.[1]

Finally, I contend that it is the moderate characteristics of the New Moon gathering that eventually enabled it to enter the mainstream, that is, to be incorporated into the cultural programs offered by community centers, synagogues, and longstanding organizations like Hillel, a Jewish collegiate student organization, and Hadassah, a Jewish women's Zionist organization. In a number of ways illustrated below, the Rosh Hodesh gathering was designed to affirm women's value in an *inoffensive* manner. The less overtly political nature of Rosh Hodesh made it palatable to a wide range of Jewish women; it was a safe way of "acting feminist" or of agreeing with an important principle of feminism—the need to respect and celebrate women—without explicitly endorsing other aspects of the feminist agenda that violated community traditions and norms. A ceremony that appeared to revive an earlier, lost, religious tradition honoring women appealed to Jewish women who were proud of their heritage and defensive of Judaism in the face of its detractors among American Christians, secularists, and feminists.

A NOTE ABOUT ROSH HODESH

The Jewish religious calendar year consists of twelve or thirteen lunar months. At the point at which the new moon becomes visible at the beginning of its cycle, Rosh Hodesh begins and is celebrated for one or two days. Since the medieval era, Rosh Hodesh has been anticipated ritually by a prayer in the synagogue on the Sabbath preceding its arrival. The prayer leader stands before the congregation and announces the day (or days) of Rosh Hodesh and then beseeches God for benefits to the individual and the Jewish people during the month ahead. On the days of Rosh Hodesh, special prayers are added to the Grace after Meals (according to Jewish law, the grace is to be recited by both men and women) and established daily prayer services, and on the New Moon prior to the New Year, the shofar is sounded at the end of the communal morning prayers. There are no specific work prohibitions associated with the day for men; as we shall see below, specific behaviors for women were honored in the breech. Different sects and circles of Jews over the centuries have augmented these practices with other rituals, special prayers, taboos, and limitations on behavior. For Ashkenazic Jews, whose religious practices (or neglect thereof) were the norm among Western Jews, Rosh Hodesh has been primarily a synagogue-centered event and, consequently, for most of its history has been the focus of male Jews.[2]

THE FIRST ROSH HODESH CEREMONY

According to Arlene Agus, one of the creators of the first Rosh Hodesh ceremony, a group of women living in New York City had been exploring women's spirituality and women's role in Jewish ritual in 1972 when they discovered that Rosh Hodesh had a unique significance for women.[3] In the Talmud and early modern custom books, they found references to work restrictions for women on Rosh Hodesh. Rabbinic exegesis provided explanations for women's link to Rosh Hodesh. Rashi, the foremost medieval commentator on the Talmud, traced the source of women's special duties to the events around the golden calf (in Exodus 32). According to a midrash (scriptural explanation) he had learned from his teacher, the Israelite women recognized the project as idolatry and refused to contribute their jewelry to build the calf. God rewarded them and their female descendants with Rosh Hodesh as a day of rest. The commentators on Rashi, the Tosafists, pointed to an elaboration of this teaching in the midrashic work *Pirke de-Rabbi Eliezer,* which explains that God acknowledged the Israelite women's virtue and bestowed upon them two rewards: "[T]he Holy One, Blessed be God, rewarded them in this world in that they would observe the New Moons more than men, and in the next world in that they are destined to be renewed like her."[4]

The women who created the modern Rosh Hodesh ceremony constructed a modern feminist rationale that illustrates their inventiveness as well as their commitment to the Jewish tradition of Torah study. They justified their innovation by interpreting rabbinic texts, starting with the ones cited above. In the original Hebrew of the passage in *Pirke de-Rabbi Eliezer, she-hen atidot le-hithadesh kemotah* is often translated "they are destined to be renewed like the New Moons." Acknowledging that "Rosh Hodesh is an obvious reference to the monthly [menstrual] cycle after which women renew themselves like the moon through immersion,"[5] Agus and her peers refused to elaborate on the immersion ritual or the biological dissimilarity of women. Instead, they understood women's future restoration to refer to women's eventual equality with men. They based their conclusion on a talmudic midrash that teaches that the sun and moon originally were created the same size. When the moon asked God whether it was wise to appoint two equal rulers, God diminished the moon's light. The moon protested, and God promised, through the prophetic words of Isaiah recorded in Isaiah 30:26, "that the light of the moon shall become like the light of the sun." Isaiah continues that prediction by anticipating that the sun will be brightened seven times its present intensity, thereby still outshining the moon, but both the midrashic author and Agus ignore this point.[6] They understood this passage to foretell the future equality of the moon and sun, a metaphor for the future equality of women and men. They found another source from the mystical tradition that taught that the sun and the moon, symbols of the male and female aspects of the Godhead, will be restored to their original equal sizes during the era of redemption.[7] A similar destiny is promised to women, they concluded. They also developed the notion that the original equality of the sun and the moon paralleled the original equality of the first man and woman: "It was a similar challenging of God's judgment in creation, in creating two equal human beings, which led to the diminution of woman's status. On the sixth day of Creation, 'God created man in his image . . . male and female he created them.' According to the Midrash, Adam's first wife, Lilith, having been created equal to Adam, refused a role of subservience and was replaced by Eve."[8]

Thus, the women found and interpreted rabbinic texts to establish a basis for egalitarianism in the beginning of time and in the future era. Their conclusions were innovative; Jewish sages did not equate the future brightening of the moon to the social status of women; they did not long for female equality, nor did they read Genesis 1 as a narrative of the creation of male and female human beings equal in power and importance.[9] The women crafted a new midrash that would be incorporated into virtually all later explanations of the modern women's celebration. Situating the gender struggle into the Creation myth and rearticulating it in a manner that foretells the equality of men and women were enormously affirming for women who identified as both feminists and religious Jews.

The creators of the modern Rosh Hodesh ceremony had no real information about the authentic women's ritual that they were seeking to revive.[10] They were unaware of any recent mode of women's Rosh Hodesh observance. Bereft in terms of liturgical resources and knowledge of Jewish women's history, they modeled their ceremony after a Sabbath evening service. Agus describes it in general terms, urging people to creatively adapt it to their needs, but she hopes that the traditional parts will be retained so as to keep some uniformity among existing ceremonies.[11] It is a women-only event held in a participant's home on the evening of Rosh Hodesh. Attendees dress in nice clothing—new, if possible—and put coins into a *pushke* (charity box) before the ceremony. The actual ceremony has five components. First, the women light a twenty-four-hour candle. The candle has a purely symbolic function, representing the moon's glow; the lighting is not a mitzvah and, in deference to Jewish law, is therefore not preceded by a blessing. Second, the participants recite a prayer or poem establishing some of the themes of the evening. Agus suggests a modern prayer by Hillel Zeitlin titled "Create Me Anew," which praises God for creating the world and for allowing the renewal of life. This prayer is rather traditional in that it addresses God as Father and women are not subjects of the prayer.

Third, following this reading is the ushering in of the new month, the heart of the ceremony. It can take several forms, such as studying a text that pertains to the holidays or rituals connected to the month, learning about the life of a famous Jew whose *yahrzeit* (anniversary of death) occurs during the month, or commemorating a historical event that occurred during that month. The fourth component of the ceremony sanctifies the day. Agus explains that a standard kiddush (sanctification over wine), which accompanies all holy day meals, would be inappropriate; that is, because each kiddush contains a special reference to the sanctified day, and there is no kiddush for Rosh Hodesh (since it was not given that elevated a status), reciting a kiddush would require religious innovation. She suggests using *kiddush ha-levana,* a prayer customarily recited in the evenings between Rosh Hodesh and the appearance of the full moon, particularly the passage that refers to the moon as a "crown of splendor for those who are carried in the womb, who are destined to be renewed like it." A blessing over wine concludes the sanctification. The fifth component is the communal meal, a sumptuous feast such as would be held on a Sabbath or holiday evening. The innovative element here is that round foods are preferred: the meal begins with two round or crescent-shaped rolls or *chalot,* and the several courses might include food that can be considered symbolic of renewal. The meal includes singing Rosh Hodesh songs, the psalms of Hallel, or the tunes typically sung on the holidays that would occur in the upcoming month. The meal concludes with the Grace after Meals, which contains the traditional Rosh Hodesh additions.

Nowhere does this ceremony articulate egalitarian feminism. Feminism is expressed in the doing of the ritual itself, in the gathering of women for a meal in which they conduct virtually all the components of a traditional holiday meal: an act of charity preceding the holiday, candle lighting, sanctification over wine, study, singing, feasting, and blessings. Though there is no violation of Jewish law in it, such a meal conducted outside a familial or communal context with the deliberate and unlamented exclusion of males is definitely subversive. This rebellious message is, at the same time, obscured by the women's demonstration of pious gratitude to God (the King and Father) and their deference to the directives of religious law issued by (male) religious authorities over the ages.

Feminism was divisive for every religious or ethnic community, and thus its adoption among religious and minority women occurred later. Jewish religious feminists were wary of manifesting disloyalty to the Jewish community and provoking the wrath of other Jews. Two decades after the first ceremony, Agus explained that the ceremony was a way to express feminist ideals without intruding on the usual familial and communal celebrations. The traditional basis for women's observance of Rosh Hodesh gave Jewish women a valuable link to the past, she writes, and "it promised embattled feminists credibility and leverage in a conservative community skeptical of change." The women creating the ritual were establishing a separate space for women, Agus writes, "that did not require leaving our homes within Judaism." They were "seeking inclusion without revolution."[12]

Although the character of the first Rosh Hodesh ceremony owes much to the idiosyncrasies of its founders, who were fairly conservative in their personal religious observances, I maintain that the Jewish context of a new moon ritual is likely to obscure the power struggles that gave rise to it. In Jewish culture, the moon is not a revolutionary image. It is described as the ruler of the night sky along with the stars, but the sun trumps them all in its greater constancy, brightness, and power. Although the moon is central to the establishment of the Jewish calendar, the sun's position relative to the earth is considered in the addition of leap months seven times every nineteen years.[13] The appearance of the new moon is not special enough to merit the prohibition of work, a sign of sanctity in Judaism. Symbolically, it is difficult to associate the moon with powerful, social actors who have an overt impact on daily life. The moon evokes themes of nature, and in a Jewish context these usually point to the majesty of God as creator and God's rule over all of the cosmos; the social realm, again, is diminished in importance. The moon's association with women's menstrual periods and reproductive functions means that it has been most useful to represent women's uniqueness and distinctiveness from men, rather than evoking the challenge to achieve parity with them.

The contemporary moon midrash does have the capacity to be an expression of a feminist conviction that women have not received what is due to them, and it could inspire them to demand what is rightfully theirs. However, the story actually affirms women's current subordinate status and removal from power; after all, the source of female/moon subordination lies with God and not with males/sun. The question of power is rather muted, for the male sun cannot be blamed for the female moon's loss; the darkened moon enacts no revenge; and God acknowledges his excessive severity and dispenses compensation. The meaning of the future renewal is also unclear. In the meantime, women are granted Rosh Hodesh as their own—but this is hardly significant in the Judaic scheme of things: Rosh Hodesh has no work restrictions (this would be the sign of a sanctified day); and since men are not enjoined to complete women's tasks on Rosh Hodesh, the custom of women refraining from work involves no real reward.[14] Of course, a woman's new moon ritual does not need to incorporate the moon midrash, and it can incorporate material expressing the struggles involved in building a new, feminist society—such ceremonies were constructed, as will be shown below. However, overt expressions of the feminist struggle did not typically get fixed into Rosh Hodesh ceremonies. A better place for these was the Passover seder, the mealtime storytelling ritual revolving around the themes of oppression and the struggle for freedom. Women's seders, first held in 1976, became the preferred venue for the elaboration of explicit egalitarian feminism in a ritual context.

THE CEREMONY DIVERSIFIES

Jewish feminism spread rapidly during the 1970s.[15] Ezrat Nashim was itself a product of the popular religious revival that began to sweep the Jewish community in the late 1960s, spawning informal learning circles, alternative communities, and a remarkable increase in scholarship and popular writing devoted to Jewish history, literature, and the arts. Jewish feminism grew out of the alternate and informal groups, and Jewish feminism benefited from the passionate attentions lavished on the Jewish cultural heritage. The North American Jewish Students' Network sponsored its first national Jewish women's conference in 1973, and some national organizations and conferences followed, but the movement was largely local and diffuse. Achieving equality within established religious movements had to occur first on the national level because of the centralized structure of the non-Orthodox denominations. Progress was already evident in the mid-1970s: the Reform movement had approved the ordination of women as rabbis and graduated its first in 1972, and the investiture of women as Reform cantors began a few years later. The Reconstructionist movement, its seminary open to women since its founding in 1968, ordained its first woman rabbi in 1974. The Rabbinical Assembly of the Conservative movement permitted the counting of women in the synagogue minyan in 1973, and various constituencies and decision-making bodies within the movement moved slowly toward permitting rabbinic ordination of women (achieved in 1985). Girls and women serving as ritual actors in the synagogue services of these three denominations was still novel and potentially controversial, but it was becoming more widespread. The influence of feminism could be discerned in some sectors of Orthodox Judaism, and in 1972 an all-women prayer group was organized in New York. Across all denominations, religious education for girls was expanded and extended, and within the religious movements and in secular institutions undergraduate and graduate Jewish studies became increasingly available to Jewish women. In turn, they became teachers, rabbis, scholars, or simply knowledgeable members of the Jewish community. Feminism also had made its mark in the refashioning of life cycle rituals, most notably in the crafting of new baby-naming ceremonies for girls, and in spurring the use of gender-neutral and gender-inclusive language in prayer books.

Yet these achievements did not preclude the desire among some women to develop new women's rituals and to embellish and reshape existing ones. Most Jewish women did not have access to religious settings in which they were honored as equals; new women-only religious gatherings were especially attractive to feminists whose experience of Jewish religious life had been profoundly patriarchal and who were not alienated from Jewish tradition. The inclusion of women in rituals and institutions previously closed to them strengthened rather than weakened the desire in some women to develop women-only structures alongside traditional ones. These offered benefits not available in mixed settings. Only in women-only settings did women feel free to explore their new identity as Jewish women. Feminism had taught them that the personal was political, and together with other women they became aware of how their personal and intimate lives were bound up with matters of religion. They could recount and reflect on their place in the transmission of tradition from one generation of Jewish women to the next. Honoring the women's chain of tradition was expressed in a ritual that became virtually standard at the start of Rosh Hodesh and other women-only rituals: participants introduce themselves by their maternal lineage, in contrast with the traditional mode of being named according to paternal lineage, and through this naming they claim religious authority. In this context—and perhaps especially at this early point in the growth of awareness—men's presence was not that desirable. Consequently, most Rosh Hodesh groups tended to foster a high level of intimacy.

According to an informal survey from the mid-1990s of Rosh Hodesh group leaders, Rosh Hodesh groups were usually initiated by one or two women who had heard of the ritual, or by a woman who had experienced a Rosh Hodesh ceremony in one city and started one in the city to which she relocated. Some groups were a collection of friends, with new people added "by invitation only"; some groups were open to all; and some alternated between both approaches (this remains the norm for many Rosh Hodesh groups to this day). The principal attendees were women in their twenties or thirties. The basic elements of the first Rosh Hodesh ceremony—study, celebration, eating—were adapted by each group to shape its ceremony according to local and personal needs.[16] The groups resisted erecting overt hierarchies of authority within them. The ordination of women as rabbis did not result in moving women's Rosh Hodesh groups into the synagogue or being sponsored there; rather, women rabbis served as models, guides, and resources to lay-led groups. Indeed, women rabbis seeking or holding pulpits were deeply invested in building egalitarian mixed-gender communities and were not as likely to be drawn to Rosh

Hodesh groups.[17] The Jewish Women's Resource Center, operating out of the National Council of Jewish Women in Manhattan, and the Woman's Institute for Continuing Jewish Education in San Diego supported and archived the new ceremonies and liturgies but otherwise exerted no control.

More resources for feminist celebrations became available over the course of the 1970s: there were new women's rituals, new prayers and poetry, and essays on women's history that could be mined for material. A survey of Rosh Hodesh liturgies reveals a wide range and variety of material geared toward Jews of all outlooks and levels of observance, from those who prefer traditional prayers to those who use gender-inclusive language, gender-neutral language, and female God-language. Rosh Hodesh groups produced rituals and prayers that were subsequently used in other settings, such as the Cup of Miriam (discussed below). In synagogues and standard home-based religious celebrations, most participants seek comfortable, familiar rituals and texts. Rosh Hodesh groups were experimental and innovative, and there was a general understanding that ceremonies were malleable, fluid, and would not necessarily satisfy all participants on every occasion. An attitude of inclusiveness, openness, and flexibility was considered essential to feminism, and this influenced the group dynamics.[18]

The Rosh Hodesh ceremony should be put in the context of the growing feminist spirituality movement, a specific form of cultural feminism. Feminist spirituality appears in many forms, but there are five principles upon which there is general agreement. First, the goal and reward of feminist spirituality is the empowerment of women, which may also be articulated as healing. Second, ritual is regarded as a tool of this empowerment and the means of communicating with the sacred. Third, there is a reverence for nature, and nature may be personified as the goddess. Fourth, women are especially revered for their connection to nature, and women's biological functions are given much attention in the spiritual practices and explanations. Finally, spiritual feminists believe that gender has been a key factor in shaping historical epochs, and they believe their activities facilitate the transformation of patriarchal society into one more beneficial to humanity as a whole and women in particular.[19]

The acceptance of feminist spirituality is evident in *Miriam's Well: Rituals for Jewish Women around the Year,* the first published anthology of Rosh Hodesh rituals. This book appeared in 1986 and its popularity is evident by its three reprints (1990, 1994, and 1996). The author, Penina Adelman, culled material from Rosh Hodesh groups that began to meet in the 1970s in Minneapolis, Philadelphia, and Boston primarily, as well as New York and Jerusalem. Her volume is a full sourcebook, offering thirteen very detailed ceremonies as well as notes on the reaction of the participants to the activities in which they were engaged. These ceremonies involve extensive preparation and time commitment; each one includes song, story, meditation or visualization, dance or movement, text study, food, and a ritual purification of the spirit. The ceremonies in *Miriam's Well* manifest the distinctive elements of feminist spirituality: the participants emphasize the healing and empowering functions of women's rituals, they are comfortable with the idea of feminized divinity (expressed in their prayers to the kabbalistic vision of a female facet of God, Shekhinah), and women's biology is central to their concerns and liturgical expressions. The women featured in the rituals in *Miriam's Well* express great satisfaction with the women-only setting, and the leaders are convinced that the bonds between the women transcend all other distinctions between them, such as differences in sexual identity.[20]

The importance of women sharing their personal lives with other women—indeed, the absence of men is key—is the meaning of the book's central metaphor, Miriam's well: according to a rabbinic midrash, Miriam's merit caused a miraculous well to appear alongside the Israelites wandering in the desert for forty years, and women telling stories to other women is a comparable life-sustaining phenomenon.[21] Great honor is paid to participants who disclose their dreams, hopes, sorrows, and the tales left to them by their forebears. One could say that the storytelling reflects the value in Judaism of expounding the words of Torah, but as the women are expounding on their lives, it is more precisely an enactment of the feminist conviction that women's empowerment starts when women tell each other their stories. Only women can generate authentic knowledge of themselves in relation to the sacred because it has been omitted from the religious traditions transmitted by men. In defining Jewish feminist ways of relating to God, this storytelling is what Rabbi Laura Geller has called "the Torah of our lives."[22] In the ideal Jewish ritual life imagined by Adelman and her followers, only one out of the year's twelve New Moon celebrations would include men, and Adelman admits that it was never enacted.[23]

The themes of healing, women's connection with nature, and women's wisdom converge in the editor's elaboration of the moon midrash. When Agus interprets the phrase from *Pirke de-Rabbi Eliezer*, "they are destined to be renewed like the New Moons," she implies it means that women would one day be equal to men. In contrast, Adelman believes that it points to women's *distinction* from men. This is first subtly indicated in her translation of the phrase as "and in the future world too they will be rewarded for their firm faith in God, in that, like the new moons, they too, may monthly be rejuvenated."[24] For Adelman, renewal and rejuvenation consist of women's unique wisdom that includes a knowledge of nature, as well as the ability to synchronize biological processes to the natural rhythms of the world and to other women.

All the principles of feminist spirituality described above can be found in Adelman's moon midrash, which begins with the Exodus from Egypt.

> In our wilderness wandering we learned to speak to the heavens and find answers written in the shapes of clouds . . . the desert sustained us all with the same umbilical cord.
>
> Is it any wonder that we who had emerged from the Sea of Reeds together into the wilderness of Sinai all began to live by one rhythm? And is the wonder any greater that the cycles of the moon reverberated in every woman at the same time, in the same way? As soon as the moon was born anew in the sky, each woman began to bleed.[25]

After the incident of the golden calf, the reward given to women included knowledge: "the moon would teach us about the rhythms of the seasons and the months of the year." Certain women would guard the memories of the songs, the postures, the foods, and the fragrances "so that we could tell our daughters and granddaughters in years to come." This idyllic period eventually ended.

> As the Jewish people traveled beyond their desert existence, women began to menstruate on different days, each in her own unique relationship to the moon.
>
> The women at Sinai had taken this eventuality into account. They had prayed to the Shekhinah, Moon of Israel, for guidance. If the sacred knowledge of the months were lost, the Shekhinah let them know that in a future time when women sought this monthly wisdom once again, it would be rediscovered as easily as moving aside a rock to uncover the fragrant plant beneath. Then the ritual would be reinstated through a community of women who remembers, as in a distant dream, how the moon once called to them at Sinai.
>
> We are that community.[26]

Women connect to God spiritually through their bodies, especially through their menstrual cycles. Adelman and other Jewish women who accept this spiritual feminist belief valorize the identity of female with nature and male with culture. Traditional Judaism's perception of women as physical, corporeal, earthy—summarized in the word *gashmiyut,* a term of disdain—is turned into a point of honor.[27] It is not clear whether one can say that nature is deified in the moon midrash. That is, whereas at first glance it seems that the moon is the object of worship—for Jews, this would be tantamount to idolatry and regarded with horror—but, more likely, the moon is simply the visual manifestation of the Shekhinah. Elsewhere in the book Shekhinah is understood to refer to "the Indwelling Presence of God which is everywhere" and, in kabbalah, the feminine aspect of the divine.[28]

The theatrical quality of the midrash is characteristic of the Rosh Hodesh ceremonies featured in *Miriam's Well.* Some of the ceremonies are quite exciting and cathartic, deliberately moving the participants in and out of intense emotional states. The participants seek the thrill of being part of an ancient drama, situating their lives within a far larger and meaningful saga that has engaged Jews for centuries. The ritual for Rosh Hodesh Nisan involves a symbolic reenactment of leaving Egypt. The Hebrew name for Egypt, Mitzrayim, is understood as the Hebrew *metzarim* (narrow straits), and all the participants form a narrow canal through which one person must squeeze. They liken this to birth through the vaginal canal, and the participants are instructed to imagine themselves feeling enormously constrained and hampered, and then released with great joy.[29] This dramatic and highly programmed mode of worship requires a certain love for an expressive behavior set within planned contours, much like play or art. Some women would be uncomfortable with that experience, and others would simply find it unappealing. Furthermore, most religious Jews, who are admittedly used to the contrivances that accompany any ritual performance, do not experience ritual as so transparently fabricated or designed so obviously to produce strong emotions.

The rituals described in *Miriam's Well* are a radical expression of the desire apparent among the alternative religious communities formed in the 1970s and 1980s to create a less cerebral and more embodied form of worship, as well as to develop theologies that were experiential, less "in the head" than "from the heart." Sociological studies of baby boomers have shown that in contrast to that of previous generations, their religious observance has been more individualized and experiential.[30] Perhaps connected to this tendency was the conflation of ceremonies commemorating national, communal events with opportunities to focus on one's personal, individual life. The feminist movement began by challenging the conventional boundaries between what was considered personal and what was considered political, and this was articulated in the slogan "the personal is political." While consciousness-raising galvanized women toward fighting for political change or reforming communal structures to be more egalitarian, it also set in motion a turn toward a more therapeutic focus on the individual.[31] The communal structure of Jewish ritual and worship acts as a force that keeps this individualizing tendency in check.

The convergence of personal and communal is apparent in the ritual object of Kos Miriam, the Cup of Miriam, invented in the late 1980s by a Rosh Hodesh group. The story of Miriam's well was concretized by the use of a vessel containing water, and during the Rosh Hodesh ritual it was an object of meditation and a source for inspiring greater elaboration on the ways that women receive and transmit spiritual strength. New and revived interpretations and elaborations on the figure of Miriam that were emerging in and outside of Rosh Hodesh groups were recalled. Stories of Miriam's oppression as a slave in Egypt and her role within her family served as a model for women dealing with their personal crises. The ritual drinking of water from the Kos Miriam and the accompanying meditation pull the individual Jewish woman into the narrative of her people's history.[32] The fact that in America the incorporation of a Kos Miriam during the Passover seder is no longer a sign of religious radicalism is a testimony to the way that the ritual harmonizes with other features of Judaism: the centrality of the Exodus myth and the theme of redemption, the frequent use of table rituals, and the compatibility of Kos Miriam with Kos Eliyahu—the Cup of Elijah symbolizing the hope for redemption. Miriam is also emblematic of a feminism that does not disrupt community. She evokes the passions of the Exodus story, but as Aaron and Moses's sister, Miriam represents an image of women living in a loving and usually cooperative manner with men.

The renaissance of Jewish writing that began in the late 1960s continued into the 1980s and had an obvious impact on Rosh Hodesh gatherings. There was a tremendous upsurge in the number of popular publications dealing with Jewish women's history, religious experiences, and literary expression. This included translations of classical midrash pertaining to women, new midrash authored by women, feminist additions to the Passover seder and Purim celebration, and new liturgy incorporating feminist prayers and feminine and gender-neutral God-language. The material in these popular publications contributed to the growing number of Rosh Hodesh groups and were incorporated into them, as the invention of Kos Miriam demonstrates, resulting in diverse ways of acknowledging women's ties to the New Moon.

New academic research on Jewish women, spurred by Jewish feminism, intersected with contemporary women's revival of Rosh Hodesh. In the mid-

1980s Chava Weissler began to disseminate her research on late medieval *tkhines,* Yiddish supplicatory prayers, which she attributed to women authors. Weissler did not unearth evidence that Ashkenazic women recognized Rosh Hodesh as a holiday specific to them, nor did she find references to observances they followed on that day, but she examined many tkhines that were designed to be recited on the New Moon.[33] In the 1990s, the research of Susan Sered showed evidence of specific women's Rosh Hodesh ceremonies prior to the one created in 1972. Sered found that women living in Jerusalem who had originated from Kurdistan, Yemen, and Turkey had distinctive ways of honoring Rosh Hodesh that were not shared by men. They would visit cemeteries and Rachel's Tomb on the day before Rosh Hodesh; on the day itself they would light candles as a mode of asking divine intercession, and they avoided work (specifically sewing and laundry).[34] Rosh Hodesh leaders applauded Weissler's and Sered's research as giving legitimacy to their feminist efforts at prayer or to create new liturgy; to them it refuted charges that women's desire to pray together and create their own prayers "originated in non-Jewish, hence insidious, influences."[35] The new research added more proof to the feminist claim that women had their own religious convictions and practices independent of men.[36]

However, these premodern traditions have had little direct effect on the substance of contemporary women's Rosh Hodesh practices. Modern American women simply do not feel the need to curtail their work, recite tkhines, light candles, or visit cemeteries on Rosh Hodesh (except for ultra-Orthodox women, who continue to recite tkhines). There seems to be only one obvious effort to revive the Ashkenazic women's custom of reciting tkhines on Rosh Hodesh. In 1992 Rivka Zakutinsky published *Techines: Voices from the Heart,* a collection of new tkhines for an American Orthodox audience. Zakutinsky was deeply impressed by the Ashkenazic women's piety exemplified by her tkhines-reciting mother: her compositions closely follow the traditional tkhine supplicatory template, and they are to be recited in Yiddish, with the worshiper glancing at the English translation for understanding. Half of the tkhines in her volume are connected to the New Moon. Like the older tkhines, they are meant to be recited by women privately at home or in the synagogue during the Sabbath service when the upcoming New Moon is announced.[37] Zakutinsky's revival of an older form of women's Rosh Hodesh is in striking contrast to liberal women's efforts to rejuvenate women's sense of themselves as religious agents.

There are, however, Orthodox women who are determined to pray with other women, lead the prayers, and chant the Torah for the congregation.

Perhaps one can regard Orthodox women's establishment of women's *tefillah* (prayer) groups as an expression of the same mix of impulses that triggered the creation of women's Rosh Hodesh ceremonies. A women's tefillah group (Orthodox halakhah has not conferred upon women the right to constitute a minyan) is a assemblage of women who meet separately from men to pray one of the established regular prayer services, minus the prayers requiring a quorum of men. The first tefillah group made its appearance in New York in 1972, at the beginning of the Jewish feminist movement and at the time of the creation of the first modern Rosh Hodesh ceremony.[38]

A women's tefillah group shares with the new Rosh Hodesh ceremony key elements: each is a separate gathering of women whose purpose is to develop their spiritual lives independent of men, to nurture a feeling of community with other women, to study and celebrate their Jewish heritage as women, and to worship together.[39] The preeminent tefillah group in Israel, Nashot HaKotel (Women of the Wall), which has met on Rosh Hodesh since 1988, defends its existence partly on the traditional texts affirming Rosh Hodesh as a women's holiday, as does the Montreal women's tefillah group, which has met on Rosh Hodesh since 1982. However, most tefillah group activists regard a regular meeting on the morning of Rosh Hodesh as too disruptive of their work schedule and (if they are married with children) their family's routine. Only one of the forty women's tefillah groups that currently designate themselves as part of the women's tefillah group network in North America meets on the morning of Rosh Hodesh; the rest meet on Sabbath morning no more than once a month, and only four are scheduled to be proximate to the Sabbath on which the New Moon is announced.[40] Orthodox women are particularly averse to being perceived as too innovative; they pray only with the versions of the prayer book endorsed by Orthodox rabbis, and their creative additions (beyond the existence of the group itself) consist of acknowledging female life cycle transitions in the service when they arise among the members of the congregation. It is not obvious that participants in women's tefillah groups accept the talmudic teaching that Rosh Hodesh is a woman's holiday. They are firmly committed to upholding Jewish law, and they regard a Rosh Hodesh ceremony involving ritual or liturgical innovation as something that only non-Orthodox women would find meaningful. A women's tefillah group is, to them, less radical than a Rosh Hodesh ceremony.[41]

Ironically, the discovery of earlier women's Rosh Hodesh prayers and practices, and the emergence of Orthodox women's tefillah groups, may actually highlight the novelty of the recent Rosh Hodesh ceremonies. The

"Moondance." This painting (original in color) is inspired by Rosh Hodesh celebrations and their connection to women. Used with the permission of Judith Margolis, http://www.judithmargolis.com.

liturgies of Rosh Hodesh ceremonies are, in important ways, discontinuous with the past. New tkhines, which have been incorporated into Rosh Hodesh ceremonies, are distinct from traditional tkhines in a number of ways. In their desire to give affirmation to the sanctity of women's bodies, they are more focused on women's biological functions. In addition, they are designed to be recited by a single individual in the midst of a community of supportive women, and they are offered only by another woman when she revises one to reflect her unique situation.[42] God images and prayer language are also distinctive, especially those addressing a feminine God and the moon as her representation.

Contemporary innovative Rosh Hodesh liturgy and rituals are also unprecedented when they remove the supplicatory element entirely. Some new liturgies reject the hierarchical relationship of the worshiper and God characteristic of traditional Jewish prayer; instead, they appear to be primarily women talking to women, and women talking with women. Women engaged in this discussion may reflect on their connection to God or even praise God directly through a blessing (*berakha*). However, they relate to the divine as only a beneficent and readily available presence, rejecting the classical Jewish belief in a personal deity who is the ruler of the universe and who guides history (and bestows disease and ill fortune) in order to reward and or punish as part of a divine plan. Alternatively, God may be portrayed an immanent presence within themselves and within nature. Worship of God may be dispensed with; the women turn to each other for help in achieving spiritual connection.[43] The theological outlook implicit in these contemporary prayers is not unique to Jewish women, of course, but typical of a modern perspective that places the locus of control within human beings.

ROSH HODESH ENTERS THE MAINSTREAM

The entrance of Rosh Hodesh ceremonies into the mainstream of Jewish communal life became evident in the mid-1990s. One obvious sign of this was that *Miriam's Well* went into its fourth printing in 1996, and in the same year the full range of Rosh Hodesh ceremonies described above was anthologized by Susan Berrin in *Celebrating the New Moon: A Rosh Chodesh Anthology.* In addition to descriptions of new ceremonies, prayers, and poems, the volume also contains reflections on the traditional holiday and liturgy. The book also includes an annotated directory of Rosh Hodesh groups, first assembled in 1992 by Beth Edberg and updated by Berrin in 1994. There is information on fifty-six ceremonies in Canada and the

United States submitted by the contact person of the Rosh Hodesh group, and the descriptions are not uniform or consistently detailed. According to the data, forty-four of the Rosh Hodesh groups included special rituals in their celebration; many of these mentioned that they utilized the rituals described in *Miriam's Well.* Thirty-five included study (some groups included ritual and prayer), which consisted most frequently of a presentation or lecture on a topic, followed by a discussion; some groups reported studying traditional texts. Twenty-five indicated that their gathering had the features of a friendship circle in which life cycle rituals were celebrated together or the participants had been meeting together as a group for years. Only four of the fifty-six groups celebrated Rosh Hodesh by conducting a prayer service along conventional lines on the morning of Rosh Hodesh.[44] Currently, according to my review of available literature and anecdotal evidence, there are more Rosh Hodesh gatherings than in the 1990s. Study programs seem to be the most common. Most of these are private gatherings of women who examine a book, study a text, or arrange for the appearance of a guest lecturer to discuss a topic of interest.

Another sign of the acceptance of Rosh Hodesh is its appearance within mainstream Jewish communal organizations. Synagogues have become involved in fostering Rosh Hodesh groups. Searching through the Web, one can find Modern Orthodox, Conservative, Reconstructionist, and Reform synagogues that announce in their newsletters the regular meeting of a Rosh Hodesh study group. Not all of these are led by synagogue personnel or meet in the synagogue, but they receive the support of the professional staff and the institutions' communication services. Rabbis and Jewish educators regard Rosh Hodesh as a good programmatic device for enhancing the religious lives of the women in their community. These institution-based Rosh Hodesh programs testify that Rosh Hodesh has been brought into the mainstream of American Jewish culture and, in some cases, professionalized.

Rosh Hodesh women's events are becoming a regular feature of Jewish programs for college-age Jews. At the 2002 Hillel Program Professionals Conference, a workshop was offered on why and how to design activities around Rosh Hodesh. The national Web site for Hillel contains examples of more than a dozen Rosh Hodesh programs that were successfully executed on campuses throughout the United States. Among the social, educational, or ritual experiences described was a brief lesson about Miriam and her role in the Passover story and then eased into an art activity consisting of painting and adorning tambourines; another offered a lecture by a Chabad Hasidic woman and a local female psychologist, with the focus on "the mystery of the mikveh." Some of the programs indicate that there is a regular Rosh Hodesh group that meets on the campus. Most, but not all of these events, are for women only.[45]

Two significant educational outreach efforts centered around Rosh Hodesh have been fostered by Hadassah, the Women's Zionist Organization of America. In 1997, the organization began developing and publishing educational material to be used at Hadassah study groups. In 2000, Hadassah joined with Jewish Lights Publishing to produce the second of two volumes of educational material, this one intended for women's Rosh Hodesh gatherings. Titled *Moonbeams: A Hadassah Rosh Hodesh Guide,* the volume offers nine topics of study, including the history and observance of Rosh Hodesh, Jewish self-hatred, medical ethics, women and Israeli law, and women rabbis. Each month's material features English translations of religious texts or an excerpt from a modern speech or essay, with editorial introductions situating the text within its historical context. These are followed by questions for discussion, as well as suggested activities and programs. The volume is designed for non-Orthodox women who have attained a high level of achievement in secular education; it is an attempt to bring their Jewish literacy to a higher level and to see the Jewish intellectual heritage as a source for making life decisions and for fostering communal activism on behalf of women.[46] The monthly programs do not offer an opportunity for worship or for spiritual activity other than studying religious texts. Worship and ritual are topics of discussion only.

One of the most interesting and innovative programs recently developed for Rosh Hodesh is designed for teenage girls. Rosh Hodesh: It's a Girl Thing! was developed by Kolot: The Center for Jewish Women's and Gender Studies, housed in the Reconstruction Rabbinical College, with lead funding from the Hadassah Foundation.[47] Mental health professionals, educators, and feminists, as well as Rosh Hodesh pioneers like Agus, Adelman, and Berrin, designed the program. It is a Rosh Hodesh girls group led by a woman who facilitates discussions and activities of many modalities—art, dance, music, cooking—that are fun, help girls celebrate their strengths, guide them in social interactions with other girls, and learn about their own religious and ethical Jewish heritage as a source of that strength. The program was designed to teach adolescent girls to respond critically and responsibly to the messages of American popular culture that promote sexist body-consciousness, consumerism, and dangerous behaviors such as eating disorders, unhealthy and degrading sexual activities, drugs, and drinking. The material was first piloted in different communities (including Orthodox, Reform, Conservative, Russian immigrant, and mixed groups) and is now available to all. However, unlike previous Rosh Hodesh groups, this one involves training and mentoring of group leaders, a scripted program, and ongoing consultation and support. Participants sign up in advance to form a group of a dozen or so girls, and there is a small fee. A group or organization interested in the program must make a serious financial commitment to purchase the rights to the material and the professional help. At this early date, indications are that the program has been very successful. The mothers of the girls typically make their daughters go to the first meeting, according to one of the supervisors of the Los Angeles program, but the girls are "hooked" by the end of the meeting and attend willingly after that.[48]

The Rosh Hodesh women's ceremony has expanded and diversified since its creation in 1972, and explanations for its success must take note of its compatibility with American religious culture. It is demanding of neither time nor labor, and it is scheduled just once a month. The holiday rationale is simple, the structure is flexible, and the actual events are designed to be entertaining, stimulating, and conducive to social bonding. American Jews, who demonstrate a diminished capacity for worship requiring formal expressions of praise and supplication, have shaped the day into a social occasion that celebrates their ethnic and religious heritage. Rosh Hodesh liturgies and programs typically do not explicitly advocate feminist activism, but they do promote a feminist consciousness and affirm the value of women's experiences.

The last thirty years have seen a virtual revolution of American Jewish women's religious lives, and the Rosh Hodesh ceremony is one of many new rituals that have been created in this time. Jewish girls raised within religious families are likely to regard women's special connection to Rosh Hodesh as a part of Jewish tradition, and many will take for granted the existence of special Rosh Hodesh women's gatherings. The increasing sophistication and diversity of women's Rosh Hodesh gatherings reflect the institutionalization of feminism in American Jewish life, as well as the success of American Jewish women in transmitting their pride at being Jewish women to the next generation.

NOTES

This essay has benefited from the insight and assistance of Phyllis K. Herman, Karen Fox, Michael Rosen, David Ackerman, Sally Goodis, Elizabeth Say, and Stephanie Jackson, as well as numerous women who shared with me their reasons for and against participating in Rosh Hodesh gatherings.

1. Catherine Bell, *Ritual Theory, Ritual Practice* (New York: Oxford University Press, 1992), 221, also 140–41, where Bell regards the "strategic" dimensions of ritual as primary. On the function of ritual for American Jews, see Vanessa Ochs, "A Matter of Belonging," in *Still Believing: Jewish, Christian and Muslim Women Affirm Their Faith,* ed. Victoria L. Erickson and Susan A. Farrell (Maryknoll, NY: Orbis, 2005).

2. On the practices of Rosh Hodesh that prevailed among American Ashkenazic Jews, see Irving Greenberg, *The Jewish Way: Living the Holidays* (New York: Summit, 1988); Isaac Klein, *A Guide to Jewish Religious Practice* (New York: Jewish Theological Seminary, 1979). On kabbalistic modes of observing the day, which were more prevalent among Sephardic and Mizrahi Jews, see Moshe Hallamish, *Kabbalah in Liturgy, Halakhah and Customs* (Ramat Gan: Bar-Ilan University Press, 2000), 537–66. Some Ashkenazic and Sephardic and Mizrahi practices associated with Rosh Hodesh are discussed below. My description of the synagogue-based Rosh Hodesh rituals reflects general Jewish practice.

3. Arlene Agus was the first to document the modern Rosh Hodesh ceremony. See "This Month Is for You: Observing Rosh Hodesh as a Woman's Holiday," in *The Jewish Woman: New Perspectives,* ed. Elizabeth Koltun (New York: Schocken, 1976), 84–93. An expanded version of Agus's original article, "Examining Rosh Chodesh: An Analysis of the Holiday and Its Textual Sources," appears in *Celebrating the New Moon: A Rosh Chodesh Anthology,* ed. Susan Berrin (Northvale, NJ: Jason Aronson, 1996), 3–22.

4. The midrash is found in chapter 45 of *Pirke de-Rabbi Eliezer,* a volume of legends written ca. 750 C.E. The remarks of Rashi (Rabbi Shelomo Yitzhaki, 1040–1105) and those of his pupils and descendants, the Tosafists, are found in Rashi's commentary to the Babylonian Talmud Megillah 22b. Agus found reference to the opinions of Rashi and the Tosafists in *Mekore Haminhagin,* no. 38. She cites specific work prohibitions mentioned in Babylonian Talmud Megillah 22b, in the book of responsa by Simeon ben Zemah Duran known as *Sefer Tashbetz,* section 3, no. 244; in *Sefer Hemdat Yamim,* vol. 1, 23b–24a; and in *Mishnah Berurah,* nos. 421–24. She found other references to the women's holiday in Mishnah Taanit 1:6 and *Sefer Hahasidim,* no. 121.

5. Agus, "This Month Is for You," 86, paraphrases the opinion of the sage known as Or Zaruah cited in J. D. Eisenstein, *Otzar Dinim Uminhagim,* 377. The author does not discuss further the ritual of women's water immersion following her period of menstruation.

6. Agus, "This Month Is for You," 85. The source of the midrash is Babylonian Talmud Hullin 60a. Isa. 30:26 reads, in full (JPS translation), "And the light of the moon shall become like the light of the sun, and the light of the sun shall become sevenfold, like the light of the seven days, when the Lord binds up His people's wounds and heals the injuries it has suffered."

7. Agus, "This Month Is for You," 86. According to Agus, this teaching is from *Sefer Hemdat Yamim* 1:25. She credits Rabbi Daniel Shevitz for this and other mystical references.

8. Agus, "This Month Is for You," 86. The first appropriation of the Lilith story

for feminist purposes occurred in 1972 as well; see Judith Plaskow Goldenberg, "The Jewish Feminist: Conflict in Identities," in the special women's issue of *Response: A Contemporary Jewish Review* 18 (Summer 1973): 15–21. For later uses of Lilith themes, see Jody Elizabeth Myers, "The Myth of Matriarchy in Recent Writings on Jewish Women's Spirituality," *Jewish Social Studies* 4 (Fall 1997): 3–7; Enid Dame, Lilly Rivlin, Henny Wenkart, and Naomi Wolf, *Which Lilith? Feminist Writers Create the World's First Woman* (Northvale, NJ: Jason Aaronson, 1998).

9. See Judith Baskin, *Midrashic Women: Formations of the Feminine in Rabbinic Literature* (Hanover, NH: University Press of New England, 2002), chap. 2.

10. It is unclear whether they were aware of the reference to women engaged in petty gambling games on Rosh Hodesh, an activity certainly nonspiritual in character, in the ethical will of Eleazar of Mainz (d. 1357) in *Hebrew Ethical Wills*, ed. Israel Abrahams (Philadelphia: Jewish Publication Society, 1926), 210–11.

11. Agus, "This Month Is for You," 89.

12. Arlene Agus, "Examining Rosh Hodesh," in *Celebrating the New Moon: A Rosh Chodesh Anthology*, ed. Susan Berrin (Northvale, NJ: Jason Aronson, 1996), 4.

13. In contrast, the moon as symbol and reality holds more power in Islam, where the lunar year is never "corrected" by the position of the earth in relation to the sun.

14. This and other women's rituals that incorporate the reenactment of myths relating to women's power are discussed in Myers, "The Myth of Matriarchy."

15. See Sylvia Barack Fishman, *A Breath of Life: Feminism in the American Jewish Community* (New York: Free Press, 1993).

16. There were women-only Rosh Hodesh study groups that had no ritual component to them, but these are not the focus of this essay. Ruth Berger Goldston and Merle Feld "drew on the knowledge of about a half dozen women who had been involved to starting twelve to fifteen groups in the last two decades" to make their observations, found in "Starting and Growing a Rosh Chodesh Group," in *Celebrating the New Moon: A Rosh Chodesh Anthology*, ed. Susan Berrin (Northvale, NJ: Jason Aronson, 1996), 86n3.

17. This observation was made to me by Rabbi Karen Fox, who received her ordination from the Reform movement in 1978.

18. Judith Plaskow, *Standing Again at Sinai: Judaism from a Feminist Perspective* (San Francisco: HarperCollins, 1990), 67.

19. This description is taken from Cynthia Eller, the foremost academic expert on the movement, in her *Living in the Lap of the Goddess* (Boston, Beacon, 1995), 3–4. Eller is particularly careful to emphasize the lack of agreement within the movement. Although these five principles are central, there is much disagreement over the specifics of each. The term "feminist spirituality" is sometimes used interchangeably with "cultural feminism," and there are those who carefully define the parameters of each—the former more concerned with the quest for gender equality and the latter for the inclusion of feminine values into life—but this serves no purpose in my analysis. See Eller, *Living in the Lap of the Goddess*, 45, 45n.

20. Penina V. Adelman, *Miriam's Well: Rituals for Jewish Women Around the Year* (1986; repr., New York: Biblio Press, 1990), 7.

21. Adelman elaborates on the central role of storytelling in the Rosh Hodesh ceremony: the stories "provide a sense of the oral tradition of Jewish women known from earliest times, as when Lilith commiserated with Eve over their troubles with Adam. [This is a reference to the modern midrash on Lilith and Eve composed by Judith Plaskow; see note 8 above.] As most oral material has been left unwritten we have recorded some exchanges verbatim, serving as examples of the potential in all of us, realizing that *since they were told in the presence of women only,* we are providing a link with the past" (*Miriam's Well,* 14; emphasis added).

22. Laura Geller, "Encountering the Divine Presence," in *Four Centuries of Jewish Women's Spirituality: A Sourcebook,* ed. Ellen M. Umansky and Dianne Ashton (Boston: Beacon, 1992), 244. In her discussion of the origins of Second Wave feminism, Sara Evans writes, "The growth of the women's movement thus depended less on specific ideas than on the ability of women to tell each other their own stories, to claim them as the basis of political action." See Evans, *Tidal Wave: How Women Changed America at Century's End* (New York: Free Press, 2003), 29–31.

23. The ritual is described in Adelman, *Miriam's Well,* 24, 25. Adelman explains,

> Rosh Hodesh groups on whose experiences this book is based have never marked the new moon with both men and women. What we present here is our ideal for a Rosh Hodesh celebration. Until now this has been a hope and dream of the women who regularly observe the new moon together. Such a joint Rosh Hodesh would be the culmination of regular meetings of men or women only who have been exploring their unique relationships to God and to each other. Thus, *Rosh Hodesh Tishre* would become a yearly reunion of men and women focusing on the insights gained in the separate groups the previous year. (114n1)

24. This is based on the version in Louis Ginzberg, *Legends of the Jews,* trans. Paul Radin (Philadelphia: Jewish Publication Society of America, 1968), 3:122, as cited in Adelman, *Miriam's Well,* 7.

25. Adelman, *Miriam's Well,* 28.

26. Ibid., 28–29.

27. This equation of female to nature and men to culture is characteristic of feminist spirituality, and is expressed openly by Adelman, *Miriam's Well,* 4. The embodied spirituality expressed in this and other Rosh Hodesh texts, as well as the articulation of a type of Jewish ecofeminism, is examined by Ron H. Feldman, "'On Your New Moons': The Feminist Transformation of the Jewish New Moon Festival," *Journal of Women and Religion* 19/20 (2003): 26–51. Feldman points out (35–38) that the feminists who, in their Rosh Hodesh ceremonies, proudly accept their status as *gashmiyut,* do not seem to find value in the *mikvah,* the ritual of water immersion mandated by Jewish law after menstruation. He suggests that this would imply that women need purification.

28. Adelman, *Miriam's Well,* 15.

29. Ibid., 60–66.

30. Wade Clark Roof, *A Generation of Seekers: Spiritual Journeys of the Baby Boom*

Generation (San Francisco: HarperCollins, 1993). The data in this study were collected during the 1980s.

31. Evans, *Tidal Wave,* chap. 4, describes this as an inevitable result of the particular dynamics of Second Wave feminism and describes its divisive as well as creative effects within the feminist movement.

32. Penina V. Adelman, "A Drink from Miriam's Cup: Invention of Tradition among Jewish Women," *Journal of Feminist Studies in Religion* 10, no. 2 (1994): 163.

33. Chava Weissler, *Voices of the Matriarchs: Listening to the Prayers of Early Modern Jewish Women* (Boston: Beacon, 1998). Weissler began speaking about and publishing her research on tkhines in the 1980s, and much of this material was revised and collected in her book. Weissler did not discover the existence of the female prayer leader—the *firzogerin* or *zogerke*—but she certainly brought new attention to the role. For more on this, see *Voices of the Matriarchs,* 9, 9n.

34. Susan Starr Sered, *Women as Ritual Experts: The Religious Lives of Elderly Jewish Women in Jerusalem* (New York: Oxford University Press, 1992). Specific to Rosh Hodesh is her article, "Rosh Chodesh Observances among Older Sefardic Women," in *Celebrating the New Moon: A Rosh Chodesh Anthology,* ed. Susan Berrin (Northvale, NJ: Jason Aronson, 1996), 78–80.

35. Arlene Agus voiced these desires in 1976, in response to finding rabbinic midrashim linking women to Rosh Hodesh. See Agus, "Examining Rosh Chodesh," 4. Chava Weissler addresses this issue in part 3 of *Voices of the Matriarchs.*

36. See Tracy Guren Klirs, "Tkines for Rosh Chodesh: Women's Prayers of Devotion," in *Celebrating the New Moon: A Rosh Chodesh Anthology,* ed. Susan Berrin (Northvale, NJ: Jason Aronson, 1996), 49–65.

37. Rivka Zakutinsky, *Techines: Voices from the Heart* (Brooklyn, NY: Aura Press, 1992). Her tkhines are unlikely to become popular even among Orthodox women because the language of prayer for American Orthodox women is Hebrew. Weissler, *Voices of the Matriarchs,* 159, points out the sentimentality inherent in Zakutinsky's choice of language; unlike most of their Ashkenazic foremothers, American Orthodox women do not have to resort to the vernacular.

38. I am unaware of a source for the history of women's tefillah groups (see note 48 below for a description of two specific groups). Much has been written about them, as they are quite controversial. For a review of rabbinic rulings on the subject, see Aryeh Frimer and Dov Frimer, "Women's Prayer Services: Theory and Practice," *Tradition* 32, no. 2 (1998): 5–118.

39. Indeed, it is this association with feminism, which is evident as well in the participants' mastery and performance of the public functions of communal prayer (leading the service, chanting Torah, giving a discourse on the Torah), that has led more conservative women and men to denounce participants as illegitimately deviating from tradition.

40. Bonna Devora Haberman, "Nashot HaKotel: Women in Jerusalem Celebrate Rosh Chodesh," in *Celebrating the New Moon: A Rosh Chodesh Anthology,* ed. Susan Berrin (Northvale, NJ: Jason Aronson, 1996), 66–77, with reference to the textual precedents on p. 67. Norma Baumel Joseph, who helped establish the Mon-

treal group in 1982 and has been instrumental in sustaining it ever since, writes, "Our Rosh Chodesh services continue the traditions of our female ancestors, in regard to both celebrating the day and joining in prayer." See Joseph, "Reflections on Observing Rosh Chodesh with My Women's Tefillah Group," in *Celebrating the New Moon: A Rosh Chodesh Anthology,* ed. Susan Berrin (Northvale, NJ: Jason Aronson, 1996), 111–16, quotation on p. 114. For a full listing of women's tefillah groups, see http://wtgdirectory.helping.org.il or http://www.edah.org/tefilla.cfm.

41. Sari Abrams, leader of the Women's Tefillah Group in Los Angeles, and Norma Baumel Joseph, interview by the author, March 2003. Joseph writes, "Those of us who participate in this tefillah group do so out of a deep concern for the laws of Judaism and with a profound sense of obligation to pray. We are not attempting to leave our community nor have we turned our backs on its traditional way of life. Rather, we are seeking a vehicle of deeper involvement, an expression of greater commitment, within an Orthodox framework" ("Reflections," 112).

42. Weissler, *Voices of the Matriarchs,* 164–67. Weissler also points out that the greater biological focus is due to the composition of tkhines for life cycle events primarily, but also because of the contemporary desire to positively affirm women's bodies.

43. A good example of this is Ruth Lerner's "Meditation for the New Moon," in *Celebrating the New Moon: A Rosh Chodesh Anthology,* ed. Susan Berrin (Northvale, NJ: Jason Aronson, 1996), 182–83. Marcia Falk has written prayers for Rosh Hodesh (she intended that these be recited by men as well as women) that do not address God at all; see Falk, *The Book of Blessings: New Jewish Prayers for Daily Life* (San Francisco: HarperCollins, 1996), 396.

44. Berrin, *Celebrating the New Moon,* 267–92.

45. See http://www.hillel.org.

46. Carol Diament, ed., *Moonbeams: A Hadassah Rosh Hodesh Guide* (Woodstock, VT: Jewish Lights, 2000).

47. Its creation and implementation was funded by Hadassah, and other family and Jewish communal foundations have supported it as well. I thank Mindy Shapiro, project director, for samples of program material and speaking to me about Rosh Hodesh: It's a Girl Thing!

48. Catherine Steiner-Adair, a clinical psychologist and member of the National Advisory Board for Rosh Hodesh: It's a Girl Thing!, describes the need for the program and the logic of its curriculum in the foreword to the *Sourcebook for Leaders.* Stacey Barrett, director of Youth Education Services and Israel Programs, Bureau of Jewish Education of Los Angeles, spoke to me about the Los Angeles group.

CHAPTER TEN

MIRIAM'S OBJECT LESSON

Ritualizing the Presence of Miriam

VANESSA L. OCHS

From the 1980s to the present, a plethora of new Jewish women's rituals has been created by American Jewish women. Typically, the creators—among them artists, musicians, writers, curators, liturgists, scholars, educators, clergy, feminist philanthropists, and communal activists—have innovated in their homes, studies, studios, and informal worship spaces. Others have worked within the institutional frameworks of Jewish women's groups, philanthropies, and synagogues.

These new rituals address spiritual lacunae broadly felt by Jewish women. They reclaim, refashion, and revise the traditional ways. They have come about as conscious responses and practical adjustments to contemporary needs and realities. They have also unfolded more haphazardly, examples of bricolage that are spontaneous and playfully inventive. All these new rituals preserve a connection to the Jewish past and establish a palpable sense of continuity. At the same time, however, they initiate and mask radical departures.

While many people joyfully embraced these new rituals at the time of their emergence, others, more resistant to innovation, regarded them with suspicion, hostility, or intolerance. At best, they may have viewed the new rituals as newfangled ideas that would fade away. At worst, they may have seen these rituals as mocking or endangering the holy, inherited practices of the community. Indeed, with the passage of time, some of the innovations have receded, but others are becoming standard practice in many sectors of American Jewry. There are, in fact, young people who have grown up witnessing these new rituals performed in their synagogues or grandparents' homes, and they cannot imagine a "proper" Judaism without them.

The emergence of new women's rituals is well documented.[1] Two aspects of the new rituals, however, deserve greater attention. The first is the role that physical objects play in the generation of the rituals. The second is the role that Miriam the prophetess plays in both the objects and rituals. In this essay, I will suggest that the new rituals depending on objects linked to Miriam have taken hold readily because they have been perceived as less provocative than other innovations.

OBJECTS

That the role of objects often goes without mention in the study of new ritual is not surprising. In the academic study of religions, it is commonly assumed that when a new ritual practice emerges, first an idea or situation is generated, and subsequently the objects needed to give it form and shape are then found or created. The objects are considered as props, so to speak. For instance, in a historical context, it is commonly supposed that the *idea* of commemorating the Exodus from Egypt preceded the ritual eating of matzah. Likewise, the *idea* of remembering those who perished in the Shoah preceded the emergence of Holocaust works of art, museums, and memorials. According to this logic, objects—along with spoken liturgies and actions—develop to concretize or enact ideas and beliefs. But when one studies religion from the vantage of material culture (a most masterful work is Colleen McDannel's *Material Christianity*), one sees that the process is just as often reversed: a ritual practice can emerge because a concrete object has been created or has become available.

Starting with the object, as it is created and used in lived religious experience, goes against the grain of conventional Jewish study, which typically originates with the consideration of a written sacred text. However, as Jewish texts have been male-generated and the study of such texts has been, until modernity, the province of men, it is not surprising that one might wish to look at objects to understand more accurately the practices of Jewish women, both in the past and present. As Harvey Goldberg writes, "The ethnography of contemporary communities teaches that there is much Jewish belief and practice that is not recorded in or derived from written texts. . . . Field experience also reveals that women are involved in aspects of religion from which we see them as excluded."[2]

Two particular objects generated by Jewish women, a Miriam's cup (Kos Miriam) and a Miriam's tambourine (*tof Miriam*), function as conduits through which new women's rituals are constructed, tried out, introduced, popularized, and transmitted. Establishing the authenticity of new Jewish women's spiritual practices and reifying their existence, the objects offer opportunities for contemporary Jewish women of diverse affiliations and ages to express themselves as Jews.

I have chosen to examine these objects of Miriam for two reasons. First, they have proven themselves to be popular. In 2000, the Judaica catalog *Hamakor Gallerie* featured on its cover both a Miriam's cup and a Miriam's tambourine seder plate. The catalog offered many other Miriam-related objects: a Miriam's tambourine matzah tray, a Miriam's tambourine silk tallit and matching bag set, a Miriam's tambourine crocheted head covering, two different works of art depicting Miriam, and Ellen Frankel's *The Book of Miriam.* On the store's Web site, one could search directly for Miriam's objects under the heading, "There's something about Miriam," playing on the title of a popular movie. In 2000, at the National Havurah Summer Institute retreat, a number of women in attendance sported different T-shirts with images of Miriam and of Miriam and the dancing women. In Jewish homes throughout the United States, not only commercially made Miriam's cups and tambourines are displayed; there are the ones that have been handcrafted by adults and children as Jewish art projects. "Objets de Miriam" are clearly filling a void and creating a niche.

There is a second, perhaps more significant, reason for examining these objects of Miriam: they demonstrate ways in which Jewish women have gently, and sometimes surreptitiously, "struggled to retrieve a usable past."[3] That is, the objects have allowed women to stay linked to traditional ways while simultaneously preserving their freedom to critique, adapt, and transform. These new objects and the rituals to which they have become linked reveal a strategy of resistance more readily available to women than that other tool of resistance, written language, which has been, historically, more accessible to men. The objects allow Jewish women to gain presence, power, and voice without subjecting themselves to being silenced, censured, or cut off. In the cup and tambourine, one can witness feminist strategies or "coding," as Joan Radner calls it,[4] artful ways in which women of many cultures quietly, often covertly and symbolically, oblige their tradition to be adaptive while at the same time disguising their transformational activities. In deciphering the coding of these objects, the "feminist messages" that are "a common phenomenon in the lives of women, who have often been dominated, silenced and marginalized by men," one perceives ways through which Judaism evolves for women—and the ways in which women themselves shape it. Coded objects contain hidden, subversive energies, which both protect and guide women yearning for and moving toward greater liberation.[5]

WHY MIRIAM, NOW?

Before observing how each of these objects functions gently to connect, transform, and destabilize, we must note that it is neither coincidental nor arbitrary that both objects are linked to Miriam the prophetess. Why is it that Miriam is emerging through these objects to represent Jewish women in a ritual context? Is it strategic, coincidental, or a bit of both? Why is it that through these objects, the biblical Miriam (or a contemporary version of Miriam who resonates with the maker of the object) becomes present, and not some other ancient figure?

For over twenty years, Miriam has become a powerful, rallying image for Jewish women ritual innovators, representing what Lily Rivlin (director of the documentary *Miriam's Daughters Now,* chronicling women's ritual innovations) describes as "how Jewish women's feminist consciousness widens tradition." Through the objects, Jewish women identify with Miriam, sometimes even going so far as to rename themselves Miriam. As Rabbi Lynn Gottlieb writes in *She Who Dwells Within,* "The women of my Rosh Hodesh group felt that my experience with the story of Miriam, my gifts as a story teller, and my life as a woman rabbi were a sign that I should take on the name Miriam."[6]

IN THE BEGINNING, THERE WAS LILITH

To understand why Miriam has become a role model for many Jewish women since the 1980s, we must explore her predecessor, Lilith, in effect the "poster girl" of Jewish feminists of the 1970s. In the rabbinic legends, Lilith is Adam's first wife, who assertively claims equality with her partner (specifically, she desires also to be "on top"). Lilith is dispatched from the garden and a more compliant wife, Eve, takes her place. Thereafter Lilith is marginalized and silenced; vilified, she becomes known as the threat to new mothers, the demonic snatcher of newborn babies. Jody Myers, in her essay "The Myth of Matriarchy in Recent Writings on Jewish Women's Spirituality," articulately describes the role Lilith played for Jewish feminists in the early 1970s.

> [T]he tale of Lilith functioned to justify and explain male dominance and to frighten and coerce women into socially acceptable behavior. Judith Plaskow may have been the first to use Lilith as a rallying cry for Jewish feminism in 1972, but wider dissemination came in 1976 with Aviva Cantor's article in the opening issue of the first Jewish feminist

> journal, *Lilith Magazine*. . . . Cantor points out that the explicit misogyny in the original Lilith story is useful for making Jewish women both angry and brave. . . . Cantor did not revise the Lilith myth, but she did argue that there was an essence to it that was free of male bias and closer to the Genesis story: the ideals of women's struggle for independence, courage in taking risks, and "commitment to the equality of woman and man based on their creation as equals by God."[7]

When Lilith emerges in the work of Jewish feminist poets and writers, she tells her own story of the creation of woman and man, restating her platform for sexual and gender equality. She offers an enticing role model, an alternative to the compliant Eve. Lilith, empowered by an anger she embraces, speaks her piece and makes demands rather than waiting for concessions. Neither nice nor accommodating, she will be called "shrill and strident." Should her actions lead her to a place outside the camp, there is no risk: already an outsider, she is alienated, marginal, and has nothing to lose.

However effective a standard-bearer Lilith may have been for dissidents, her disenfranchisement is problematic for insiders: those Jewish women wishing to transform Jewish practice and culture more slowly, without risk to personal status and without bringing undue attention to themselves. There are also other limitations to Lilith's myth, as Myers describes:

> It is difficult to integrate Lilith into the Torah when she is simply not there; acknowledging her would accentuate women's feelings that neither are they. . . . Second, the Lilith legend reinforces the view of woman as victim and implies that her essential morality arises from her victimized status. . . . The problems this raises for individual and communal consciousness are manifold. In its favor, though, one could argue that ritualized storytelling of victimization may be an effective therapeutic tool in a world in which people do abuse one another. This myth would have only transitional value; I would think that it is too negative to be the narrative foundation of one's individual or communal identity.
>
> Finally, generating attractive qualities for Lilith poses a challenge. She can be refashioned as an independent woman who seeks equality, but the tale cannot exist without her disdain for men. . . . Most women who are creating new liturgy, ritual, and exegesis seek a more positive tone and aspire to live within a harmonious mixed community. They are loathe to be labeled as man-haters, and they tend to avoid Lilith altogether.[8]

Enter Miriam. If Lilith kills babies, Miriam—as midwife and guardian of Moses-in-the-basket—saves them. If Lilith stands at the shores of the Sea of Reeds threatening pregnant women, Miriam—standing in the very same place—celebrates the successful birth of a people through a dangerous, narrow, wet passageway. Miriam leads the women who emerge out of slavery and into freedom and works alongside powerful men, her brothers Aaron and Moses. She has the women's respect and, by leading a song of deliverance, gives voice to their memories and hopes. Miriam works gracefully, yet critically, within the system. Powerful, but not egoistic, Miriam stands for a set of positive virtues that include healing, inspiration, foresight, courage, cooperation, nurturance, and the capacity to celebrate all victories along the journey. She mentors younger women and girls who have a dim memory of Judaism in which women count less, or not at all.

This version of Miriam who emerges after Lilith is the latter-stage Jewish feminist: her consciousness has already been raised and awakened. She speaks to "Miriams" in a Jewish world being realigned daily by incremental small gestures made by women rabbis, cantors, federation executives, seminary professors, synagogue presidents, professors of Jewish studies—and, just as important, Jewish women in their communities and homes. Miriam's anger is not debilitating: well channeled and well supported by many sisters who echo her voice, it affirms women's different ways of knowing and acting in the world. Confident, the new Miriam feels empowered to "integrate the personal with traditional rituals" and make them her own.[9] She stands for any Jewish woman who is a ritual expert, amateur or professional, who widens tradition, transforming it just as she transforms sacred texts and ritual objects, moving toward active repair of the community.

In the current social climate, a woman can claim this Miriam—cooperative, patient, and ready to negotiate—as her role model and still remain within the mainstream. Unsurprisingly, Hadassah, in its 2000 publication *Moonbeams: A Hadassah Rosh Hodesh Guide,* includes Miriam among the four Jewish women to be studied by Hadassah chapters—even by those who resist identifying themselves as feminists "because of the many negative associations."[10] Hadassah members studying Miriam are encouraged to portray Miriam's character, "complex and beautiful," through artistic media[11] and to share their creative representations. Miriam's traits highlighted in the Hadassah guide include her intelligence, courage, and leadership among women (not surprisingly, traits valued within the Hadassah organization). She is praised for her human capacity to err, her goodness,

Seder plate with "Miriam's Dance" is an example of the use of Miriam in traditional rituals. The painting/collage on glass (originally in color) illustrates the passage from the Book of Exodus in which Miriam and Israelite women dance at the Sea of Reeds. Used with the permission of Lucy Rose Fischer, http://www.lucyrosedesigns.com. Photo credit: Sid Konikoff.

her defiance of Pharaoh, and her lifetime of merits that preserved her people.[12] She has power, stature, loveliness, and a place at the table.

The Miriam who is emerging in this generation in America has clearly not been transmitted, directly and unchanged, from the pages of the ancient biblical texts, midrash, or later legends. Bringing this new Miriam into being required that Jewish memory be shaped through feminist midrash, creating and emphasizing Miriam's centrality and efficacy in the Exodus story and beyond. Though in the biblical text and midrash we get glimpses of her spiritual, political, and familial importance and influence, she was, according to Judith Plaskow, "by no means accorded the narrative attention the few texts concerning her suggest she deserves."[13] In particular need of repair, Plaskow suggests, is the biblical tendency to hint at Miriam's importance as a leader of women and as a prophetess and, at the same time, to undercut it by failing to narrate her rise to leadership. The silence led Plaskow to imagine that there must have been a trove of "other Miriam traditions that were excluded from the Torah."[14] Thus, creators of Jewish feminist midrash were challenged to undo and correct androcentric transmission. Mere glimpses of Miriam in action would be replaced with fleshed-out scenarios that readily captured the imagination of readers, activists, and ritualists, and served to encourage women to look toward Miriam as a role model and to be inspired by her. The makers of new midrashim[15] were well aware that recovering Miriam through study and the creation of feminist midrash could lead to new practice and new theology. The new midrashim, works of imaginations stirred up by biblical texts and their lacunae, validated new myths lived out by women and reified through the performance of rituals. Midwives for Miriam in her new incarnation, the new midrashim would stabilize and transmit contemporary angles on her legend, making her narrative accessible and giving it the solidity and weight of written expression and, through ritual, the weight of practice.

We turn now to the objects themselves.

MIRIAM'S CUP

Miriam's cup (Kos Miriam) did not initially emerge within the Passover seder but within women's Rosh Hodesh (New Moon) groups. Penina Adelman offers her telling of the ritual's origin. In 1979, she heard the midrashic legend of Miriam's well told at a Philadelphia Rosh Hodesh group. This became the metaphor that framed Adelman's influential book of rituals and teachings, *Miriam's Well,* which would become the official "how-to" book of Rosh Hodesh groups. Adelman recounts that a decade later, "The women in the Boston Rosh Hodesh group made the leap into action from the text I had written, meditating on the image of Miriam's well and creating the ritual of drinking from the cup of Miriam in their own homes. Thus, the constant interplay between written word, spoken word and ritual act generates ever-evolving forms of the ritual."[16]

She writes of how this particular symbolic form came into being naturally and spontaneously. One of the initiators reflected, "[I]t was as if *Kos Miriam* already existed and was just waiting to be discovered." Adelman brings her attention back to the physical cup: "By sanctifying an object that is portable and small enough for a child to hold, Jewish women have made the well more accessible to more people. Every home can have a Cup of Miriam. They have also taken a bold step by making a physical object represent an ethereal well named for a woman."[17]

The cup began to appear at feminist and women's seders. By 2004, it was finding a place at many family and community seders as well. Miriam's cup, already filled with water or collectively filled with water from each person's cup, holds a symbolic drink for Miriam: she, like Elijah, "visits" the seder meal. But there is a difference. The prophet Elijah wafts in dramatically though the door at the seder's end and offers a vision of healing in a messianic future. The prophet Miriam is there from the beginning: she is with the people—in the kitchen, at the table—an engaged participant in the repair of the world.

Various blessings for the water the cup invariably holds and liturgical evocations of Miriam are emerging. Now, as the practice continues to consolidate, one often hears people ask, "How do *you* do the Miriam's cup ritual?" Though there is no single role the cup plays within the seder, using it or pointing it out at the very beginning of the seder or at the end, linked to Elijah's ritual, are two frequent choices. Anecdotal evidence suggests that people often consider performing any Miriam's cup ritual after having received the cup as a gift, having purchased one to compliment one's Passover paraphernalia, or having made one as a Jewish art project. Often a newly received or acquired Miriam's cup is set out on a seder table, across from or next to Elijah's cup, so as to balance it and put both cups into a "his/hers" relationship. Once Miriam's cup is in place, it inevitably functions much in the same way as the orange on the seder plate, providing an occasion for discussion: What is that, what does it mean, what is it for, how did it get started?

The source of instructions for the ritual a group selects might be an article in *Lilith* or *Hadassah* magazine or a handout from a women's seder. Of late, Miriam's cup rituals are included in new family haggadot, such as *A Night of Questions: A Passover Haggadah,* a product of the Reconstructionist movement.[18] In that Haggadah, setting out Miriam's cup and offering a blessing or reflection are presented as neither choice nor novelty. Rather, Miriam's cup exists alongside the familiar practices of antiquity, such as the sign of the paschal lamb, or the practices that have accrued over the ages, such as the singing of Had Gadya. Before blessing the first cup of wine, celebrants are instructed, "Place Miriam's Cup, filled with spring water, on the seder table"[19] and recite, "Miriam's well reminds us that our journey has both direction and destination—to a place where freedom is proclaimed for all."[20] Only a marginal note provided by Rabbi David Teutsch hints at the ritual's novelty. "Miriam's Cup has become part of the seder ritual," he writes, effectively repressing the object's innovative quality when he adds that "its origin lies in the Midrash." That is, the ritual is legitimate because it can be linked to a venerated text of antiquity.[21]

Miriam's cup is engaged once again in *A Night of Questions* after reciting the plagues and before singing Dayenu when it is raised, and one recites Exodus 15:20–21, Miriam's song and timbrel dance at the sea. At this point, the text invites people to rise from the table and to join in a Miriam's dance of one's own. As marginal notes by Lori Lefkovitz read, "We can only imagine that these timbrels had the status of religious ceremonial objects. Today we might remember to take candlesticks. Back then, a good Jewish girl made sure she had her drum."[22] Miriam's cup is engaged a third and final time before the door is opened for Elijah. This time a blessing for water is recited, one sips from the cup, and sings "Miriam Hanevi'ah" in which Elijah's song is given new words by Leila Gal Berner. Elijah's cup, which is conventionally poured before the seder begins and is neither touched nor drunken from, at this time receives, in this version, some wine from each participant's cup. Thus the new ritual of Miriam's cup reframes the practice of the traditional ritual, making it more communal and democratic in nature.

Miriam's cup has become familiar among the Modern Orthodox as well. In the 2001/2002 calendar of the Jewish Orthodox Feminist Alliance (JOFA), images of Miriam and her timbrel from medieval haggadot are provided, with the intention of proving there is a legitimate place for feminists at the seder table. Social acceptance of Miriam's cup among the Modern Orthodox is also demonstrated in *The Outside World,* Tova Mirvis's 2004 novel. Her character Naomi dresses up as Miriam for her family's seder, one which will marry "new ideas to ancient traditions."[23] Naomi provides an assortment of dress-up clothes for her female guests so they can be "miniature, Modern Miriams."[24] She places a cup of Miriam next to Elijah's cup on their seder table: "This, a latter-day addition to the age-old traditions of the seder. She was using a cup Ilana (her daughter) had made years before, gluing onto it seashells and beads from old necklaces. She had saved it for years, bringing it out each Pesach as the cup of Elijah. But this, she knew, was the use it was truly intended for."[25] Naomi's guest, Tzippy, who has never seen a cup of Miriam, stares at it. Instead of appraising it with a critical eye, she finds strength in the object: "[S]he stared at it, and it steadied her."[26]

"Thanks for the Chair" tambourine. Used with the permission of Betsy Teutsch, http://www.kavanahcards.com/tambourines. Photo credit: Benj Kamm.

MIRIAM'S TAMBOURINE

Following the appearance of Miriam's cup, Miriam's tambourine (*tof Miriam*) appeared simultaneously in two different communities: American Jewish feminists of various denominations and Lubavitch Hasidic women. Neither group appeared aware of the other's innovation.

A Miriam's tambourine, as it has come to be known, can be either a tambourine especially decorated with images or calligraphy to designate that it is, in some way, akin to the timbrels played by Miriam and the Israelite women, or it can be a generic tambourine provided for use by Jewish women in an educational or celebratory setting.

Jewish Feminists' Use of Miriam's Tambourine

Among Jewish feminists, Miriam's tambourine is said to give witness to the voice of women that resists being silenced. Although Miriam's tambourines are sometimes played or displayed at women's Rosh Hodesh groups, Jewish healing services, or bat mitzvah dancing, their primary usage has been at women's seders. They are set out on the tables by the organizers and designate the space as one where Jewish women can joyously celebrate a reframed Passover story together. Participants carry and play the tambourines as they join in a circle and snake-dance around the room singing one of the many newly composed Miriam-inspired songs, such as the popular "Miriam's Song" by Debbie Friedman, which recalls Miriam dancing with her timbrels along with the women after crossing the sea. Based on my observations since the early 1990s at many women's seders, most women begin holding their tambourines somewhat self-consciously and tap them, tom-tom like, to keep the beat of the music. Those musically trained will use their tambourines more artfully: shaking them, waving them in arcs, tapping out more complicated rhythms, beating the tambourines against their legs. At the evening's end, many women (even those who initially hesitated to take up their tambourines and join the dancing) will reflect that participating in a seder that made tambourines available helped them feel like Miriam or like the Israelite women who danced with her.

The tambourines are used across the denominations. Like Miriam's cup, they appear in both liberal settings and among the Modern Orthodox as well. This is portrayed in Mirvis's novel: Shopping with her grown daughter, Naomi stares into the store window of a New Jersey Judaica shop, and a display of handmade tambourines catches her eye. "She felt a rush of desire to buy one. It seemed silly to want it. What would she do with it, she wondered. . . . They were so pretty, but it wasn't just that. She didn't want to look at it. She wanted to grab it and rattle it against her hip and shake out some greater feeling. As if this music could rouse her."[27]

Encouraged by her daughter to buy one, she remembers that Miriam was the character she had enjoyed studying most in her Women of the Bible class. Miriam, using her tambourine, she reflects, helped the reluctant Israelite women realize they could sing and dance: "Naomi wished someone would pull her in. She wanted not the tambourine but what it could unlock. While she waited for her purchase to be rung up, she turned it over and examined it, as if it contained a message for her."[28]

The sentiment this character expresses echoes that of many women I interviewed at women's seders where tambourines were provided. Having the tambourine in one's hand, in the presence of other Jewish women, unlocked the possibility of identifying with Miriam and other powerful women of the Bible.

The Philadelphia artist and calligrapher Betsy Platkin Teutsch appears to be the first to have marketed professionally designed Miriam's tambourines. In 1992 she created a tambourine with the express purpose of providing moral and financial support for the Women of the Wall (WOW) and the International Committee for Women of the Wall. She called it "Thanks for the Chair." (She had previously made hand-decorated tambourines that were privately commissioned.) The image on the tambourine, originally painted in acrylics and then mass reproduced, is of a women's service at the wall. On the women's side of the *mechitzah* are nine adult Jewish women and two young girls in the midst of a Torah service. The women's head coverings—the head scarves of the Orthodox, the flat and pillbox *kippot* of the liberal movements—depict the range of ways Jewish women are now attiring themselves for prayer. Some women wear prayer shawls—even one white-haired grandmother. The woman reading from the Torah appears to be wearing a tallit-poncho, perhaps reminiscent of one Woman of the Wall leader who wears this very kind of prayer shawl. A tenth adult woman, representing Miriam the prophetess, holding a tambourine in her hand, flies over the top of the mechitzah to complete the prayer quorum. Unlike conventional portrayals of Miriam as a beautiful young lady, she is a grown woman, her hair peppered with grey.

Teutsch provides this note explaining the iconography with each tambourine:

> Since one picture is worth a thousand words, I have created a tambourine to share with you in honor and in support of Women of the Wall who have been fighting far too long for the right to daven and read Torah at the Western Wall. The men keep throwing chairs at these women, over the *mechitzah* at the Kotel, and these chairs have become an important symbol of their struggle. In Jewish tradition, an empty chair signifies the absence and the desired presence of someone important. The chair of the Bratslavers comes to mind, as does the chair of Eliyahu (*Elijah*) at a circumcision. Since Miriam is the analogue of Eliyahu, I would like you to join me in inviting Miriam to help make the *minyan* at the Wall and once again lead the women of Israel. This piece is titled, "Thanks for the Chair!" The words read, "This is the chair

of Miriam" (echoing the opening words at a Brit Milah, "This is the chair of Elijah").

The theme of reversal underlies Teutsch's concept. The chair that the violent ultra-Orthodox men have hurled over the mechitzah will no longer silence, humiliate, or physically injure the praying women. The men are made to provide a chair of honor for the prophetess Miriam who has come to grace the women's Torah service as the tenth woman who will make their prayer quorum possible. Teutsch has said, "What the piece does is to turn that symbol of humiliation into celebration. . . . It's kind of a gentle protest, an assertion of something positive. It's a tongue-in-cheek way of making a statement. . . . Despite whatever abuse we are taking from the Israeli establishment, we're going to persist, and we will prevail."[29]

Teutsch then created, for this cause, a second mass-produced tambourine, "Women at the Sea." Less overtly political than the first one, it depicts a multigenerational group of Jewish women resembling a cross between the biblical Miriam and the Israelite women and a group of contemporary Jewish women at a Jewish renewal retreat. Teutsch describes its message: "When we celebrated our liberation from slavery at the shores of the Red Sea, our voices were loud and clear. This design captures that moment of Jewish women's spiritual expression, led in song, prayer, and celebration by Miriam, and declares that the sound of women's voices, so vibrant as we crossed the sea, shall be silenced no longer."[30]

Teutsch has sold several thousand tambourines, raising thousands of dollars for Women of the Wall. She created other mass-produced tambourines, now available in Judaica stores and on Web sites. Teutsch's new tambourines include one for Bat Kol, a feminist yeshiva in Jerusalem, with a circle of women sitting around a table studying in a library whose bookshelves blend into the walls of Jerusalem. There is the "Hallelujah Rainbow Psalm" tambourine in which the text of Psalm 150 is written in seven concentric circles, each in the order of the rainbow. There is the healing tambourine with Miriam's prayer, "Please God, send healing now," a "Daughters of the Moon Tambourine," and a Purim tambourine. As of this writing, the most recent is the all-purpose "Shalshelet Tambourine" to be used, as her advertisement suggests, "at drumming circles, or to accompany song and dance at baby namings, *b'not mitzvah,* weddings, seders, Shabbat dinners—or at any celebration where ancient rhythms are welcome. To create an heirloom, guests can sign the back with an indelible pen." Teutsch has been told that however and wherever her tambourines have been used or displayed, they have had the power to "touch and shape a life moment."[31] She believes that the tambourines that have been most meaningful to recipients are those that have been specifically commissioned for bat mitzvah girls. How any or all of the tambourines will eventually be used in liturgy and as "objects de Judaica" remains to be discovered. As Teutsch says, "We'll find out."

There is no single way in which the tambourines have been used ritually, aside from their use in women's seders. They have never been incorporated in the regular worship of Women of the Wall—not surprisingly, as the women in Jerusalem have taken pains to avoid bringing additional attention to themselves. When the International Committee for Women of the Wall met in Brooklyn at the home of activist Phyllis Chesler to celebrate the Israeli Supreme Court's 2000 ruling that WOW could indeed pray in their fashion at the wall (a ruling that would be rescinded in April 2003), a tambourine was taken off Chesler's shelf and was gently tapped while the group posed for photographs to mark the occasion. It seems as if being displayed is the primary way the tambourines are used now; indeed, Teutsch's tambourines can often be found in the homes and offices of Jewish feminists, either hung on the wall or placed on a shelf or table. They typically announce that the owner is committed to achieving spiritual freedom for Jewish women.

Lubavitch Women's Use of Miriam's Tambourine

When the tambourine appeared in Lubavitch women's communities in 1992, it reflected the steadfast faith many women had in God. Comparing themselves to Miriam, they introduced tambourines that helped them feel and demonstrate optimism that the time of redemption was near.

According to a report of Lubavitch Hasidim who maintain that their rebbe is the messiah, their rebbe, Menachem Mendel Schneerson, gave a discourse on January 15, 1992, introducing the significance of both Miriam and tambourines for the women in his community. He said, "So, too, in the final Redemption, the righteous women must, and certainly do—trust so completely in the immediate Redemption that they will begin immediately in the last moments of exile to play music and dance for the coming of the complete Redemption."[32]

That night,

> [H]undreds of Jewish women gathered in Brooklyn, New York, with tambourines and live music to dance and rejoice for the coming Redemption. During the distribution of dollars the next day, the 12th of *Adar* I, 5752 (January 16, 1992), a representative from this group, Mrs.

> Chava Cohen, gave the Rebbe a tambourine and said, "This is for the Rebbe, *Shlita.* With this tambourine the women danced yesterday with joy that breaks through all limitations. With a deep trust in the revelation of the Rebbe, *Shlita,* King Moshiach, immediately and actually to the complete Redemption." The Rebbe answered with a radiant smile, "This [tambourine] you are most probably leaving with me." The Rebbe handed her a second dollar and, referring to psalm 150, said, "This is for the *'Tziltzilei Teruah'* [Clanging Cymbals]. This is how they are referred to in *Tehillim. Es Zoll Zein In A Gute Sha'ah* [It should be in a good and auspicious hour]."[33]

This tambourine had been decorated with the words "Yechi Adoneinu, Moreinu V'Rabeinu, Melech HaMoshiach, L'Olam Va'ed. (Long live our Lord, master and teacher, the King Messiah, forever and ever)." Previously, the rebbe had accepted boxes containing the signatures of Lubavitch women, worldwide, proclaiming their belief that he was the messiah (*moshiach*) and that the time of redemption was imminent.

On Chabad's Web site, the significance of a tambourine in the Bible is explained in order to suggest that modern Jewish women, like Miriam, also possessed sufficient strength to herald the impending redemption they believed was immanent. It was prevalent sentiment that the rebbe would not die, but would be "raised up" as the messiah.

> [I]t was Miriam, with her deep well of feminine feeling, who truly experienced the bitterness of *galut* (exile and persecution). And it was Miriam, with her woman's capacity for endurance, perseverance and hope, who stood lonely watch over the tender, fledging life in a basket at the edge of a mammoth river; whose vigilance over what would become of him and his mission to bring redemption to her people never faltered. . . . Miriam and her chorus brought to the Song at the Sea the intensity of feeling and depth of faith unique to womankind. Their experience of the bitterness of *galut* had been far more intense than that of their menfolk, yet their faith had been stronger and more enduring. . . . Today, as we stand at the threshold of the ultimate redemption, it is once again the woman whose song is the most poignant, whose tambourine is the most hopeful, whose dance is the most joyous. . . . Today, as then, the woman's yearning for Moshiach—a yearning which runs deeper than that of the man, and inspires and uplifts it—forms the dominant strain in the melody of redemption.[34]

In 1994 Lubavitch women worldwide used tambourines—selling them, decorating them, practicing dancing with them in women's groups—as they kept vigil for their dying rebbe, and anticipated they would use them to welcome the messiah. In that period, many Lubavitchers believed that the rebbe would be "raised" as the messiah. Lubavitch women I spoke with said that they needed to be the ones who, acting behind the scenes, would have the optimism and strength to allow the community to emerge from this crisis. Tambourines were distributed to every Lubavitch woman and girl, and they were carried everywhere during the last weeks of the rebbe's life. One could say that the tambourines were the women's equivalent of the electronic "messiah beepers" that Lubavitch men carried during that period: they were emblems of preparedness and, hence, sustained and professed belief.

Some tambourines were left unadorned; others were decorated with imagery of a heavenly Jerusalem or pictures of the rebbe. Often they were tied with multicolored ribbons. I was told that decorated tambourines had been hung in the hospital unit where the rebbe lay, and ICU nurses were instructed to shake them at the moment he became revealed as the messiah. At the rebbe's funeral, women carried tambourines in diaper bags, tote bags, and stroller pockets. A few women danced with their tambourines in Crown Heights soon after the funeral, but this gesture was suppressed by those who considered it inappropriate.

Following the rebbe's death, his earlier discourse concerning women and tambourines and his acceptance of the tambourine the women had given him have both been frequently used as prooftexts of the claim that he is, indeed, the messiah.

Several years later the decorated tambourines are still hanging in Lubavitch homes. To the best of my knowledge, they are no longer carried as a constant accessory. Even just a year after the rebbe's death, in Crown Heights, I found only one decorated tambourine for sale: a small one, painted sky blue, decorated with a small decoupaged image of the rebbe, along with the words in Hebrew, "Welcome, King Messiah."

Still, the tambourines have kept a quiet presence. In her 2003 ethnography of Hasidic girls, Stephanie Levine describes how tambourines were being used in slightly subversive ways. On one anniversary of the rebbe's death, she writes, "Rochel traipsed off to the main synagogue with her tambourine: women are supposed to carry tambourines to herald the coming of the Messiah. This was a sign of supreme faith; few of the other women had brought tambourines."[35] (In fact, Rochel, Levine's informant, believes that the messianists are engaging in idol worship; her bringing a tambourine—which she still owned—was meant as an ironic gesture, "the ultimate act of mockery.")[36] Wellen also observes tambourine making as an activity among Lubavitch girls of the Bais Rivka School. On a class trip, a teacher, intending to entertain and occupy her students, gave them bare tambourines and the materials with which to decorate them: "[T]his was art with a purpose. Now the girls would have their own personalized instruments to usher in the Messianic era."[37] The girls decorated the tambourines, but they took pleasure in refusing to do so precisely as their teacher suggested. For the girls, then, the tambourines were being used once again as sites of quiet intergenerational rebellion.

Currently tambourines are being used in outreach (*kiruv*) efforts by the Chabad organization. The women's circle of Chabad of Manhattan's Upper West Side, considered among the "trendiest" Chabad houses, held a workshop in April 2006 in anticipation of Passover. Women were invited to come study about Passover and prepare themselves spiritually while decorating Miriam's tambourines with the help of an artist.[38]

Thus, among the Lubavitch women, Miriam's tambourines no longer signify the same acute belief in an impending redemption. They are, however, still being created and displayed to recall and cultivate a trait historically attributed to faithful Jewish women: the capacity to rebel against spiritual apathy, hopelessness, and despair.

CONCLUSION

In many respects, Miriam's cup and tambourine do similar work. They introduce a practice or the possibility of several variations of practice. The growing presence of these objects in different contexts—spiritual, decorative, commercial, educational—allows one to view them as standard Jewish "equipment" one might desire or need. With increased exposure, and with some consolidation of practice, any off-putting novelty of either object wears off and one begins to experience them as familiar, slowly accepting their familiarity and authenticity.

The cup and the tambourine are finding their place within the canon of traditional Jewish ritual objects. Each time one gives or receives the objects on a meaningful occasion, each time one sees them displayed, or advertised and described in popular Jewish magazines and newspapers, the establishment of the objects and the rituals they occasion seem more normative. In an article titled "Recasting Jewish Rituals with Modern Addition" appearing in the *New York Times* on April 12, 2003, Debra Nussbaum Cohen quotes Professor Lori Lefkovitz regarding the presence of the new objects. She says,

"Of course there's always invention, liturgical and ritual, in religious life, to meet the needs of any given moment. The trick is to meet a contemporary need in a way that will quickly look like it came from Mount Sinai." The very appearance of a *New York Times* article about the objects affirms and reifies the presence of Miriam's cup and Miriam's tambourine in Jewish life.

The objects make the new rituals tangible, accessible, performable, concrete, and repeatable. They function as signs, indicating that the owner, holder, or displayer of the object feels empowered to participate—even just for one time—in a new Jewish woman's practice; that the space in which the object is used or displayed is hospitable to new forms of Jewish women's expression.

Being objects of the acceptably rebellious Miriam, the cup and the tambourine and the new rituals they evoke seem more readily acceptable to increasing numbers of tradition-bound, conservative individuals or communities, those who tend to be particularly anxious about innovation. Because Miriam—however powerful and imaginative—is a faithful daughter who supports the collective enterprise of her people, objects linked to her are "safe." Miriam's radical nature is obscured within objects so mundane, domestic, and innocuous that it feels nonthreatening.

Strategically disguised, Miriam's new objects innovate through this same innocuous nature. The objects appear so humble, so simple: the cup evokes the domestic, a household item, and the tambourine is like a child's toy. Neither object points to the women's agenda it facilitates. Furthermore, if an artist or youngster makes the object, or if is linked to a fund-raising project, attention is diverted from its ritual use. In this way, Miriam's objects foreground the political, aesthetic, educational, or philanthropic implications of the object and background their religious nature. Predictably, the cup and tambourines have evaded strong gestures of rejection, opposition, or control from Jewish men, women, or institutions that could so easily be antagonized by new ritual objects or practices. (The Israeli Ministry of Religion has yet to pose a fine for possession of a Miriam's cup, and even the playing of a Miriam's tambourine at the wall, which might incite violence, is still legal.) I believe this is because the objects do not compete with existing practices. Moreover, they do not displace or challenge other sacred objects: the cup does not replace the kiddush cup or Elijah's cup; the tambourine does not replace the shofar. The objects beacon Miriam's presence, but they do not dislodge male figures such as Moses or Elijah.

The objects share other significant similarities. First, they have originated outside the synagogue. Created for use in homes or in women's gatherings, the objects are free of constraints or sanctions that might have been imposed by rabbis, ritual committees, or fellow congregants had they been intended for use within the public rule- and tradition-bound space of the synagogue. Second, while scripture inspires the objects, no sacred text drawn from Torah or rabbinic literature mandates or specifies a particular ritual use of the objects or a particular form they must take. Consequently, the objects and those who use them engage in no text-based transgression. Finally, the objects create new opportunities to honor Jewish women's leadership. They do so by depicting leadership (social, liturgical, and creative) as a venerable Jewish women's tradition with biblical roots.

In both the cup and the tambourines we encounter a new Miriam who watches Moses from a distance as he floats toward the rescue she anticipates. Through these objects, she watches Jewish women of the present, who float toward their own rescue, from the distance of time that is simultaneously of antiquity and of an imagined redemptive future. This Miriam knows how to protect and influence indirectly and from the margins; she knows how to wait, how to seize the right moment, and when to celebrate. In these objects and the rituals that accompany them, this Miriam lives.

NOTES

1. *Nashim: A Journal of Jewish Women's Studies and Gender Issues,* nos. 9–10 (2005). See especially Lori Lefkowitz and Rona Shapiro, "Ritualwell.Org—Loading the Virtual Canon, or: The Politics and Aesthetics of Jewish Women's Sexuality," no. 9 (2005): 101, available at http://muse.jhu.edu/journals/nashim.

2. Harvey Goldberg, *Jewish Passages* (Berkeley: University of California Press, 2003), 23.

3. Jack Wertheimer, ed., *The Uses of Tradition* (New York: Jewish Theological Seminary, 1992), 328.

4. Joan Newlon Radner, ed., *Feminist Messages: Coding in Women's Folk Culture* (Urbana: University of Illinois Press, 1993), vii.

5. Radner, *Feminist Messages,* vii.

6. Lynn Gottlieb, *She Who Dwells Within: A Feminist Vision of a Renewed Judaism* (New York: HarperCollins, 1995), 110.

7. Jody Myers, "The Myth of Matriarchy in Recent Writings on Jewish Women's Spirituality," *Jewish Social Studies* 4, no. 1 (1997): 3, available at http://iupjournals.org/jss/jss4-1.html.

8. Ibid., 5.

9. Lily Rivlin, *Miriam's Daughters Celebrate,* VHS (New York: Filmmaker's Library, 1986).

10. Carol Diament, ed., *Moonbeams: A Hadassah Rosh Hodesh Guide* (Woodstock, VT: Jewish Lights, 2000), 103.

11. Ibid., 156.

12. Ibid., 104–10.

13. Judith Plaskow, *Standing Again at Sinai: Judaism from a Feminist Perspective* (San Francisco: HarperCollins, 1990), 39.

14. Ibid.

15. Aside from Plaskow, other authors of the feminist midrash include: Gottlieb, *She Who Dwells Within;* Ellen Frankel, *The Five Books of Miriam* (New York: Grosset/Putnam, 1996); Alicia Ostriker, *The Nakedness of the Fathers: Biblical Visions and Revisions* (New Brunswick: Rutgers University Press, 1997); Norma Rosen, *Biblical Women Unbound: Counter-Tales* (Philadelphia: Jewish Publication Society, 1996); Vanessa Ochs, *Sarah Laughed: Modern Lessons from the Wisdom and Stories of Biblical Women* (New York: McGraw-Hill, 2005).

16. Penina Adelman, *Miriam's Well: Rituals for Jewish Women Around the Year* (New York: Biblio Press, 1990), 114.

17. Ibid., 117–18.

18. Joy Levitt and Michael Strassfeld, eds., *A Night of Questions: A Passover Haggadah* (Elkins Park, PA: Reconstructionist Press, 1999).

19. Ibid., 29.

20. Ibid.

21. Ibid.

22. Levitt and Strassfeld, *A Night of Questions,* 63.

23. Tova Mirvis, *The Outside World* (New York: Knopf, 2004), 298.

24. Ibid., 301.

25. Ibid., 298.

26. Ibid., 299.

27. Ibid., 18.

28. Ibid., 119.

29. Betsy Teutsch, personal communication with the author.

30. *ICWOW 1999 Newsletter* insert. This tambourine is still widely available. On the *Hamakor Gallerie* Web site (http://www.jewishsource.com) it is described in this way: "Women at the Sea Tambourine. A true celebration of womanhood! Whether you dance and sing with your tambourine, or prefer to simply display this beautiful instrument on a shelf in your home, it is a unique piece of feminine Judaica that can be enjoyed in many ways."

31. Betsy Teutsch, personal communication with the author.

32. "The Rebbe as Moshiach—Based on Torah Sources," 1998, available at http://www.moshiach.net/blind/itmotrw.htm.

33. Ibid.

34. http://www.chabad.org/parshah/article.asp?AID=2744.

35. Stephanie W. Levine, *Mystics, Mavericks, and Merrymakers: An Intimate Journey among Hasidic Girls* (New York: New York University Press, 2003), 105.

36. Ibid.

37. Levine, *Mystics, Mavericks, and Merrymakers,* 109.

38. "Chabad Women's Circle: Tambourine Design with Morah Dina Eber, Teacher, Artist" (Chabad of the West Side, 2006), available at http://www.chabadwestside.org/templates/photogallery/photogallery.asp?AID=376786.

CHAPTER ELEVEN

FINDING HER RIGHT PLACE IN THE SYNAGOGUE

The Rite of Adult Bat Mitzvah

LISA D. GRANT

Adult bat mitzvah is a uniquely American phenomenon. Reports suggest that thousands of American Jewish women have studied for and celebrated a ceremony of bat mitzvah over the past thirty years. For more than fifteen years sociologists of religion, social workers, psychologists, educators, historians, and journalists have all been drawn to explore how this adolescent rite of passage has been adapted to serve adult Jewish women's needs. This research tells us that women seek out this opportunity in order to publicly affirm their Jewish and, more particularly, their religious identity.[1] These women are looking for greater comfort and connection in their synagogue communities. They want to become literate and confirm their legitimate place in the public arena of Jewish ritual practice. Though they are learning normative synagogue "skills" in order to actively participate in and even lead parts of the service, their very participation can have a profound impact on reshaping the norms for worship in their particular synagogue community and ultimately American Judaism.

There is scant documentation regarding when the phenomenon of adult bat mitzvah began, but from all accounts it appears to have gained its initial momentum as a grassroots initiative, most likely arising out of the Havurah movement of the 1960s. One of the earliest records of "belated" b'not mitzvah (plural) appears in the *Jewish Catalog,* first published in 1971.[2] Similarly, one of the earliest studies on adult bat mitzvah pointed to countercultural influences that supported this form of "do-it-yourself" Judaism.[3] Other reports from the 1970s and 1980s describe private, individual ceremonies that mostly took place outside synagogues at college Hillels, Jewish summer camps, and hotel conference rooms.[4] In a relatively short time span, however, this do-it-yourself approach was co-opted by many Reform, Conservative, and Reconstructionist synagogues as rabbis and educators began to see adult bat mitzvah as a way to strengthen attachment to the congregation and Jewish practice in general, and to increase attendance and participation in worship.

While no definitive statistics have been gathered, an estimated five hundred synagogues across North America offer adult b'not mitzvah classes among their array of adult learning and religious offerings. In general, both men and women are welcome to participate in these programs in Reform, Conservative, and Reconstructionist congregations. In practice, however, the vast majority of participants are women. In addition, the adult bat mitzvah phenomenon is far more prevalent in the liberal movements of American Judaism, though it is not unheard of in Modern Orthodox congregations. For instance, Chana Kotzkin cites Liberty Jewish Congregation, a Modern Orthodox synagogue in suburban Baltimore, as having initiated an adult bat mitzvah class in 1976.[5] Anecdotal evidence, however, suggests that other forms of women's study are more common in Modern Orthodox circles than is adult bat mitzvah, which typically focuses on building synagogue "skills," competencies that a much higher percentage of Orthodox women already possess.

The curriculum and ceremony differ quite significantly from synagogue to synagogue and across denominational lines as might be expected. Hebrew reading literacy is almost always part of the program. Despite these differences, the programs share a common goal, which is to help women become more comfortable and "literate" within their particular synagogue setting. To that end, in recent years both the Women's League for Conservative Judaism and the Union for Reform Judaism (URJ) have published curriculum guides[6] for adult bat mitzvah that have been sold or distributed to over eight hundred congregations.[7] Perhaps the largest group of women who collectively participated in a ceremony of adult bat mitzvah was at the 1996 National Hadassah Convention in Miami Beach, with 122 women as celebrants and over 1,000 in the congregation.[8] Hadassah held such mega-ceremonies at their national gatherings for several years. Since 2000, many of the Hadassah regions now facilitate adult bat mitzvah programs and ceremonies, sometimes in partnership with a local synagogue.[9] These programs may appeal to women who are more strongly connected to Hadassah than they are to a synagogue, or to women who belong to a synagogue that does not offer an adult bat mitzvah program. The nondenominational nature of Hadassah and its focus on peer leadership and Jewish peoplehood are other features that distinguish Hadassah's program from a synagogue-based experience.[10]

Various studies and journalistic reports[11] suggest that women who participate in a ceremony of adult bat mitzvah range in age from their early twenties to their nineties. However, the majority appear to fall within the mid-life years of late thirties to early sixties. Most of these women begin their studies without being able to read Hebrew and with almost no understanding of synagogue ritual. The 1990 National Jewish Population Survey showed that women were more than twice as likely as men not to have received any Jewish education.[12] Though the gender gap in Jewish education is narrowing, there are still large numbers of Jewish adults, both men and women, who have had minimal Jewish education as children and did not become bar or bat mitzvah at age twelve or thirteen. For example, a family education survey conducted in 1999 of almost 2,000 individuals from 38 congregations in metropolitan Chicago showed that 49 percent of respondents did not become bar or bat mitzvah as a child. Seventy-six percent of the survey respondents were women.[13]

How can we understand the adult bat mitzvah phenomenon in the context of ritual innovation and change? What are the elements of this ritual? Why is it so meaningful for the participants? What impact are the women "graduates" of adult bat mitzvah programs having on ritual life and practice in their synagogues? What are the implications of these changes for Jewish life in America?

This chapter addresses these questions by building on the existing literature and adding new voices to the stories of women who choose this path of Jewish learning and observance. It showcases the experiences of fifteen women who celebrated an adult bat mitzvah in the last several years to illustrate the impact of the experiences on them as individuals and on their synagogue communities. They range in age from their mid-thirties to their late seventies. The data come from interviews with five women from a Conservative synagogue who were interviewed one year and again three years post–bat mitzvah,[14] plus interviews and/or written testimony from four other women from Conservative congregations, four from Reform, and two from unaffiliated congregations. These fifteen women represent a diverse group. Three are Jews by choice; seven are mothers of school-aged children; two are lesbians; and three had no children at the time of the study. As part of this research, interviews were also conducted with rabbis and educators from three Conservative congregations, three Reform congregations, and one Reconstructionist congregation that offer adult bat mitzvah programs.[15] These numbers are relatively small, but the themes that emerged in these stories are wholly consistent with research conducted by many others across disciplines. The impacts described in all of these studies can be summarized into three key points. In virtually all cases, women who participate in a program of learning leading to a ceremony of adult bat mitzvah feel a stronger sense of Jewish identity and become more comfortable in worship in their synagogues. In addition, in many but not all cases, women develop a strong commitment to ongoing Jewish learning. Thus, adult bat mitzvah is a powerful learning and ritual experience that has the potential to redirect women's lives and change the culture of worship in their synagogues.

EVOLUTION OF ADULT BAT MITZVAH

For most of history, study and prayer, central elements of Jewish experience, were practiced and enacted in public almost exclusively by men. Jewish women expressed their piety and marked their experience privately, at home, in ways quite different from those of their male counterparts. In effect, men owned the Great Tradition, while women developed their own small traditions that were generally understood as peripheral to "authentic" Jewish experiences.

In the twentieth century, though study and worship were still held up as exemplars of Judaism, they were not a significant part of the lives of the majority of American Jews, either men or women. Public Judaism was expressed much more frequently through communal involvement, not ritual practice.[16] Even Jewish communal leaders were typically Jewishly illiterate and disengaged from most ritual activity and religious practice.

Over the last few decades Jewish communal leaders have increasingly recognized that Jewish learning is essential to sustaining a vibrant and meaningful American Jewish community. As a result, we have witnessed a burgeoning growth of adult Jewish learning in synagogues, Jewish Community Centers, and independent institutions. In most cases, women populate these classrooms in far greater numbers than men.[17] Women want to claim their place at the study table to deepen their knowledge, to strengthen their own Jewish identity, to learn how to be better transmitters of Jewish tradition, and to enrich the ritual observances they choose to perform.

The rise of feminist consciousness and the impact of the Jewish countercultural movement in the latter part of the twentieth century primed women to seek access to the study table of the Great Tradition and to demand that this tradition respond to their experiences.[18] As women's religious roles expanded over the last part of the twentieth century, so did their desire to mark their experience through ritual. This impulse for ritual creativity is as much a product of general American cultural influences as it is a response to perceived gaps in Jewish religious practice. The feminist movement led women to demand that what might once have been private spiritual expression should take place in the public domain. In fact, religious feminists created, improvised, and reinterpreted ritual because they found "the performance of long-suppressed rituals and the making of newly improvised rituals to be invaluable for maintaining their solidarity, courage, and imaginative resource."[19]

Thus, over the last thirty years, we have witnessed a flourishing of Jewish ritual innovation to mark women's life experience, adding female voices and gender-neutral language to liturgy, creating new rituals such as brit bat (baby naming) ceremonies for girls, mid-life passages, healing services, and ceremonies to ritualize divorce, and reclaiming old ceremonies for new purposes, such as using *mikvah* (ritual bath) to help heal the emotional pain of miscarriage, sexual abuse, and abortion. There is an abundance and seemingly ever-expanding number of women's centers, books, journals, and Web sites that document and support these innovations.[20]

In some ways adult bat mitzvah seems to represent a perfect outgrowth of these impulses toward increased Jewish learning and ritual innovation. It provides a way for women to find their place in the Great Tradition of study and worship, while at the same time acknowledging women's experience and elevating it to the public realm. However, whereas the ritual innovations described above are all attempts to make Judaism more responsive to women's experience, adult bat mitzvah is not about changing the system but about seeking legitimacy within an existing framework.

Adult bat mitzvah emerged out of the spirit of American innovation and individualism, but the impetus for engaging in it for most women is toward conformity rather than change. There is a paradox in the outcome, however. While the women are searching to master the liturgy and feel competent and authentic in a particular religious community, their involvement ultimately can lead to reshaping what is normative and authentic for that community.

WHO ARE THE WOMEN WHO BECOME ADULT BAT MITZVAH?

The research on adult bat mitzvah provides us with a rich portrait of the women who embark on a course of study culminating in a public religious expression of their commitment to Judaism. They come from diverse backgrounds and have different initial motivations. Some women come from assimilated backgrounds; some are converts who are discovering Judaism for the first time. Others are looking to fill in the gaps in their education and to find answers to questions about identity and belonging. Some are inspired to start the process by the Jewish educational accomplishments and ritual performance of their daughters and granddaughters. Some are looking for meaning after experiencing a life transition or challenge—a birth, a death, a child entering school, a career change, and so forth. Others are seeking to resolve "unfinished business" that may have left them feeling alienated or betrayed by their family and their tradition. Regardless of starting point, all are seeking to become fully enfranchised participants in Jewish ritual life.

In most synagogues, women who choose to undertake an adult bat mitzvah participate in a lengthy course of study prior to the ceremony. Clearly, they have made a sincere and serious commitment to Judaism. They are also making a clear statement of need. They are goal-oriented learners who embark on a course of study in order to participate more actively, comfortably, and confidently in worship. In some cases, it is the motivation to learn rather than the actual ceremony that brings them to classes initially. Such women seemed almost reluctant to associate their decision with a spiritual need. Typical remarks among informants include: "Remember, I didn't come for the bat mitzvah. I wanted to learn trope,"[21] or "It wasn't the bat mitzvah per se. I was looking to figure this all out in a safe way."[22] Occasionally, women would speak about the social needs that were their initial impetus. For example, Ann, an audiologist with two young daughters, said, "At first, I did it on a dare. My friend and I challenged each other to see if we could learn to read Hebrew."[23] Similarly, Linda, a mother of children enrolled in day school, wrote that she signed up "because so many of my friends from Schechter were doing it so I decided I might as well do it also."[24]

It may be that these women were reluctant to attribute their initial motivations to a desire for some sort of ritual marking of their religious identity. Many American Jews may be uneasy with ritual expression, especially when the liturgical language is foreign and unfamiliar. But, as the learning process progresses, even the most hesitant seem to report having great excitement about and deriving deep meaning from the ceremony. They begin to appreciate publicly marking a transition and an affirmation of their commitment to Judaism.[25] As Beth Cousens notes in her 2002 study,

Marian Weissman, who had an adult bat mitzvah, went on to become an active member of her congregation and a Judaic artist. Used with the permission of Bill Aron, http://www.billaron.com.

"the ritual helps them officially and with distinction mark a 'before' and 'after' period in their lives."[26]

The women highlighted here used similar words to describe their experiences. Rachel, a former stage manager, described her bat mitzvah ceremony as a "goal post, marking the beginning of a journey toward greater involvement in religious life."[27] Louise, a stay-at-home mom, called it a "turning point in my life."[28] Karen, a synagogue administrator who had recently moved, said, "It was my entrée into the community. It served as a launching pad for my involvement in a wide range of activities at the temple."[29]

ADULT BAT MITZVAH: RITUAL OR CEREMONY?

Scholars have long noted the important role ritual plays in defining relationships and transmitting family and group values.[30] Life cycle rituals in particular are intended to connect individuals to one another and to their common heritage. They commemorate continuity with the past and play a critical role in shaping collective memory, which in turn builds group cohesion and reinforces a sense of communal affiliation.[31]

"Ritual" is a term than can have a variety of different usages and meanings. It is commonly understood as something that follows a set of formal, predictable, repeatable behaviors. In the broadest sense, ritual is a way of bringing symbolic meaning into everyday reality. In a religious context, these choreographed actions are usually preceded or accompanied by liturgical language.[32] When effective, the ritual moment not only marks a transition from one state to another but also connects the performer to God and community.

Victor Turner, one of the pioneers in ritual studies, distinguishes between *ritual* as a transformative rite and *ceremony* as a rite that confirms the existing social structure rather than transforming it. Ceremony is performative; ritual is *trans*formative. As elaborated by Ronald Grimes, "[W]hen effective rites of passage are enacted, they carry us from here to there in such a way that we are unable to return to square one. To enact any kind of rite is to *per*form, but to enact a rite of passage is also to *trans*form."[33]

The political scientist Charles Liebman applied this distinction to a Jewish framework. He notes the difference between *ritual,* which is stylized, repetitious behavior that is explicitly religious, and *ceremony,* which is designed to affirm the individual's membership in a particular religious community.[34] Ritual, he claims, is fixed by tradition, while ceremony is more flexible and adaptable to changing needs and expectations. Ritual is controlled by the elite, whereas ceremony is more of a grassroots, folk expression. Writing in the 1990s he noted a decline in ritual practice among American Jews, but a flourishing of ceremony as an American expression personalizing and customizing Judaism to suit individual preferences and needs.

This impulse toward personalization and customization has grown even stronger in the past two decades. Americans of all religions have moved away from the institutionally based "dwelling-oriented" spirituality of the

1950s to a "seeking-oriented" spirituality where faith is no longer inherited but negotiated, sought out not within a single religious tradition but patched together from many. The notion of religious freedom has become equated with the consumer's right to pick and choose religious behaviors based on what is meaningful at any given time.[35]

In this consumer-oriented society, contemporary Jews choose their level of engagement based on what they feel is meaningful much more often than they do out of a sense of commitment to an obligatory, normative tradition.[36] As Steven M. Cohen and Arnold M. Eisen write, "If they have come to a particular observance, it is because of an experience of its meaning. In most cases, that significance is highly personal in the most basic sense; wrapped up in biography and family. If the meaning disappears over time, the observance will cease."[37]

In this context, adult bat mitzvah fits within Liebman's conception of ceremony. Like the adolescent ceremony it imitates, many women perform the rite and affirm their Jewish identity and belonging. Although they may feel more comfortable with worship, they all do not necessarily increase their level of observance or go on to become active in ritual or other aspects of synagogue life. The rabbis and educators interviewed were unequivocally positive about what the adult bat mitzvah experience means for the participants and their synagogues, but they also acknowledged that not everyone is equally affected. As profound and wonderful as the experience may be, for some the meaning simply does not stick. Like their adolescent counterparts, they engage in an intensive spate of learning that culminates in a meaningful ceremony, and then they resume old patterns of marginal affiliation. The voluntary and fluid nature of this commitment is reflected in the remarks one adult bat mitzvah made about some of her classmates: "For some of the women in my class, I feel almost as if it was an expediency thing. They wanted to become bat mitzvah because it was the thing to do. And get it over with. When I see some of them, I can't even remember that they were in the class! Because they never ever come to Shabbat services. I guess that's the way with anything."[38]

In such cases, adult bat mitzvah is an affirmation of the status quo. As one rabbi said, "It's a way to make your Jewish adulthood official." This is no small thing. The fact that women feel the need for this public statement is solid proof of how significantly women's status has changed. As women claimed equal status in other aspects of American life, they felt equally entitled to publicly claim their connection to Judaism through this rite of initiation.

By all reports, standing on the bimah, reading from Torah, and leading a congregation in prayer are deeply moving moments in time. But for some women, the experience exists in the moment and then seems to fade. For many others, however, the experience moves from being simply performative to transformative. Women do indeed change their behaviors, observing more mitzvot personally and increasing leadership roles in their synagogue. In such cases, the ceremony becomes ritual. The rite of affirmation does become a rite of passage. As one rabbi observed, "I think it's a transforming and transcendent moment in the life of a person." It is these women who are so personally transformed who are making an impact on their synagogues as well.

CEREMONIAL DETAILS

The exact details of the experience itself vary depending on the denomination, size, and culture of the synagogue. Some synagogues have large group classes of twenty or more with a single ceremony once every two years. Others have smaller groups where individual women or groups of two to five may celebrate together after a lengthy period of study. Since the goal is for participants to be able to comfortably and confidently participate in the worship experience, the service structure of their ceremony conforms to what is normal for that particular synagogue community. These features are driven by denominational affiliation and the specific cultural norms of each congregation. Despite variations in group size and preparation, there are many shared dimensions. Typically, students learn about the key elements of the worship service. Most women in Reform, Conservative, and Reconstructionist synagogues learn how to chant Torah and/or haftarah as well. As the date of the ceremony approaches, participants are often asked to write a personal narrative that chronicles where the bat mitzvah experience fits into their "Jewish journey." In some cases, the rabbi will use these statements to craft an individualized blessing for each woman. In other cases, they are put together in a booklet for guests and congregants. In Conservative and Reconstructionist congregations, the ceremony almost always takes place in the Shabbat morning service. In Reform synagogues, the ceremony may be on a Friday night or Saturday morning.[39] In large groups, participants often divide up and lead different parts of the service. All are called up for an aliyah to the Torah. Many chant from the Torah and/or haftarah (Prophets), and some even deliver a *dvar Torah* (homiletic discourse on the Torah portion).

As we saw earlier, the grassroots beginnings of adult bat mitzvah largely gave way to the institutionalization of the experience as more and more rabbis and educators realized this was a way to build critical mass and set a standard for achievement through the adult bat mitzvah ceremony that many others will strive to emulate.[40] As one rabbi remarked, "Adult bat mitzvah is a great way of getting people on the bimah. Getting them to give *Divrei Torah* and read Torah." Indeed, the goal seems to go beyond simply filling the pews to getting women to be active leaders in worship.

Given the turn inward toward self-definition of religious values and practice, there still are women who seek to celebrate an adult bat mitzvah outside an institutional framework. Cousens notes one such case where the woman "had never found a prayer service in which she felt comfortable,"[41] so she created her own and held the ceremony in her home. Such an approach fits well within American values of individualism and subjective ordering of one's own independent religious expression. Similarly, an Internet site called adventurerabbi.com offers a wilderness-based "invigorating approach to Judaism," and will customize retreats and life cycle events, including adult bar or bat mitzvah, to suit individual needs. Interestingly, adventurerabbi.com appears to target Jews who are not affiliated with congregations. They are not seeking to build affiliation and critical mass but to meet each individual's personal needs. As such, their program appears to be quite short—six sessions plus the ceremony, as compared to a synagogue-based program, which is typically two years or longer.

IMPACT ON THE WOMEN THEMSELVES

What characterizes the differences in these women after they have culminated their adult bat mitzvah studies? Three themes dominate the research conducted over the last several years. As a result of their study and ceremonial marking of their accomplishments, participants feel a stronger sense of Jewish identity, they develop a strong commitment to ongoing Jewish learning, and they become more comfortable and connected to ritual and their synagogues.

The first two themes occur frequently as a result of any positive experience of adult Jewish learning. Learning builds meaning, which leads to a stronger sense of self as a Jew. This may not result in any outward change in behavior, but it does build self-confidence and commitment to Jewish practices the women choose to observe. As Audrey, a musician who had never felt comfortable with her Judaism, wrote, "There is also no question that being able to read Torah and Haftarah gives me a stronger sense of identity and of my membership within the community, my synagogue 'family.'"[42] Others, such as Stephanie, spoke in more general terms: "Taking this class has made me feel more Jewish."[43] Similarly, Linda wrote, "I can't say enough about how the bat mitzvah class changed my Jewish life. I felt after the bat mitzvah a true sense of belonging to the adult community."[44]

Likewise, many women develop an excitement about and commitment to ongoing Jewish learning. Here, we do note a behavioral change. Of the fifteen women represented in this study, nine were involved in some form of ongoing adult Jewish learning after the bat mitzvah experience. For some, this entailed learning additional prayers and new parts of the service, such as chanting haftarah. Others attended weekly Torah study sessions, and spoke of taking a variety of short- and long-term topical classes of adult Jewish study. One chose to work for a Jewish educational institution after becoming bat mitzvah and is now considering applying to cantorial school.

The third theme is what distinguishes this experience from many other forms of adult Jewish learning: its emphasis on ritual. The rabbis and educators who teach in these programs do not just teach *about* Judaism; they teach the students *how* to be a Jew. A review of different published curricula demonstrates that adult bat mitzvah courses focus not just on providing students with a basic foundation in Jewish literacy but teaching behavioral aspects of Jewish life, particularly public worship and the performance of mitzvot. For example, the Hadassah *Eishet Mitzvah Curriculum Guide,* their program of adult bat mitzvah, sets out three goals: to gain Jewish knowledge; to improve Hebrew language fluency; and to observe mitzvot.[45] The curriculum published by the Women's League of Conservative Judaism describes two different types of classes. One set focuses on the development of Hebrew reading proficiency and synagogue skills so that students can not only participate but also lead parts of the Shabbat morning service. The other set of classes focuses on building Jewish literacy, enriching the commitment to participating in prayer, and creating "a community of learners that will serve as a role model for adult learning and engagement throughout the synagogue community."[46] Similarly, the course of study outlined in *Rediscovering Judaism,* a bar and bat mitzvah guide for adults, includes behavioral components that address personal religious practices and observances, family relationships, an individual's obligation to engage in social action, and to make a commitment to ongoing Jewish study.[47]

Women who enroll in these classes want to be full participants in worship. They want to know about Judaism and how to practice being Jews in the public arena of the synagogue. Many are also expressing a commitment to increased religious observance. Learning to read Hebrew and to chant Torah and haftarah, standing on the bimah, wearing a tallit, and performing ritual all make these women feel more connected to their synagogue community and more complete as Jews.

These activities can be described as spiritual practices, "a cluster of intentional activities concerned with relating to the sacred."[48] In contrast to a "seeking-oriented" spirituality that focuses more on self-interest and meaning than it does on behavior, this practice-oriented approach demands action. According to the sociologist of religion Robert Wuthnow, a practice-oriented spirituality requires a commitment to prayer and reflection on one's relationship to God.[49] This form of religious expression allows room for personal exploration but also demands participation in a religious tradition. There is a moral dimension to these practices, meaning that rather than letting "desire be one's guide," an individual commits to following a "set of rules and tries to do what is right."[50] In other words, a practice-oriented spirituality requires the individual to buy in to a normative religious community.

THE IMPACT OF ADULT BAT MITZVAH ON SYNAGOGUE RITUAL LIFE AND PRACTICE

As we have seen, for many women, the adult bat mitzvah marks their embarkation into such a practice-oriented spirituality that results in increased involvement both in worship and other aspects of synagogue life. The rabbis and educators interviewed estimated that more than half of each graduating class goes on to become synagogue regulars, meaning they continue to attend services almost every week after celebrating their b'not mitzvah. Written and oral testimony shows the adult bat mitzvah "graduates" often go on to assume significant leadership positions in their synagogues, serving as board and various committee members, sisterhood officers and presidents. One woman became a youth group advisor; another became the chairperson for the change initiative at her synagogue. Two helped establish healing services. Most continued their Jewish learning in some significant and ongoing way. All of these activities serve the congregation, but they also have the potential to change it in subtle and obvious ways from simply increasing the ranks of women in leadership positions to actually changing synagogue programs and practices.

The type of ritual activity adult bat mitzvah graduates pursue seems to depend largely on the culture of their particular synagogue. For example, women in synagogues that have a strong culture of lay participation in services will often continue to take on service leadership roles. Rachel, who celebrated her adult bat mitzvah in June 2002, belongs to an eight-hundred-member unaffiliated, egalitarian synagogue that relies heavily on lay leaders in worship. Members who want to become service leaders are required to take a course. Rachel completed this class and led her first service within six months of celebrating her adult bat mitzvah. Audrey, Linda, and Louise belong to a large Conservative synagogue where many members regularly read Torah. All three of them spoke about having read several times since they became bat mitzvah. Louise, who became an adult bat mitzvah in 1996 and has continued Jewish study, chants Torah on a monthly basis. Audrey, who celebrated her ceremony of adult bat mitzvah by reading Torah in the summer of 2000, chanted haftarah for the first time in April 2003, on the occasion of her husband's sixtieth birthday. Linda, who was in the summer 2002 class from the same synagogue, wrote, "Since the bat mitzvah I have read Torah twice and am always asking for another reading. I did a reading prior to the bat mitzvah also. My goal is to read at least seven times and I am hoping that will be in time for Shavuot 2004!"[51]

Even synagogues where laypeople do not read routinely from the Torah or take on other leadership in worship note an increase in attendance at services and involvement in other aspects of synagogue life. The educator at a six-hundred-member Conservative synagogue said, "Almost without exception the people have become more involved in synagogue programs. They go on to learn more. They participate more actively in services. They join the committees and the board, and it has rubbed off on their kids."[52]

As suggested by this last remark, the adult bat mitzvah experience can have an impact on other family members as well. Linda noted how her involvement inspired her husband to want to read Torah as well. She wrote, "The bat mitzvah was the best thing I have ever done and it has enriched my life and our family life as well. I used to think just because my kids attend Schechter that was enough, but I realize how much more there is for us to do and achieve. My husband now wants to read Torah. Of course like most adults he hasn't read since his bar mitzvah, but he sees so many of our friends and his wife doing it and he feels inspired!"[53]

This impact also spills over to other members of the congregation. One rabbi of a Reform congregation noted that the sanctuary on the date of the adult bat mitzvah ceremony is as full as it is on the high holy days. The seats are filled not only with family members of the five or six participants but with members of the community who come to support and celebrate with their fellow congregants.

Along with their increased synagogue roles and engagement in Jewish learning, many women begin to feel ready and capable of confronting questions of meaning. For some women, the adult bat mitzvah experience has a profound impact on emerging or evolving systems of belief. For instance, for Susan, a music librarian, and Louise, a community volunteer, both in their early fifties, the bat mitzvah classes awakened long dormant reflections about God. As Louise said, "I think [the class] very much affected my belief in God. Because there was a time that I questioned it, that I wasn't sure, and now I'm sure. It's something that's so empowering—that feeling that it's not random."[54] Other women find more powerful emotional connections to the Jewish people and Jewish history. Nina, a woman who felt alienated from Judaism since childhood when her family decided girls did not need to attend Hebrew school, came back to Judaism through the encouragement of her adult son. One year she went to her son's synagogue for Yom Kippur services, and as she wrote in her adult bat mitzvah statement, "To my amazement, it was the most beautiful service I ever attended. The rabbi was incredible. I felt as if she were speaking only to me. My entire Jewish life changed that night. I started to think about myself as a Jew and started to learn about the history I had long since dismissed."[55]

CHANGING ROLES AND CHANGING PRACTICES

Over the past several decades, the feminist movement has had a profound impact on American Judaism, which is demonstrated by women achieving equal rights in public expression of ritual, as well as the influence they have had on the nature of public ritual itself. However, the initial impetus for adult bat mitzvah did not derive from activists pushing for change, nor was it strongly promoted by mainstream leadership, at least for the first two decades. Indeed, few if any of the women whose voices we hear in the research and reports described their decision to become adult bat mitzvah as a feminist statement. Likewise, scholarship on women's ritual innovation in Judaism generally does not point to adult bat mitzvah as a new form of spiritual expression. Women who enroll in adult bat mitzvah programs are not seeking to innovate and reinterpret Jewish ritual; they are seeking to fit into existing ritual patterns. These existing ritual patterns, however, were changed through feminist activism. In other words, adult bat mitzvah could not have been conceived of as an option without the pioneering accomplishments of many early feminists who became the first rabbis, scholars, and Jewish communal service professionals.[56] As more and more of these elite women assumed public roles, other women began to feel that they, too, could be legitimate participants in public ritual. The problem, however, was that as women claimed their egalitarian rights, they began to realize that they lacked the knowledge and skills to perform them.

Hence, the motivation for adult bat mitzvah. Thus, this quiet folk revolution not only changes the lives of American Jewish women, it also is changing the nature of Jewish ritual practice.

In the late 1980s and early 1990s, the sociologist Stuart Schoenfeld conducted the first studies about adult bat mitzvah. His research reflects a contemporary and widely expressed feminist belief that full equality for women can only be achieved "when the informal conservatism which keeps women out of positions of real influence is overcome and when mainstream Judaism incorporates new ideas and rituals which reflect the female as well as the male experience."[57] Complete egalitarianism remains illusive, but the nature of the informal conversation has changed dramatically and irrevocably since that time. Women have indeed made deep and lasting marks on American Judaism, claiming their place on the bimah and in the boardroom, and marking significant moments in their lives through public ritual expression. Certainly in liberal Jewish communities and even in Orthodox ones as well, American Jewish women understand they are entitled to full citizenship and all its rights therein. But they want to exercise these rights with a sense of authenticity. In essence, they perceive adult bat mitzvah as their citizenship exam. As one rabbi remarked, "After the bat mitzvah, they tell me when they're participating in services or on the bimah (even an aliyah) they don't feel as fraudulent. It's as if they are saying, 'I'm doing it right and I have every right to do it.'"[58]

Adult bat mitzvah is about fitting into a normative Jewish framework. However, as more women achieve this milestone, they change what is normative for their given community. Through the performance of this ritual, they strengthen the existing system and group structure. But as they become stronger, more confident, and more informed as Jews they also effect subtle changes in the system. As Sally Moore and Barbara Myerhoff write, "Ritual may do much more than mirror existing social arrangements and existing modes of thought. It can act to reorganize them or even help to create them."[59]

For example, an earlier study focused on five women from a suburban Conservative synagogue who became adult bat mitzvah in the summer of 1996.[60] They were among a class of eleven. Since that time at that synagogue new classes are formed every two years, ranging in size from twelve to twenty, so that over seventy women have celebrated adult bat mitzvah in the past eight years. More than twenty of these women are now among the regular Torah readers at this congregation. Every year more women wear *tallitot,* read from the Torah, and serve in significant leadership roles. They start new program initiatives. They inject new life into old practices. Every class has a mix of ages. As women see the accomplishments of their peers, they imagine the possibility for themselves. By virtue of numbers alone, they shift the status quo. More members are more active in ritual and know how to pray, which can change the nature of congregational singing. More people see a commitment to religious practice as something normal and fulfilling as well.

It is not just in terms of increased numbers that the impact can be felt. The women who participate in adult bat mitzvah classes are not among the elite. They are ordinary people who go from marginal involvement to become strong, active, and more knowledgeable participants. They want to claim a place within normative Jewish tradition, but they also bring a feminine ethic to the public sphere. This influences organizational structures and how decisions are made. It empowers women whose voices would have been totally excluded or silenced a short while ago. Rachel, for example, is a lesbian who had no Jewish education as a child. She was reluctant to join a synagogue for many years, feeling alienated from the mainstream. Through a friend she learned about a congregation that was fully welcoming to gays and lesbians and joined the choir. Shortly after that, she signed up for the adult b'not mitzvah class and spent three years in intensive study. At her ceremony, which she celebrated with two other women, she spoke these moving words about her new relationship with Torah study and her sense of belonging to and participating in an evolving tradition:

> Ultimately, what I think is important—is that we can read a Torah portion and engage in a dialogue about it. When we study and struggle over such important ideas with others, a sense of community develops. . . . This study keeps our tradition alive. It is truly awesome to think that shortly I will be reading from the Torah in the same words, with much the same melodies that my ancestors for over two thousand years have done before me. But remember that I am a woman and a lesbian . . . and I realize that if it were not for the tradition of struggling with the Torah and allowing our tradition to evolve, that my standing here today would be an impossibility.[61]

The more knowledgeable women from all backgrounds and perspectives become the more self-confident and assertive they become. As more women gain the skills and increase their comfort in prayer and public ritual performance, the more likely they are to embrace the practice-oriented spirituality that Wuthnow proposes. This makes them more committed and engaged, both in personal meaning making and public ritual expression.

The life course of one of the women interviewed for this research provides evidence of this trend. Karen, the daughter of Holocaust survivors, grew up as a Reform Jew. She attended Reform Jewish summer camp and was involved in her synagogue youth group as a teen but, as she describes it, "really didn't know much at all." She served as an administrator at a Conservative synagogue for several years. When she and her young family moved to a new community, they decided to join another Conservative synagogue. As we learned earlier, Karen signed up for the adult bat mitzvah class almost immediately; she saw this as her way into this new community. After celebrating her adult bat mitzvah in 1998, she became involved in sisterhood and enrolled in a two-year program of adult Jewish learning. In 2001, she was appointed chairperson of her synagogue's change initiative. She attends Shabbat services weekly, wears a tallit, reads Torah every few months, and is considered an influential and well-respected lay leader.

Karen's reflections on her growth since the bat mitzvah focuses on two things. First, she notes how her increased Jewish knowledge and comfort with Jewish ritual practice makes her more confident and perhaps more critical of the worship experience. She no longer feels the need to conform precisely to the status quo at her synagogue; she is empowered to make informed decisions about how and where she wants to worship. As a new leader in the community, she may indeed be on the path toward shaping change in the nature of services at her congregation. She said, "I'm more secure in who I am as a Jew as a result of the adult bat mitzvah experience. I have a much better sense of what I like and don't like and feel comfortable expressing my opinions. I'm starting a process of fanning out to see what other kinds of Jewish religious experiences there are to help shape what I want for myself."[62]

This newfound independence was evident in her reflections about the next steps she wanted to take. She said, "I'm taking an online writing course right now. I'd really like to travel and write about Jewish life in different communities around the world. Also, I'd like to do some *hevrutah* study, something more self-directed." Consistent with her sense of empowerment, Karen also seemed to be thinking seriously about the nature of her involvement in the synagogue. She felt she was spending too much time supporting organizational and program initiatives for the synagogue and not enough time on her own religious life. As she said, "Learning to chant Torah was an awesome experience. I wanted to do it my whole life. By now,

I thought I'd be onto the next rung. I think I would get a lot more spiritually out of the synagogue if I learned to *daven* than I do arranging meals and flowers for the sick people. I wish it could be more balanced."[63]

Karen embodies the rabbinic precept that study leads to action. She is thoroughly identified as a Jew, but not complacent. She has adopted a practice-oriented spirituality and sees herself as a full participant in Jewish life. Her musings about where she wants to direct her energies and her yearnings for a more meaningful religious life represent the confluence of her American individualism and her Jewish sense of belonging. She is deeply rooted in the community, but now sees herself as having a voice in how this community will continue to grow to reflect her needs.

Rabbi Abraham Isaac Kook is often quoted as saying, "Let us renew the old and sanctify the new." The American rite of adult bat mitzvah affords Karen and thousands of women like her the opportunity to do just that. These women have "renewed the old" by adapting a rite intended to mark the chronological transition to adulthood, infusing it with new meaning. Through bat mitzvah, they are saying that becoming a Jewish adult means developing certain basic skills and competencies in order to participate fully in community. They are also saying that this can happen at any point in the life cycle. Though the public affirmation of belonging sometimes is enough, for most, the adult bat mitzvah ceremony marks a step along a longer journey. These women "sanctify the new" as they deepen their religious lives through ongoing Jewish learning, *and* stronger connections, *and* more varied contributions to community. As their own lives are changed, they too change their communities (in their families, their synagogues, and the larger Jewish community). The full extent of these changes has yet to be realized, but the signs suggest that the trajectory will represent a blending of American individualism with Jewish practice. As these women strive to find personal meaning within Judaism, they will make sure that their needs as women are met and that their place as public and full participants in Jewish ritual life will endure.

NOTES

1. Stuart Schoenfeld, "Integration into the Group and Sacred Uniqueness: An Analysis of Adult Bat Mitzvah," in *Persistence and Flexibility: Anthropological Perspectives on the American Jewish Experience,* ed. Walter P. Zenner (Albany: State University of New York Press, 1987); Schoenfeld, "Ritual Performance, Curriculum Design and Jewish Identity: Towards a Perspective on Contemporary Innovations in Bar/Bat Mitzvah Education," *Bikurim* 6, no. 2 (1989): 19–22; Schoenfeld, "Interpreting Adult Bat Mitzvah: The Limits and Potential of Feminism in a

Congregational Setting," in *Jewish Sects, Religious Movements, and Political Parties,* ed. Menachem Mor (Omaha, NE: Creighton University Press, 1991); Schoenfeld, "Ritual and Role Transition: Adult Bat Mitzvah as a Successful Rite of Passage," in *The Uses of Tradition: Jewish Continuity in the Modern Era,* ed. Jack Wertheimer (New York: Jewish Theological Seminary, 1992); Nancy Ellen Kahn, "The Adult Bat Mitzvah: Its Use in Female Development" (Ph.D. diss., Smith School of Social Work, 1993); Lisa D. Grant, "Adult Bat Mitzvah: An American Rite of Continuity," *Courtyard* 1 (Winter 2000): 142–71; Grant, "Restorying Jewish Lives Post Adult Bat Mitzvah," *Journal of Jewish Education* 68 (Fall–Winter 2003): 34–51; Beth Cousens, "Adult Bat Mitzvah as an Entrée into Jewish Life for North American Jewish Women" (working paper for Hadassah International Research Institute on Jewish Women, 2002); Chana Kotzin, "Ascending the Bimah: Jewish Women 'Come of Age': The Growth of Adult Bat Mitzvah in America during the 1970s" (paper delivered at the Jewish Feminist Research Group, New York, February 18, 2002).

2. Albert Axelrad, "Belated Bar/Bat Mitzvahs," in *The Second Jewish Catalog* (Philadelphia: Jewish Publication Society, 1971).

3. Schoenfeld, "Ritual and Role Transition."

4. Schoenfeld, "Integration into the Group and Sacred Uniqueness"; Ruth Mason, "Adult Bat Mitzvah: Changing Women, Changing Synagogues," *Lilith* 14 (Fall 1989): 21–24.

5. Kotzkin, "Ascending the Bimah."

6. Lisa D. Grant, *Aytz Ha'yim He: She Is a Tree of Life: Adult Bat Mitzvah Curriculum* (New York: Women's League for Conservative Judaism, 2001); *Adult B'Nei Mitzvah: Affirming Our Identities* (New York: UAHC Press, 2002).

7. These estimates are based on correspondence with Francie Schwartz, URJ adult learning coordinator, Department of Lifelong Jewish Learning, February 17, 2004, and Lisa Kogen, program director of the Women's League for Conservative Judaism, February 5, 2004.

8. Charles Strouse, "Mazel Tov," *Sun-Sentinel* (Fort Lauderdale, FL), July 16, 1996.

9. Dr. Carol Diament, national director of education for Hadassah, e-mail correspondence with the author, January 28, 2004.

10. Claudia Chernov, senior editor, National Jewish Education, Hadassah, e-mail correspondence with the author, August 2004; Barbara Spack, Hadassah National Chair of Jewish Education (1993–99), telephone interview by the author, August 24, 2004.

11. Reports of adult bat mitzvah ceremonies appeared regularly in the Jewish press from the late 1980s onward. See, for example, Mason, "Adult Bat Mitzvah"; Robert Goldblum, "Daughter of the Book," *Baltimore Jewish Times,* August 14, 1992; Strouse, "Mazel Tov"; "At 28, a Woman Finally Feels Like a Jewish Adult," *Forward,* January 24, 2003; "UConn Student Turns to Judaism," *Connecticut Jewish Ledger,* November 29, 2002; Ellen Jaffe-Gill, "Adult Bar and Bat Mitzvah: Meaningful at Every Age," available at http://www.ujc.org (accessed February 12,

2004). An article on the subject even appeared in the secular press in the summer of 2003: David Van Biema, "A Ritual for All Ages," *Time,* July 7, 2003.

12. Sylvia Barack Fishman and Alice Goldstein, *When They Are Grown They Will Not Depart* (Waltham, MA: Cohen Center for Modern Jewish Studies, 1993).

13. Linda Seidman and Sharon Milburn, *Family Education Survey* (Chicago: Community Foundation for Jewish Education of Metropolitan Chicago, 2000).

14. Grant, "Adult Bat Mitzvah"; Grant, "Restorying Jewish Lives."

15. Pseudonyms are used for all informants.

16. Jonathan Woocher, *Sacred Survival: American Jewry's Civil Religion* (New York: American Jewish Committee, 1986).

17. Steven M. Cohen and Aryeh Davidson, *Adult Jewish Learning in America: Current Patterns and Prospects for Growth* (New York: Florence G. Heller/JCC Association Research Center and the Jewish Theological Seminary of America, 2001); Lisa D. Grant, Diane T. Schuster, Meredith Woocher, and Steven M. Cohen, *Journey of Heart and Mind: Transformative Jewish Learning in Adulthood* (New York: Jewish Theological Seminary, 2004).

18. Hasia R. Diner and Beryl Lieff Benderly, *Her Works Praise Her: A History of Jewish Women in America from Colonial Times to the Present* (New York: Basic Books, 2002).

19. Tom Driver, *Liberating Rites: Understanding the Transformative Power of Ritual* (Boulder: Westview Press, 1998), 9.

20. Among the many examples of published works of creative ritual are Penina Adelman, *Miriam's Well: Rituals for Jewish Women around the Year* (Fresh Meadows, NY: Biblio Press, 1986); Debra Orenstein, ed., *Lifecycles: Jewish Women on Life Passages and Personal Milestones* (Woodstock, VT: Jewish Lights, 1994); E. M. Broner, *Bringing Home the Light: A Jewish Woman's Handbook of Rituals* (San Francisco: Council Oak, 1999); Debra Nussbaum Cohen, *Celebrating Your New Jewish Daughter: Creating New Jewish Ways to Welcome Baby Girls into the Covenant* (Woodstock, VT: Jewish Lights, 2001). The journal *Kerem: Creative Explorations in Judaism,* ed. Gilah Langer and Sara Horowitz, also includes articles on new ritual in virtually every issue. http://www.ritualwell.org, sponsored by Ma'yan, the Jewish Women's project of the Jewish Community Center in Manhattan, posts rituals and material to support women in creating and using them.

21. Interview with Roberta, October 19, 2001.

22. Interview with Rachel, February 6, 2003.

23. Interview with Ann, September 30, 2001.

24. Written testimony from Linda, March 9, 2003.

25. Kahn, "The Adult Bat Mitzvah."

26. Cousens, "Adult Bat Mitzvah as an Entrée into Jewish Life," 16.

27. Interview with Rachel.

28. Interview with Louise, September 25, 2001.

29. Interview with Karen, March 3, 2003.

30. Arnold Van Gennep, *The Rites of Passage,* trans. Monika B. Vizedom and Gabrielle L. Caffee (1909; repr., Chicago: University of Chicago Press, 1960);

Victor Turner, *Dramas, Fields, and Metaphors: Symbolic Action in Human Society* (Ithaca: Cornell University Press, 1972).

31. Barbara Myerhoff, *Number Our Days* (New York: Dutton, 1989); Paul Connerton, *How Societies Remember* (Cambridge: Cambridge University Press, 1989).

32. Clifford Geertz, "Religion as a Cultural System," in *The Interpretation of Cultures* (New York: Basic Books, 1973).

33. Ronald Grimes, *Deeply into the Bone: Re-Inventing Rites of Passage* (Berkeley: University of California Press, 2000), 121.

34. Charles Liebman, "Ritual, Ceremony and the Reconstruction of Judaism in the United States," in *Jews in America: A Contemporary Reader,* ed. Roberta Rosenberg Farber and Chaim I. Waxman (Hanover, NH: Brandeis University Press, 1999), 308.

35. Robert Wuthnow, *After Heaven: Spirituality in America since the 1950s* (Berkeley: University of California Press, 1998).

36. Bethamie Horowitz, *Connections and Journeys: Assessing Critical Opportunities for Enhancing Jewish Identity* (New York: UJA-Federation, 2000); Steven M. Cohen and Arnold M. Eisen, *The Jew Within: Self, Family, and Community in America* (Bloomington: Indiana University Press, 2000).

37. Cohen and Eisen, *The Jew Within,* 93.

38. Interview with Louise.

39. The Modern Orthodox synagogue cited in Chana Kotzkin's research also held the adult bat mitzvah ceremony on a Friday evening. Here, the ceremony consisted of English readings only and a communal Oneg Shabbat celebration after services.

40. Joy D. Levitt, "Embracing the Tradition: Changes for Jewish Women in Religious Life," in *Voices for Change: Future Directions for American Jewish Women* (sponsored by Hadassah: The Women's Zionist Organization of America and the Maurice and Marilyn Cohen Center for Modern Jewish Studies Institute for Community and Religion, Brandeis University, 1995); Mark Washofsky, *Jewish Living: A Guide to Contemporary Reform Practice* (New York: UAHC Press, 2001).

41. Cousens, "Adult Bat Mitzvah as an Entrée into Jewish Life," 13 (page refers to offprint edition).

42. Written testimony from Audrey, March 6, 2003.

43. Written testimony from Stephanie, March 13, 2003.

44. Written testimony from Linda.

45. *Eishet Mitzvah Curriculum Guide* (Jewish Education Department, Hadassah, the Women's Zionist Organization of America, 2001).

46. Grant, "*Aytz Ha'yim He,*" iv.

47. Kerry Olitzky and Ron Isaacs, *Rediscovering Judaism: Bar and Bat Mitzvah Guide for Adults* (Jersey City, NJ: Ktav, 1997), xiii.

48. Wuthnow, *After Heaven,* 170.

49. Ibid., 178.

50. Ibid., 184.

51. Written testimony from Linda. At this synagogue, anyone who has read from

the Torah at least seven times is presented a Tikkun during Shavuot services each year.

52. Eleanor Fried, education director, interview by the author, March 11, 2003.

53. Written testimony from Linda.

54. Interview with Louise.

55. Narrative statement, Nina, June 1, 2002.

56. Rela Geffen Monson, "The Impact of the Jewish Women's Movement on the American Synagogue," in *Daughters of the King: Women and the Synagogue,* ed. Susan Grossman and Rivka Haut (Philadelphia: Jewish Publication Society, 1992).

57. Schoenfeld, "Interpreting Adult Bat Mitzvah," 207.

58. Interview with Rabbi B., March 2003.

59. Sally F. Moore and Barbara G. Myerhoff, *Secular Ritual* (Assen/Amsterdam: Van Gorcum, 1977), 5.

60. Grant, "Adult Bat Mitzvah."

61. D'var Torah delivered at her ceremony of adult bat mitzvah, Rachel, June 2002.

62. Interview with Karen.

63. Ibid.

TIMELINE OF JEWISH AND U.S. FEMINISM

Note: This timeline juxtaposes Jewish feminism with feminism in the United States, with events in U.S. feminism set in italics. It begins in the nineteenth century when the campaign for suffrage began and when Reform Judaism began to consider how to integrate women into the public world of Jewish worship.

Timelines are chronological snapshots. They focus on "firsts." In decades when there is little activity it is important to keep in mind the ongoing work that is building on the pioneering events that preceded it.

1848

The first Women's Rights Convention is held in Seneca Falls, New York, where participants write and sign a Declaration of Sentiments, modeled on the Declaration of Independence, asserting women's natural right to equality in all spheres.

1851

First use of a family pew and the abolition of a separate women's gallery within the synagogue in Congregation Beth El in Albany, New York, where Isaac Mayer Wise is rabbi.

1855

Die Deborah, a German-language supplement of the English-language weekly *The Israelite,* is first published by Reform rabbi and leader, Isaac Mayer Wise, in Cincinnati, a strong supporter of women's suffrage. It ceases publication in 1902.

1869

Susan B. Anthony and Elizabeth Cady Stanton form the National

Woman Suffrage Association, which is dedicated to influencing Congress to pass an amendment to the Constitution for women's suffrage.

Lucy Stone and Henry Blackwell help form the American Woman Suffrage Association, which is dedicated to voting rights for women through amendments to state constitutions.

1890

Ray Frank delivers a sermon and leads prayers at an opera house in Spokane, Washington, on Yom Kippur.

Ida B. Wells, African American journalist and publisher, launches an anti-lynching crusade.

1893

The Jewish Women's Congress is held as part of the Religious Parliament at the Colombian Exposition in Chicago.

The National Council of Jewish Women is founded as the first national organization to unite Jewish women to promote Judaism. The organization has been consistently committed to social welfare and political reform, the needs of mothers and families, and the importance of Judaism and educating Jewish women.

1895

The American Jewess, the first independent English-language paper published by and for Jewish women in the United States, is founded by Rosa Sonneschein, who served as its editor. It ceased publication in 1899.

1909

The Uprising of the 20,000, a strike against clothing manufacturers, occurs in the New York garment industry, initiated by young immigrant Jewish working women in the Shirtwaist Makers Local 25 of the International Ladies Garment Workers Union. These young women attract the attention of the labor movement and of the suffrage movement because of their unanticipated boldness and courage to take organized political action on behalf of workers. Clara Lemlich, who will become a major leader in the labor movement, calls on workers to strike.

Solomon Schechter creates the Teachers Institute, which opens the Jewish Theological Seminary to women students and offers Jewish higher education to men and women on an equal basis.

The First permanent chapter of B'nai B'rith Women is founded in San Francisco to promote socializing among families of American Jewry's oldest and largest fraternal and service organization. B'nai B'rith women would develop service, youth, and political work, and ultimately embrace feminism. In 1990 they became an independent, self-governing organization. In 1995 the organization was renamed Jewish Women International.

1911

The Triangle Shirtwaist Factory fire claims the lives of 146 workers, mainly Jewish women. They are seen as martyrs in the struggle to transform labor conditions and labor relations in the United States.

1912

Hadassah, the Women's Zionist Organization of America, is founded. It became the most successful American women's volunteer organization in history and the most popular American Jewish organization, as well as the largest Zionist organization in the world. It blends Zionism, social feminism, and a practical idealism.

1913

The National Federation of Temple Sisterhoods in Reform Judaism is founded, enabling women to focus on congregational life in an unprecedented way. The organization is renamed Women of Reform Judaism in 1993.

1915

Teachers Institute of the Jewish Theological Seminary of America creates a professional teacher training curriculum that enables women to prepare for careers in Jewish education.

1916

Jeannette Rankin (R-Montana) is the first woman elected to Congress.

1918

Women's League, the women's division of the United Synagogue of America, the lay organization of Conservative Judaism, is founded by Mathilde Schechter.

1920

The Nineteenth Amendment to the Constitution passes, giving women the right to vote.

1921

The Jewish Woman, a quarterly magazine of the National Council of Jewish Women, begins publication. It is designed to provide the "first organized record of Jewish womanhood's aspirations and successes." It ceases publication in 1931 and is revived as *Council Woman* in the 1940s and 1950s.

Martha Neumark, a seventeen-year-old student at Hebrew Union College, launches a two-year-long debate on the ordination of women rabbis. The college's board of governors denies her the right of ordination despite an affirmation of the principle of gender equality by the Central Conference of American Rabbis.

1922

The first bat mitzvah is held in the United States. Judith Kaplan Eisenstein, daughter of Rabbi Mordecai Kaplan, is called to the Torah at the Society for the Advancement of Judaism in New York, his synagogue.

1923

The Equal Rights Amendment to the Constitution is first introduced into Congress.

1925

Pioneer Women, the Labor Zionist women's organization in the United States, is officially founded as a separate and independent group, emphasizing the importance of women in the American Zionist movement. It changes its name in 1981 to *Na'amat* to parallel the Israeli organization.

1927

Women's American ORT (the Russian acronym that stands for the Distribution of Artisanal and Agricultural Skills) is founded to support the work of training and rehabilitating impoverished Jews in Russia and of refugee settlement in Russia and Europe. Throughout the twentieth century, the organization responded to the needs of resettlement and training that resulted from war and the establishment of the State of Israel. By the 1970s, Women's American ORT became the financial backbone of the entire organization.

1934

Amit, the largest religious Zionist organization in the United States, is founded as an autonomous group when it separates from the men's organization. It supports religious technical education schools in Israel as well as children's homes and youth villages.

1939

Helen Levinathal is awarded a master of Hebrew literature but not rabbinic ordination by the Jewish Institute of Religion, despite her completion of the rabbinical curriculum.

1953

Professor Saul Lieberman formulates a clause to be inserted in the marriage contract that both husband and wife agree that the husband will come to a Jewish court and a civil court for arbitration if necessary, thus ensuring women the right to a religious and civil divorce.

Simone de Beauvoir's Second Sex *is published in English.*

1954

Stern College for Women is established at Yeshiva University to provide a modern baccalaureate program with a strong emphasis on Jewish studies.

1955

The Conservative Committee on Jewish Law and Standards issues a minority opinion written by Rabbi Aaron Blumenthal that permits women to be called to the Torah to pronounce a blessing (aliyah). This position was adopted more broadly in the 1970s and today is the norm of Conservative synagogues.

The Daughters of Bilitis, the first lesbian organization in the United States, is founded.

1963

Betty Friedan publishes The Feminine Mystique, *which identifies the limits placed on women's lives that constrain them to their roles as wives and mothers.*

Congress passes the Equal Pay for Equal Work Act.

1964

Congress passes the Civil Rights Act, including Title VII, which prohibits discrimination in employment on the basis of race, color, religion, national origin, or sex.

1966

The National Organization for Women is founded as a grassroots, civil rights lobby for women, followed by the founding of Women's Equity Action League and National Women's Political Caucus.

1968

Shirley Chisholm (D-New York) is the first African American woman elected to Congress.

1968–69

The women's liberation movement flourishes through groups like New York's Redstockings and Boston's Bread and Roses.

1969

The New York Conference of the United Methodist Church forms a task force to discuss women's issues, calling on the church to renounce the "unchristian formula of male superiority."

The Stonewall Riots occur in New York City when police attempt to raid a gay bar. Gay men and lesbian women resist police attacks, launching the gay liberation movement.

Late 1960s

The first women's *tefillah* (prayer) group is founded at Lincoln Square Synagogue in Manhattan on the festival of Simhat Torah. Women convene their own Torah reading apart from men to be in keeping with Jewish law. These groups, based in Orthodox communities, have proliferated throughout Israel, Canada, and the United States.

1970

Trude Weiss-Romarin publishes in the *Spectator,* the journal she edits, "The Unfreedom of Jewish Women," in which she articulates the liabilities of women in Jewish law.

Rachel Adler writes in *Davka,* a small countercultural journal published in Los Angeles, a highly influential and much reprinted critique of the status of women in Jewish tradition, titled "The Jew Who Wasn't There."

Robin Morgan publishes the edited collection Sisterhood Is Powerful. *(Shulamit Firestone's* The Dialectic of Sex *and Kate Millet's* Sexual Politics *also appear that year.)*

The Equal Rights Amendment to the Constitution is reintroduced into Congress.

1971

The National Women's Political Caucus forms to lobby for women's rights within the legislative process and to enforce an "equal pay" act and Title VII of the Civil Rights Act, which outlaws sex discrimination.

Ms. Magazine's *first issue appears (the feminist publication with the largest circulation, but one of hundreds published nationwide).*

1972

The Equal Rights Amendment passes Congress and is returned to states for ratification. The amendment, originally drafted in 1923, fails ratification.

Ezrat Nashim confronts the Rabbinical Assembly of Conservative Judaism with its statement of demands which is a public affirmation of women's equality in all aspects of Jewish life. The group consists of highly educated young women, most of whom grew up in the Conservative movement, and many are members at the time of the New York Havurah, a countercultural fellowship.

Sally Priesand is ordained as the first woman rabbi in Reform Judaism at Hebrew Union College of Cincinnati, Ohio.

Congress passes Title IX of the Higher Education Act outlawing sex discrimination in any educational program that is federally funded.

1973

The National Black Feminist Organization is founded.

The Supreme Court establishes a woman's right to a safe and legal abortion throughout the United States in Roe v Wade.

Saul Berman publishes "The Status of Women in Halakhic Judaism" in *Tradition,* an Orthodox journal.

The Committee on Jewish Law and Standards passes a *takkanah* (ruling) allowing women to count equally with men in the minyan if the rabbi of a congregation has consented.

The North American Jewish Student Network convenes the first national Jewish women's conference in New York City, attracting 500 participants.

Rabbi Daniel I. Leifer and Myra Leifer create a baby naming ceremony for their daughter, Ariel, and a *pidyon ha bat* (redemption of the firstborn normally only for the first son). They publish the rituals in the first collection of essays on Jewish feminism.

Mary Daly publishes Beyond God the Father: Toward a Philosophy of Women's Liberation, *a feminist analysis of Christianity. Daly continues to publish many books that offer feminist critiques of the church and Western religion.*

1974

Sandy Eisenberg Sasso is the first woman ordained by the Reconstructionist Rabbinical College.

The Jewish Feminist Organization (JFO) is formed. Though short-lived, it brings together both secular- and religious-oriented feminists to advance an agenda of equal participation in all aspects of Jewish culture.

The Coalition of Labor Union Women (CLUW) is founded to unite women workers.

1975

Barbara Ostfeld-Horowitz is ordained the first Reform female cantor by Hebrew Union College.

Combahee River Collective, a nonhierarchical socialist, African American feminist group, is organized. Its members assert that feminism is an essential element of the struggle against racial and economic injustice.

Catholic women organize a conference in Detroit titled "Women in Future Priesthood Now: A Call to Action." It is attended by 1,200 women while another 500 are turned away.

The Reform movement publishes *Gates of Prayer,* a newly revised prayer book (siddur), and the Prayer Book Commission upholds the principle of equality in liturgical language.

The First International Women's Conference is held in Mexico City.

1976

The Jewish Women's Resource Center is founded to document and support the modern Jewish women's movement. It provides an archive and library, as well as a setting for study and self-help groups. It grew out of the New York Women's Center, which was founded by students affiliated with the Jewish Feminist Organization, and was directed by Rabbi Nina Beth Cardin and Rabbi Carol Glass. In 1982 it was housed by and affiliated with the New York Section of the National Council of Jewish Women.

Lilith: The Independent Jewish Women's Magazine is founded by Susan Weidman Schneider and Aviva Cantor, and continues publication under Schneider's editorship.

The first feminist seder is held in New York City by the "Seder Sisters" using a women's Haggadah, which is subsequently published in *Ms. Magazine* by E. M. Broner.

Elizabeth Koltun edits *The Jewish Woman in America: New Perspectives,* a collection of essays on Jewish feminism drawn from a special issue of *Response Magazine,* a Jewish countercultural magazine, and supplemented by other essays.

The Episcopal Church recognizes the ordination of women priests.

Charlotte Baum, Paula Hyman, and Sonya Michel write *The Jewish Woman in America,* the first book-length study of American Jewish women inspired by feminism.

1977

The Women's Institute for Continuing Jewish education is founded by Irene Fine in San Diego and is among the first to publish women's interpretations of Jewish texts as well as women's rituals.

The National Conference on Women held in Houston, Texas, with 2,000 delegates and 18,000 observers.

The National Women's Studies Association is founded.

Drisha Institute for Jewish Education is founded in New York City by Rabbi David Silber to provide women with the opportunity to engage in serious study of traditional Jewish texts as a nondenominational institution of higher Jewish education. It provided the first opportunity for Orthodox women to have access to study these texts and methods.

1979

The Conservative movement's commission on the ordination of women rabbis recommends after two years of meetings across the United States that women should be allowed to become rabbis.

1981

Cantor Deborah Katchko-Zimmerman founds the Women Cantors Network.

Blu Greenberg publishes *On Being a Jewish Feminist,* making the case for Orthodox feminism.

Jewish women form Feminists against Anti-Semitism, which defines itself as both Zionist and feminist. The group responded to international women's meetings organized by the United Nations where Zionism is labeled as racist in the 1975 conference declarations. The meeting in Copenhagen in 1980 was the final catalyst in creating the organization.

This Bridge Called My Back: Writings of Women of Color *is published, marking the emergence of multicultural feminisms.*

Professor Jane Gerber is the first woman elected to serve as the president of the Association for Jewish Studies.

Sandra Day O'Connor is the first woman appointed to the U.S. Supreme Court.

1982

Evelyn Beck publishes an edited volume, *Nice Jewish Girls,* the first discussion of lesbian issues in Jewish and Jewish feminist life.

Letty Pogrebin, an editor at *Ms. Magazine,* publishes "Antisemitism in the Women's Movement" to decry anti-Zionism, Christian feminist attacks on Judaism as the root of sexism, and other indignities in the June issue of *Ms. Magazine.*

1983

The Jewish Theological Seminary faculty votes to admit women to its rabbinical school.

1984

The Los Angeles feminist conference "Illuminating the Unwritten Scroll: Women's Spirituality and Jewish Tradition" is organized by Rabbis Laura Geller and Patricia Karlin-Neumann. They address the following question: "What is the nature of women's religious experience?" and declare these issues to be paramount in the next generation of Jewish feminism.

The American Jewish Congress focuses its annual United States—Israel dialogue in Jerusalem on the topic, "Woman as Jew, Jews as Women."

Jewish women form a permanent Jewish Women's Caucus within the Women's Studies Association.

Geraldine Ferraro is the first woman to be nominated to run for vice president of the United States.

1985

The United Nations sponsors a gathering of 14,000 women in Nairobi, Kenya, to place women's rights on the human rights agenda.

Amy Eilberg is the first woman ordained in Conservative Judaism by the Jewish Theological Seminary.

The Women's Tefillah Network is formed to unite Orthodox women's groups in the United States.

The Conservative movement publishes a new prayer book, *Sim Shalom,* that offers a small degree of gender equality in liturgical language, including an alternative *Amidah* (central prayer) evoking the biblical matriarchs.

1986

Women members of the Association for Jewish Studies meet for the first time to form a women's caucus.

1987

Erica Lipitz and Marla Rosenfeld Barugel are ordained as cantors by the Cantors Institute of the Jewish Theological Seminary.

American Jewish women join together at the Western Wall in Jerusalem to pray collectively, in violation of custom.

1989

Israeli Women of the Wall and the International Committee for Women of the Wall appeal to Israeli court for the right to pray together at the Western Wall, the first time that religious rights of Jewish women were argued in a court of law.

The Reconstructionist movement publishes a new prayer book (siddur), *Kol haneshamah,* with gender-inclusive language in Hebrew and English.

1990

Bridges: A Journal for Jewish Feminists and Our Friends, an independent journal of fiction, poetry, essays, visual art, and reviews, is founded. The journal has created space for Jewish lesbian and working-class voices, and engages with a multiethnic feminist movement concerned with antiracism, economic justice, peace, and lesbian and gay issues.

The Los Angeles Jewish Feminist Center is founded. Rabbi Sue Levi Elwell serves as its first director.

Judith Plaskow's *Standing Again at Sinai: Judaism from a Feminist Perspective* is published, the first book-length work of Jewish feminist theology.

1992

Rabbi Sharon Kleinbaum is appointed senior rabbi of Beth Simchat Torah, New York, the largest gay and lesbian synagogue in the world.

The International Coalition for *Agunah* Rights is founded by Norma Joseph (Canada), Alice Shalvi (Israel), and Rivka Haut (United States). The coalition works to educate and bring attention to the plight of *agunot,* women whose husbands are either unwilling or unable to grant a Jewish divorce, and because of Jewish law these women cannot remarry.

1993

Marcia Falk publishes *The Book of Blessings: A Feminist-Jewish Reconstruction of Prayer,* the first serious effort to bring a feminist perspective to the writing of Jewish liturgy.

The Rabbinical Council of America endorses a two-part prenuptial agreement mandating a level of support for a wife in the event of separation until divorce is concluded, and requiring both partners to agree to the arbitration of a religious court regarding divorce. The decision is a direct result of a struggle by Orthodox feminists, including Norma Baumel Joseph and Rivka Haut.

Ma'yan: The Jewish Women's Project of the Jewish Community Center in Manhattan, is founded. It sponsors a woman's seder, classes, a library and archive, and gatherings for Jewish women.

The Reform movement publishes a "gender-sensitive" liturgy to supplement their prayer book, *Gates of Prayer*.

1995

The Jewish Women's Archive is founded under the directorship of Gail Reimer in Brookline, Massachusetts. Its mission is to uncover and communicate American Jewish women's history. It is a pioneer in the technology of collecting and disseminating history.

Diane Cohler-Esses is the first Syrian Jewish woman to become a rabbi. She is ordained at the Jewish Theological Seminary.

1996

The Jewish Orthodox Feminist Alliance (JOFA) is founded by Blu Greenberg.

1997

The first international conference on feminism and Orthodox Judaism is held in New York City. One thousand people registered for the event, and conferences have since been held yearly.

Hadassah-Brandeis Institute opens at Brandeis University. (It was originally called the International Research Institute on Jewish Women.) It is currently codirected by Sylvia Barack Fishman and Shulamit Reinharz, and is committed to interdisciplinary and international research on issues of Jewish women and gender.

Paula E. Hyman and Deborah Dash Moore publish *Jewish Women in America: An Historical Encyclopedia* in two volumes.

1998

Nashim: A Journal of Jewish Women's Studies and Gender Issues is cofounded by the Hadassah-Brandeis Institute and the Schechter Institute of Jewish Studies in Jerusalem.

The Barbara Dobkin Award in Women's Studies is created as a new category of the Jewish Book Council's National Jewish Book Award. The award is created by friends of Barbara Dobkin, a philanthropist who supports a number of Jewish women's initiatives and is a leader in Jewish communal life.

2000

Jewish Women Watching, an anonymous group, launches its first campaign to draw attention to sexism and other forms of discrimination in the Jewish community. They send 1,500 Jewish new year's cards to the press and prominent members of the Jewish community with the message, "Sexism is a Sin." They have conducted yearly actions since.

2001

Advancing Women Professionals and the Jewish Community is founded by Shifra Bronznick to close the gender gap in women's leadership in the Jewish community. This organization promotes leadership of women professionals within Jewish communal institutions and is a catalyst for change to create equity in those institutions. The organization undertakes projects to transform the Jewish communal structure and to assure that women and younger leaders are represented in all community undertakings.

Danya Ruttenberg publishes the edited volume *Yentl's Revenge: The Next Wave of Jewish Feminism.*

Rela Mintz Geffen is appointed president of Baltimore Hebrew University.

2003

Tobin Belzer and Julie Plec publish the edited volume, *Joining the Sisterhood: Young Jewish Women Write Their Lives.*

2004

Rennert Forum in Judaism of Barnard College presents a national conference titled "Jewish Women Changing America: Cross-Generational Conversations."

2006

Dina Najman is appointed "spiritual leader" or *kehilat orach* of Manhattan.

CONTRIBUTORS

Andrew Bush is a professor of Hispanic studies and Jewish studies at Vassar College, where he served as the first director of the Jewish Studies Program and is among its founders. He is the author of *The Routes of Modernity: Spanish American Poetry from the Early Eighteenth to the Mid-Nineteenth Century* (2003) and many articles on Spanish literature and American Jewish culture and theorizing diaspora. He is author most recently of "Post-Zionism and Its Neighbors," in *Judaism,* "Benjamin's Baroque," in *Never-Ending Adventure: Studies in Medieval and Early Modern Spanish Literature in Honor of Peter N. Dunn* (2002), and "Overhearing Hollander's Hyphens: Poet-Critic, American-Jew," in *diacritics* (2000).

Karla Goldman is a historian-in-residence at the Jewish Women's Archive in Boston and is the author of *Beyond the Synagogue Gallery: Finding a Place for Women in American Judaism* (2000). During 1991–2000 she taught American Jewish history at Hebrew Union College-Jewish Institute of Religion in Cincinnati, where she was the first female member of the faculty.

Lisa D. Grant is an associate professor of Jewish education at the Hebrew Union College-Jewish Institute of Religion, New York School. Her research interests include adult Jewish learning and the role of Israel in American Jewish life. Her research has appeared in the *Journal of Jewish Services, Courtyard, Jewish Education News,* and *Conservative Judaism.* She cowrote "Teaching Jewish Adults," in *New Jewish Teachers Handbook* (2003), and *A Journey of Heart and Mind: Transformative Learning in Adulthood* (2004).

Norma Baumel Joseph is an associate professor of religion at Concordia University in Montreal, Quebec. She started the women and religion specialization at Concordia. Her doctoral dissertation was an analysis of gender in the legal decisions of Rabbi Moses Feinstein. She has edited a volume of *Nashim* on food, gender, and identity, and has published many articles on women and Orthodox Judaism and women and Jewish law.

Adriane B. Leveen received her Ph.D. in 2000 from the University of California at Berkeley. After teaching at Hebrew Union College-Jewish Institute of Religion in Los Angeles from 2000 until the end of 2003 she joined Stanford University as a senior lecturer in the Hebrew Bible in the Department of Religious Studies. She has published in the *Journal for the Study of the Old Testament* and *Prooftexts* on the politics of memory and burial practices in the biblical world. She also coedited an award-winning anthology of the poetry of Stanley Chyet and is a contributor to the forthcoming *Women's Torah Commentary* and a volume on healing in Judaism. Her book *Memory and Tradition in the Book of Numbers* will appear in 2008.

Rochelle L. Millen is a professor of religion at Wittenberg University. She is the editor of *New Perspectives on the Holocaust: A Guide for Teachers and Scholars* (1996), and the author of *Women, Birth, and Death in Jewish Law and Practice* (2004).

Deborah Dash Moore is Frederick G. L. Huetwell Professor of History and the director of Jewish studies at the University of Michigan. She is the author of, among other books, *At Home in America: Second Generation New York Jews* (1981); *To the Golden Cities: Pursuing the American Jewish Dream in Miami and L.A.* (1994); and *GI Jews: How World War II Changed a Generation* (2004). Among her coedited works are *Divergent Jewish Cultures: Israel and America* (2001), and *Jewish Women in America: An Historical Encyclopedia* (1997).

Jody Myers is on the faculty of the Religious Studies Department at California State University, Northridge, and directs the Jewish Studies Interdisciplinary Program. She has written several articles on the emergence of modern messianic and religious Zionism, as well as a book, *Seeking Zion: Modernity and Messianic Activism in the Writings of Tsevi Hirsch Kalischer* (2003). She has also written several articles on contemporary religious expression, including "The Midrashic Enterprise of Contemporary Jewish Women," *Studies in Contemporary Jewry* 14 (2000); "The Myth of Matriarchy in Contemporary Jewish Women's Spiritual Writings," *Jewish Social Studies* 4 (Fall 1997); and "The Secret of Jewish Femininity: Hiddenness, Power, and Physicality in the Theology of Orthodox Women in the Contemporary World," in *Gender and Judaism: The Transformation of Tradition,* ed. T. M. Rudavsky (1995).

Pamela S. Nadell is a professor of history and the director of the Jewish Studies Program at American University. Her book *Women Who Would Be Rabbis: A History of Women's Ordination, 1889–1985* (1998) was a finalist for the National Jewish Book Award and a main selection of the Jewish Book Club. She is also the author of *Conservative Judaism in America: A Biographical Dictionary and Sourcebook* (1988), editor of *American Jewish Women's History: A Reader* (2003), and coeditor of *Women and American Judaism: Historical Perspectives* (2001).

Vanessa L. Ochs, Ida and Nathan Kolodiz Director of Jewish Studies at the University of Virginia, is an associate professor in the Department of Religious Studies at the University of Virginia. She has written *Sarah Laughed: Modern Lessons from the Wisdom and Stories of Biblical Women* (2005), *The Jewish Dream Book* (with Elizabeth Ochs) (2003), *Words on Fire: One Woman's Journey into the Sacred* (1990, 1999), and *Safe and Sound: Protecting Your Child in an Unpredictable World* (1995), as well as dozens of articles in national newspapers and magazines. She is the coeditor of *The Book of Jewish Sacred Practices* (2001). In 1991–92 she was awarded a Nonfiction Writing Fellowship by the National Endowment for the Arts.

Riv-Ellen Prell is a professor of American studies at the University of Minnesota. She is the author of *Prayer and Community: The Havurah in American Judaism* (1989), which was awarded the National Jewish Book Award. She has also written *Fighting to Become Americans: Jews, Gender, and the Anxiety of Assimilation* (1999), which was a finalist for the Tuttleman Award given to the best book in Jewish women's studies in 1999–2000. She is the coeditor of *Interpreting Women's Lives: Feminist Theory and Personal Narratives* (1989).

Shuly Rubin Schwartz is I. Lehman Research Professor of American Jewish History at the Jewish Theological Seminary of America, where she also serves as dean of List College. She is the author of *Emergence of Jewish Scholarship in America: The Publication of the Jewish Encyclopedia* (1991), and *The Rabbi's Wife: The Rebbetzin in American Jewish Life* (2005), the first study of rabbis' wives in America. She has written a wide range of articles, and serves on the editorial board of the *Encyclopedia of Women and Religion.*

CHAVA WEISSLER is Philip and Muriel Professor of Jewish Studies at Lehigh University. She is the author of *Making Judaism Meaningful: Ambivalence and Tradition in a Havurah Community* (1989), and *Voices of the Matriarchs: Listening to the Prayers of Early Modern Jewish Women* (1998). At present, she is studying the Jewish Renewal movement in North America, with a focus on issues of gender and spirituality.

INDEX

Page numbers in italics refer to illustrations

Ackerman, Paula, 119
Adelman, Penina, 240–44, 248, 249, 264–65
Adler, Rachel, 40–43, *41*, 58–59
Adult bat mitzvah: as ceremony, 287; in Conservative Judaism, 288, 290; elements of, 288–89; and empowerment of women, 18–19; evolution of, 279–80, 282–83; impact on synagogues, 280–89, 291–93, 294–96; in Orthodox Judaism, 300n39; participants, 281, 282, 283–86, 289–91; promoted by denominations, 280, 288–89; in Reform Judaism, 124; as ritual, 288; seeking legitimacy within tradition, 18, 283
Agunah, 22n17, 156–58, 170, 202–3
Agus, Arlene, 233, 234, 235–36, 241
'Aliyot, 158
ALEPH: Alliance for Jewish Renewal. *See* Jewish Renewal
Alpert, Rebecca, 146, 215–16, 217
Androcentrism: in Bible, 7, 85, 94, 95, 102n10, 263–64; in halakhic process, 31, 34–35, 36; in language of God, 32–33, 124; in liturgy, 33, 63
Aronson, David, 162
Asherah, 88, 103n28
Assimilation, 6, 21n14, 112–13, 143
Autobiography: of Conservative rabbis, 226n46; as empowerment tool, 241; forms of, 225n23; gender differences in, 219–20; and Second Wave feminism, 254n22
Axelrad, Albert S., 169

Balin, Carole B., 217
Bar mitzvah, 139. *See also* Adult bat mitzvah
Bat mitzvah: in Conservative Judaism, 156; first, 119, 138–39; and Judaism as evolving religious civilization, 147; in Orthodox Judaism, 189
Bell, Catherine, 23n25, 232
Berman, Phyllis: on being woman rabbi, 77n22; on God and gender, 72; on male God language, 62; on Shekhinah, 71; on Yah, 64–65
Berner, Leila Gal, 266
Berrin, Susan, 248–49
Beth Jacob schools, 186
Bible: androcentrism in, 7, 85, 94, 95, 102n10, 263–64; connection to *The Red Tent* of, 95–96, 99–100; feminine images of God in, 88; feminist commentary, 83, 84–92, 100, 215, 234–35; patriarchal foundations of, 13, 89; as polemic, 87; role models in, 2, *2*, 10, 18, 87, 214–15, 235, 241, 244, 260–64, 276; tradition of commentary, 89, 91. *See also* Torah
Birth rituals: in Orthodox Judaism, 189, 206n18; in Reconstructionist Judaism, 220–21

Blank, Debra Reed, 216
Bloom, Jack H., 213
Blumenthal, Aaron H., 158, 167
B'nai Or Religious Fellowship, 53
Book of Blessings (Falk), 33
Breitman, Barbara, 64
Brevis, Anna Bear, 155
Brickner, Barnett, 119–20
Brit ahuvim, 43
Brooks, Marcia, 71

Cantor, Aviva, 260–61
Cantor, Debra, 219
Cardin, Nina, 170, 171, 173
Carlebach, Shlomo, 53, 58
Celebrating the New Moon: A Rosh Chodesh Anthology (Berrin), 248–49
Central Conference of American Rabbis (CCAR), 116–17, 127
Chabad Hasidism, 57, 271–74
Chained women. *See* Agunah
Charry, Dana, 166
Chosenness concept, 141–42, 151n24
Civilization: ancient Israelite, 85, 86, 88–89, 102n11, 103n28; Judaism as, 139–40, 142, 148; Judaism as evolving religious, 146–47; and law, 137
Cohen, Gerson D., 158, 160, 161–62, 164
Cohen, Marcia Baltimore, 163
Cohen, Shay J. D., 168
Cohen, Steven M., 287
Community: importance of unity in, 236; maintaining through worship, 243–44; narratives, 42; and practice-oriented spirituality, 291; ritual as affirmation of membership in, 286; Rosh Hodesh rituals create, 232
Complementary feminism. *See* Essentialist feminism
Confirmation services, 118–19
Conservative Judaism: accommodations to modernity, 15–16, 154–56; adult bat mitzvah in, 280, 288–89, 290; agunah issue, 170; 'aliyot in, 158; bat mitzvah in, 119; celebration of gender differences in, 171–72; criticism of Jewish feminism, 2–3; development of, 153; education of women, 155–56; guiding principles of, 137; Jewish mother/wife role in, 154–55; male dominated lay leadership of, 128; minyan in, 7, 159, 172, 238; mitzvah in, 156; women as leaders in, 154–55; women rabbis in, 159–64, *169,* 216
Conservative Judaism, 160–61, 164–69
Cousens, Beth, 284–85, 289
Cover, Robert, 41–42
"Create Me Anew" (Zeitlin), 235
The Creation of Feminist Consciousness (Lerner, Gerda), 216
Cultural feminism, 17–18, 232. *See also* Essentialist feminism
Cumulative revelations, doctrine of, 39–40
Cup of Miriam. *See* Miriam's Cup

Dalsheimer, Helen, 120
Daniels, Cindy, 163
Democratic principles: diversity, 143; and folkways, 144; freedom of choice, 144; and gender equality, 35, 139; individualism, 286–87, 289; primacy in Reconstructionist Judaism, 145
Denominations: assumptions shared across, 4; and decentralization of American Judaism, 3. *See also specific branches of Judaism*
Diamant, Anita, 84, 92–100
Difference feminism. *See* Essentialist feminism
Dinah, 86, 93
Diversity: in haggadot, 146; within Orthodox Judaism, 205n3; value of, 143
Divorce, 22n17, 156–58, 170, 202–3

Ecological feminism: in Jewish Renewal, 56, *56*; Shekhinah as Mother Earth, 69, 81n66; women's identification with nature, 240, 242–43, 254n27
Edwards, Lisa A., 214
Egalitarian feminism, 58–59, 68, 231–32, 237–38
Eilberg, Amy, *169*; on effect of exclusion of women, 215; on gender bias against women rabbis, 217; on symbolic exemplarhood, 213; writing women's history, 216–17
Ein Sof, 60
Eisen, Arnold M., 287
Eisenberg (Sasso), Sandy, 148, 216, 220–21

Eisenstein, Ira, 148
Eisenstein, Judith Kaplan, 138–39
Eishet Mitzvah Curriculum Guide (Hadassah), 290
Elat Chayyim, 51
Elijah's cup, 265, 266
Elwell, Sue Levi, 51, 127, 215–16, 222
Empowerment of women, 5; and adult bat mitzvah, 18–19; and autobiography, 241; and folkways, 144; ritual objects as signs of, 275; rituals as tools for, 240; segregation furthers, 239, 241, 246, 248; using language of God for, 65–67, 70. *See also* Rosh Hodesh rituals
Engendering Judaism: An Inclusive Theology and Ethics (Adler), 40
Enlightenment: and Jewish feminism, 5–7, 8, 9; and Judaism, 21n12; and Reform Judaism, 109
Environmental stewardship: in Jewish Renewal, 56, *56*; Shekhinah as Mother Earth, 69, 81n66; women's identification with nature, 240, 242–43, 254n27
Epstein, Louis, 157
Essentialist feminism, 58–59, 68, 70, 71
Esther, Queen, 2, *2*
Ethical Cultural Society, 138
Ethical monotheism, 137
Ethics and ethos, 141
Evans, Jane, 118, 120
Eve, 87, 214–15
Expanding the Palace of Torah: Orthodoxy and Feminism (Ross), 34
Ezrat Nashim, 159, 160, 162–63, 168, 238

Faces of Light Religious Fellowship, 53
Falk, Marcia, 33
Family life, 163, 166. *See also* Jewish mother/wife role
Federation of Temple Sisterhoods, 125
Feinstein, Moshe, 37, 199, 200
Feminism: development of, 19, 236. *See also* Jewish feminism
Firestone, Tirzah, 216
First International Jewish Feminist Conference (1988), 198
Fishman, Sylvia Barack, 201, 202
Flam, Nancy, 124
Folkways: as bridge between modernity and tradition, 142–43; development of, 136, 142, 150n10; as foundations for authority, 15; and haggadot, 145, 146; kashrut as, 143–44; and minhag, 139; and mitzvot, 135, 139, 142; portability of, 143–44; Protestant influence on, 140–42
Frankel, Zechariah, 153
Freedman, David Noel, 91–92
Freedom of choice, 144
Freiberg, Stella, 116
Friedan, Betty, 163
Friedman, Debbie, 124, 268
Frimer, Aryeh, 201, 202
Frimer, Dov, 201, 202
Frishman, Elyse, 127
Frymer-Kensky, Tikva, 86, 87, 89, 91–92
Functional interpretation, 150n10

Gafni, Mordecai, 76n16
Gates of Repentance, 214
Gay and lesbian issues, 4, 127–28, 215–16, 222
Gaylin, Willard, 163
Geertz, Clifford, 23n25
Geller, Laura, *218*; and adoption of new rituals, 212, 220; and Judaism with women at center, 223; and modern midrash, 241; and perspective of women rabbis, 123–24
Gender differences: in autobiography, 219–20; celebrated in Conservative Judaism, 171–72; in Jewish education, 281; in Jewish Renewal, 79n50; Rosh Hodesh rituals emphasize, 241–43; Shekhinah highlights, 60–61, 67–68; traditional, 242–43, 254n27
Gender discrimination: bar mitzvah as classic example of, 139; faced by women rabbis, 126, 128, 172–73, 217, 219
Gender equality: and accessibility to language, 259; across denominations, 4; and affirming religious adulthood, 287, 297; ʾaliyot, 158; confirmation services, 118–19; Conservative Judaism accommodations to, 15–16; demands of, 5; as democratic ideal, 35, 139; elusiveness of, 294; and halakhah, 30, 147; in Jewish education, 146; in Jewish Renewal, 12–

Gender equality (*continued*)
13, 57–59; in lay leadership, 146–47; and Lilith, 261; in marriage, 43, 167; midrashic basis for, 234–35; negative effect on family life, 166; Orthodox women's response to, 183–85, 188, 190, 199, 204; *vs.* pluralism, 173; Reconstructionist Judaism contribution to, 146; as religious principle, 169; women as normative Jews, 40–41
Gender roles: and assimilation, 6; change through traditional, 154–55; in egalitarian feminism, 59; fostered by synagogue gift shops, 118; Jewish mother/wife role: balance with working life, 217, 219; Conservative Judaism praised, 154–55; feminist impact on, 163; and Shekhinah, 68–69
Gender stereotypes: and essentialist feminism, 59; and Shekhinah, 60, 70–71
Gilligan, Carol, 31, 219
Ginzberg, Louis, 157
Glueck, Nelson, 120, 121
God: adult bat mitzvah and reflections about, 293; androcentric images of, 32–33, 215; in contemporary Rosh Hodesh liturgy, 248; experiential relationship with, 54; feminine images of, 58, 59, 88, 89, 103n28; feminist assertions about, 8; gendered nature of, 12–13; in kabbalah, 60; multiple images, 52; names of, 87, 88; unfolding of intentions over time, 38–40. *See also* Language of God; Shekhinah
Goddess worship, 10, 85, 88, 101n7, 103n28, 240
Goldbard, Arlene, 64, 71
Goldberg, Harvey, 258
Goldstein, Elyse, 222
Goldstein, Ruth, 155
Golinkin, David, 156
Goren, Shlomo, 197, 199
Gottlieb, Lynn, 168, 214, 260
Gottschalk, Alfred, 121
Graubart, David, 166
Green, Arthur, 166
Greenberg, Betty, 154–55
Greenberg, Blu, 204
Grimes, Ronald, 286
Grossman, Susan, 221
Gumbiner, Avraham, 193

Hachen, Debra, 217
Hadassah: and adult bat mitzvah, 280–81, 290; and Rosh Hodesh, 250, 262–63
Hafetz Hayim, 186
Hagar, 87, 214–15
Haggadot: feminist, 127; and folkways, 145, 146; instructions for use of Miriam's Cup in, 265–66
HaKohen, Yisrael Meir, 186
Halakhah: and accumulating revelation, 39–40; and 'aliyot, 158; androcentrism of, 31, 34–35, 36; based on gender equality as goal, 30, 147; celebration of gender differences in, 171–72; centrality to Judaism, 31–32, 35–36, 139, 143; community development of, 41, 42; Conservative Judaism accommodations within framework of, 154–56; continuum of decision making, 167; flexibility of, 36, 37, 41, 135–36; and Jewish feminist theology, 30–32; and Jewish Renewal, 79n42; and minhag, 139; and mitzvot, 135–36; neglect of, 36–37; and ordination of women, 164; in Orthodox Judaism, 183, 185; ritual exemptions for women, 188–89; ritual obligations for women, 192–93. *See also* Agunah; Minyan
Halevy, Judith, 51
"Hannah, Jessica, Bessie—Me?" (Schiff), 166
Hasidim: gender roles, 57; and Jewish Renewal, 53, 54; Lubavitch, 271–74
Hauptman, Judith, 165
Haut, Rivka, 197–98, 202
Havurot, 148
Head coverings, 171, 190
Hebrew Union College (HUC), 116–17, 120
Heckelman, Tziporah, 162
Helfgott, Esther Atlshul, 169
Hermeneutics of remembrance, 28, 32, 45n8
Hermeneutics of suspicion, 28, 45n8, 89
Heschel, Susannah, 132n44, 227n62
Hierarchy, 32, 33–34, 35, 62
Hirsch, Samson Raphael, 206n13

Hodes, Natalie Lansing, 120
Homemaker role. *See* Jewish mother/wife
Horowitz, Barbara Ostfeld, 121
"How to Be a Jewish Working Mother" (Cohen, Marcia Baltimore), 163
Hyman, Paula E., 6, 165

Idelson, Shirley, 215–16
Inclusion: demands, 14; in denominations, 15; equality more than, 30–31; without equality, 10
Individualism in American religion, 286–87, 289
International Committee for Women of the Wall, 269
Israelites (ancient): biblical women as representative of fate of, 87; culture, 85, 86, 88–89; religious practices of women, 102n11, 103n28

Jacob, 100
Jacobson, Matthew, 8
Jewish education: after adult bat mitzvah, 290; as equalizer, 38; gender equality in, 146; gender gap, 281; growth of adult, 282; logical outcome of, 162; in Orthodox Judaism, 185–89, 202; by Rosh Hodesh groups, 249–50; of women, 155, 206n14; of women, premodern, 206n13; women's contribution to men's, 29, *29*. *See also* Adult bat mitzvah; Women's tefillah groups (WTGs), Orthodox
Jewish family: and assimilation, 6; balance with working life, 219; as embodiment of Western values, 6; feminist impact on, 163; fostered by synagogue gift shops, 118; and Miriam, 241
Jewish feminism: and adult bat mitzvah, 293–94; critics of, 2–3; demands of, 9, 11–12, 282–83; early, 238; and Enlightenment, 5–7; expressed through ritual, 236; and halakhic process, 30–32; and Lilith, 260–62; and Miriam, 262; overview of, 1–4, 5, 8; and Second Wave feminism, 7, 8; as sociological issue, 30–31; as threat to Orthodoxy, 36–37; tools of, 3; traditional approach, 12; transnational nature of, 3–4, 27; types of, 17–18, 20n3, 58–59; women rabbis as agents for, 212, 222–23
Jewish identity, 289–90, 296
Jewish Institute of Religion (JIR), 117, 120
Jewish mother/wife role: and assimilation, 6; balance with working life, 217, 219; Conservative Judaism praised, 154–55; feminist impact on, 163; fostered by synagogue gift shops, 118; rabbis as, 173; Shekhinah as, 68–69
Jewish Orthodox Feminist Alliance (JOFA), 199
Jewish Renewal: characteristics of, 54–55; ecological feminism in, 56, *56*; gender differences in, 79n50; and gender equality, 57–59; and halakhah, 79n42; membership, 55, 57, 76n14; power structure of, 64, 66; roots of, 53, 75n6; Shekhinah in, 12, 52, 58, 59–60, 61–62, 63, 65–70; women rabbis, 216
Jewish Study Bible (Reinhartz), 90
Jewish Theological Seminary (JTS), 153, 155–56
Johnson, George, 168
Judaism and the New Woman (Priesand), 212–13, 215
Judaism as a Civilization: Toward a Reconstruction of American-Jewish Life (Kaplan), 136
Judaism-in-the-home project, 155

Kabbalah: and feminine power, 77n26; and Jewish Renewal, 58; Shekhinah in, 12, 59–60, 66, 67
Kaddish: and Orthodox Judaism, 189–90, 190, 207n23; and synagogue involvement, 48n51
Kagan, Ruth Gan, 63
Kamsler, Harold M., 162
Kaplan, Mordecai Menachem: background of, 136; and bat mitzvah, 119; and development of Reconstructionist Judaism, 137–38; expectations of gender equality in lay leadership, 146–47; and foundation of feminist positions, 145; and Judaism as evolving religious civilization, 146–47; on mitzvot, 135–36; and pluralism, 142

Kashrut, 142, 143–44
Keesler, Darin, 96
Ketubah: bride's status in, 169; as commercial contract, 42–43; reform of, 157
Kippot (skullcaps), 171
Kohut, Rebekah, 115
Kolodny, Debra, 58, 65, 67–68
Kook, Avraham Yitzchak, 38
Kosmin, Barry A, 172
Kos Miriam. *See* Miriam's Cup
Kraemer, David, 169
Krauthammer, Joy, 51, 64, 73

Langer, Sidney, 201
Language: gender equality and accessibility to, 259; Hebrew literacy, 280, 281; use of American idiom, 139
Language, liturgical: androcentric, 33, 63; gender inclusive, 124, 147, 214; using maternal lineage, 239; Yiddish as, 191, 245, 248
Language of God: androcentric, 32–33, 124; to empower women, 65–67, 70; Jewish Renewal, 61–62, 63–65; non-anthropomorphic, 64–65; traditional, 62–63
Lauterbach, Jacob, 219
Lay leadership: and adult bat mitzvah, 280, 288–89, 291–93; in Conservative Judaism, 128, 154–55; and decline of Sisterhoods, 125; gender equality in, 146–47; Jewish literacy of, 282; in Jewish Renewal, 66; in Reform Judaism, 115–16, 117, 118
Lefkovitz, Lori, 266
Legal tradition. *See* Halakhah
Lerner, Gerda, 216
Lerner, Stephen C., 165
Lesbian issues, 4, 127–28, 215–16, 222
Lesbian Rabbi (Alpert, Elwell and Idelson), 215–16
Levine, Stephanie, 273–74
Levinthal, Helen, 117
Lewis, Ellen, 217
Lieberman, Saul, 157–58, 160
Liebman, Charles, 148, 286
Life on the Fringes: A Feminist Journey toward Traditional Rabbinic Ordination (Ner-David), 216
Life passages, honoring, 17, 189, 219–22, 227n58
"The Lifestyle of Low Fertility: The Changing Needs of Jewish Women" (Johnson), 168
Lilith: in midrash, 235; reclaiming, 214–15; role in early Jewish feminism, 18, 260–62
Lilith, 29, *29*
Linn, Louis, 166
Liss, Janet B., 217
Listfield, Chaim, 166
Liturgy: androcentric language in, 33, 63; feminist interpretation of, 127; gender inclusive language, 124, 147, 214; for Rosh Hodesh, 240–44, 248
Lubavitch Hasidim, 271–74

Male bias. *See* Androcentrism
Marder, Janet, 127, 219
Marriage: as commercial transaction, 42–43; contract, 42–43, 157, 169; gender equality as threat to, 167; in Orthodox Judaism, 189. *See also* Divorce
Meisleman, Moshe, 201
Memory: autobiography of women rabbis, 219–20; biography to reclaim, 216; forming content of, 30; holiness of female, 95; present compared to, 98
"Menstrual Taboos, Jewish Law and 'Kovod Tsibbur'" (Kamsler), 162
Merow, Andrea, 173
Midrash: affirming women's subordinate status, 237; basis for gender equality in, 234–35; Miriam in, 241, 263–64
Mikvah use, reappropriating, 222
Milgram, Goldie, 217
Minhag, 139
Minyan: in Conservative Judaism, 7, 159, 172, 238; in Orthodox Judaism, 7, 190, 197; and women's tefillah groups, 45, 208nn34
Miriam: contemporary identification with, 260; family role of, 244; in midrash, 241, 263–64; revisioned, 18, 262–63, 276; and ritual objects, 18
Miriam's Cup: and authenticity of new rituals, 258–59; instructions for use of, 265–66; as nonthreatening, 244, 275–

76; origin, 264–65; as traditional, 274–75
"Miriam's Song" (Friedman), 268
Miriam's tambourine, 267; and authenticity of new rituals, 258–59; as nonthreatening, 275–76; as traditional, 274–75; used by Jewish feminists, *267,* 268–71; used by Lubavitch Hasidic women, 271–74
Miriam's Well: Rituals for Jewish Women around the Year (Adelman), 240–44, 248, 249, 264–65
Mirvis, Tova, 266
Miscarriages, rituals for, 221
Mitzvot: as determinant of Jewishness, 143; and folkways, 15, 135, 139, 142; goal of traditional, 142; and halakhah, 135–36
Modernity: and Conservative Judaism, 15–16, 154–56; folkways as bridge between tradition and, 142–43; Judaism's compatibility with, 5–6; and Orthodox Judaism, 18, 39, 182, 183, 204; and status of women, 6
Modern Orthodoxy. *See* Orthodox Judaism
"Modern Orthodoxy and the Challenge of Feminism" (Ross), 34
Monson, Rela Geffen, 163
Moon: in creation midrash, 234; in power structure, 234, 237; as source of knowledge, 242; as visual manifestation of Shekhinah, 60, 242, 243
Moonbeams: A Hadassah Rosh Hodesh Guide (Hadassah), 250, 262–63
Moore, Sally, 294
Mores, 140–41
Myerhoff, Barbara, 294
Myers, Jody, 260
"The Myth of Matriarchy in Recent Writings on Jewish Women's Spirituality" (Myers), 260

Nadell, Pamela, 159–60
Naming ceremonies, 220–21
National Council of Jewish Women (NCJW), 114
National Federation of Temple Sisterhood (NFTS): impact of, 114–16; lay leadership, 118; name change of, 125; and ordination of women, 120; and Sisterhood Sabbath, 117
National Women's League: agunah issue, 157; and development of egalitarian consensus, 161–64; and lay leadership, 154–55; viability, 170–71; women rabbis, 160, 161–64
Ner-David, Haviva, 216, 222
Neumark, Martha, 116
The New Haggadah, 145
New Moon rituals. *See* Rosh Hodesh rituals
New York Times, 274–75
Night of Questions: A Passover Haggadah, 265–66
"Nomos and Narrative" (Cover), 42
North American International Coalition for the Women of the Wall, 198
Novick, Leah, 68–69, 73, 80n64
Nusbacher, Ailene, 201–3

Offner, Stacy, 222
Orthodox Judaism: and adult bat mitzvah, 280, 300n39; birth rituals, 189, 206n18; diversity within, 205n3; and divorce, 202–3; education of women, 185–88, 206n14; and halakhah, 36, 183, 185; Jewish feminism as threat to, 2–3, 16, 36–37; minyan in, 7, 190, 197; and modernity, 18, 34, 39, 182, 183, 204; and ordination of women, 216; ritual practices of women in, 188–93, 204; role of change and innovation in, 182, 183; role of tradition in, 183; stereotype as oppressive to women, 181; and Torah, 137; use of Miriam's Cup, 266; women's response to gender equality, 183–85, 188, 190, 199, 204; women's roles in, 34. *See also* Women's tefillah groups (WTGs), Orthodox
Ostow, Mortimer, 165, 166–67
Outlook, 160, 161–64
The Outside World (Mirvis), 266
Ozick, Cynthia, 7, 30–31, 47n38

Pardes, Ilana, 87
Passover. *See* Seders
Patriarchy: in ancient Israelite culture, 85, 86, 102n10; in Bible, 13; distorted monotheism, 91; imperative to confront,

Patriarchy (*continued*)
30; in *The Red Tent,* 94; and sexual abuse, 86
Pearl, Chaim, 167
Phylacteries, 171–72
Pirke de-Rabbi Eliezer, 234, 241
Plaskow, Judith: on halakhah, 30–32; and hierarchical dualism, 32, 33–34; and language of God, 32–33; and Lilith, 260; methodology of, 28, 30; on Miriam in Torah, 264; and parameters of Jewish feminist theology, 40; on Shekhinah, 66–67; theology of, 27, 28–34; workability of model of, 36
Pluralism, 142, 173
P'nai Or Religious Fellowship, 53
Positive Historical School of Judaism, 153
Power structure: in ancient Israel, 86, 88–89; in Jewish Renewal, 64; and Miriam, 244, 262–64; moon in, 234, 237; personal as element of, 243–44; in Reform Judaism, 15; and rituals, 232; women's tefillah groups as challenge to Orthodox, 204–5. *See also* Lay leadership; *headings beginning with* rabbis
Practice-oriented spirituality, 290–91
Prager, Marcia, 63, 65
Pragmatism, 141–42
Prayer: and Conservative Judaism, 7, 158–59, 172, 238; modern, 235; and Orthodox Judaism, 7, 190, 191–92, 197; at Western Wall, 198–99, 246, 269, 270; women rabbis and new, 124; women's exemptions, 188; women's obligations, 192–93; Yiddish as language of, 191, 245, 248. *See also* Language, liturgical; Women's tefillah groups (WTGs), Orthodox
Prayer shawls, 171, 172, 190
Prell, Riv-Ellen, 171
Priesand, Sally: feminist critique of Judaism by, 212–13, 215; ordination of, 120–21, 152n42, 216; retirement of, 128
Prinz, Deborah R., 214

Rabbis: Conservative Judaism, *169,* 226n46; Jewish Renewal, 54, 57; male as normative, 77n22; promotion of adult bat mitzvah by, 291; sexual abuse by, 76n16; as symbolic exemplars, 213–14. *See also* Women rabbis
Rabbis, Orthodox Judaism: and dissatisfaction of women, 182; and education of girls, 186, 187–89; and women's tefillah groups, 193, 195–98, 199–201, 202
Radner, Joan, 259
Ramah camps, 158
Raphael, Geela Rayzel, 61, 65, 67
Rashi, 233–34
Reading the Women of the Bible (Frymer-Kensky), 91–92
Rebecca, 87
Reconstructionist Judaism: adult bat mitzvah in, 280, 288–89; birth rituals in, 220–21; development of, 137–38, 147–49; inclusion in, 15; as indigenous American Judaism, 144–45; and Passover, 145–46; primacy of democratic principles in, 145; use of Miriam's Cup, 265–66; women cantors, 238; women rabbis, 148, 216
Rediscovering Judaism, 290
The Red Tent (Diamant): connection to Bible of, 95–96, 99–100; popularity of, 84, 96; readers' commentary on, 96–99; religious practices of women in, 103n28; story in, 92–95
Reform Judaism: activism of women, 112–16; adult bat mitzvah in, 124, 280, 288–89; bat mitzvah in, 119; confirmation services in, 118–19; and Enlightenment, 109; and ethical monotheism, 137; as leader in inclusion, 15; liturgical language of, 124, 214; membership of, 116; power structure of, 15; Sisterhoods, 112–13, 114–16, 117, 118, 120, 125–26, 127–28; and synagogue architecture, 109, 110–11, 112; women as prayer leaders, 117, 119; women in congregational governance, 115–16, 120. *See also* Women rabbis in Reform Judaism
Reinhart, Adele, 90
Religious education. *See* Jewish education
Religious feminism, 16
Responsa: and minyan, 197; repercussions of, 36
Riets 5 responsum, 197

Riskin, Shlomo, 201
Ritual objects: becoming part of tradition, 274–75; emergence of new, 18, 240; relationship to rituals, 258–59; seder plate, *263*; as signs of empowerment, 275; tambourines, *2*, 90, *90*; and tradition, 259. *See also* Miriam's Cup; Miriam's tambourine
Rituals: birth, 189, 206n18, 220–21; *vs.* ceremonies, 286; as empowerment tools, 147, 240; halakhic exemptions for women, 188–89; halakhic obligations for women, 192–93; importance in Judaism of, 231; for invisible life passages, 227n58; measure of success of, 23n25; in Orthodox Judaism, 182, 189, 206n18; overview of new, 257; performance of uncommanded, 200; performed outside synagogues, 231; performed publicly, 282–83; and power structure, 232; in Reconstructionist Judaism, 220–21; in *The Red Tent,* 93; relationship of ritual objects to, 258–59; replication of male practices by women, 196, 204; role of, 48n51, 136–37, 286–88; role of tradition in, 286; transformative effects of, 18–19, 286, 294; women-centered, 17, 219–22; women rabbis and adoption of new, 211–12. *See also* Adult bat mitzvah; Rosh Hodesh rituals
Rivlin, Lily, 260
Role models: biblical, 10, 87; Emma Goldman, 20n3; Esther, 2, *2*; Lilith, 18, 214–15, 235, 260–62; Miriam, 18, 241, 244, 260, 262–64, 276; women rabbis as, 215
Rosh Hashanah service, 214
Rosh Hodesh rituals, *247*; accepted by mainstream, 248–51; create community, 232; elements of, 235–36, 239, 240–44; for girls, 250–51; and maintenance of status quo, 237; and Miriam, 262–63; and Miriam's Cup, 264–65; origin of modern, 233–37; Orthodox, 246; premodern, 233–34, 245, 253n10; structural flexibility of, 231–32, 240; and Women of the Wall, 246; and women rabbis, 221–22; and women's tefillah groups, 194–95
Rosie the Riveter, 2, *2*
Ross, Tamar, 34–40, 42, 193–94

Sasso, Sandy Eisenberg. *See* Eisenberg (Sasso), Sandy
Schachter-Shalomi, Zalman: and Conservative Judaism, 153; and Gafni, 76n16; and Jewish Renewal, 53, 54; and Shekhinah, 58, 61; on Yah, 64, 79n46
Schechter, Mathilde, 154
Schechter, Solomon, 154, 155
Schiff, Ellen F., 166
Schneerson, Menachem Mendel, 271–73
Schnirer, Sarah, 186
Schoenfeld, Stuart, 294
Schorsch, Ismar, 160
Schwarz, Sidney, 168
Second Wave feminism: divisions in, 10; and ethnicity, 22n20; and family, 163; growth of, 254n22; and Jewish feminism, 7, 8; role models of, 2, *2*
Seders: haggadot for, 127, 145, 146; Miriam's tambourine at, 268–69; and Reconstructionist Judaism, 145–46; revisioned, 221, 227n62; ritual objects, 244, *263*; as venue for egalitarian feminism, 237–38. *See also* Miriam's Cup
Seeking-oriented spirituality, 286–87, 289, 291
Sered, Susan, 245
Sexual abuse/harassment: in androcentric reading of Bible, 94, 95; and patriarchy, 86; by rabbis, 76n16, 132n44; of women rabbis, 217
Shapiro, Miriam, 167
Shapiro-Reiser, Rhonda, 70, 72
Shekhinah: artistic dimensions, 72–73; empowers women, 65–67, 70; as Jewish mother, 68–69; in Jewish Renewal, 12, 52, 58, 61–62, 63, 65–70; in kabbalah, 59–60, 66, 67; and men, 70, 80n55; as metaphor, 70–72; moon as visual manifestation of, 242, 243; as Mother Earth, 69, 81n66; as negative image, 80n57; reinforces anthropomorphism of God, 71
She Who Dwells Within (Gottlieb), 260
Shoub, Myra, 168

Siegel, Seymour, 166
Sigal, Philip, 159
Silverman, Althea Osber, 154–55
Silverstein, Alan, 168
Simon, Carrie Obendorfer, 114
Sisterhoods. *See* National Federation of Temple Sisterhood (NFTS)
Sisterhood Sabbath, 117
Skolnic, Benjamin, 169
Skullcaps, 171
Social constructivist feminism. *See* Egalitarian feminism
Social heritage, Judaism as, 140
Society for the Advancement of Judaism (SAJ), 138
Society (non-Jewish): changes in, 36–37; democratic principles of, 15, 143, 144, 286–87, 289; and folkways concept, 140–42; Judaism's compatibility with, 5–6; Judaism's sense of difference from, 8–9; norms, 7; pragmatism in, 141–42; and synagogue architecture, 156; women's activism in, 113
Soloveitchik, Joseph B., 187, 200–201
Sons of Light Religious Fellowship, 53
Soria, Karen, 213–14
Spiritual feminism, 240–44, 253n19
Spitzer, Julie, 127
Standing Again at Sinai (Plaskow), 27, 28, 30
Sternbuch, Moshe, 36
Stern College, 187, 202
Sumner, William Graham, 140–42
Swidler, Leonard, 167–68
Switkin, Linda, 166
Symbolic exemplarhood, 213–14
Symbols. *See* Ritual objects; Role models
Synagogue architecture: Conservative Judaism, 156; Reform Judaism, 109, 110–11, 112; women's section, 26, 207nn23, 241
Synagogues: ancient, 168; gift shops in, 118; historical presence of women in, 191; impact of adult bat mitzvah on, 280–89, 285–86, 291–93, 294–96; kaddish and involvement in, 48n51; ritual objects for use outside of, 275–76; and Rosh Hodesh, 249; women as not Jews in, 47n38
Szold, Henrietta, 155
Tallitot (prayer shawls), 171, 172, 190
Talmud, 7, 187
Tamar, 87
Tambourines, *2*, 90, *90*, *267*. *See also* Miriam's tambourine
Teachers Institute, 155
Techines: Voices from the Heart (Zakutinsky), 245
Tefillin / tefillot (phylacteries), 171–72, 190
Teubal, Savina, 51
Teutsch, Betsy Platkin, 2, *267*, 269–71
Teutsch, David, 266
Textuality, role of, 13–14
"Thanks for the Chair" tambourine (Teutsch), *267*
Tiferet, Hanna, 61–62, 67
Tikkun ha-lev, 54–55
Tikkun olam: in Jewish Renewal, 54–55, *56*; and kabbalah, 60. *See also* Environmental stewardship
Tkhines, 245, 248
Torah: and adult bat mitzvah, 288; androcentrism of, 7, 263–64; centrality in Orthodox Judaism of, 137; language of God in, 62; midrash, 234–35, 237, 263–64; Orthodox women dancing with, 190; premodern study by women, 206n13; reclaiming, 30; study by Orthodox women. *See* Women's tefillah groups (WTGs), Orthodox
Tradition: of affirming religious adulthood, 287, 297; androcentric, 282; of biblical commentary, 91; changing fundamentals of, 28, 30; changing without challenging, 10, 18, 259, 275, 293–94, 297; folkways as bridge between modernity and, 142–43; and hierarchical society, 35; importance of, 22n24; integrating Lilith within, 261; and Orthodox Judaism, 183, 186; and ritual objects, 259, 274–75; role of ritual in, 286; seeking legitimacy within, 18, 283, 293–94; of women's presence in synagogues, 191; and women's tefillah groups, 195–96
Transvaluation process, 138
Trible, Phyllis, 83, 89
Turner, Victor, 286
Twersky, Mordechai, 201

Umansky, Ellen, 32
Ungar, Andre, 162
University of Judaism, 155–56

Victim status, 261

Waldman, Nahum M., 169
Waskow, Arthur, 53
"The Ways of a Woman" (Tiferet), 67
Weibershul, 26, 207nn23
Weilerstein, Sadie Rose, 155
Weinberg, Abigail, 65–66, 71–72
Weinberg, Jeanette, 120
Weinberg, Sheila Peltz, 219
Weinberg, Yehiel, 39
Weiss, Avi, 197, 201
Weissler, Chava, 245
Wenger, Beth, 159–60
Wicca worship, 10
Wiessman, Marian, *285*
Wise, Isaac Meyer, 112
With Roots in Heaven (Firestone), 216
Wolfe-Bank, David, 58
"Women and the Commandments" (Listfield), 166
"Women and Torah in Talmudic Judaism" (Swidler), 167–68
"Women at the Sea" tambourine (Teutsch), 270
Women cantors, 121, 238
"Women in the Synagogues of Antiquity" (Cohen, Shay J. D.), 168
Women of Reform Judaism (WRJ), 125–26, 127–28
Women of the Wall (WOW), 198–99, 246, 269, 270
Women rabbis: and adoption of new rituals, 211–12, 220–22, 239–40; as agents for feminist Judaism, 16, 212, 222–23; in Conservative Judaism, 159–64, *169,* 216; gender and perspective of, 123–24; gendered-based employment issues, 126, 128, 172–73, 217, 219; and inclusion of gays and lesbians, 222; in Jewish Renewal, 216; as not normative, 77n22; opposition to, 219; in Orthodox Judaism, 216; in Reconstructionist Judaism, 148, 216; as role models, 215; self-knowledge of historicity, 225n23; as symbolic exemplars, 213–14
Women rabbis in Reform Judaism: first, 120–21, 128, 152n42, 216; leadership roles, 126–28; movement for, 116–17, 119–21; organization of, *122,* 123, 217; professional integration of, 121, 123
Women's organizations: feminism as threat to, 168, 170. *See also* Women's tefillah groups (WTGs), Orthodox; *specific organizations*
Women's Rabbinic Network (WRN), *122,* 123, 217
Women's tefillah groups (WTGs), Orthodox, 193–98; attendance at, 201–2; and minyan, 45, 208nn34; origin of, 187, 194–95; and rabbis, 193, 195–98, 199–201, 202; and Rosh Hodesh, 245–46; and tradition, 195–96; as ultimate challenge to power structure, 204
Women's Tefillah Network (WTN), 196, 197–98
The Women's Torah Commentary, 215
Wuthnow, Robert, 291

Yah, 64–65, 79n46
Yeshiva University, 187
Yiddish, 191, 245, 248

Zakutinsky, Rivka, 245
Zeitlin, Hillel, 235
Zimmerman, Sheldon, 132n44
Zionism, 8